Kierkegaard and the Question Concerning Technology

Kierkegaard and the Question Concerning Technology

Christopher B. Barnett

BLOOMSBURY ACADEMIC
NEW YORK • LONDON • OXFORD • NEW DELHI • SYDNEY

BLOOMSBURY ACADEMIC
Bloomsbury Publishing Inc
1385 Broadway, New York, NY 10018, USA
50 Bedford Square, London, WC1B 3DP, UK
29 Earlsfort Terrace, Dublin 2, Ireland

BLOOMSBURY, BLOOMSBURY ACADEMIC and the Diana logo are trademarks of
Bloomsbury Publishing Plc

First published in the United States of America 2019
This paperback edition published in 2021

Cover design: Maria Rajka
Cover image: View of Copenhagen, Denmark between ca. 1890 and 1900, Library of
Congress, Prints & Photographs Division, Photochrom Collection, [LC-DIG-ppmsc-05746]

Library of Congress Cataloging-in-Publication Data
Names: Barnett, Christopher B. (Christopher Baldwin), 1976- author.
Title: Kierkegaard and the question concerning technology / Christopher B. Barnett.
Description: New York: Bloomsbury Academic, 2019. | Includes bibliographical
references and index.
Identifiers: LCCN 2019008162 (print) | LCCN 2019013542 (ebook) |
ISBN 9781628926682 (ePub) | ISBN 9781628926699 (ePDF) | ISBN 9781628926668
(hardback: alk. paper)
Subjects: LCSH: Kierkegaard, S²ren, 1813-1855. | Technology.
Classification: LCC B4377 (ebook) | LCC B4377 .B365 2019 (print) |
DDC 198/.9–dc23
LC record available at https://lccn.loc.gov/2019008162

ISBN: HB: 978-1-6289-2666-8
       PB: 978-1-5013-7834-8
       ePDF: 978-1-6289-2669-9
       eBook: 978-1-6289-2668-2

Typeset by Deanta Global Publishing Services, Chennai, India

To find out more about our authors and books visit www.bloomsbury.com and
sign up for our newsletters.

And at the touch of Love everyone becomes a poet.

Plato, *Symposium*

FOR LUKE, CALEB, PAUL, AND MONICA GRACE

Contents

Preface

Overview of the philosophy of technology

The philosophy of technology has grown steadily since its inception, although its development has hardly proceeded in linear fashion. Carl Mitcham traces the field's origin at least as far back as Robert Boyle (1627–91) and Isaac Newton (1642–1727), who sought to understand the world in terms of the principles of mechanics.[1] Yet, it was not until the latter half of the nineteenth century that the philosophy of technology as such began to emerge. A key thinker in this regard was Ernst Kapp (1808–96), who, like Karl Marx, sought to understand technology in terms of Left-Hegelian materialism. In fact, Kapp coined the phrase *Philosophie der Technik*,[2] which became popular in Germanophone scholarship, particularly among those interested in what Mitcham calls "engineering-philosophy discussions."[3] Still, it would be another century before the term became commonplace outside of Germany.[4]

That is not to say, however, that the philosophy of technology lay dormant until the 1980s. On the contrary, the discipline had already pressed into the academic mainstream in the mid-twentieth century, albeit under the guise of phenomenology and existentialism—a point to which this study will return. Moreover, by the 1970s, "there began to be a proliferation of publications"[5] on the subject, and this shift was followed by the formation of the Society for Philosophy and Technology in the United States. Monographs were soon to follow, including Langdon Winner's *Autonomous Technology: Technics-out-of-Control as a Theme in Political Thought* (1977), Don Ihde's *Technics and Praxis: A Philosophy of Technology* (1979), and Albert Borgmann's *Technology and the Character of Contemporary Life* (1984).

At this stage, the philosophy of technology largely received its orientation from "six forefathers": Martin Heidegger, Lewis Mumford, Jacques Ellul, Hans Jonas, Günther Anders, and Arnold Gehlen.[6] In this group, Heidegger loomed largest, not only due to his reputation as one of the seminal philosophers of the twentieth century but also due to his influence on subsequent thinkers concerned with technology, such as Borgmann, Hubert Dreyfus, and Andrew Feenberg. Though not exactly forming a "school," these forefathers nevertheless held two basic traits in common: (i) a preoccupation with the "historical and *transcendental* conditions that made modern technology possible" and (ii) an ostensible, if not necessarily explicit, desire to "return to some prior, seemingly more harmonious and idyllic [relationship] . . . between nature and culture."[7] In other words, the philosophy of technology emerged as a discipline "interested in technology writ large,"[8] placing particular emphasis on how technology has come to shape modern society, often in detrimental fashion.

Over time, however, the forefathers of the philosophy of technology have exercised diminishing influence on their field. Ihde argues that the trend is now toward "a more pragmatic, more empirical, and more concrete approach to technologies."[9] Such an approach, he adds, improves upon the work of Heidegger and his peers, precisely to the extent that it eschews metaphysical concerns about the "essence" of technology and, instead, attends to "the differing contexts and multidimensionalities of technologies."[10] Doubtless this change reflects, at least to some extent, the so-called "end of metaphysics," which, in the postmodern, postindustrial West, underlies discourse in economics, education, and politics. But Ihde sees a shift in technology itself, which is increasingly moving away from "mega-machine industrial technologies" and toward "micro-processes that include *nano-*, *info-*, *bio-*, and *genetic* technologies."[11] The upshot, he suggests, is something new—namely, technological innovation that seems to resist the dystopian analyses characteristic of much early philosophy of technology. As Ihde puts it, "Philosophies of technology need to renew themselves constantly, just as the technologies themselves change."[12]

Still, Ihde's distinction between "older" and "newer" technologies not only points forward to the evolution of the philosophy of technology but also points backward to a fissure in the very foundation of the discipline. For the phrase "philosophy of technology" itself bears different meanings. On the one hand, when the words "of technology" are taken to indicate "the subject or agent," the philosophy of technology might be seen as "an attempt by technologists or engineers to elaborate a technological philosophy."[13] On the other hand, when "of technology" is taken to indicate "a theme being dealt with," the philosophy of technology is better understood as "an effort by scholars from the humanities . . . to take technology seriously as a theme for disciplined reflection."[14] For Mitcham, the former approach is "more pro-technology and analytic,"[15] promoting a "general philosophical elaboration and social application of the engineering attitude toward the world."[16] In contrast, the latter approach is "more critical and interpretive,"[17] often finding expression in "attempts to defend the fundamental idea of the primacy of the nontechnical."[18]

With these distinctions in mind, Ihde's claim that the philosophy of technology is leaving behind older metaphysical concerns seems shortsighted, if not downright erroneous. That is to say, Ihde is doubtless right that, at present, the engineering philosophy of technology is undergoing a resurgence, not least due to the cultural-cum-technological reasons adduced above. Nevertheless, whether or not this resurgence will last, or whether or not it is the best way to approach technology, remains an open question. After all, the so-called "humanities philosophy of technology" is grounded in the very rudiments of human experience—namely, the attempt to understand the nature and purpose of things "in sacred myth, in poetry, and in philosophic discourse."[19] It is hardly necessary, then, that technology be evaluated solely (or even primarily) in terms of its technical features, and it would seem self-evident that "non- or transtechnological perspectives"[20] offer valuable ways of considering technology's place in human society. Moreover, it may even be the case that non-technological thinking stands as a "balance to an over-rationalized, over-managed form of life that becomes distorted and oppressive precisely to the extent that it is unable to allow any other 'take' on reality than its own."[21] Indeed, might not Ihde's call to move on from the ostensibly antiquated views of Heidegger (and others) be seen as an effort, however nascent, to foreclose on the kind of thinking that resists the totalizing grasp of efficient reason and yet longs for a "horizon of promise"[22] beyond what human beings can build or know? Would it not be valuable, then, to keep such a horizon open, to persevere in asking questions that refrain from treating the world in reductive fashion? Such, at any rate, are the kinds of questions that this book hopes to ask, chiefly in and through the thought of Søren Kierkegaard.

Kierkegaard's relation to the philosophy of technology

At the outset, it should be said that the basic purpose of this text—namely, to explore the relationship between Kierkegaard's thinking and the question concerning technology—falls squarely within the camp of the "humanities philosophy of technology." So, for those who have renounced such an approach, it may not be of much interest, except perhaps as a chronicle of a now-outmoded way of confronting the subject matter. Nor will it likely appeal to those who believe that *theology* has no place in the philosophy of technology, whether because, on the one hand, theology entails the kinds of non-technological concerns that the field is trying to abandon, or because, on the other hand, theology seems to proffer existential "answers" to human problems in a manner that paradoxically corresponds to technical efficiency. And yet, not only does Kierkegaard write about theological topics himself, but his thinking in general and his ideas about technology in particular came to exercise influence on later theologians. Consequently, a project such as this one cannot eschew theological considerations, despite the fact that it is also seeking to engage the philosophy of technology.

This balancing act is, I hope, reflected in the book's title—namely, *Kierkegaard and the Question Concerning Technology*. Of course, this name echoes Heidegger's famous treatise, *Die Frage nach der Technik* (1953), but I have chosen it for thematic purposes too. As will become clear, it is doubtful that Kierkegaard can be considered a "philosopher of technology" in the strict sense of the term. While *technologies* (buses, print media, and so on) turn up a number of times throughout his writings, he rarely employs the abstract term "technology." In other words, Kierkegaard neither directly nor systematically addresses technology but, rather, does so in ad hoc fashion, making an observation here or offering a discursive reflection there. For those who already know Kierkegaard's work, this approach should not come as a surprise. Kierkegaard was a great critic of *das System*, and this opposition to supposedly objective or presuppositionless thinking is manifested in his own literary style, which is alternately pious, painstaking, playful, and polemical—or sometimes all at once. Thus, his thinking about technology cannot be excised from the idiosyncratic nature of his authorship. To the extent that he has something worthwhile to say about technology, he does so precisely as one resistant to addressing the issue in a systematic manner.

It is clear, then, how this book *cannot* proceed. But is there a way forward, given the lack of direct, sustained engagement with technology in Kierkegaard's writings? Here is where the book's title becomes pertinent. For if it is true that Kierkegaard offers nothing in the way of a methodical response to technology, it is also true that he was aware that the rise of the modern, secular world—a problem with which he was famously concerned—cannot be understood without also attending to the rise of technology. Of course, writing at the midpoint of the nineteenth century, his vantage point on modern technology was far more limited than that of a Heidegger or a Herbert Marcuse: Kierkegaard could not decry the deleterious effects of hydroelectric plants and tourism on natural landscapes,[23] nor could he criticize the military-industrial complex and its promotion of nuclear armament.[24] In other words, there is a real sense in which Kierkegaard encountered modern technology just as it was becoming a "problem" or a subject for philosophical reflection. After all, Kapp's *Baselines of a Philosophy of Technology* (*Grundlinien einer Philosophie der Technik*, 1877)—one of the founding texts of the philosophy of technology—was published over twenty years after Kierkegaard's death. Hence, in the vein of thinkers such as Jean-Jacques Rousseau and Karl Marx, Kierkegaard views technology not as an independent theme but as a component of wider intellectual and social issues. In that regard, Kierkegaard might be said to belong to the *background* of the philosophy of technology, rather than to the discipline as such. Thus, to call this project *Kierkegaard as Philosopher of Technology* (or something along those lines) would be inappropriate on both a historical and a methodological level. The open-ended theme of "questioning" is more suitable to Kierkegaard's actual capacity as an interlocutor with technological issues.

But there are also constructive reasons to think of Kierkegaard's relation to technology in terms of "questioning." In other words, this approach does not just reflect Kierkegaard's abjuration of systematic thinking or the limitations of his sociohistorical *Weltanschauung*; on the contrary, it suggests that questioning itself is of positive value in thinking about technology. Here is where the allusion to Heidegger is especially apt. In his treatise, *Gelassenheit* (1959),[25] published in English as *Discourse on Thinking*, Heidegger argues that the poverty of modern thinking is that it has been reduced to a merely calculative function. That is to say, rather than consider "the meaning which reigns in everything that is,"[26] contemporary thought begins with a set of given conditions and then calculates how they might be put to this or that use. Such calculative thinking is "justified and needed in its own way."[27] However, its supremacy in modernity has entailed a distorted and furious approach to the world. As Heidegger explains, "Calculative thinking computes. It computes ever new, ever more promising and at the same time more economical possibilities. Calculative thinking races from one prospect to the next. Calculative thinking never stops, never collects itself."[28] Thus constituted, calculative thinking abstracts the thinker from existence, effectively bracketing "local" considerations of culture and tradition. Through "modern techniques of communication" and through the "great industrial corporations of the leading countries," this phenomenon has come to affect the whole of Western society, uprooting people from hearth and home (even if, physically, they remain there) and thereby revealing "a different world":

> The world now appears as an object open to the attacks of calculative thought, attacks that nothing is believed able any longer to resist. Nature becomes a gigantic

gasoline station, an energy source for modern technology and industry. This relation of man to the world as such, [is] in principle a technical one.[29]

With this in mind, Heidegger quotes the American chemist and Nobel laureate, Wendell Meredith Stanley (1904–71), who predicted that soon "life will be placed in the hands of the chemist who will be able to synthesize, split and change living substance at will."[30] This is an unnerving statement, Heidegger adds, but even more unnerving is "our being unprepared for this transformation."[31]

What response, then, does Heidegger recommend? His answer is famously elliptical—and more will be said about Heidegger as this book unfolds—but it is perhaps best summed up by the phrase "meditative thinking."[32] This is precisely the sort of thinking that has lost purchase in the technologized West, for it is seen as "floating unaware above reality," profiting "nothing in carrying out practical affairs."[33] And yet, says Heidegger, such assumptions refuse to acknowledge the essence of human nature, namely, that "man is a *thinking* . . . a *meditating* being."[34] Moreover, calculative thinking often mischaracterizes meditation, which does not position one above reality but, rather, directs one to "that which concerns us, each one of us, here and now; here, on this patch of home ground; now, in the present hour of history."[35] To attend to "what lies close" is to root oneself in reality, and it is from this "rootedness" that a free relation to technology is made possible.[36] In other words, when one thinks meditatively, one is able to attend to "that which shows itself and at the same time withdraws," to focus on "the mystery" that permeates all of life, including technology.[37] Borrowing from German mystics such as Meister Eckhart (c.1260–c.1328), Heidegger refers to this approach as *"releasement toward things"* (*Gelassenheit zu den Dingen*), because it does not cling to a single way of viewing the world.[38] The one who practices *Gelassenheit*, then, is able to use technology without forgetting that it "remain[s] dependent on something higher."[39] Only in this disposition, which is both a "yes" and a "no" to technology, will a "new ground and foundation" be uncovered, so that human creativity might be revitalized.[40]

As has been noted, Heidegger's approach to technology is not without its detractors. Still, he remains a principal figure in the philosophy of technology, and his insight into the decline of meditative thinking seems almost prescient in the twenty-first century—a point underlined by Nicholas Carr's *The Shallows: What the Internet Is Doing to Our Brains*, nominated for a Pulitzer Prize in 2011, which traces the exacerbation of this problem by the rise of net-based information technologies. Thus, it is not surprising that, according to Richard Rojcewicz, Heidegger's work on technology "remains unsurpassed—indeed, unequalled—in its radicality."[41] If, then, Heidegger's call to ponder or to question technology remains valuable (if not flawless), it makes sense to turn to someone like Kierkegaard, who himself encourages this very mode of thinking. After all, not only does Kierkegaard's authorship delve into topics such as the origin and end of the created world, the essence of human nature, and the question of the good life, but it does so against the backdrop of a modern, technologically determined society. Moreover, as a literary and rhetorical stylist, Kierkegaard writes precisely as one who aims to elicit "reflection," "contemplation," or "meditation." As he explains in an 1848 journal entry, his task is to foster a "God-fearing reflection" (*Reflexion*), a "simplicity armed with reflection," which, in opposition to the modern subjugation of thought to calculation, seeks to "comprehend that one cannot comprehend."[42] In this undertaking, Kierkegaard's anticipation of Heidegger is unmistakable.[43] Moreover, in his attention to theological concerns in general and to spiritual upbuilding in particular, it might even be said that Kierkegaard offers a richer and more suasive response to modernity's culture of calculation.

The volume's structure

The basic claim of this study is that Kierkegaard's oeuvre is capable of stimulating reflection on the question concerning technology—a thesis that will be developed over six chapters. Chapter 1 will survey technology's development in Western culture, while Chapter 2 will examine the same issue in nineteenth-century Denmark, paying particular attention to those technologies that Kierkegaard would have encountered. Far from being exercises in historical curiosity, these chapters will demonstrate that Kierkegaard lived in a time of immense and varied technological change. Thus, they will properly contextualize many of his sociopolitical concerns, which, as will be argued, cannot be separated from the rise of technology as a dominant force in Danish (and, by extension, Western) society.

Chapters 3 and 4 will explore Kierkegaard's evaluation of technology in the modern world. The former will investigate direct references to technology in Kierkegaard's authorship, whether in his published or unpublished writings, and it will look for issues and/or themes that have a bearing on the philosophy of technology. Here, urbanization and mechanization will prove significant, along with Kierkegaard's recognition that modernity is generally moving toward an objective way of framing the world. Chapter 4, in turn, will focus on what is inarguably Kierkegaard's greatest contribution to thinking about technology—namely, his early critique of information technology. It will be argued that his 1846 text, *A Literary Review*, which is well known for its censure of "the present age," cannot be fully understood without taking into consideration the rise of print media and, with it, the ever-increasing role of information technology. But these considerations will raise an ostensible conflict. After all, Kierkegaard himself was a *user* of print technology—a practice that would appear uncontroversial vis-à-vis his publication of *books* but quickly verges on contradiction as regards his so-called "attack on Christendom," in which Kierkegaard adopts the methods (and message?) of the popular press.

After demonstrating that Kierkegaard wrestled with the question concerning technology, Chapter 5 will seek to apply Kierkegaard's insights to a concrete technological problem—to wit, the rise of Google and its systematic ordering of net-based information. As is well known, Kierkegaard was a great critic of what he saw as the Hegelian project of systematic, objectified knowledge. What this chapter will argue is that Kierkegaard's criticism of Hegelianism is applicable to Google, one of today's most dominant cultural influences. Google is a multinational corporation, whose eponymous search engine has revolutionized the way in which internet users seek and process information. The company claims to serve the common good, insofar as it renders information more accessible and thus more "useful." But is the systematic collection and distribution of knowledge necessarily beneficial? Drawing on the thought of Kierkegaard, this chapter will argue to the contrary. Specifically, it will show how Google's mission recalls Kierkegaard's concerns about Hegelianism and "the system's" abstraction of knowledge from existence. Moreover, it will demonstrate that, particularly in his upbuilding discourses, Kierkegaard both promotes and fosters an alternative way of seeing or thinking—namely, *Betragtning* ("meditation" or "contemplation"), which centers the existing person and so is propaedeutic to an earnest engagement with reality. In the age of Google, it will be determined, reading Kierkegaard is akin to therapy.

Chapter 6 will conclude this study by pondering the nature of a Kierkegaardian response to modern technology. With this in mind, it will begin by highlighting Kierkegaard's influence on the humanities philosophy of technology in the twentieth century. It is not within the purview of this study to examine this influence in toto, though a few key points will be developed. First, it will be shown that a number of Kierkegaard's insights regarding modern technology influenced the thought of later philosophers—namely, Walter Benjamin, Martin Heidegger, and his onetime student Herbert Marcuse (1898–1971), along with a pair of French philosophers, Gabriel Marcel (1889–1973) and Jacques Ellul (1912–94). While the philosophical consequence of Kierkegaard's writings can hardly be limited to these five authors, it is hoped that this chapter will flesh out some important points of convergence and divergence, thereby stimulating further interest in the Dane's impact on the philosophy of technology.

And yet, it will also be reasoned that Kierkegaard's greatest influence on this question may lie in *theology*.[44] To be sure, the list of twentieth-century theologians who draw on Kierkegaard's authorship and its intellectual-cum-spiritual repercussions is a veritable "Who's Who," including Karl Barth (1886–1968), Henri de Lubac (1896–1991), and Jürgen Moltmann (1926–). However, this chapter will concentrate on three theologians in particular—namely, Romano Guardini (1885–1968), Paul Tillich (1886–1965), and Thomas Merton (1915–68). Not only do Guardini, Tillich, and Merton utilize Kierkegaard in order to formulate a Christian response to technological dominance, but their respective ways of appropriating his legacy represent a classic fissure in Christian thought and practice: is the Christian called to *elevate* fallen society or to *detach* from it? While Guardini and Tillich tend to side with the former perspective, Merton has an unmistakable sympathy for the latter. But Kierkegaard, with his eschatological approach to the subject, was more radical than each of these critics of technology—a point that situates him as a liminal thinker for theologies of technology, though, perhaps, it is just this liminality that makes him valuable.

At this point, it will be clear that Kierkegaard's position over against technological society was largely negative. And yet, as Chapter 5 argued, it may be that Kierkegaard's negativity can be put in service to the good, offering a crucial counterbalance to the blithe endorsements of technology that preponderate today. In short, there is scope for nuance in Kierkegaard's thinking on technology—a fact that should come as no surprise to anyone familiar with his sophisticated literary style and skill, not to mention his meticulous studies of human existence, the relationship between faith and reason, and so on.

Indeed, if anything, it may be that Kierkegaard's thought is *too* nuanced to link him to any particular "school" in the philosophy of technology. At different points, his oeuvre seems to resemble Christian mysticism, critical theory, expressionist poetry, phenomenology, and Sartrean existentialism—sometimes all in a single volume! Hence, in the end, this treatise will conclude as it started: Kierkegaard's ultimate value as a thinker on technology does not lie in any one "answer" but, rather, in his ability to compel persons to interrogate who they are and how they should relate to others, including those skills and techniques that facilitate their interaction with the world around them—in nuce, to ask the question concerning technology.

Christopher B. Barnett
Cooperstown, New York
December 2018

Acknowledgments

Taken as a whole, this book is a new and original work. However, it should be noted that Chapter 5 was previously published in *Kierkegaard's God and the Good Life*, edited by Stephen Minister, J. Aaron Simmons, and Michael Strawser (Bloomington, Indiana: Indiana University Press, 2016), pp. 130–51. I am grateful for permission to reproduce it in this setting.

Finally, before moving on to the book itself, a few words of acknowledgment are in order. I would like to thank my colleagues and students at Villanova University, who provide a stimulating yet hospitable academic environment. I would also like to thank Villanova's College of Liberal Arts and Sciences and Dean Adele Lindenmeyr for granting me a "Research Semester" in fall 2018 to wrap up this years-long project. Special thanks are due to a number of scholars working in the academy and in Kierkegaardiana who have had a hand in the development of this study: Michael Burdett, Andy Burgess, Jack Caputo, Lenny DeLorenzo (and others at the University of Notre Dame's McGrath Institute for Church Life, where I spoke on Kierkegaard in March 2018), Josh Furnal, Jacob Given, David Gouwens, Vincent McCarthy, Stephen Minister, George Pattison, Marcia Robinson, Aaron Simmons, Jon Stewart, and Michael Strawser. Alas, such a list cannot itemize countless scholars who have helped in subtle yet significant ways—whether with a word of encouragement, a provocative question, or simply by listening—but my gratitude remains all the same. Lastly, I am grateful for the interest and support of Haaris Naqvi and everyone at Bloomsbury.

As with all such endeavors, the origins of this project are manifold, ranging from scholarly presentations to pedagogical instruction (I've been regularly teaching a course called "God, Spirituality, and Technology") to film and literature and even to casual conversations with friends at the little-league field. However, there has been no greater impetus than my family—my wife Stacy, who is ever supportive, but especially my children Luke, Caleb, Paul, and Grace. Talking with my kids about technology, about its benefits as well as its dangers, has spurred me to think more deeply about this issue, so that my advice, however unwelcome, will at least be informed! I hope that my own desire to ask the question concerning technology—a desire kindled by Kierkegaard more than any other thinker—will encourage them to do the same. To them, then, I dedicate this book.

Abbreviations for Kierkegaard's Works

Danish[1]

SKS   *Søren Kierkegaards Skrifter* (1997–2013)

Pap.   *Søren Kierkegaards Papirer* (1909–48)

English[2]

CUP1   *Concluding Unscientific Postscript to "Philosophical Fragments,"* Vol. 1 (1992)

EO1   *Either/Or*, Vol. 1 (1987)

EO2   *Either/Or*, Vol. 2 (1987)

EUD   *Eighteen Upbuilding Discourses* (1990)

FT   *Fear and Trembling* (1983)

JP   *Søren Kierkegaard's Journals and Papers*, Vols. 1–7 (1967–78)

KJN   *Kierkegaard's Journals and Notebooks* (2007–)

LD   *Letters and Documents* (1978)

M   *"The Moment" and Late Writings* (1998)

PC   *Practice in Christianity* (1991)

PV   *The Point of View* (1998)

SLW   *Stages on Life's Way* (1988)

SUD   *The Sickness unto Death* (1980)

TD   *Three Discourses on Imagined Occasions* (1993)

UDVS   *Upbuilding Discourses in Various Spirits* (1993)

WA   *Without Authority* (1997)

WL   *Works of Love* (1995)

References to Kierkegaard's Works

Given its subject matter, I hope this book will find a broad audience—scholars and students, to be sure, but also non-specialist readers. Thus, I have made its critical apparatus as straightforward as possible and have tried not to overburden it with footnotes. Quotations from Kierkegaard's published work generally have been taken from the current standard English translations of his work, *Kierkegaard's Writings*, issued by Princeton University Press under the direction of Howard and Edna Hong. On occasion, however, I have elected to provide my own translations of Kierkegaard's writings, and, when appropriate, I have made a note of that decision. Accordingly, the standard Danish edition of Kierkegaard's works, *Søren Kierkegaards Skrifter* (SKS) is also indicated.[1]

Quotations from Kierkegaard's *Nachlaß* have been taken from two places: either *Søren Kierkegaard's Journals and Papers* (JP), the seven-volume set arranged by the Hongs, or the new *Kierkegaard's Journals and Notebooks* (KJN), which is under the general editorship of Bruce H. Kirmmse. As with the published writings, I have cross-referenced the journals and papers to SKS as well,[2] though, in rare instances, I have needed to use the older *Papirer*.[3] In addition, a register of abbreviations has been included, and complete documentary information can be accessed in the Works Cited section.

1

A General History of Technology

In the year 1811—just two years before the birth of Søren Kierkegaard—the population of Denmark was one million.[1] In contrast, the population of England and Wales in 1801 was over nine million[2] and that of France nearing thirty million.[3] Each of those nations would experience remarkable population growth over the course of the nineteenth century, but the Denmark into which Søren Kierkegaard was born was still very much an agricultural nation: "75–85 per cent of this population was rural, with roughly 70 per cent directly engaged in agriculture."[4] The country's lone metropolis was also its capital, Copenhagen, whose 100,000 residents[5] represented but a tenth of London's populace.[6]

On the surface, then, it might seem as if the rise of technology in nineteenth-century Denmark is an inconsequential topic. One might suppose that, to whatever extent there was technological development during that time period, it was a mere byproduct of progress elsewhere in Europe and, furthermore, a negligible force in a country of farmers and fishermen. At the same time, however, one might start with similar premises and reach a different conclusion—namely, that the arrival of modern technology in Denmark was momentous, precisely because it largely came from the outside and therefore unsettled a nation whose social order had changed little since the Middle Ages. Indeed, as will be argued, the latter is much closer to the case. During the first half of the nineteenth century, Denmark was rocked by a series of economic, military, political, and technological changes, so much so that, by the time Kierkegaard died in 1855, it was a far different country than the one he knew as a child. The task of this chapter is to outline these developments, paying special attention to technology. Not only will this topic cast light on the broader context of Kierkegaard's authorship, but it will indicate that Kierkegaard's engagement with the key social questions of his day was inseparable from the question concerning technology.

The task of this chapter is to sketch a general history of technology and, in turn, to clarify a point that many already intuit—that the evolution of world history is bound up with the evolution of technology. "The hand-mill gives you society with the feudal lord; the steam-mill, society with the industrial capitalist,"[7] as Karl Marx famously put it. One need not subscribe to such a reductive view to see that it contains merit. Of particular concern here will be the rise of what is now often referred to as "information technology," which, following Johannes Gutenberg's implementation of movable type printing in 1439, played a decisive factor in Europe's slow but inexorable turn to a "knowledge economy," that is to say, a society centered on "the systematic supply of knowledge and systematic training in applying it," so that information, rather than material goods, becomes "the central 'factor of production' in an advanced, developed economy."[8] It is critical to survey this development, since, as will be seen, Kierkegaard was principally concerned with information technology or, as he preferred, "the press" (*Pressen*).

Modernity and the ascent of technology

To confront the origins and development of technology is to confront a story of daunting proportions. After all, as John Dyer has commented, the first "technology upgrade"[9] goes back to the very beginning of human civilization—in his example, to God's clothing of Adam and Eve in the Garden of Eden (Gen. 3:21). This suggestion draws on the Bible, but archaeologists agree that the evolution of the genus *Homo* goes hand in hand with that of technology: roughly one million years ago, *Homo erectus* began to develop "sophisticated stone tool technology"[10] in advance of the arrival of *Homo sapiens*, the only extant human species. The archaeological record is based as much on the development of instruments for industry and cooking as it is on biological markers such as cranial capacity.

And yet, even if one moves beyond the abysses of prehistory, there is a surfeit of complications. Questions about the cultural development and expression of various technologies abound. For example, printing, gunpowder, and the compass all have Chinese origins but, at least initially, failed to transform China as they did Western culture.[11] Likewise, a "wave of technology emanating from China and India rolled across the Islamic world of the eighth and ninth centuries AD,"[12] but these innovations were often put in service to Muslim piety. For example, "Indian astronomical tables" were used for *'ilm al-miqat*—a manner of time-keeping by which a muezzin was able "to determine the five daily canonical hours of prayer."[13] Such nuances underscore the fact that there is no simple "history of technology" and, likewise, no universal or culturally neutral way of speaking about "technological progress." What is seen as an advance in one culture may be received as a retrogression in another—a point borne out by ongoing tensions between the Orient and the Occident on the nature and significance of technological development.

Consequently, this survey of the rise of technology will restrict itself to Western culture, with particular attention on the centuries postdating Gutenberg's printing press. This is not to imply that Western technology can be neatly detached from extra-Occidental contexts. And yet, at the same time, a number of characteristics have come to distinguish technology in the West. Keld Nielson summarizes them as follows:

> The ability to extract mechanical energy from fossil fuel through inventions like the steam engine and the internal combustion engine: mass production through the integration of the extraction of raw materials with transport systems, production

facilities and sophisticated systems of distribution of wares to masses of consumers; the widespread use of technological standards and unified measuring systems; a permanent increase in mechanical precision in tool-making and manufacture; an intimate and active relation to capital and investments; the use of scientific knowledge in the development of products and production methods; and the high priority given to renewal through investments in research and development.[14]

Such features have become so ubiquitous in the West as to seem banal. Right now, as I write this, I am looking out of my office window. Bare maple and birch trees extend over rooftops bearing the last remnants of a recent snowfall; beyond them lies the low, pallid cloud cover of a February morning, which, here and there, reveals patches of pale azure. There are a few animals around as well: a black squirrel (a common species in the northeastern United States) perches on a branch nearby, and a skein of geese fly north and quickly leave my field of vision. This could be an almost timeless scene, but, at second glance, the world described by Nielson above is unmistakable. The squirrel exchanges his branch for a series of wires, which run on a grid throughout the neighborhood. These wires, of course, provide a variety of telecommunication services (electricity, telephone, cable, internet, etc.), and they have been put there by multibillion-dollar corporations such as PECO and Verizon. Moreover, every house that I can see accommodates one or two motorized vehicles—themselves constructed and sold by multibillion-dollar companies—in an adjacent driveway. Farther in the distance, just out of view, runs a two-lane thoroughfare that facilitates a steady flow of traffic, the vast majority of which is powered by large, fuel-burning machines, including commercial trucks carrying sundry goods and even bigger vehicles (buses, in particular) moving people from destination to destination. And, finally, an airplane passes overhead and vanishes into the western horizon. It is an enormous piece of equipment, holding perhaps 200 persons and their belongings, and yet its internal combustion engine is capable of bringing it to a speed of almost 600 miles per hour. Hence, if the flight I'm watching is bound for Chicago, it will make the nearly 700 mile trip from Philadelphia in around 90 minutes—an almost impossibly efficient journey, for which the airplane's owner (another multibillion-dollar corporation) charges hundreds of dollars per ticket—indeed, through an advanced telecommunications system such as a computer website!

A scene such as this one can be observed from most windows in the Western world, and it serves as a précis of the current state of technology in the West. As late as the fourteenth century, Europe was still a predominantly agricultural civilization, whose technological innovation either came from the outside or differed from other cultures "in quantity rather than in essence."[15] Since that time, however, Europe and its Western progeny (North America and Australia, above all) have been transformed into highly mechanized, essentially urban societies, whose fundamental preoccupation lies with the systematic gathering and distribution of goods and services for the sake of monetary profit. The factors leading to this change are profuse, but, broadly speaking, two developments demand particular emphasis: (i) the proliferation of cities oriented toward exchange and (ii) technological innovations stemming therefrom.

The growth of Western urbanization

The great Belgian historian Henri Pirenne famously argued that Europe's development as a distinct continent, led by a number of autonomous (or relatively autonomous) northern cities, can be traced back to the ninth century.[16] The rise of Islam in the East and the threat of Muslim invasion not only legitimized the prevailing Frankish Empire but encouraged it to turn away from the Mediterranean Basin—long the cradle of European civilization—to the "forces of the north."[17] Later in the century, this shift in the balance of power would be reinforced, when the Carolingian Empire was "parcelled out" to "local dynasties"—a move that stabilized Europe and "was, on the whole, beneficial for society."[18] It was at this time that, according to the so-called "Pirenne Thesis," a class of persons dedicated to facilitating commerce between northern Europe's various administrative outposts arose. Eventually these "merchants"—a term derived from the Latin *mercari* ("to trade")—would grow in stature, transcend the limitations of feudal culture, and orient Europe toward an economic system based on the flow of goods, information, and services.

Whether or not one adopts Pirenne's theory in toto, it is nevertheless clear that urbanization—and, with it, an economy "catering to trade and handicraft production"[19]—played a key role in technological development. For example, the clustering of tradespersons in Europe's cities meant that various groups, from guilds of master craftsmen to less cohesive bands of apprentices and laborers, were able to focus on the manufacture and exchange of commercial goods. In turn, "new modes of production involving many steps and division of labor were perfected,"[20] and with increased productivity came increased profits. Thus, "banking systems emerged, making it easier to direct the flow of money toward trade, building and production, and the rising trading companies started to use double-entry bookkeeping."[21]

The success of Europe's burgeoning urban culture, as well as the upsurge of its attendant trading conglomerates, resulted in the establishment of cities abroad. Starting with the Portuguese and the Spanish, European merchants sought to expand their opportunities for trade and, with it, for wealth. Explorers were commissioned not only to espy new territories but also to extricate "commodities and raw materials from around the world."[22] This was the beginning of colonialism, and it resulted in a cycle of technological development: urbanization entailed trade and the technological means by which to trade (goods, transport, etc.); the more these conduits were acquired, the more productivity grew and, along with it, the inevitability of exploration and colonization; yet, in order to facilitate this expansion, more technology was needed, thereby spurring further innovation and urbanization. It is for this reason that Sam Bass Warner, Jr., could argue, albeit with a degree of humor, that "urban history might serve as the focus of an entire liberal arts curriculum,"[23] since the disciplines that are so often identified with Western civilization—namely, the arts and the sciences—should be understood "with explicit reference to the urban dimension where they each intersected."[24] Richard Rodger takes this notion a step further, insisting that cities were not just *sites* where Western culture was cultivated but, indeed, *participants* in that very cultivation: "The town was not simply the theatre; it was an actor, too."[25]

This notion was vividly displayed during the eighteenth and nineteenth centuries—a period in which Western cities, having grown steadily for centuries, now "skyrocketed."[26] In the words of the contemporaneous English scholar Robert Vaughan, it was "the age of great cities," during which "the world has never been so covered with cities as at the present time, and society generally has never been so leavened with the spirit natural to cities."[27] That rapid technological change also occurred during this epoch was hardly an accident. Industrialization—or the process by which a given society evolves from a predominantly agricultural model to one centered on the production and distribution of goods and services through large-scale technical operations—was one of modernity's "dual revolutions," and it cannot "be understood apart from the story of urban growth."[28] After all, the concurrence of urbanization and industrialization is due to the structure of cities themselves, which function "simultaneously [as] markets, service centers, and sites of production," thereby requiring "strong economic bases."[29] Unlike rural settlements, cities cannot sustain themselves from the land and, therefore, "have to produce something to sell in return for food."[30] It is here that technology becomes almost indistinguishable from the urban project, since technology is a means both to produce and to convey commercial goods, not to mention a commercial good in and of itself.

An example of these interrelationships can be seen in Great Britain. James Watt's steam engine, developed in the latter half of the eighteenth century, made it possible to deliver mechanical power wherever "fuel could be found or imported."[31] This convenience led to the explosion of mining in places such as the West Midlands and Yorkshire, and "with the expanding mines came ramshackle housing, new streets, and shops."[32] Eventually, these settlements "turned into towns, and towns . . . became cities, as industrial development continued."[33] A similar course would transform Glasgow into one of the largest cities in the UK: once a modest town, the steam engine extended Glasgow's textile productivity, and soon the River Clyde was dredged to make room for barges and larger ships. These changes sparked economic growth, and various factories "sprouted up on vacant land in central districts, as workers poured into the city hoping to find jobs."[34] Nor was this pattern unknown in Europe's oldest and most established towns. The number of factory workers in Berlin soared by nearly 300 percent in the first half of the nineteenth century, and ancient cities such as Lyon and Barcelona experienced similar growth.[35] Indeed, it appears that cities already "famous for their artisanal manufacturing made a gradual transition to factory production, using their resources of skilled labor, capital, and marketing savvy."[36]

Overall, then, the influence of urbanization on technological advancement is hard to overestimate. While it is true that entrepreneurs and inventors were largely responsible for the development of various technologies, their ventures were both encouraged by and dependent on the proliferation of urban centers, especially in Europe, for cities made available the basic ingredients of technological growth—transportation, information, and an abundance of skilled labor.

Technological innovation in the "Age of Great Cities"

If technology began to flourish with the rise of European city life, it is also true that specific technical devices tended to emerge from the principles and needs of Christian monasticism, especially in its Benedictine form. Indeed, whereas the earliest Christian monks were located in places such as Syria and Egypt and often led lives of solitary asceticism,[37] Benedict of Nursia's "Rule" reoriented Western monasticism in the sixth century. It was not, admittedly, the very first monastic guidebook. But unlike the preceding "Rules" of Basil the Great and Augustine of Hippo—both of which tended to emphasize the importance of communal living and "love more than obedience"[38]—*The Rule of Saint Benedict* made duty, order, and manual labor central to its mission.[39] As its opening prologue states: "Through the toil of obedience you may return to him from whom you have separated by the sloth of disobedience."[40]

This emphasis on active labor as a component of religious life was "integral to massive technological development," insofar as the Benedictines, in their attention to external matters, "carried with them not merely a new religion but also new practical arts."[41] Already in the twelfth century, Arnold of Bonneval noted that monks were using "waterpowered machines for milling, fulling, tanning, blacksmithing, and other industries," and such developments were independently attested in *De diversis artibus*—a contemporaneous text by a German Benedictine known as Theophilus, who details the "religiously motivated codification of all the skills available for the embellishment of a church."[42] Nor was this solely a Benedictine movement. At the Abbey of St. Victor in Paris, a number of Canons Regular articulated philosophically what had been implied in Benedictine practice. For example, Hugh of St. Victor's *Didascalicon* (c. 1130) presents "a secular schematization of all human knowledge, which, for the first time, includes the mechanic arts."[43] In particular, Hugh argues that "there are four branches of knowledge only": "the theoretical, which strives for the contemplation of truth; the practical, which considers the regulation of morals; the mechanical, which supervises the occupations of this life; and the logical, which provides the knowledge necessary for correct speaking and clear argumentation."[44] Hugh divides mechanical knowledge into several subdisciplines, including commerce and medicine,[45] yet adds that each branch "pursues merely human works."[46] That is to say, whereas God "works" in his creation and sustenance of the cosmos, and nature "works" by actualizing the potentialities latent in creation, human beings work by virtue of their "own reasoning," which seeks to supply by artistry what they otherwise lack. As Hugh writes, "Want it is which has devised all that you see most excellent in the occupations of men."[47]

This philosophical appreciation of human work was "unprecedented" at the time, though, by the high medieval period, "all the arts, including the mechanic arts, were [considered] a part of the good life."[48] Indeed, the technological advances that have come to characterize the modern West were primarily inaugurated during the Renaissance—a period that Nielson approximates with the "fifteenth to seventeenth centuries,"[49] during which "European intellectuals began to become aware of technological progress not as a project . . . but as an historic and happy fact."[50] Perhaps the most crucial of these innovations was Gutenberg's printing press, and its impact will be assessed below. But it was hardly alone in shaping Western culture. The possibility of European colonization and the concomitant rise of transatlantic trade was dependent on "the development of the full-rigged ship, armed with guns, and the design of new astronomical methods of navigation."[51] Other advances naturally followed. There were slow but steady improvements "in mining techniques, in the extraction and processing of metals, in the design and use of firearms, in fortification, in the design and use of ships, and in the construction of harbors, canals and bridges."[52] Such developments were the means by which nation-states were able to grow, in terms of both commercial efficiency and military conquest.[53]

By the eighteenth century and the so-called Age of Enlightenment, the West was in the throes of a full-blown technological revolution, with attention now shifting to the provision of more stable energy sources. In previous eras, "the chief energy source had been the muscle power of men or animals,"[54] and thus there were intrinsic limitations to the amount of available energy, from the challenges of accumulating manpower (a problem that slavery could only incrementally diminish) to the expensiveness of feeding both human and animal workers. Meanwhile, natural energy sources such as water or wind represented tantalizing yet inefficient options, circumscribed by geography, unreliable output, and/or the need for capital. Watt's steam engine, however, ameliorated many of these difficulties, converting "accumulated solar energy in the form of wood, coal or oil to mechanical motion" and, in doing so, paving the way for the rise of "steam turbines, internal combustion engines and jet engines that have the same function."[55] As these devices improved and manufacturing increased, vocational schools and engineering societies were founded, leading to better communication among engineers and therefore "more precision and more uniformity" in the process of production.[56] Eventually, this development resulted in the so-called "American system of manufacture," whereby "one part of a mechanical device could be manufactured with such precision that without individual fitting it could be replaced by a similar part from another similar mechanical device."[57] This step paved the way for assembly-line production, which the Ford Motor Company inaugurated in 1914.[58]

It was also around this time that scientists became directly involved in the technological process. This trend began in the textile industry, where "university-trained chemists discovered ways to produce dyes synthetically," but quickly expanded to other industries, resulting in the rise of the "industrial research and development laboratory."[59] Today, such laboratories have become standard within corporations and governments, and they have advanced "a very large part of the technological breakthroughs of the last hundred years."[60] For that reason, new technological devices and ever-expanding technological horizons are now the anticipated outcomes of Western social organization. In other words, it is no longer possible—as it would have been, say, in medieval Benedictine monasteries—to see technology as an expedient that facilitates the practice of a higher, nontechnical end. Instead, technology is understood as an end in itself: technology is now the goal of the modern West's most powerful institutions, inasmuch as it is inseparable from "life, liberty, and the pursuit of happiness." As Nielson puts it, "The modern Western style of living, health and welfare would be unthinkable without Western technology."[61]

As has been seen, no one technology can be said to have wrought all of these changes, nor can they be chalked up to a single political development or scientific discovery. The rise of the modern West is a profoundly complicated event, and, to borrow from Charles Taylor, there are "many stories"[62] regarding its provenance. And yet, even if this is true, it is nevertheless the case that one innovation ranks above the rest, since it rapidly intensified the emergent urban and technological tendencies of medieval Western culture. This innovation is the printing press.

"The Gutenberg Galaxy"

The primal media for human language are the "folds" of mucous membrane that extend across the larynx—the "vocal cords." Hence, from an anthropological point of view, written language is essentially a byproduct of vocal speech, but its derived quality by no means reduces its importance. Even in primitive human cultures, marks and symbols were carved into assorted media, from "strips of bark" to "chunks of broken pottery."[63] Later, the ancient Sumerians developed a more stable medium for written communication, using clay tablets to record everything from commercial transactions to religious stories.[64] But this method proved cumbersome, and, over time, other media for written language were tested. The Egyptians fashioned scrolls from the fibers of papyrus plants, while the Greeks and the Romans used a parchment made from animal skin.[65] Yet, these methods, too, presented difficulties. Scrolls were costly and inefficient, and so the search continued for an ideal literary medium.

An ostensible solution was found when the codex was developed during the first century CE. Originally consisting of sheets of parchment sewn "between a pair of rigid rectangles of leather,"[66] the codex allowed scribes to write on *both* sides of a sheet of parchment, thereby condensing information and, in turn, lowering production costs. Moreover, since codices were typically smaller than scrolls, they were not only easier to transport from one place to another but also easier to use: "Finding a particular passage, an awkward task with a long roll of text, became a simple matter of flipping back and forth through a set of pages."[67] With this innovation, the exchange of information in the West slowly but surely increased, and literacy followed suit, albeit even more slowly. Indeed, access to codices was limited to a "relatively small group of privileged citizens,"[68] often from religious contexts. So, while the codex—or, as it is now known, the book—emerged as the best vehicle for written language, it had yet to be perfected in such a way that it could be "produced and distributed cheaply, quickly, and in abundance."[69]

Johannes Gutenberg's printing press effected precisely this change. It appeared during what Lewis Mumford has dubbed Western society's "eotechnic phase," that is to say, "the dawn age of modern technics."[70] During this period, which laid the groundwork for the "multiplication of machines and the increase of power,"[71] there was a general movement toward organization and efficiency. Mumford cites the "mechanical clock," with its ability to organize social habits and interaction, as the inaugurator of Western systematization, though he adds that the printing press is "second to the clock in order if not perhaps in importance."[72] As has been noted, the origins of print technology are manifold: the Chinese "first experimented with block printing and moveable type,"[73] and a number of other civilizations, from the Korean Peninsula to present-day Turkey, contributed to this development. Yet, it was the German blacksmith, Johannes Gutenberg, who "perfected the invention, and from Germany it spread to all the world."[74]

At the time, Europe still had a predominantly agricultural economy, despite the pull to urbanization.[75] It was also a time "of stagnation in politics and Church affairs."[76] Gutenberg's resourceful invention, which "used the physical action of the paper- or wine-press to transfer the ink from typematter to dampened paper with one even and forceful impression,"[77] would soon render prior eras obsolete. By the 1450s, not only had the famed *Gutenberg Bible* appeared but so had a number of other documents, from poems to dictionaries. Moreover, an ominous employment of Gutenberg's invention was discovered: the press was used to issue propaganda and indulgences in order to promote military resistance to the expanding Ottoman Empire.[78]

There was, then, a certain ambivalence about Gutenberg's invention. Its ability to disseminate information could be used for good or for ill. But its import was more than instrumental. The ever-increasing availability of printed matter also *shaped* Western culture. According to Mumford, the biggest change concerned the turn to mechanical control and reproducibility:

> Printing was from the beginning a completely mechanical achievement. Not merely that: it was the type for all future instruments of reproduction: for the printed sheet, even before the military uniform, was the first completely standardized product, manufactured in series, and the movable types themselves were the first example of completely standardized and interchangeable parts. Truly a revolutionary invention in every department.[79]

Moreover, there were significant changes in the dissemination and the consumption of information. After Gutenberg, books became commodities and reading, "a possibility for countless numbers of people."[80] Scholars became "authors," who wrote for the sake of distribution. Phrases such as "mass readership" and "reading public" entered the popular lexicon.[81] For the first time, reading became a form of entertainment, even as its possibilities for sociopolitical subversion multiplied. Absolutist regimes sought to control these changes with censorship—a tack that, as will be seen, was tried in Denmark.

And yet, in the end, the tug of the expanding publishing market, coupled with the influence of the Enlightenment, rendered censorship efforts ineffectual.[82] Louis XVI's director of the book trade office, Guillaume de Malesherbes, once put it this way: "Because the law prohibits books the public cannot do without, the book trade has had to exist outside the law."[83] There was, in short, no stopping this radical shift. "The printing press served as the main instrument in the creation of a new political culture."[84] Indeed, that republican pamphleteers such as Thomas Paine in the American colonies and Camille Desmoulins in France used the press to foment revolution was an inexorable application of print technology. It was no longer possible to restrict public opinion to a handful of authorized voices.[85] On the contrary, there were as many opinions as there were presses, and the organization of Western government now had to adapt to this change.

But it may be that such political occurrences are mere symptoms of a deeper and more substantive transformation. In his well-known treatise, *The Gutenberg Galaxy: The Making of Typographic Man*, Marshall McLuhan argues Gutenberg's innovation actually produced a "psychic transformation"[86] in Western people. It was not just that the printing press facilitated the transmission of information; rather, it presented information in such a way that a "visual homogenizing of experience" occurred, thereby consigning "auditory and other sensuous complexity to the background."[87] Following the Hungarian theorist György Kepes,[88] McLuhan thereby argues that printed material inculcates a private, "fixed" perspective on reality, which conceals as much as it reveals.[89] Whereas any given image was once a "plastic organism," print abstracts it from wider sensual experience and situates it on the page for the sake of a "compartmentalizing or specialist outlook."[90] This way of looking at things—namely, as a "consistent series of static shots or 'fixed points of view' in homogenous relationship"—"will become the great program of the Gutenberg era, the source of wealth and power unknown to any other time or technology."[91] In other words, "printed books, themselves the first uniform, repeatable, and mass-produced items in the world, provided endless paradigms of uniform commodity culture for . . . succeeding centuries."[92]

Here, of course, McLuhan is sketching a notion that he later summarized in his memorable phrase: "the medium is the message."[93] By this he means that technology has an influence far beyond what it does or transmits, since the technological medium itself shapes our perception of reality and, eventually, how we interact with the world. For example, one might assume that the printing press is beneficial just to the extent that it is used to print beneficial material and deleterious just to the extent that it is used to print deleterious material. On this view, the technology itself is intrinsically neutral, and thus the primary question facing the user of the press has to do with *content*. But McLuhan sees it otherwise. For him, the question of content serves as a distraction from the subtle ways that a technology such as the printing press reorients human knowing and acting. As he writes, "The effects of technology do not occur at the level of opinions or concepts" but, rather, through the alteration of "patterns of perception."[94]

Of course, one may quibble with the degree to which McLuhan advances his thesis. However, with regard to Gutenberg's innovation, there is no question that it changed the course of human history—not just in terms of *what* it disseminated but also in terms of *how* it did so. As Nicholas Carr has shown, the printing press quite literally expanded the vocabulary of the English language, including "new words [that] encapsulated abstract concepts that simply hadn't existed before."[95] Thought began to deepen and, with it, consciousness: "As our ancestors imbued their minds with the discipline to follow a line of argument or narrative through a succession of printed pages, they became more contemplative, reflective, imaginative."[96] A "literary ethic" emerged, which came to permeate every field of human endeavor, including science, which would eventually boast two of the most impactful books of the modern era—Charles Darwin's *On the Origin of Species* (1859) and Albert Einstein's *Über die spezielle und die allgemeine Relativitätstheorie* (1916).[97] In short, there is no development in the modern West untouched by Gutenberg's press, whether in literature, politics, religion, or science. To encounter an abundance of printed material—and the ideas contained within—is simply part and parcel of what it means to be a modern person.

Conclusion

A visit to any bookstore or newspaper kiosk should be enough to demonstrate that the printed word remains prominent today. That is not to imply, however, that the medium is stagnant. With the advent of electronic media in the twentieth century, the changes wrought by Gutenberg have been accelerated, arguably at breakneck pace. To be sure, if Walter Ong is right that "writing and print and the computer are all ways of technologizing the word,"[98] it is also the case that the word has never been as technologized as it is today. People are now reading in countless places and through countless means, including television screens, laptop computers, and handheld devices such as phones and tablets. It stands to reason, then, that a shift from the printed page to the digital screen will entail further changes in human behavior and thought. As Carr notes, "The world of the screen . . . is a very different place from the world of the page,"[99] and this claim has already been confirmed not only in popular experience but, increasingly, in psychological and sociological research as well.

As this study unfolds, the question of electronic media will demand further attention. First, however, it is important to explore Kierkegaard's own sociohistorical location, which gave him a unique perspective on technology in general and on print technology in particular. One might say that he lived in the advanced Gutenberg era—an era in which books, newspapers, magazines, and periodicals flourished, and the birth of the computer was imminent.[100] Hence, despite not having any personal knowledge of electronic media, Kierkegaard's insights regarding the press of his day have remained relevant in the twenty-first century and, indeed, may even appear prophetic.

Technology in Golden Age Denmark

Whereas Chapter 1 tendered a general history of technology, this chapter concerns the development of technology in Denmark as such. Here the operative question will be: which technological advances, particularly in the eighteenth and nineteenth centuries, came to shape Denmark during Kierkegaard's lifetime? In this connection, the expansion of the print media will demand primary consideration. And yet, Copenhagen's transition from a sleepy "market town"[1] to a modern European cultural center—whose leaders hoped "to remake . . . in the image of Paris"[2]—involved the arrival of a variety of technologies. Tracing these currents will lay the groundwork for Chapter 3, in which Kierkegaard's reflections on modern technology will be investigated. For, in the end, it is only in understanding Kierkegaard's *experience* of modern technology that we can properly assess his ideas about it.

Technological change in nineteenth-century Europe

Kierkegaard was a son of the nineteenth century. Thus, he lived in the wake of the American and French Revolutions and, therefore, on the far side of "a great divide in human history."[3] With these events, the ancien régime had been toppled and "could never be restored."[4] As a result, the nineteenth century became an era in which the consequences of revolution were realized. For many, this meant that the era would be remembered as a highpoint of human achievement: "Our century [is] superior to any that have gone before it,"[5] wrote the British scientist Alfred Russel Wallace. Others were less effusive, while also recognizing the century's import. The Swiss critic Jacob Burckhardt—who was in the same audience as Kierkegaard during Friedrich Schelling's Berlin lectures of 1841—noted that the nineteenth century was defined by "the mutability of things" and "the multiformity of modern life," since "the last three generations have experienced an infinitely greater variety of things"[6] than their predecessors.

Of course, at the heart of this modern experience was technology, so much so that one might think of the so-called "industrial revolution" as the revolution most characteristic of the nineteenth century.[7] This was a point already recognized at the time. For example, Wallace details the century's "new departures," which have "profoundly affected many of our habits, and even our thoughts and our language."[8]

He goes on to list no fewer than *thirteen* technological inventions, from railroads and steamships to electrical lighting and anesthetics.[9] What is more, he maintains that previous time periods, even when considered as a whole, cannot rival the nineteenth century's technological progress:

> We find only five inventions of the first rank in all preceding time—the telescope, the printing-press, the mariner's compass, Arabic numerals, and alphabetical writing, to which we may add the steam-engine and the barometer, making seven in all, as against thirteen in our single century.[10]

And this is to say nothing of various "theoretical discoveries," including "organic evolution,"[11] which likewise have outnumbered the rest of human history. It is for this reason that Wallace believes that "the age in which we live merits the title I have ventured to give it of—The Wonderful Century."[12]

Historians may quibble with Wallace's estimation of the nineteenth century's singularity, but the fact remains that it was a period of stunning technological change. Nowhere was this process more advanced than in Great Britain: "Just as the French Revolution of 1789 provided an ideal and a model even when the ideal was tarnished and the model misleading, so the British industrial revolution was treated both as a precursor and as a 'classic' case history in its own right."[13] Indeed, it was in Britain that a number of technical innovations were developed—most notably the steam engine, which made possible "the first sizeable factory industry"—and where a series of "new social problems" emerged in turn.[14] Writing about the northern city of Manchester, whose population swelled during the first half of the nineteenth century, Alexis de Tocqueville remarked that the "land is given over to industry's use," resulting not only in a "black smoke" so dense that the "sun seen through it is a disc without rays," but also in "wretched dwellings" that serve as a "home of vice and poverty."[15] If the upshot of such "progress" was monetary profit and better technology, those benefits came dearly. As Tocqueville concluded, "From this filthy sewer pure gold flows. Here humanity attains its most complete development and its most brutish; here civilization works its miracles, and civilized man is turned back almost into a savage."[16]

As the century passed, industrialization spread from Britain to the rest of Europe. By 1850, Europe had 15,000 miles of railway, and that number would more than triple by 1870.[17] Coal and iron ore production soared as well, particularly in the Ruhr Valley of Germany—"continental Europe's first great industrial zone."[18] What's more, these momentous changes were but precursors to even greater ones. The internal combustion engine appeared in the latter half of the nineteenth century, and, soon after, the automobile was developed. Equally important was the development of public electric power stations. The first one opened in Britain in 1881,[19] but decisive advances were made by Thomas Edison, whose station on Pearl Street in New York City was dedicated exclusively to the supply of incandescent lighting.[20] So successful was Edison's model that, by 1890, electric utilities had already spread across the United States and into Europe.[21]

Hence, not long after Kierkegaard's death, the Western world was already entering the so-called "Second Industrial Revolution," a "new culture of change" in which technology led to the "redefinition of time, space, and human social and economic relationships."[22] And yet, one might wonder, what of Denmark itself? How did the residents of this small nation—which was not quite on the outskirts of European affairs but hardly a main player in the manner of a France or a Germany—experience "The Wonderful Century"?

Denmark in "The Wonderful Century"

Denmark began the nineteenth century as an "overwhelmingly rural and agrarian society."[23] However, like other modern European nations, its base of power was centered in urban areas, especially in Copenhagen. During the seventeenth and eighteenth centuries, "a narrowly based urban absolutism"[24] came to dominate Danish commerce, culture, and government from the capital city. And yet, this arrangement would be challenged and, in some ways, overturned in the nineteenth century. Political turmoil, economic volatility, and social reform led Denmark to shift, however slowly, "to a broadly based rural and democratic regime."[25] The story of how this came about is a complex one—far too complex to thoroughly explore here—but it is worth highlighting the role that technology played in these changes. As will be seen, the printing press and its social effects loomed large in this regard. But other technological innovations were also present in Denmark, albeit in varying degrees and in varying contexts.

Agricultural reform

In his seminal work, *Kierkegaard in Golden Age Denmark* (1990), Bruce Kirmmse explains that a series of agricultural reforms rocked Danish society during the first decade of the nineteenth century. Underlying these changes was the restructuring of land ownership in the countryside: in order to facilitate "technical improvements and more rational, intensive agriculture," the government compelled the owners of great rural estates "to sell their copyholdings to their tenants so that they could get on with rationalizing the cultivation of their own lands."[26] Within the first decade of the nineteenth century, the majority of "peasant farms had passed over to self-ownership," and, in turn, the "government offered many prizes, cash incentives, educational programs, etc. in order to encourage the peasants to use new agricultural techniques."[27] Strictly in terms of output, the results were more than promising. There was an "enormous jump in productivity," coinciding with a "fifty percent increase in grain prices,"[28] and consequently many farmers experienced newfound wealth. But others— the so-called "cottagers," who did not own any land—suffered because their "labor obligations to the great landlords actually increased as more and more copyholders went free."[29] This situation persisted until late in the nineteenth century, when the "beginnings of mechanization"[30] reduced the need for human labor in the grainfields and, at last, the cottagers were able to take work in new industries.

The fate of Denmark's farmers may seem like a historical trifle, but, notably, Kierkegaard's own roots lie in the Danish peasantry. Kierkegaard's grandfather, Peder Christian, was a peasant hired to tend the small churchyard (*kirkegaard*) adjacent to the parish church in Sædding—a West Jutland hamlet located on the eastern side of Ringkøbing Fjord, which borders the North Sea. It is a windswept place, which, if not as forbidding as legend has it,[31] is nevertheless modest and far removed from the bustle of cosmopolitan life. Famously, Kierkegaard's father, Michael Pedersen, worked the same land as a young boy but, around 1768, left Sædding in order to apprentice with his uncle in a Copenhagen shop. That he needed formal permission to do so indicates the lowly status of the Kierkegaard family. As Peter Tudvad explains:

> In order to be able to acquire a trade license, one had to . . . be able to show an identification of incompetence, dismissal, or freedom. As a peasant's son, M.P. Kierkegaard was able to be supplied by the owner of the estate where he was born—namely, parish priest Nikolaj Satterup. Under his hand and seal, on 20 December 1777, Satterup gives ". . . *Michael Pedersen Kierkegaard*—who belongs to my annex estate and, due to his parents' poor circumstances and for the sake of many children, has been in *Copenhagen* from his 12th year for 9 years, and is still with his maternal uncle, Mr. *Niels Andersen*, hosier—an identification of freedom to be and to reside where he wants to."[32]

Thus, M. P. Kierkegaard knew the tumultuousness of the eighteenth and the nineteenth centuries well—the instrumentalizing reform of Danish agriculture and the sociocultural changes, both good and ill, stemming therefrom. Moreover, he experienced firsthand the transition from the rural peasantry to the urban bourgeoisie, and, famously, he struggled to negotiate this tension throughout his life. Even as his business ventures flourished, making him "one of the richest men in the country,"[33] he sustained an "unbroken connection with the religious awakening movement of the faraway West Jutland village of [his] childhood,"[34] especially by participating in Copenhagen's Moravian society (*Brødresocietet*), an important Pietist organization during the first half of the nineteenth century.[35]

It was principally through Pietism that Søren Kierkegaard, too, evinced his roots in the Danish peasantry, for otherwise he was a product of the city. Indeed, when Kierkegaard journeyed to Sædding as a twenty-seven-year-old, he did so with a mixture of fascination and bewilderment, waxing poetic about rural vistas ("the sheep drifting home; dark clouds, broken through . . . by bright beams of light") and yet alarmed by the poverty there.[36] Never one to spend much time away from Copenhagen, Kierkegaard found the journey itself equally challenging. He left Copenhagen by coach, boarded a "shabby" fishing boat in the port of Kalundborg, disembarked in the Jutland town of Aarhus, and then continued on by carriage to Sædding, requiring various stops in between.[37] The trip home, however, fared somewhat better. Arriving back in Aarhus, Kierkegaard booked a passage on "the supermodern, well-equipped steamship *Christian VIII*, so the crossing took only six hours."[38]

Such details are intriguing, because they indicate that Kierkegaard's social context was not qualitatively different than our own. He experienced the tension between the modern city and the hoary countryside, between the latest technology and its fading antecedents. As will be seen, such a tension would have presented itself to him in a variety of ways, not least in the myriad of technological advances that characterized his epoch.

Technological development

Transportation

Kierkegaard's era was positioned at the intersection of older forms of transportation (horseback riding, horse and carriage, sailing, etc.) and newer ones (steamship, automobile, various sorts of rail transport, including railways, subways, and trolleys, etc.). In Denmark, for example, the first railway line opened in 1847 under the leadership of Søren Hjorth. Hjorth had visited England in the 1830s and, while there, studied "the use of steam road and rail vehicles."[39] Upon returning to Denmark, he became the technical director of the nation's first railway line, which ran from Copenhagen to Roskilde—a distance of roughly twenty miles. Later, with support from the great Danish scientist Hans Christian Ørsted, Hjorth became a pioneer in the generation of electricity, unveiling an electric motor at the 1851 Great Exhibition in London and continuing to design electrical apparatuses until his death in 1870.[40]

Also appearing in Denmark in the mid-nineteenth century was the "omnibus," so named because "these carriages were available to everyone,"[41] as opposed to the private carriages owned by elites. Unsurprisingly, the country's first omnibus service was established in Copenhagen, with carriages—drawn by horses at first—taking an approximately five-mile route from Amagertorv in the city center to the Western suburb of Frederiksberg. Notably, Kierkegaard's family home as a youth was on Nytorv—a mere quarter mile from Amagertorv. Thus, the omnibuses, which "drew attention to themselves with their brightly painted coachwork,"[42] would have been a familiar sight to Kierkegaard from a young age.

As has been suggested, Kierkegaard was also aware that sea travel was changing in Denmark. Given the arrival of railroads, which facilitated the speed of transportation overland, the nation needed to improve the ferry service that linked its larger land masses (the Jutland peninsula as well as the islands of Funen and Zealand) to the hundreds of smaller islands surrounding them.[43] The first steam-powered ferry in Denmark was the *Caledonia*. Acquired in England in 1819, it demonstrated that the external combustion engine made it possible to conduct ferry service regardless of maritime conditions.[44] Other steamers were added to the Danish fleet in due course, and, by the 1850s, these ships were constructed with "inbuilt railway tracks and movable decks," thereby "allowing rapid continuous rail connections to all parts of

Denmark."[45] Similar accommodations would be made when automobile ownership began to rise in the 1930s, eventually making Denmark one of the world's leading shipbuilders.[46]

Of course, Kierkegaard did not live long enough to see the automobile: the German engineer Karl Benz would not unveil the world's first motorcar until 1886. However, he would hardly have been surprised at such a development, given the impact the external combustion engine had already made on Danish transport. In addition to his voyage on the *Christian VIII*, Kierkegaard traveled by steamship on a number of other occasions, including his trip from Copenhagen to Berlin (via Kiel) in October 1841 and his return journey in March 1842.[47] He traveled by railroad as well. In May 1843, on a particularly trying trip (from Copenhagen to Berlin via three stopovers), he boarded a train in the Prussian city of Stettin (now Szczecin, Poland) and took what would have amounted to a ten-hour train ride, albeit "in an armchair in an empty first-class carriage."[48]

None of this is to say that Kierkegaard was a connoisseur of modern methods of transportation. In fact, as will be discussed in the following chapter, he found such travel taxing and instead preferred to take what he called "air baths"—"gently undulating carriage rides"[49] to destinations on the outskirts of Copenhagen, where there were forests in which to walk and restaurants in which to dine. Modern transportation moved more people to more places at a faster rate, but it could not provide the quiet detachment that Kierkegaard himself desired.

Industrialization

As with developments in transport, the nineteenth century was a busy time for scientific and technological research in Denmark. After declaring the nation bankrupt in 1813— ironically, the year of Kierkegaard's birth—King Frederik VI sought to advance new avenues for trade and increased investment in the sciences.[50] Here, again, Ørsted was a leader. He discovered electromagnetism in 1820 and, while unsure of how to appropriate it, nevertheless understood the value of applying scientific principles to quotidian life. In 1829, Ørsted founded the Polytechnic Institute (*Den polytekniske Læreanstalt*, now known as *Danmarks Tekniske Universitet*), and, in 1842, he inaugurated the Society for the Spread of Natural Science (*Selskabet for Naturlærens Udbredelse*). But his approach to scientific and technical matters was broad enough to include metaphysical-cum-religious ones. In 1850, not long before his death, Ørsted published *The Spirit in Nature* (*Ånden i naturen*)—a collection of assorted talks and papers, the goal of which was to establish the underlying unity of science and religion.[51]

If Ørsted represented the expansive, conciliatory side of Denmark's turn to the sciences—indeed, Kierkegaard himself was an admirer of Ørsted, even considering him a scientist who reflects "the calm, the harmony, the joy"[52] in nature—there were cruder expressions as well. Following a geological survey in the mid-1830s, the South Jutland chemist and geologist Johan Georg Forchhammer determined that Denmark had an abundance of chalk and clay, in addition to "limited amounts of coal."[53] Consequently, the nation sought to ramp up its production of Roman concrete, especially on the

Baltic island of Bornholm, where several cement plants were opened in Kierkegaard's lifetime.[54] Moreover, Portland cement was imported from England and Germany, in order to provide further support for the nation's industrialization.[55] Joakim Garff sets the scene vividly:

> The 1840s were the first decade of steam power in Denmark, and during his wanderings along the ramparts Kierkegaard could see how, one after the other, the windmills went over to steam-driven grindstones. This efficient power source penetrated from the suburbs to the outskirts of the city and was soon within the ramparts of the city itself; factory chimneys sprung up everywhere.[56]

Such growth indicated a burgeoning economy, but problems were not far behind: "People complained about the noise and the stinking coal smoke . . . and before long the entire town was full of smoke and steam."[57]

Yet, it was not just heavy industry that saw an uptick at this time. For example, the growing possibility of harvesting wind energy—a tempting prospect for a nation surrounded by the sea—made Denmark an early leader in aerodynamics and wind technology, particularly through the efforts of Poul la Cour and Hans Christian Vogt.[58] But there were more conspicuous developments as well. Those structures (or structural aggregates) by which culture is formed and reproduced—whether through technological implements such as communicative media or through the habits and practices that order a given society—underwent a variety of changes precisely in Kierkegaard's era. As will be seen, the arrival of these so-called "cultural technologies"[59] would indelibly stamp Denmark and its people.

Cultural technologies

One of the first modern cultural technologies to impact Danish society was the daguerreotype—an early method of making photographs, consisting of a "jewellike images produced on polish plates of silver-plated copper."[60] Louis Daguerre unveiled this highly technical process[61] in 1839, and, by 1842, the Viennese daguerreotypist Joseph Weninger had set up a makeshift studio on Bredgade in Copenhagen. This was a milestone in Danish culture. Just two years earlier, the Parisian businessman and tourist Aymard Neubourg captured what has become a well-known daguerreotype of the sculptor Bertel Thorvaldsen.[62] In contrast, Weninger's enterprise was commercial, charging "a few of eight rixdollars" for a "reasonably clear portrait in fifteen seconds."[63] He was successful, so much so that he eventually drew "competition from a Dane named Alstrup, who installed himself in a small shop at the Royal Gardens and produced pictures for five rixdollars apiece."[64]

Other Danish industries appropriated this model, using the latest technical advancements to turn a considerable profit. In 1847, J. C. Jacobsen founded Carlsberg Brewery, naming it for his son Carl. It was a success story not unlike that of the Kierkegaard family. J.C.'s father Christen was the son of a Jutland farmer, requiring a "passport" to move to Copenhagen in 1800.[65] He apprenticed as a brewer for a time and, eventually, started his own brewery in 1826. Christen was so devoted to science that he attended lectures by Ørsted and, in turn, emphasized the need to incorporate modern technology into the brewing process, becoming the first Danish brewer to use the thermometer. He passed down this approach to his son J.C.:

> Recommended by his father, J.C. Jacobsen followed H.C. Ørsted's lectures in chemistry, and H.C. Ørsted who also took a special interest in the fermentation industries and the brewing business thus sowed the seeds of J.C. Jacobsen's lifelong commitment both to science and to "developing the art of making beer to the greatest possible degree of perfection."[66]

Later in life, J. C. Jacobsen "founded the world's first brewery-owned and -run research facility, the Carlsberg Laboratory,"[67] which he anticipated would deepen the connection between science, brewing, and business. Ironically, however, the discoveries made at the Carlsberg Laboratory extended well beyond pilsner: it was the Laboratory's chemist, S. P. L. Sørensen, who first developed the concept of pH—a scale for measuring acidity and basicity, which has gone on to make an impact in a variety of fields, from medicine to oceanography.[68]

One might argue that brewing, particularly once it transitioned from artisanal to industrial manufacture, emerged as part of the modern "entertainment industry," given its centrality to sporting events, concerts, and the like. With that in mind, it is striking that, just as Carlsberg was on the verge of developing into one of the world's leading beer producers, Copenhagen saw the arrival of its most famous amusement park—namely, Tivoli Gardens.[69] Tivoli was opened in August 1843, just six months after Kierkegaard published his early masterpiece, *Either/Or*. The park was the brainchild of Georg Carstensen, an officer in the Danish army, who had come to admire the various "pleasure gardens" found in major European cities, especially Jardin de Tivoli in Paris and Vauxhall Gardens in London. Indeed, in 1841, Copenhagen's Tivoli began with a pair of "Vauxhall-Concerts" in the Rosenborg Castle Gardens, featuring music, food, fireworks, and "thousands of oriental lamps."[70] Two years later, Carstensen opened a permanent "Tivoli & Vauxhall" at its current location outside Vesterport in Copenhagen, and the park immediately drew much attention. In 1844—its first full season—Tivoli attracted nearly 400,000 visitors, which was "over three times the population of Copenhagen itself."[71] As George Pattison has noted, such popularity was at least partly due to its provision of a kind of virtual world, where "visitors could slip off their everyday identity and become tourists in some vaguely defined land to the east and south of Denmark."[72] The latest technology no doubt contributed to this effect. Tivoli boasted a "range of attractions," including a "steam roundabout, a roller-coaster, [and] a daguerreotype studio,"[73] not to mention various means of entertainment, from a pantomime theater to a diorama—the latter, notably, another invention of Louis Daguerre.

Kierkegaard only makes a handful of references to Tivoli in his authorship, though, at the same time, he comes to place great stress on modernity as "the age of the crowd and the age of the aesthetic."[74] Thus it is not hard to see how Tivoli—which yoked modern cosmopolitanism and technology to such an extent that one Danish satirist depicted it, quite literally, as hell for the nation's peasantry[75]—would be implicated in Kierkegaard's criticism of "the present age." Still, the bulk of Kierkegaard's ire was directed at Denmark's burgeoning print media, which emerged as a powerful force in his own lifetime.

Print technology and the publishing industry

In considering the fate of Denmark's publishing industry, it is ironic if also fitting that France plays a key role. Following the French Revolution, "the [Danish] press was . . . subjected to a strict censorship law and severe penalties."[76] The regent and future king of Denmark, Frederick VI, "issued a long series of ordinances and decrees to discourage in advance those who might entertain liberal or revolutionary sympathies."[77] These measures sought to protect Danish Church as well, even going so far as to proscribe "assaults upon the existence of God or the immortality of the soul."[78] It was a decision that proved effective for a time. Despite a handful of exceptions—most notably, the author and Francophile activist Peter Andreas Heiberg—most "intellectuals [took] up a moderate position with respect to social and political reforms."[79]

Things began to change, however, during the 1830s. Led by Henrik Nicolai Clausen—a theologian and one of Kierkegaard's professors at the University of Copenhagen—a group of over 500 scholars, businessmen, and even military officers presented the king with the *Freedom of the Press Petition*.[80] It was a sign, however delicately conveyed, of "the nation's waning belief in the legitimacy of the absolute monarchy."[81] Long paranoid of an uprising, Frederik recognized that his response to the petition must be decorous yet firm. He issued a public reply stating that, despite the request of "our dear and faithful servants," "no one other than ourselves alone is capable of judging what is truly in the best interests of both parties."[82] This move turned out to be a mistake. Frederik's authoritarian rhetoric became a rallying point, even as his subsequent attempts to appease the public were distrusted.[83] After all, "as late as 1842, twenty-two of the country's twenty-four daily newspapers were subjected to censorship."[84]

Eventually, as will be seen, Kierkegaard would insert himself into the debate about the freedom of the press. But what must be underlined here is the basic point that, by Kierkegaard's era, print technology had become a presupposition in Danish society. The question, then, was not whether there would be a press, but how or if the press could be regulated by the government.

This dilemma was, in fact, central to the tension between old and new, between the ancien régime and the emerging democratic society—a point recognized by not only political doyens but also the intellectuals coming of age during the 1830s. Among the latter was a linguistics student by the name of Johannes Ostermann, who, in November 1835, published a lecture entitled "Our Latest Journalistic Literature." According to Ostermann, the desire to control the press betrays an emphasis on content rather than on form. Yes, he admits, there is a glut of "gutter papers" on the market, and these frequently manage with "untruths and probably more often with half-truths and almost always [without] decency of expression."[85] But, he goes on to explain, the very existence of dubious publications serves "to promote a greater good":

> About six years ago, the reading of papers was still very rare among the lower classes, and it was therefore very necessary that something absolutely exceptional occur that really accorded with popular taste in order to awaken the desire to read, and we can think of nothing more sustainable to this end than that mockery of "the great."[86]

The press, then, has promoted literacy and social engagement, even when its immediate aims have lain with mere titillation. In broader terms, the press has provided a forum in which persons can express political concerns. While this opportunity can lead to "attacks on the government," it is also the case that "some action by the government can give cause for complaints."[87] With that in mind, Ostermann ends with an ostensibly modest proposal: "Let us guard ourselves against a one-sided deification of this or that party, but let us also recognize the good wherever we find it."[88]

The restraint of Ostermann's rhetoric is misleading, however. Far from a slight modification of Danish social life, "the rise of liberal journalism and the subsequent defense of press freedom was the most important political event of the 1830's."[89] The rising generation of liberal leaders—most notably, the journalist Orla Lehmann—not only "favored a constitution with a broader franchise," but developed a brand of "National Liberalism," which wed a platform of constitutional reform to an enthusiastic embrace of popular Scandinavianism.[90] Of course, such tendencies did not go unopposed, eliciting criticism from "the owners of the great estates, the older and more powerful bureaucrats, the clergy, and most of the literary and poetic establishment."[91] But what united these debates was how they were carried out—namely, through Copenhagen's burgeoning press, which facilitated arguments in various ways, from staid editorials to satirical ripostes to burlesque cartoons. It was a culture not all that different from what is encountered on the internet today—where sanctioned news media receives competition from blogs, chat rooms, Twitter, YouTube, and so on—albeit on a scale of a mere "6,000 families with an academic education."[92]

To be sure, even in such limited fashion, the print media had come a long way in Denmark. The nation's first printing shop was established by the German publisher Johann Snell in 1482.[93] Snell came to Odense—the largest city on the Danish island of Funen—at the behest of Bishop Karl Rønnov, who tasked him with publishing a breviary.[94] Over the next few decades, itinerant German printers were common in Denmark,[95] and, by the time of the Reformation, the "Danish book market had changed in a quite dramatic way."[96] No longer were the Danish presses "dependent in the first place on ecclesiastical patronage," but, rather, they issued a considerable number of so-called "secular" works in the vernacular.[97] In fact, by 1525, nearly half of the books printed in Denmark lay in fields other than religion, with the largest percentage of these concerning education and law, though political and scientific tracts appeared as well.[98] And this is to say nothing of Danish-language books published outside the country, for example, in Lübeck (where Snell was based) and in Paris.[99]

This slow but "steady"[100] trend toward the secularization of the printed word accelerated in the seventeenth century. Bookbinders and booksellers circumvented state (and, with it, ecclesial) control by utilizing a "commercial network of common tradespeople"[101] to hawk their wares in the marketplace, rather than in and around governmental institutions. Still, due to limited resources (the cost of paper, the need to procure "type supply" from Germany, and so on),[102] print runs remained relatively small. But the situation began to change in the mid-eighteenth and early nineteenth centuries. By the year 1800, there were close to thirty printing businesses in Denmark, some of them—such as the one founded by Søren Gyldendal in 1770—already quite large and destined to usher in "the modern book market of the next century."[103]

Also significant—perhaps especially so in light of Kierkegaard's response to the press—was the rise of Danish periodicals. The nation's first journal appeared in 1720, roughly ten years after *The Tatler* debuted in London, and over the ensuing decades around 200 literary periodicals would turn up in Denmark.[104] Most of these periodicals enjoyed brief runs and dallied in "miscellaneous content,"[105] but they nevertheless served a larger purpose. The publication of journals, particularly in the common tongue of Danish, introduced "Enlightenment ideas and bourgeois culture to Denmark and [educated] the Danish middle class audience, so as to transform it into a discriminating public."[106] A key figure in this movement was Jens Schelderup Sneedorff, whose journal, *The Patriotic Spectator* (*Den Patriotiske Tilskuer*), sought to disseminate the virtues of the Enlightenment "throughout the middle classes" and, in turn, to elevate the status of Denmark in Europe. As he once put it: "It is not the size of a country or the number of inhabitants but the number of those thinking that determines the possible progression of science and literature. A smaller nation can by the spreading of good taste vie with a larger. It may surpass it."[107]

The objectives of publishers such as Sneedorff received a boon when, in 1770, the Danish press was granted unprecedented freedoms by Johann Friedrich Struensee—the German physician who, on account of King Christian VII's mental illness, came to govern Denmark for a tumultuous sixteen-month period. Struensee viewed himself as a rationalist, and he even edited a controversial Germanophone periodical during the 1760s.[108] Hence, as he saw it, the "unlimited freedom to print books and texts was intended to stimulate the impartial investigation of the truth, enlighten the misunderstandings and errors of earlier eras and advance the common good."[109] In actual fact, however, dissension erupted. Journals and pamphlets disputed issues ranging from the price of grain to the standing of the Danish state church to "nepotism in the distribution of [governmental] offices."[110] Some of these debates were as scurrilous as they were fervent: "Queen Caroline Matilda's love affair with Struensee—combined with the recent diminution of the punishments for sexual offences—was particularly newsworthy."[111] When, in January 1772, Struensee's regime was toppled by a coup, it was not long until "control of the press was reasserted,"[112] albeit under somewhat different parameters than before. As Henrik Horstbøll explains:

> The Chief Constable of Copenhagen was authorized to fine printers or authors heavily for offensive polemics, especially any touching on the state or government.

The great experiment with freedom of the press was over; post-publication censorship and self-censorship had replaced pre-publication censorship. Unlimited freedom of the press was succeeded by limited press freedom.[113]

As has been seen, this "limited press freedom" effectively held until Kierkegaard's era, indeed, with restrictions *added* by royal decrees in 1799 and 1810.[114] Thus it is not surprising that, when Kierkegaard entered the University of Copenhagen in 1830, Danish publishers had reduced their output "by a third compared with the 1790s."[115]

This point explains why Ostermann's call for increased press freedom, along with the efforts of figures such as Clausen and Lehmann, was so significant. It represented the reemergence or, better yet, the reassertion of republican values in Denmark. But herein lies confirmation of an additional point: print technology is one of the key premises of republicanism. After all, the liberal exchange of information is an ideal only realized in the wake of printing press, that is, after the means of such an exchange had become readily available—a symbiosis famously underscored by the First Amendment to the American Constitution.[116] Hence, to the extent that Western monarchies failed to withhold the press, the rise of a representative form of government was all but ineluctable.

Once again, Denmark serves as a case in point. The Danish crown's long-standing effort to control the press began to flag in the 1830s, so much so that, by the 1840s, "official censorship was challenged by a flurry of satirical publications."[117] Moreover, it was around this time that Copenhagen began to see the introduction of a variety of newspapers, each aiming to address a particular segment of society:

> *Berlingske Tidende* (Berling's Times) was the paper for loyal officials; *Corsaren* (The Pirate) was read both by gentlemen and their servants; *Fædrelandet* (The Fatherland), founded in 1834, appealed to young liberal intellectuals; the more radical *Kjøbenhavnsposten* (The Post of Copenhagen) addressed craftsmen and artisans. *Flyveposten* (The Fly Post) was a scandal-sheet, while the little-read *Aftenposten* (Evening Post) was subsidized by Christian VIII's Secretariat for Favors (*nådessager*), set up for this purpose.[118]

It is worth noting that *each* of these papers turns up in Kierkegaard's authorship,[119] demonstrating not only their salience in the Danish society but also his own connections to journalism—connections that, as will be seen, decisively if also puzzlingly marked his response to the modern world.

To be sure, in arguably the most important political event of Kierkegaard's lifetime, the liberal demand for press freedom would not only prevail in Denmark but, in fact, lead to the adoption of a new constitution. On June 5, 1849, King Frederick VII endorsed an agreement that "entailed the king sharing previously unlimited power with a parliament elected by universal suffrage of the male population."[120] This was by no means a radical revolution. Not only was it handled diplomatically, but, as has been noted, the realignment of institutional structures followed the prior "development of a middle-class public, which was the true prerequisite for growth towards democracy."[121]

And yet, it is worth adding that the extent of constitutional enfranchisement remained a cause célèbre. Lehmann himself "expressed the sentiment that in his view power should only be exercised by 'the intelligent, the educated and the rich,'"[122] and this issue would remain contested throughout the remainder of the nineteenth century.

Still, the nation had come a long way since the days of censorship, and the fall of the absolute monarchy would leave an indelible mark on Danish society.[123] Kierkegaard himself realized this point, even though his response was otherwise ambivalent. For, as will be seen, he believed that the press had ushered in a new and treacherous historical era. The task of modern persons was to learn to cope with this change.

Conclusion

George Pattison has recently noted that, although Kierkegaard tends to ignore the everyday challenges facing denizens of the modern West, he does encourage people to "seek to be human, in, with, and under the culture conditions of our own time, which, for us as for Kierkegaard, means doing so in the culture of modern urbanity."[124] Whether or not Pattison is right about the first point is worth pondering as this study proceeds. However, the business of the present chapter has been precisely to show how Kierkegaard's experience of "modern urbanity" was very much bound up with technology—with the arrival of scientific methods of agriculture and transport, with the nascence of various technical devices and cultural industries, and, perhaps above all, with an upsurge of publishing outlets that were destined to reform Danish political life. If, then, Kirmmse and others[125] are right to view Kierkegaard's writings within the context of Golden Age Denmark, this chapter has also demonstrated that Golden Age Denmark is inextricable from, and therefore inexplicable without, modern technology.

And yet, one might wonder, what does Kierkegaard himself *say* about technology? In other words, granted that Kierkegaard lived an era of technological change, and granted that such a change influenced his life in a variety of ways, what did he actually think about it? It is the task of the next chapter to investigate just these questions.

Kierkegaard on the Rise of Technological Culture

After two chapters, this study has covered significant historical ground. Not only has it surveyed the history of technology, underlining the West's slow but certain turn toward urbanization and instrumentalization, but it has also examined the rise of modern technology in Denmark, demonstrating that Kierkegaard lived in a time of decisive scientific, technical, and political change. These topics may seem ancillary to the book's principal aim—namely, to come to a better understanding of Kierkegaard's response to the question concerning technology—but they have been highlighted for two reasons. First, they have helped to clarify the so-called "spirit of the whole" (*Geist des Ganzen*)[1] of Kierkegaard's life. Indeed, in order to read Kierkegaard well, one must not limit oneself to his writings alone but, in addition, explore the range of conditions that made his authorship possible. What has been shown here, then, is that Kierkegaard's age was one of technological, and not merely philosophical, system building. Second, and just as importantly, the preceding chapters have demonstrated that Kierkegaard's sociohistorical location is by no means qualitatively different than our own: both eras feature ever-expanding technological implementation, increasingly rapid transport, patent industrialization and mechanization, the use of technology in and for personal entertainment, and the near ubiquity of print media. Hence, when Kierkegaard grapples with questions about technology, it should now be clear that, in a number of ways, his questions are our questions too. After all, to paraphrase Hans-Georg Gadamer, a text is best understood when it is understood "to make a true claim about something that is an issue for us in our time and place."[2]

With these points in mind, it is now time to attend to what is effectively the fulcrum of this study—an examination of Kierkegaard's own response to technology. Here, the task is not to explore what preceded Kierkegaard's reflections on technology (the subject of the first two chapters), nor is it to consider the application of his thought to the philosophy of technology (the subject of two upcoming chapters). Rather, the point is to concentrate on those texts in which Kierkegaard himself discusses technology. This task will begin by examining passages that make reference to "technology" or to other related terms, though it will soon be apparent that Kierkegaard employs this language relatively infrequently and often ambiguously. As a result, it will be essential to extend the investigation further, namely, to places in Kierkegaard's authorship where he mentions specific technologies or sociopolitical issues related to modern urbanity and technology.

With this point in mind, two general categories of reference demand consideration: (i) those concerning the *form* of modern life, particularly as determined by technology, and (ii) those concerning the *content* of modern life, particularly as determined by theoretical developments such as the rise of the natural sciences. This division between form and content is heuristic in nature; it is not meant to suggest that the two can be neatly separated. Indeed, as will become clear in Chapter 4, Kierkegaard's early critique of information technology precisely concerns how the formal exchange of information in modernity (through the technology of the printing press) begets an attendant way of understanding the world. As persons familiar with the philosophy of technology will recognize, this insight raises meta-questions about the priority of technology in relation to a scientific *Weltanschauung* or vice versa. But unlike Heidegger, who argues that modern technology emerges out of modern science,[3] Kierkegaard does not attend to this issue per se. What's decisive for him is not the abstract question about "the essence of technology" but, rather, the more practical concern about technology's vitiation of our moral and religious lives.

References to technology in Kierkegaard's authorship

The most salient feature of Kierkegaard's direct references to "technology" is how scarce they are. For example, the Danish word for "technology" is *teknologi*, and Kierkegaard does not use it a single time in his writings, whether published or unpublished. Likewise, neither the adjective "technological" (*teknologisk*) nor the related modifier "technical" (*teknisk*) turns up once in Kierkegaard's authorship. The noun *Teknik*— which is cognate to *la technique*, the term preferred by Jacques Ellul when speaking about technology— makes an appearance in Kierkegaard's 1838 work, *From the Papers of One Still Living*. But this reference has nothing to do with "technology" in the modern sense of the term. Rather, amid a series of prefatory reflections on Danish literature, Kierkegaard contrasts the "masterly technique [*Teknik*]" found in "the short stories by the author of *En Hverdags-Historie*" with the "solitary, dramatically charged lines" in the poetry of Steen Steensen Blicher.[4] Here, then, Kierkegaard employs *Teknik* in its antique sense, recalling the Greek word *technē*, which concerns "not only . . . the activities and skills of the craftsman but also . . . the arts of the mind and the fine arts."[5]

Thus it would seem that this inquiry can barely get off the ground. And yet, it is striking that Howard and Edna Hong—the late husband-and-wife team responsible for the standard English translations of Kierkegaard's writings—*do* occasionally use the word "technique" when translating Kierkegaard's journal and papers. Moreover, the Hongs even list "technology" as a category in their index to Kierkegaard's journals and papers. Why is this the case?

With regard to the first point, an 1854 journal entry provides a notable case study. As is typical of the writings leading up to, and during, Kierkegaard's so-called "attack upon Christendom," this passage juxtaposes the teachings of the New Testament with

Christianity as it is practiced in Denmark. Whereas the former enjoins the individual believer to relate to God, the latter "interjects between [the individual] and God the middle term: the others, society, the human race."[6] What this amounts to, Kierkegaard clarifies, is the idolization of the human order, since, while "God is the being for whom to be is to be the concept," "man is the being for whom the numerical is the way to power."[7] Thus, human beings tend to band together for the sake of accruing power—a tendency seen preeminently not only in the "business of nationality and the state"[8] but also in the Church, which too often props up these institutions. It is with this in mind that the notion of "technique" slips into Kierkegaard's argument. The co-option of divine worship by the state church, he adds, is a sign that people will "use every human *technique* and trick in the bag"[9] in order to prevent the individual from relating to God as God.

While "technique" is not a poor rendering of Kierkegaard's Danish in this context, it is not precise either. Indeed, as adumbrated, this passage does not mention *Teknik* at all. Instead, Kierkegaard uses the terms "eminent skill" (*Virtuositet*) and "doing tricks" (*at gjøre Kunster*). The former, of course, is a word often applied to a great artist ("she displays virtuosity on the cello"), while the latter phrase is typically used of animals ("my dog is great at doing tricks"). Thus, Kierkegaard is indicating that, even though human beings are capable of demonstrating great technical skill, they are not above employing their skill for the coarsest of reasons. Human talent, however dazzling, may amount to little more than animal tricks—pleasant, entertaining, and ultimately devoid of meaning.

An 1851 journal entry not only anticipates this point but deepens it. Under the heading "Decline in Christendom," Kierkegaard blames human "cunning"[10] (*List*) for cheapening Christian discipleship. As he explains, Christ's ministry began with a call to follow him as "the prototype" (*Forbilledet*), but, in time, his example was distorted into an "object of admiration."[11] "In short," Kierkegaard concludes, "the human technique of getting rid of everything called discipleship or imitation prevails everywhere."[12] This, at any rate, is the translation provided by the Hongs. But Kierkegaard does not use the term *Teknik*. Rather, in this case, he utilizes the noun *Taktik*—a cognate of the English "tactic," which is indeed etymologically related to the Greek *technē*, albeit with rational rather than practical connotations. To put it in rough terms, the tactician is one whose preparations are implemented by the technician. Thus, Kierkegaard's application of *Taktik* implies that human beings are not just adept at acquiring power over against God but, in truth, prepare to do so.

The above two examples demonstrate a couple of notable points. First, on a linguistic and hermeneutical level, that words such as *teknologi* and *teknik* are lacking in Kierkegaard's oeuvre hardly means that related terms or concepts are absent—a contention underscored by the Hongs's insistence on rendering *Virtuositet* and *Taktik* as "technique." Second, the identification of Kierkegaardian "buzzwords" that might indicate an interest in technology now becomes a matter worth investigating. And yet, a degree of interpretive sensitivity is needed, since Kierkegaard's vocabulary predates and thus lacks the shared terminology of later philosophical discourse on technology.

Does Kierkegaard employ any recurring words that signify a philosophical concern with technology—for example, in the way that *Paradox* marks his thinking on Christianity or in the way that *Gestell* epitomizes Heidegger's later philosophy of technology? As noted above, the Hongs register "technology" in their index to Kierkegaard's journals and papers.[13] Does a clue lie there? The first entry indicated by this heading stems from 1846, the year in which Kierkegaard (among other things) published *A Literary Review*. Like that work, this passage considers the changes wrought by Western society's turn to technology and to science, though the term *teknologi* as such does not appear. Rather, in an ironical vein, Kierkegaard imagines a play regarding the "extravagance of the natural sciences" (*Naturvidenskabernes Extravagance*).[14] He compares modern scientists to the Sophists of the ancient world: just as the latter deigned to sell *arête* in the marketplace, so do the tools and discoveries of modern science require "huge sums" of money and untold hours of labor.[15] The reward, however, is dubious. Kierkegaard remarks that political and religious leaders celebrate scientific progress, but, due to the "insane speed by which one discovery displaces another,"[16] money is often wasted and laborers exploited. Thus, he envisages the play ending "with a revolt by some of the craftsmen who rip down the booths and smash everything to pieces."[17]

It is certainly a telling passage, which hints at some of Kierkegaard's broader critiques of modern *Wissenschaft*—namely, that it peddles facts and figures for profit but, precisely because of its concern for objectivity, fails to encourage individual ethico-religious development. That this entry, then, should be explicitly linked with the theme of "technology" (rather than, say, of "science") is questionable; it presumably has to do with Kierkegaard's comical allusions to a "giant microscope" and his repeated use of the word "discovery" (*Opdagelse*).[18] A society devoted to science, he suggests, is a society enamored by discoveries, and, while he does not deny that such discoveries might be exciting or helpful, he is clear that such a society is *ipso facto* restless. Intriguingly, this restlessness comes from within and from without, driven by the monetary and political expediency of applauding the new and improved but also by a global exchange of ideas that only augments such desires. As Kierkegaard quips, "A report comes that someone in China (by a series of remarkable discoveries communication had been amazingly accelerated) had discovered a microscope of even higher magnifying power which could be constructed very easily. Thus, the giant microscope had lost all its worth (before it was even ready!)."[19] What is striking here—particularly in anticipation of an upcoming discussion of *A Literary Review*—is that Kierkegaard associates improved communication with technological discovery. In other words, he perceives the symbiosis between information technology and industrial technology: better communication facilitates manufacturing, even as improvements in the exchange of information rely on the implementation of devices such as the printing press and so on.

Broadly speaking, then, this journal entry implies that the term *Opdagelse* functions as a kind of surrogate for *teknologi*. But the matter is not so simple. In point of fact, Kierkegaard uses *Opdagelse* almost 100 times in his authorship, its plural *Opdagelser* over 30 times, and the verb *opdage* more than 300 times. Given the various ways that one might speak of "discovery" in English—from Christopher Columbus's "discovery" of America to the "discovery" of one's favorite restaurant—it is not surprising that Kierkegaard's Danish is equally ambiguous. Indeed, Kierkegaard himself not only highlights this issue in *Works of Love* but uses it as an occasion to distinguish between what people typically mean by "discovery" and "discovering" and the manner in which love (*Kjerlighed*) understands those terms. He begins by underlining the cultural situation in nineteenth-century Denmark:

> Discovering [*at opdage*] is praised and admired in the world. On the one hand, one who does not discover something or who discovers nothing is rated very low. In order to designate as eccentric someone who goes around lost in his own thoughts, one often says, "You can just bet that he doesn't discover anything." And if one wants to single out someone as especially shallow and obtuse, one says, "He for sure didn't invent gunpowder," which of course hardly needs to be done in our day, since it has already been invented; so it would be even more dubious if someone in our time were to think that he was the one who had invented [*opfundet*] gunpowder. Oh, but to discover something is so admired in the world that it is impossible to forget the enviable fate of having invented gunpowder![20]

Modernity, then, is a time in which discovery is correlated to intelligence: one is valuable to society just to the extent that one *discovers*. This point bears more rhetorical weight in Danish. In contrast to the English word "discover," which literally means "the opposite of covering up," the Danish *opdage* is related to the word for "day" (*Dag*) and, in turn, the phrase "to bring to light" (*bringe for dagen*). If, then, to discover is to cast light on a given object, it only makes sense that *Opdagelse* is a key component of what is now known as "the Age of Enlightenment" (*oplysningstiden* or, quite literally, "the time of lighting up").

And yet, Kierkegaard goes on, the modern emphasis on discovery is problematic in the ethico-religious sphere. For example, it is lamentable that society rewards the one who makes "discoveries even with regard to evil, with regard to sin and the multitude of sins, [who is] the shrewd, sly, foxy, perhaps more or less corrupt observer who can really make discoveries."[21] Such a person, in fact, is increasingly common in modernity, a period in which, "compared with ancient times," "everyone is a judge of human nature."[22] Recalling an argument he develops in *A Literary Review*, Kierkegaard implies that this cultural shift is owing to the print media, since what would otherwise be unthinkable in a private relationship (that one would *desire* to discover evil in the other) is now the modus operandi of the public sphere: "If . . . someone pretends that he had discovered how fundamentally shabby every human being is, how envious, how selfish, how faithless . . . that person conceitedly knows that he is welcome, that it is the yield of his observing, his knowledge, his story that the world longs to hear."[23] "In public, in company," he later concludes, "the one tempts the other to divulge what he has discovered."[24]

If a person is to opt out of this economy of hostility, she has to prioritize the love (*Kjerlighed*) of God and of neighbor. This may come across as glib advice, but

Kierkegaard clarifies that such love will be "laughed at" and "mocked" precisely because it militates against society's orientation toward discovery.[25] In fact, the lover does not discover but *hides*:

> The one who loves discovers nothing [*opdager Intet*]; therefore he hides the multitude of sins that could be found through discovery [*Opdagelse*]. The life of the one who loves expresses the apostolic injunction to be a child in evil.[26] What the world actually admires as sagacity is knowledge of evil—whereas wisdom is knowledge of the good. The one who loves does not have and does not want to have knowledge of evil; in this regard he is and remains, he wants to be and wants to remain, a child.[27]

Underlying this passage is a pointed, albeit underdeveloped, Aristotelian-cum-Thomistic epistemology of participation.[28] As Kierkegaard clarifies, when one comes to know something, one comes to share in that object: "At the basis of all *understanding* lies first and foremost an *understanding* between the one who is to understand and that which is to be understood."[29] Thus the one who gains knowledge of evil epistemically interacts with evil, and, while Kierkegaard grants that this interaction is by degrees, he adds that it cannot help but engender a relativism inimical to ethico-religious development: "To become better or seem to be better by means of comparison with the badness of others is, after all, a bad way to become better."[30] To be sure, in such a context, the one who shuns evil and gives precedence to love will look naive, even idiotic.[31] As Kierkegaard puts it, "In these times much is done so that such a loving person, who has a great understanding of the good and does not want any understanding of evil, looks like a deranged person."[32]

A related, if not identical, point is found in the *other* journal entry that the Hongs list under "technology." This passage stems from 1854 and, as it happens, is loaded with historical references that are likely unfamiliar to readers today. In particular, Kierkegaard alludes to Louis-Napoléon Bonaparte, who ascended to the presidency of the French Second Republic in 1848 and, after a self-coup, became the emperor of the Second French Empire in 1852. In an 1851 note, Kierkegaard reveals that he had been monitoring the rise of Louis-Napoléon (also known as Napoléon III), adding that the younger Napoléon lacks the noble composure of his renowned uncle Napoléon Bonaparte.[33] His 1854 journal entry returns to this line of thinking. Drawing on an article in *Fædrelandet*, Kierkegaard documents an incident during the Crimean War, in which Louis-Napoléon announced the capture of Sevastopol via the staged appearance of a courier on horseback—a display that Kierkegaard regarded as the cunning work of a "dramatic poet," who "is excellent for prostituting the generation."[34] Such a leader, according to Kierkegaard, is a far cry from "what Plato wanted," namely, a king who is likewise a philosopher.[35] And yet, Kierkegaard continues, Louis-Napoléon is quite suitable for modern persons, who belong to an era that promotes mass communication at the expense of intellectual and moral substance: "This generation of windbags deserves a *windbag en gros* for emperor. And how superb that all of humanity's great discoveries [*Opdagelser*] (railroads, telegraphs, etc.) are all in the direction of developing and subsidizing the condition of being a windbag."[36]

A "windbag" (*Vindbeutel*) is a person who speaks at length about a given topic but does not truly understand it—a vociferous yet superficial talker. It is perhaps unsurprising that Kierkegaard would accuse the print media of fomenting windbaggery, since, after all, newspapers and periodicals (not to mention today's internet-based media) provide a forum in which information is exchanged profusely, rapidly, and outside of the restraints of academic, governmental, and religious institutions. An unrestricted media entails an abundance of communication, and even the most ardent defender of "free speech" would grant that much of it is superficial and superfluous, not to mention scurrilous. What is especially provocative in Kierkegaard's view, then, is the suggestion that *all* technical innovations—whether in transport or in telecommunications—are in service to a culture bereft of common purpose and ultimate meaning. He does not elaborate on this point here, though it is worth flagging it for later consideration, since Kierkegaard's insight would turn up again in thinkers such as Heidegger and Thomas Merton.

Hence, in the end, the two entries grouped by the Hongs under the heading of "technology" would be more accurately classified under that of "discovery"—a term that signposts a number of pertinent Kierkegaardian insights vis-à-vis modernity in general and information technology in particular. But is "discovery" in and of itself a marker of Kierkegaard's philosophical concern with technology? In other words, would an examination of the hundreds of instances in which Kierkegaard uses this term yield an evident and coherent philosophy of technology? Here, doubtless, the answer must be "no," simply because Kierkegaard employs *Opdagelse*, *opdage*, and other associated words with just the ambiguity one would anticipate, from Cordelia's "discovery"[37] of Johannes the Seducer's coyness in *Either/Or* (1843) to Kierkegaard's passing reference to "the discovery of America"[38] in *Christian Discourses* (1848). Again, that is not to say that *Opdagelse* is irrelevant to Kierkegaard's philosophy; it is just to clarify that the term as such does not represent the "core" of his thought on technology. *Opdagelse* plays a complementary, rather than a fundamental, role.

With this in mind, and given the dearth of references to *teknologi* and *teknik* in Kierkegaard's authorship, it appears that a conceptual or terminological analysis of Kierkegaard's thought on technology is bound to disappoint. The Dane is simply not systematic enough to approach the matter in this way. Indeed, while there is an inspired, furious quality to much of Kierkegaard's literary output, his sociopolitical writings are perhaps especially so. After all, it is telling that his most overtly "political" treatise, *A Literary Review*, is tendered as commentary on a fictional novel! Of course, that is not to suggest that Kierkegaard lacked reasons for such literary elusiveness. As Ed Mooney writes, "In Kierkegaard's practice, the matters of pseudonymity, genre, and communication are interlocked, joined in the service of bringing an ethico-religious individual to life, joined in the service of increased freedom from a stifling onslaught of false authority, pervasive gossip, and sloganeering, of objective-only measures of truth."[39] Still, even if one were to grant that Kierkegaard's literary methods are worthwhile (and many would demur on this point), one would not be any closer to identifying a direct examination of "technology" or "technique" in his oeuvre. Hence, as mentioned at the outset of this chapter, it is necessary to approach this question in other ways—first by looking at how Kierkegaard associates technology with the shape or form of modern life.

Kierkegaard on the form of modern life

The first two chapters of this study have already detailed what is meant by the "form" of modern life, particularly in the West. Chapter 1 demonstrated that, on the one hand, the West has become increasingly urbanized—a trend that continues to intensify even in recent decades. For example, in 1950, a little more than half of France's population lived in cities, whereas that number was nearly 80 percent in 2010.[40] The situation in Denmark is not very different: 86 percent of Danes resided in cities in 2010, compared to 68 percent in 1950.[41] Moreover, it is expected that, by 2030, well over 90 percent of the persons in the UK will be urban dwellers.[42] The significance of this rate of expansion cannot be overestimated—to take but one example, the phenomenon of "global warming" has been partly linked to the fact that the "annual mean air temperature of a city with 1 million people or more can be 1.8–5.4°F (1–3°C) warmer than its surroundings"[43]—and, as was discussed in Chapter 2, urbanization was a process well underway in nineteenth-century Denmark. Thus, it will be important to consider Kierkegaard's reflections on life in the modern city.

The same is true of the other major focus of the first two chapters, namely, on the proliferation of instruments in the modern West. From personal devices to large-scale industry, Kierkegaard witnessed firsthand Denmark's slow but certain push toward instrumentalization. It will be crucial, then, to attend to Kierkegaard's descriptions of this development, though perhaps his experience of modern transportation will be of primary significance. Still, what is essential in both cases—that of urbanization and that of instrumentalization—is just how Kierkegaard *saw* these changes. An analysis of how the Dane understood their intellectual underpinnings will follow.

Bourgeois, busy, and crowded: The city according to Kierkegaard

In a June 1835 letter[44] to Peter Wilhelm Lund—a distant relative of the Kierkegaard family, not to mention a pioneer in paleontological and zoological studies in Brazil— Kierkegaard makes what appears to be a throwaway comment about summer excursions to the amusement park known as Deer Park's Hill (Dyrehavsbakken). While pondering the state of academic theology, Kierkegaard adds:

> To me the scholarly theological world is like Strandveien on Sunday afternoon during the Dyrehaug season—they dash by each other, yelling and shouting, laugh and make fools of each other, drive their horses to death, tip over and are run over, and when they finally come—covered with dust and out of breath—to Bakken— well, they just look at each other, turn around, and go home.[45]

Curiously, Kirkegaard returned to this observation in January 1837, adding a marginal note: "There is something strangely ironic in Copenhageners' excursions to Dyrehaug. They are trying to shake off the bourgeois dust of the city, flee from themselves—and find themselves again at Bakken."[46] While Kierkegaard's relation to Dyrehavsbakken is interesting in its own right,[47] these passages are also striking for what they reveal about

Kierkegaard's rendering of life in the modern city—namely, that it is bourgeois, busy, and crowded.

The term "bourgeois" comes from the Old French *borjois*, meaning "town dweller." By the eighteenth century, it had come to refer to those who strive to conform to social conventions and styles, and, in the wake of Marxism, it would be associated with the capitalist mercantile class as well. Kierkegaard uses two words that might be translated as "bourgeois": *borgerlig* and *spidsborgerlige*. They are obviously related to one another and bear meanings such as "middle-class," "conventional," and "respectable," though *spidsborgerlige* carries the additional connotation of "philistine"—a slang term in Kierkegaard's era, which refers to urbanites who lack culture and learning. Hence, when Kierkegaard claims that the city is "bourgeois," he is simultaneously offering a judgment on its essential purpose—namely, that it is a place where people reside for the sake of making money and enjoying a comfortable lifestyle. Hence, to the extent that cities are bourgeois, they are at bottom spaces dedicated to the temporal age (*saeculum*). As Kierkegaard puts it in early journal entry, "The bourgeois mentality or philistinism [*Spidsborgerlighed*] is essentially the inability to rise above the absolute reality of time and space."[48]

Indeed, writing in the mid-nineteenth century, when the pressures of urbanization had yet to become dire,[49] Kierkegaard depicts the modern secular city as the site of middle-class conformism. A typical *Spidsborger*, he notes, exists in a "vegetative" state, "when the hands are comfortably folded over the stomach, when the head is reclining on a soft easy chair."[50] This kind of person knows next to nothing about self-denial and, for that reason, equates the ethical life with good manners. In turn, to love the neighbor comes to mean that "when someone is asked for a pair of scissors, even though he is some distance away, he will say 'Righto!'"[51] Recorded in 1837, these droll observations anticipate Kierkegaard's intensive (and more sympathetic) analysis of the "ethical sphere" in later works such as *Either/Or* and *Fear and Trembling*, wherein "the ethical stage seems to include a strong emphasis on acceptance of social roles and institutions."[52] And yet, in these early journal entries, Kierkegaard is doing more than parodying the mores of bourgeois Copenhagen. On the contrary, and in a manner reminiscent of Marx,[53] he is describing a civic culture in which goods are not pursued as ends in themselves but as means toward financial prosperity and social influence. As he writes in an 1848 passage:

> There is constant talk in the world about wanting only the truth, etc., but something else is always implied. A journal which seeks only the truth: well, this is regarded as all right if the journal has many subscribers; to seek only the truth in this way is understandable. And why? Because the great number of subscribers shows that it is earning a lot of money.[54]

Even a thinker as renowned as Hegel, whom Kierkegaard concedes had "a pretty good head on his shoulders," falls prey to the "illusions of finitude" that shape bourgeois society: "[Hegel] became B.A., M.A., and later professor—and now begins to work. Now . . . this is the way he makes a living. And then he probably makes money on his books—there we have it again."[55]

Cities, then, are locales dedicated to bourgeois interests, especially the calculated and ceaseless pursuit of personal gain. This point leads to Kierkegaard's second observation about life in the modern city: it is *busy*. In one of his earliest academic pursuits—namely, a paper given in November 1835 before the Student Association (*Studenterforeningen*) of the University of Copenhagen—Kierkegaard seeks to demonstrate that the press is an "unorthodox and unauthorized source of political power."[56] One reason for the press's illegitimacy, argues Kierkegaard, is that it operates without a worldview capable of bringing together conservative and liberal tendencies,[57] and thus its journalistic commotion lacks the "calm circumspection"[58] characteristic of truly productive activity. In this disunity, however, Kierkegaard sees a direct link to modern bourgeois society, whose "*whole striving in our time*" is best described as "bustling busyness" (*stundesløs*).[59] As Kierkegaard goes on to explain: "It is this whole striving that I have tried to describe as one of bustling busyness (*Stundesløshed*), for bustling busyness is not action but a fitful fumbling. To use the words of a poet . . . bustling busyness is 'a restless rambling—from castles in the air—to mousetraps—and home again.'"[60]

This impression of the modern bourgeois city as a place of "bustling busyness" appears in a number of places in Kierkegaard's oeuvre. In an 1848 letter to his disabled cousin, Hans Peter Kierkegaard, he contrasts the rapidity of modern life with the "solitude" and "inwardness" of Hans Peter's circumstances.[61] While Hans Peter appears "superfluous in the obtuse eyes of a busy world," "the busy, busier, busiest haste of busy-ness" is, in fact, only "busy with wasting life and losing oneself."[62] This insight reads like an appendix to "An Occasional Discourse," which comprised the first part of *Upbuilding Discourses in Various Spirits* (1847). In that work, Kierkegaard laments "the noise of the world," which dominates "the busy life" and its "dealings from morning to night," so much so that busyness "indeed [becomes] like a spell" whereby one gets lost in a "swarming multitude of excuses."[63] No wonder, Kierkegaard concludes, that the spiritual life suffers in such a context, since, amid "the motley, teeming crowd," "excuses and the hosts of them become a general plague that nibbles off the sprout of the eternal, become a corrupting infection among the people."[64] That this crowd is synonymous with the modern bourgeois city Kierkegaard underlines in an 1854 journal entry: persons now define faith by the habits and practices of "these thousands and millions," but, for that very reason, the upshot is to "never think about it, now [to] get on with the busy activity of life . . . get married, have children, make something of yourself, be active early and late."[65]

These comments plainly link up with what Kierkegaard saw as the third defining feature of modern urbanity—that it is crowded, that it is, *summa summarum*, a crowd. Kierkegaard speaks about "the crowd" or "the many" (*Mængden*) throughout his authorship, and references to *Mængden* and *Mængde* are far too numerous (well over 500 appearances) and varied even to consider itemizing them. It is hardly surprising, then, that scholars[66] have dedicated attention to Kierkegaard's critique of "mass society" and its ties to similar accounts found in later thinkers such as Dostoevsky, Nietzsche, and Heidegger. But what is often underemphasized—at least with respect to the Dane—is that Kierkegaard's censure of mass society is ipso facto a censure of the rise of the modern bourgeois city and, by association, the technology that supports it. For example, Howard Tuttle presents Kierkegaard's protest as a response to "Rousseau and Hegel," from whom "we inherit the notion that human beings are essentially social creatures whose deepest nature is to be found in their relation to others."[67] More specifically, Hegel's prioritization of "the essentiality of reason, especially in his systematic construction of the real," drew Kierkegaard into an impassioned defense of the individual subject.[68] Hence, as Tuttle sums up, the "Hegelian and Kierkegaardian doctrines of truth are at the heart of this situation, and the divergence between Hegelian essentialism and Kierkegaardian existentialism is . . . prominent."[69] Tuttle even goes as far as to say that Kierkegaard "was the theoretician of the mass from the perspective of . . . the authentic destiny of the individual" and that, in turn, "Kierkegaard's analysis remained apart from considerations of technology, urbanism, economics, or science."[70]

Tuttle's perspective on this matter is not altogether erroneous, but it is reductionistic all the same. To claim that Kierkegaard's response to mass society is principally a theoretical concern is to forget that it also entails a *lived* encounter with modern urbanity and technology. Indeed, in a Heideggerian vein, one might say that urban-cum-technological modernity constituted the *Horizont* in which Kierkegaard's philosophical and theological concerns came to light. And this is to say nothing of Kierkegaard's direct critiques of technologies such as the printing press—critiques that were bound up with precisely the issues (say, urbanism or economics) that Tuttle would exclude. In brief, one cannot finally disentangle mass society from urban society, nor urban society from technology. To the extent that Kierkegaard was a "theoretician of the mass," his thought pertains to urbanity and technology as well.

A number of Kierkegaard's comments on *Mængden* reflect these points of connection. First, he grasped that, even though the phenomenon of the crowd is not limited to the modern world, it has nevertheless taken on a new and more perfidious form in modernity: "Here . . . is the tragedy of history. Once again the principle of the crowd (and now, with the prevalent culture and aided by the press this concept will have an utterly more frightful power than in ancient times) has been established."[71] Here, already, Kierkegaard links *Mængden* not only to the forces of history but also to changes wrought by technology. He returns to this point in an 1854 journal entry:

> Alas, in ancient days there still lived men who thought primitively about being human, what it means on the whole to be a human being, what meaning it has within itself and within the whole of existence. Lost as everyone now is from the earliest years in the man-made nonsense of numbers, no one thinks of such things.[72]

This shift from contemplative self-examination to numerical self-neglect follows from the changing demographics of Western culture. As persons have increasingly clustered in urban areas, they have increasingly isolated themselves from the vicissitudes of the natural world. Moreover, in keeping nature at bay, they have become preoccupied with business affairs, leisure, social status, technology, and so on. The *humanum* has, quite literally, crowded out *natura*.

With this in mind, Kierkegaard argues that human beings have forgotten to marvel at creation, at their relation to it, and ultimately at its divine origin. That is to say, while documents such as the Bible presuppose and thus preserve a more primeval understanding of nature, its meaning is now lost or, at least, adulterated in the context of Western urbanity. "An actual situation in nature," Kierkegaard notes, is far different than when one, "in a quiet hour . . . dressed in silk and velvet," declaims that "not even a sparrow falls to earth without God's will."[73] Such phrases may sound amenable as one strolls through a city park, ostensibly sterilized from the elements, but they take on a darker significance "in a storm, when a hurricane rages and uproots trees, and the birds in death-agony plunge to the ground."[74] In fact, Kierkegaard continues, nature remains ever stronger than humanity, as in earthquakes when "the earth opens up and swallows entire cities."[75] But these occurrences are rare, and, in the bustle of bourgeois life, people assume that nature is nothing more than scenery for their self-regarding pursuits. It is for that reason that Kierkegaard calls for a return to the natural world: "Really, we need to live more with nature if for no other reason than to get more of an impression of God's majesty. Huddled together in the great cultural centers [*Stæder*] we have as much as possible abolished all overwhelming impressions—a lamentable demoralization."[76]

Thus cities are crowded, and in them "the crowd" flourishes, insofar as the very structure of urban life (buildings, streets, transport, etc.) minimizes the influence of nature and, in turn, forestalls an encounter with life's most fundamental questions. In other words, as an existential medium, the city's message is that the human, the finite, is dominant. This arrangement, according to Kierkegaard, leads to *demoralisation*, an eradication (*de-*) of right conduct (*-moralisation*). It is a provocative claim, which countervails the general Enlightenment assumption that bourgeois society and its concomitant mercantilist ethic are liberating.[77] Thus Kierkegaard's perspective on this matter ranges beyond modern urbanity and requires the sort of far-reaching attention that cannot be given here. Still, a few points germane to this discussion are in order. First, the proximity of human beings to one another in the city, especially when combined with the relative withdrawal of nature, facilitates what Kierkegaard calls "comparison" (*Sammenligning*). It is a word that literally means "joint assessment," and, for Kierkegaard, it follows from the modern tendency to "escape into sociality,"[78] to flee from the ideals of ethico-religious existence in order to pursue the relative ends of bourgeois life. What these relative ends promise is "material well-being,"[79] but they are certain to deliver other things as well—namely, physical tension, psychological unrest, and, finally, spiritual despair.

Perhaps Kierkegaard's finest treatment of this theme turns up in "What We Learn from the Lilies in the Field and from the Birds of the Air," the second part of *Upbuilding Discourses in Various Spirits*. Not only does "What We Learn" represent Kierkegaard's most sustained and most lyrical writing about the natural world, but it explicitly sets nature in contrast to the crowded busyness of bourgeois society. For Kierkegaard, the one who ventures "out where the lily blooms so beautifully, in the field" finds an "unbroken silence" that is salutary.[80] Unlike the entertainments featured in places like Dyrehavsbakken and Tivoli—those hailed by the "barker's voice" and the "cannon's thunder"[81]—nature provides what Kierkegaard terms a "godly diversion."[82] That is to say, nature diverts not by seeking to pass the time but by pointing away from time to its eternal ground. Thus, one does not "watch" the natural world like one watches a show; rather, one *contemplates* it.[83]

Again, according to Kierkegaard, the bourgeois city's infrastructural arrangement and daily practices obviate this contemplative mode. Whereas the activity of flowers, birds, and other creatures participates in their divinely ordered purpose, work in the city is regarded as a means of making money and attaining social status. Even leisure in the city requires the means to attain it. As a result, the typical denizen of the city is consumed "with worry about making a living,"[84] and, in this worry, "imagined need" (say, the attainment of a socially respectable financial station) comes to replace "actual need" (food, clothing, shelter, etc.).[85] The identification of imagined needs arises first and foremost through comparison—a focus on what others have, rather than on what one *is* by virtue of being human. Intriguingly, Kierkegaard associates comparison with industrial labor: those who abide in the "low underground regions of comparisons" are like "miners," who gauge their worth in terms of what they acquire.[86] And yet, their material gain comes at the expense of their individuality. In trying to keep up with the others, they have become little more than "beasts,"[87]—enslaved to *Mængden*, attached to "the herd."

This state of affairs was centuries in the making, yet Kierkegaard insists that a number of institutions benefit precisely by exacerbating it. The most important of these institutions, especially in relation to technology, is the press—a topic that will merit its own chapter. Another key establishment is the government, both in its secular and sacred iterations. With regard to the former, and as sketched in the previous chapter, Kierkegaard lived through the collapse of the absolute monarchy which had prevailed in Denmark from 1661 to 1848. The monarchy's decline, then, was a historic upheaval, though, in truth, it began with the "rising tide of liberalism" in the 1830s.[88] Hence, as a youth and on into his mature years, Kierkegaard really only knew a moribund form of absolutism, attenuated by the establishment of consultative assemblies in 1831—a type of geographic representation "based on property qualifications" and thus "weighted towards the wealthy."[89] Denmark's liberals, however, continued to press for wider enfranchisement, and, when the nation's first modern constitution was ratified in June 1849, it confirmed that liberalism finally had overtaken the absolute monarchy. The consultative assemblies were supplanted by a bicameral parliament of elected officials, and the king (then Frederik VII) formally became a "constitutional monarch," limited by the parameters of the new charter.

Kierkegaard's own views on these events are notoriously ambiguous. For every commentator who argues that he was a "monarchist" and "antidemocratic,"[90] there is another who claims that he "acknowledged and even welcomed" what might be termed the "new age of 'the common man.'"[91] That such statements do not necessarily contradict one another adds to the confusion. Indeed, Kierkegaard himself claimed that his stance over against the present age ought to be described as *"armed neutrality,"* inasmuch as his authorial task was to defend "the ideal picture of what it is to be a Christian," albeit in such a way that he refused to champion himself or a given party as representative of the highest truth.[92] He elaborates on this position further in "An Open Letter," an 1851 article prompted by the Danish pastor and theologian Andreas Rudelbach who had publicly associated his own political views with Kierkegaard's critique of the state church. What provoked Kierkegaard was not Rudelbach's fundamental claim—namely, that he and Kierkegaard were opponents of nominal or "habitual Christianity"—but the suggestion that this opposition allied Kierkegaard with Rudelbach's Grundtvigian party.[93] On the contrary, Kierkegaard explains, he rejects *a priori* the Grundtvigian claim that "free institutions" are needed if "Christianity and the Church are to be saved."[94] Not only does this perspective overlook Christian history, which proves that Christianity is "able to live, according to its vigor, under the most imperfect conditions and forms,"[95] but it comically elides the distinction between Christian action, driven by faith in God and the individual's duty to conscience, and the picayune compromises of liberal politics:

> The apostles did not go around talking among themselves, "It is intolerable that the Sanhedrin makes preaching the Word punishable; it is a matter of conscience. What should we do about it? Should we not form a group and send an appeal to the Sanhedrin—or should we take it up at a synodical meeting? It is just possible that by combining with those who otherwise are our enemies we can manage a majority vote so that we can obtain freedom of conscience to proclaim the Word." Good Lord![96]

This is not to imply that Christianity is indifferent to concrete action on behalf of the neighbor—after all, Kierkegaard authored a book called *Works of Love*—nor is it to deny that there "are situations . . . in which an established order can be of such a nature that the Christian ought not put up with it."[97] No, what rankled Kierkegaard about the rise of liberalism was the attempt to identify truth, especially Christian truth, with the *vox populi*. Christianity does not bend to intellectual fashion or popular sentiment— both of which may be erroneous and are, in any event, fraught with fickleness—but submits to God's unfailing self-revelation in the person of Jesus Christ.

Thus it is fair to say that, since Kierkegaard did not think that Christianity "could be helped from the outside by institutions and constitutions,"[98] he was a political agnostic, who refused to align his own project with that of any particular political system. And yet, it would also be fair to say that he had a special antipathy for liberalism, which he feared would contribute to "the downfall of Christianity" by its implication that the truth is attained "in a social and amicable political way, by elections or by a lottery of numbers."[99] In short, Kierkegaard associated the modern phenomenon of *Mængden* with liberal politics: "The idol, the tyrant, of our age is 'the many,' 'the crowd,' statistics," he writes in an 1850 journal entry, "for voting by ballot is the productive power in relation to the deification of statistics."[100] If enough persons seem to agree on a given issue—and "seem" is an apt word, since voting assigns whole numbers to issues that are otherwise many-sided and so cannot be taken as a careful and wise articulation of a person's convictions—then that issue becomes decisive for the society in question. Put differently, laws established from numerical tallies are reckoned as true, even if they are untrue in other ways or in a higher sense.

But what, then, is the purpose of treating such laws as true? For Kierkegaard, the answer lies in "the bourgeois mentality," whose utilitarian calculus declares that one is in the right just to the extent that one accords "with a specific number" of persons.[101] Thus truth is not absolute but relative, and herein lies one of the comforts of modern urbanity and its liberal political articulation—that "everyone is so prone to set his mind at ease in a relativity."[102] Ultimately, this is the case both for those in the majority and for those in the minority, since members of each party feel secure among their particular herd, transported "to an exalted state just as opium does."[103] Moreover, in ever seeking to add to their totals, all tacitly agree that "number is the power in this world."[104] As Kierkegaard continues in an 1854 passage:

> The numerical (which as numbers increase more and more has become the law of human existence) also has the demoralizing effect that the sight of these thousands and thousands prompts men to live merely comparatively, all human existence dissolves in the nonsense of comparison, the mud of numbers, which then is even prettied up to look like something under the name of history and politics, where the whole point . . . is always that what counts is a large number of participants, that numbers confer significance.[105]

Premodern thinkers—Aristotle particularly comes to mind[106]—tended to see happiness as a consequence of virtue, both on a personal and on a political level. What pains Kierkegaard is that the modern liberal polis takes a far more reductive view: "To have it just as good as the others—this is called being happy. Whether or not the lives of contemporaries are utterly shabby or are actually worthwhile does not concern the numerical one bit."[107]

At the very least, then, Kierkegaard censures liberal politicians (*de Liberale*) for exploiting the rise of *Mængden*: "They never have had any essentially ethical outlook. They want to have the crowd on their side—otherwise they are angry with it."[108] That is neither to claim that liberals lack ethical concerns not to aver that harm alone can come from liberal reforms. And yet, since "it is not understood that the crowd itself is the evil,"[109] liberal measures are finally in vain. Hence, at his darkest, Kierkegaard fears that liberalism's indebtedness to *Mængden* will lead to ruination. Drawing on "The Tailor in Heaven," a fairy tale by the Brothers Grimm,[110] Kierkegaard writes: "The liberals are like the tailor in heaven—in order to punish a single abuse which they notice from our Lord's usurped throne, they grab God's footstool and hurl it down to earth—yes, to punish it they would willingly destroy the whole world."[111]

Still, to whatever extent Kierkegaard blamed secular politics for the crowd's escalating tyranny, he faulted the Danish state church even more. Traditionally, this has been a topic of immense interest in Kierkegaard scholarship,[112] and so it would be redundant to dwell on it in this context. Suffice it to say that Kierkegaard maintained that the state church in general, and its clerical leadership in particular, profited from the bourgeois crowd and thus refrained from promoting authentic Christianity. In an 1854 passage, to cite but one example, Kierkegaard argues that Danish Christians have been rendered "spineless" by the *Mængden*: in and through the ritual practices of the church, they profess to want "the highest," but, confident among so many like-minded persons, they partake of bourgeois comforts and flout the demands of an actual relationship with God.[113] Still worse, the Danish state church acquiesces to this arrangement:

> And this mass [of people] . . . is led by the clergy to think that they are Christians—which naturally is to the interest of the preacher because of his appointment. If they were to be told that they were not Christians, they would become furious . . . . No, but the clergy have gotten them to imagine that they are Christians, that is, they so shockingly reduce what being a Christian is supposed to mean that in a certain meaningless sense it is true that they are Christians. This, you see, is why they become insulted. And thus the mass of good, decent people is used to set upon the Christian.[114]

Put differently—and to reiterate a statement made earlier—the state church does not resist the modern dictatorship of "the crowd" but, instead, underwrites it for the sake of worldly benefit. Both privately and publicly, Kierkegaard tried to make this point to a number of the leading churchmen of his day, especially Bishop Jacob Peter Mynster,[115] but he felt ignored. Hence, in 1854, he launched what has become known as the "attack upon Christendom"—a blitz of polemical broadsides against the Danish state church, which continued almost up to his death in November 1855.

In the end, then, Kierkegaard understood that urbanization entails grim consequences: "The advance of civilization, the rise of the large cities, centralization . . . have given all life completely the wrong direction."[116] In fact, many of the most important themes of his authorship, from the need for psycho-spiritual integration to the corrupting influence of philosophical and/or political abstractions, *presuppose* the context of modern urbanity. It is not that Kierkegaard hated every aspect of city life: he patronized Copenhagen's restaurants and theaters, and he famously took daily walks around the city.[117] And yet, in his view, the one who remains in the city must be prepared to face a variety of trials, including the possibility of being martyred by the crowd. As he writes in 1854 journal entry:

> From a Christian point of view the law is this: Either go out into solitude, away from men, so that you may be able to acquire the criterion of the ideal undisturbed by the nonsense and the haggling of numbers . . . ; or if you remain among men, then you must suffer persecution—in order to preserve heterogeneity, which again insures individuality and the criterion of the ideal. But Christianity is impossible in direct continuity with the herd.[118]

This passage is dated 1854, the year that Kierkegaard's attack upon Christendom began. He would protest in the midst of Copenhagen,[119] thereby extending his claim that authentic existence involves taking "life's dailiness quite literally as one's scene of action, to walk about and teach in the streets."[120]

Kierkegaard's experience of technological instruments

It is now clear that, while Kierkegaard did not employ the terminology of the philosophy of technology, he understood that he was living in an age of "discovery" and of increasing urbanization—trends about which he was concerned and often critical. To see Kierkegaard against this backdrop is, at the very least, to recognize that Kierkegaard's "conceptual analysis of modernity" is inseparable from his "interpretation of the condition of urbanity."[121] This is simply because the city is "the fullest possible embodiment of the ideological intentions of modernity."[122] And yet, if city life is a macrocosm of the modern, what of the microcosmic components that comprise it—say, its economic structures, political conventions, or technological apparatuses? How did Kierkegaard experience these different facets of the modern city?

Of course, a few responses to this question already have been sketched, though a complete answer would require a much larger study than the present one. For that reason, and given the peculiar focus of this inquiry, attention here will be limited to technology, especially those technological instruments that came to define Kierkegaard's era. For that reason, special emphasis will be given to modern transportation.

Kierkegaard on modern transport

As seen in Chapter 2, modern methods of transport began to appear in Denmark during Kierkegaard's lifetime, and they were essential to the nation's push toward modernization. Moreover, it is clear that Kierkegaard was familiar with these mechanisms and, indeed, used them at times. But how did he respond to them, whether in intellectual or affective terms? In order to address this question, three forms of transportation will be discussed—the bus, the railroad, and the steamship.

The bus was the "first popular method of commuting, apart, that is, from walking under one's own power."[123] Initially, the bus was known as the "omnibus," the Latin term meaning "for all." In 1826, a French physician and entrepreneur named Stanislas Baudry applied the word "omnibus" to his burgeoning carriage business, which utilized large horse-drawn stagecoaches to move people in and out of Nantes.[124] Since he envisioned a mode of transport accessible for all persons, Baudry thought "omnibus" fitting, though the appellation eventually would be simplified to "bus." Baudry's enterprise was a financial success, and the concept of public transportation— principally aimed at the bourgeoisie in major Western cities—took root over the next decade. George Shillibeer started an omnibus line in London in 1829,[125] with similar services established in New York City (1827), Philadelphia (1831), St. Petersburg (1835), and Berlin (1837).[126] This was nothing less than a revolutionary development: "The egalitarian nature of buses was . . . new. Anybody who could pay the fare was welcome aboard and this made them something of a social leveller. Some of those using them might be from the upper classes and others merely shopkeepers; all were equal on the omnibus."[127]

In Copenhagen, omnibuses were established in the early 1840s, at which point they "transformed" the "urban scene" of the capital city.[128] Indeed, when an English travel writer named James Ewing Ritchie visited Copenhagen in the 1840s, he was impressed by Tivoli and, perhaps above all, the city's omnibus line:

> Never were there such omnibusses in the world before. The cushions are formed to give you as much ease as a mortal can have in a sitting posture; the windows are of plate-glass, with gilt frames and curtains; the top of the omnibus inside is beautifully painted, and the conductor has "an air and a grace" . . . easier imagined than described.[129]

Ritchie makes a number of other curious comments about Copenhagen—for instance, he stresses that, more than any other place or person, the sculptor Bertel Thorvaldsen is the city's "chief claim"[130] to fame—but most pertinent is his observation that liberalism is gaining traction in Denmark. As he puts it, "There are indications that change is near; that a new spirit is walking the earth; that the power of the people is increasing; and that its progress no man nor monarch can hinder or restrain."[131] Eventually, he predicts, the Danish crown will have to permit "the introduction of liberalism," because no monarch can "exclude the light in which all nations shall ultimately rejoice."[132]

What is fascinating is that, in associating Copenhagen's newfangled public transportation with Denmark's slow but certain turn to liberal modernity, Ritchie echoes Kierkegaard's own response to the omnibus. The Dane's first reference to the omnibus occurs in "In Vino Veritas," which comprises the first major section of *Stages on Life's Way* (1845). The overall intent of *Stages* is to exemplify different facets of Kierkegaard's so-called "spheres of existence," which, according to C. Stephen Evans, "represent different forms of inwardness or subjectivity, different configurations of caring and passion that give particular shape to human lives."[133] "In Vino Veritas" involves the aesthetic stage in general and erotic love (*Elskov*) in particular, on the latter of which a series of pseudonymous speakers are invited to expound after a bacchanalian feast. One of the final speakers is Victor Eremita or "Victorious Hermit," whose name, to be sure, indicates a withdrawn attitude toward erotic love. For Victor, eroticism all too often makes the male dependent on the female, and that is why the ideal relationship, from a masculine perspective, is "so reflective that for that very reason it would not become a relationship with her."[134] What this seems to mean is that man should suppress the destabilizing passion of eros in favor of a "false expression"[135] by which he keeps feminine immediacy at bay. And yet, Victor concludes, this prescription is not an advocacy for "the monastery";[136] in other words, he is not demanding that the bourgeois comforts of modern life—whether material or sexual—be renounced. As he explains, "The person for whom every immediate expression is only forgery, he and he alone is better safeguarded than if he entered the monastery; he becomes an Eremita even if he rides the omnibus night and day."[137]

The first takeaway here is the fact that Kierkegaard published a reference to the omnibus rather quickly after it appeared in Copenhagen. Still, it is also intriguing that Kierkegaard, writing as Victor Eremita, is already pondering how one might resist the leveling tendencies of modern technology. Sure, Victor notes, one might flee the city in a kind of religious solitude (*Klosteret*), but this measure is ineffectual and unnecessary besides. It would be better, he says, to participate in bourgeois externality (getting married, riding the bus, etc.), while maintaining a place of *interior* control—a place where the individual, deep down, remains beyond the vortex of mass society.

Kierkegaard's next mention of the omnibus is, at the same time, one of the broader and more meaningful references to modern technology in his entire authorship. It is found in *Concluding Unscientific Postscript*—another pseudonymous text, published in 1846, which is written from the perspective of Johannes Climacus. Thirty years old and a native of Copenhagen,[138] Climacus is a budding author, who nevertheless prefers to spend "the day loafing and thinking, or thinking and loafing."[139] He recalls how his literary avocation came to him on a Sunday afternoon—in fact, he mentions "Sunday afternoon"[140] twice, as if to stress its connection to the Sabbath—while resting outside of Josty's café in Frederiksberg Gardens, "that lovely garden which . . . was a pleasant diversion in the happy gaiety of the populace."[141] So he sat there, smoking a cigar and pondering the direction of his authorship. His lone certainty was that he enjoyed the "splendid inactivity"[142] of passing the time in this way—there, in the park, reveling in modern affluence. As he adds, "Although I am generally not unacquainted with the comforts of life, of all comforts indolence is the most comfortable."[143]

In short, Climacus is a member of the bourgeoisie—a contented, debonair, and somewhat waggish resident of the city. And yet, he is self-reflexive enough to realize that his bourgeois lifestyle is not so much chosen *by* him as chosen *for* him. He is going with the flow, as it were, given that the whole of modern life is maneuvering people to a place of comfort and ease:

> Wherever you look in literature or in life, you see the names and figures of celebrities, the prized and highly acclaimed people, prominent or much discussed, the many benefactors of the age who know how to benefit humankind by making life easier and easier, some by railroads, others by omnibuses and steamships, others by telegraph, others by easily understood surveys and brief publications about everything worth knowing, and finally the true benefactors of the age who by virtue of thought systematically make spiritual existence easier and easier and yet more and more meaningful—and what are you doing?[144]

Thus Climacus not only understands that his age is an age of technological innovation, but he grasps that technology's raison d'être is efficiency—what Jacques Ellul would dub *technique* roughly a century later. This development, in and of itself, does not seem to trouble Climacus. As a matter of fact, the ease of modern life provides the means, the "indolence,"[145] by which his assessment is possible.

At the same time, however, Climacus's response to the omnibus and to other modern technologies bears an important reservation. Not unlike Victor Eremita, Climacus perceives that the very shape of modern life threatens to control everyone and everything. More specifically, he worries that bourgeois amenities are bound to obscure the sorts of questions that give life meaning. With this in mind, Climacus vows to resist:

> When all join together to make everything easier in every way, there remains only one possible danger, namely, the danger that the easiness would become so great that it would become all too easy. So only one lack remains, even though not yet felt, the lack of difficulty. Out of love of humankind . . . out of genuine interest in those who make everything easy, I comprehended that it was my task: to make difficulties everywhere.[146]

It is worth adding that, also like Eremita, Climacus resists on behalf of the individual, albeit for a totally different reason: Climacus is not interested in preserving the individual's *libido dominandi* but, rather, in deepening the individual's self-knowledge in relation to eternity. For, as he will ultimately make clear, the individual's relation to the eternal is precisely a matter of giving up control, and, for that reason, it cannot be squared with modernity's technological and philosophical systems.

Kierkegaard's subsequent references to the omnibus underline this point. In a letter to Rasmus Nielsen, a philosophy professor at the University of Copenhagen,[147] Kierkegaard suggests the irony in giving the name "omnibus" to a modern method of transportation. Drawing on a reference from *Fear and Trembling* (1843), in which Kierkegaard's pseudonym, Johannes de Silentio, refers to Hegel's philosophical system as an "omnibus,"[148] Kierkegaard explains to Nielsen that "the association of ideas from omnibus to omnibus is evoked in the maxim: *de omnibus dubitandum* [all things are to be doubted]. Hence, when Johannes de Silentio calls the system 'an omnibus,' it must be understood as having a double meaning."[149] Kierkegaard makes a similar pun in an 1854 journal entry but draws a stronger connection between the omnibus as a mode of public transport and the Hegelian system as an "omnibus." As he puts it, "Personality is aristocratic—the system is a plebeian invention; by means of the system (that omnibus) everyone comes along."[150]

These last two passages recall the previous references to the omnibus, in that they evince concern about modern technology's encroachment upon the individual. And yet, they are more perspicuous in their critique: just as Hegel's system makes the individual subservient to the ends of "an abstraction—the state, etc.,"[151] so does the omnibus work for the sake of abstract end (whether it be efficient conveyance, improved economic productivity, or some combination thereof) regardless of the individual persons who use it. One might even say that, with the arrival of the omnibus, transportation begins to use persons rather than the other way around, since the first omnibuses inaugurated the practice of operating according to a fixed schedule, effectively indifferent to the interests and needs of its customers *qua* individuals.[152] That is why Kierkegaard considers both Hegelian philosophy (no matter how theoretically complex) and modern transportation (no matter how skillfully designed) to be "plebeian"—a term that can be traced back to the Greek *pleion*, which means "greater in quantity" or "very many." Thus whatever is "plebeian" belongs to "the masses" or, in Kierkegaard's parlance, to *Mængden*: Hegelianism is plebeian inasmuch as it "basically regards men, paganly, as an animal-race endowed with reason,"[153] while the omnibus is a material expression of the same idea, treating persons strictly in terms of their function within bourgeois society.

The railroad—which, as noted in Chapter 2, first appeared in Denmark in the mid-1840s—provoked a stronger response from Kierkegaard than the omnibus. Indeed, the term "railroad" (*Jernbane*) turns up twelve times in his authorship, beginning with *Either/Or* in 1843—a reference that, not incidentally, is similar to Kierkegaard's allusions to the omnibus, since it associates "the train" with bourgeois "triviality" and with "losing oneself in life's social hordes."[154] Likewise, Johannes Climacus calls modernity "the age that travels by railroad," and he implies that this technological innovation is but an extension of the epoch's basic orientation, since modernity views the past as "a receding little station on the systematic world-historical railroad."[155] Hence, in an ironical vein, he adds that the individual might as well not even bother with his or her particular destiny, because "the whole trick is to jump into a passenger car, the first the best, and leave things to the world-historical."[156]

If these passages reinforce the thrust of Kierkegaard's comments on the omnibus—comments associating modern technology with consumerist conformity and mindless efficiency—other references to the railroad suggest a deeper concern. In "The Cares of the Pagans," the first major section of *Christian Discourses* (1848), Kierkegaard argues that, just as natural organisms such as birds do not worry about the future, Christians should not fret over "the next day" either:

> The one who rows a boat turns his back to the goal toward which he is working. So it is with the next day. When, with the help of the eternal, a person lives absorbed in today, he turns his back to the next day. The more he is eternally absorbed in today, the more decisively he turns his back to the next day; then he does not see it all.[157]

Here, intriguingly, an older technology represents the Christian attitude toward life: the Christian is like an oarsman, concentrating on where he has come from (God or, to continue the analogy, the shoreline), "entirely present"[158] to the needs at hand, and thus free from worry about the future. In contrast, the pagan attitude is embodied in the modern railroad, which instantiates a concern for moving as far as possible and as quickly as possible for the sake of "earthly and worldly care," which "is basically for the next day."[159] And yet, no matter how far or how quickly the train goes, it cannot provide the peace of mind secured by living in the present. As Kierkegaard explains, "We ride so fast on trains that we arrive at a distant place the same day, but the bird is more ingenious or swifter; it travels many, many days and arrives the same day. We cannot travel that fast by train if we are to travel just as far."[160]

Kierkegaard, then, concedes the material efficacy of the railroad, but he questions the premise on which it is based—namely, that the quantifiable improvement offered by rail travel will lead to greater human happiness. Indeed, for Kierkegaard, it is just this kind of assumption that has pushed the West into a secularism so pervasive that Christian teaching is no longer intelligible. He makes this point in the second edition of his polemical bulletin, *The Moment* (1855), where he argues that the modern Christian reads the New Testament in the same way that a modern traveler reads an outdated travel guide:

> Such a handbook is not to be taken seriously by travelers in that country, but it has great value as entertaining reading. While one is comfortably riding along in the train, one reads in the handbook, "Here is the frightful Wolf Ravine, where one plunges 70,000 fathoms down under the earth"; while one is sitting and smoking a cigar in the cozy dining car, one reads in the handbook, "Here is the hideout of a robber band that attacks and beats up travelers"—here it is, here it was, since now (how amusing to imagine how it was), now it is not the Wolf Ravine but a railroad, and not a robber band but a cozy dining car.[161]

Hence, just as the modern tourist encounters a place that was once fearsome but now, under the control of technology, is simply a matter of curiosity, so has modern Christendom altered Christianity to such an extent that the New Testament appears peculiar, if also tame.

Clearly, this way of approaching modern transport—namely, as a material expression of the inner comportment of modern persons, especially members of the bourgeoisie—connects a number of Kierkegaard's references to the technologies in question. Yet, given its descriptive specificity, this particular mention of the railroad also intimates Kierkegaard's own use of rail travel. As alluded to in the previous chapter, Kierkegaard had personal familiarity with the *Jernbane*. Not only did he witness the first Danish railroad—which, opening in June 1847, provided transport between Copenhagen and Roskilde—but he also had the opportunity to encounter rail travel in Germany. Perhaps his most notable experience in this regard came in May 1843, when Kierkegaard boarded a train in Stettin, then a major Prussian seaport, en route to Berlin. The roughly 95-mile journey was scheduled to take nine to ten hours, better than half the time of a horse-drawn carriage ride. Kierkegaard purchased first-class tickets "and positioned himself comfortably in an armchair in an empty first-class carriage."[162] Hence, despite having an awkward exchange with a German conductor,[163] Kierkegaard understood well the luxurious possibilities afforded by rail travel—the quicker pace, the relative ease, and the systematic organization.

Again, though, Kierkegaard's concern is that the logic of the railroad is now being applied to every aspect of human existence, including religious life and, indeed, Christianity. In an 1852 journal entry, Kierkegaard worries that modern Christianity has adopted a technological mindset: whereas Christ proclaimed that his way is "narrow,"[164] the modern church acts as if all are saved and that everyone is on "the way which leads to life."[165] "Nowadays the way is easy," Kierkegaard adds, "it goes faster than on a train [*Jernbane*]."[166] Elsewhere he suggests that technology is influencing the manner in which persons conceive of God. Citing a book on recent Protestant movements such as the Irvingites and the Mormons, Kierkegaard suggests that their belief in divine possibility is derived from the modern preoccupation with development and speed. As he notes, "It is very characteristic, and presumably I am not wrong in assuming this to be the influence of trains and the inventions of the telegraph. In all probability . . . all these modern inventions will be employed to decide the conception of God."[167]

This last point approaches Kierkegaard's deepest apprehension regarding the railroad and other modes of modern transport. As he sees it, they represent a renewed attempt to make humanity "the measure of all things,"[168] that is to say, to view everything (even God) in terms of its human utility or its reflection of the *humanum*:

> The railroad craze is altogether an attempt à la Babel. It also fits together with the end of a cultural period; it is the last lap. Unfortunately almost simultaneously the new era began, 1848. The railroads are to the idea of centralization as a potentiation. . . . Centralization will probably also be Europe's financial downfall.[169]

What is particularly fascinating here is that Kierkegaard directly links railroads with the centralization (thus urbanization) and democratization. The great trends of modern Western society—urbanization, technology, and liberalism—have coalesced, leading to a society in which human ideals are flattened and individuals expected to pursue the purely immanent utilitarian ends of secular life. Again, Kierkegaard does not view this turn to the secular as unprecedented in and of itself, but he does think of it as a consummation, as it were, of previous attempts to establish an anthropocentric world: "The inventions which really please mankind are either tinged with the rebellion of the race against God (the tower of Babel, railroads, mass-mindedness) or, if they are related to the individual, they are inventions which satisfy his boyishness."[170] Human beings crave strength and amusement—or, to quote the Roman poet Juvenal, *panem et circenses*[171]—and the railroad is another example of this tendency. For Kierkegaard, however, these cravings occlude the individual's awareness of his or her eternal significance, of the fact that he or she is not just a number but, *qua* individual, has been willed into being by God: "Man's salvation lies precisely in his becoming a person."[172]

In the end, then, the invention and the popularization of the railroad incited Kierkegaard. It does not appear, however, that the steamship (*Dampskib*) produced the same effect. The difference may be due to timing. Whereas the railroad became an integral part of Western society during Kierkegaard's adulthood, the first steam-propelled boats dated back to the eighteenth century,[173] and the earliest seaworthy steamships appeared during the first quarter of the nineteenth century.[174] Thus the steamship was already a presupposition in Denmark when Kierkegaard came of age, and, as the mechanization of a prehistoric technology (the boat), the steamship perhaps seemed less radical, less bourgeois than the railroad or even the omnibus. Still, it is worth noting that references to the *Dampskib* do turn up in Kierkegaard's oeuvre. A number of these allusions are metaphorical. In the *Postscript*, for example, Johannes Climacus posits the suffering of a poet, who likens his pain to "a steamship in a storm, with machinery too large in proportion to the structure of the hull."[175] At other junctures, Kierkegaard mentions the steamship as part of a wider critique of Danish culture. One 1855 sketch compares Kierkegaard to a passenger on a "very large ship," with "room for one thousand passengers," who warns the captain (Bishop Mynster) that a storm or an iceberg is in the ship's path; however, the captain does not listen and "hurries down to the noisy, hilarious company in the lounge." Another late journal entry, dated September 24, 1855, compares membership in the Danish state church to purchasing "a ticket to Tivoli or a steamship, an omnibus."[176] Once the ticket is in hand, one no longer thinks of the cost but frivolously enjoys the ride. In this way, the church caters to those who "are utterly impatient to get into the sensate hustle and bustle of this life."[177] Indeed, according to Kierkegaard, Denmark's naive embrace of modern conventions and technologies—especially the "rabble newspapers"[178]—will lead to its downfall. This "small nation" and its "small city" (Copenhagen) might be likened to a "dinghy" (*Jolle*) outfitted with "machinery suited for a great steamship [*Dampskib*]": rather than drive the dinghy forward, the technology just causes it to sink.[179]

Hence, even if Kierkegaard does not criticize the steamship in the same manner as the railroad, his remarks continue to express reticence vis-à-vis modern transport. Perhaps, it is even tempting to conclude that Kierkegaard dismisses modern transportation en masse. After all, if he thought the railroad both signified and facilitated the malaise of cosmopolitan modernity, what would he think of the airplane—to date, the fastest and most efficient form of modern transport, which was already being experimented with in Kierkegaard's day?[180] Still, a more circumspect reading is possible. Kierkegaard himself traveled on steamships on a number of occasions,[181] and, as noted, he used the railroad as well. Thus, his life stands as a tacit acknowledgment of the convenience and reliability of these forms of technology, and so, whatever his objections, he clearly did not shun modern transportation altogether.

It seems reasonable to conclude, then, that Kierkegaard's criticisms of modern transportation are not blanket condemnations but, rather, expressions of apprehension. To be more specific, Kierkegaard is not as apprehensive about the technologies themselves as about their influence on humanity. This concern is twofold. On the one hand, Kierkegaard registers consistent alarm at the *pace* of modern life—a pace only exacerbated by the degree to which technology has enhanced transportation and expedited urbanization. On the other hand, he worries that, while such technical improvements are hailed as "progress," this sort of progress is superficial at best and, if adopted as a principle, catastrophic at worst. Thus, the "progress" of nineteenth-century technology, much like the "progress" made in the political realm, is actually a misnomer, since true progress, according to Kierkegaard, comes from personal ethical and religious growth. But it is just this point that the age is inclined to miss.

These conclusions will be revisited as this study continues. Yet, in closing this section on Kierkegaard's view of modern transport, it is worth appending an exchange he once had with Janus Kolderup-Rosenvinge, a law professor at the University of Copenhagen and a regular companion on Kierkegaard's strolls about the capital city. In an August 1848 letter, Kolderup-Rosenvinge playfully acknowledges Kierkegaard's love of walking, only to add that *he* prefers to move "by carriage or by ship."[182] Indeed, after dismissing the use of the omnibus, which he associates with the working classes, Kolderup-Rosenvinge highlights a particular affection for the "steamship [*Dampskib*], one of today's most brilliant *Errungenschaften*,"[183] which he recently had taken up to Elsinore on the northeastern coast of Zealand and then back to Bellevue Beach, just outside of Copenhagen. "What more can you ask?" Kolderup-Rosenvinge states,

"Three different means of locomotion in one day, and many, many miles traveled by motion into the bargain—I cannot even count them, nor do I care to."[184]

Kierkegaard's response, penned a week or so later, is similarly lively, though his point is no doubt earnest. He begins by observing that the Danish noun *Bremse* can mean both "gadfly" and "brake," and so he relishes the irony that modern forms of transport need a "gadfly"—that is to say, a "brake"—in order to decelerate: "I had read that on railroad trains something called a 'gadfly' is employed in order—yes, is this not crazy?—*to stop*."[185] For Kierkegaard, this oddity is a metaphor for "the whole development in Europe."[186] As he continues, "Throughout Europe nothing is really established at this moment—everything is movement," and yet this "vortex" is by no means salutary, because one "gets tired, becomes dizzy, yearns for a foothold, a stop."[187] But what would it even mean to stop, when every facet of Western culture, from industry to politics, is based on constant and ever-rapid progress? Kierkegaard adds that a gadfly is needed to bring an end to this tornado of revolution, but not just any gadfly will do. Here he turns his attention to Socrates, who once opposed the "Sophist vortex"[188] in ancient Athens. For Kierkegaard, the Sophists were precursors to the innovators and officials of modern society, since "Sophistry . . . always asks whither one should go instead of asking whence one should depart."[189] In contrast, Socrates made "it apparent that nothing remained fixed in this way. On the contrary, Socrates had the fixed point *behind*. His point of departure lay in himself and in the god."[190] And, eventually, "[Socrates] stopped Sophistry" in just this way.

As is well known, Kierkegaard considered his task in modern Denmark analogous to Socrates's mission centuries before. While modern persons rush ahead, championing new ways of communicating, investing, writing, and even moving, Kierkegaard remained preoccupied with what he saw as essential to human nature. That is why, as he explains to Kolderup-Rosenvinge, he remains a walker first and foremost, because only "he who fundamentally understands walking . . . understands also how it is bound up with stopping."[191] In the constant motion of the modern world, with its buses, trains, and ships (never mind automobiles and airplanes), there is increasingly little time to consider the source of this motion. Yet, if there is no *terminus a quo*, there cannot be a determinate *terminus ad quem* either. People look to the future, but the future is itself undecided, vulnerable to untold contingencies. Thus, it appears that the value in walking lies in the intimacy with which it holds person and motion together: the source of movement comes, as it were, from within. In this sense, Kierkegaard suggests, walking stands in relation to modern transport as religion does to modern Western society. Just as the walker knows how and when to stop, so "the whole European confusion . . . cannot be stopped except by religion."[192] Modernity may very well be a time of constant and ever-rapid transportation, but Kierkegaard expects that, in the end, this movement "will turn out suddenly to be religious or the need for religion."[193]

Kierkegaard on other technological developments

This chapter has shown that, even if a relatively slight portion of Kierkegaard's authorship concerns modern methods of transport, there are enough extant references to delineate his basic orientation toward the arrival of buses, trains, and steamships. The situation is no different with other nineteenth-century technological advances—that is to say, those devices and machines that came to shape modern society. Kierkegaard scatters references to these instruments in ad hoc fashion, and, while the totality of these allusions does not add up to a cohesive philosophy of technology, it nevertheless allows us to get a better sense of his relation to and understanding of some of the key technological innovations of his era. Moreover, it is clear that, as with transportation, Kierkegaard feared that the convenience and efficiency promoted by such innovations was a distraction at best and a form of anthropocentric aggrandizement at worst.

Electricity. The first widely accessible electrical supplies began to appear in the 1870s, and yet, as a source of lighting, electricity did not become dominant until after the First World War.[194] In fact, Denmark was among the slowest European countries to embrace electricity, since it was relatively "well endowed with gas supplies."[195] Nevertheless, a handful of references indicate that Kierkegaard was well aware that electricity had become an object of scientific experimentation and invention. He writes of an "electric shock"[196] in *Stages on Life's Way*, and, in an 1854 journal entry, he compares God to an "electrical machine" (*Elektriseermaskine*): neither can be touched without getting shocked.[197] This is likely a reference to the so-called Leyden jar—a crude yet potent device, developed by the Dutch scientist Pieter van Musschenbroek in the 1740s, which made it possible to store an electrical charge.[198] The success (and danger)[199] of the Leyden jar attracted the attention of the era's best scientific minds, including the French priest Jean-Antoine Nollet as well as the American polymath Benjamin Franklin, and electrical technology continued to evolve well into Kierkegaard's day and beyond. In one key discovery, for example, the Italian scientist Luigi Galvani "found that dissected frog legs twitched as though in convulsion when they were placed in contact with a spark from an electric machine."[200] He went on to modify this experiment, using different materials and even different animal parts, and eventually the process of stimulating muscles by an electrical current would be named "galvanism" after him.

Galvanism is of particular import here, insofar as Kierkegaard himself took an interest in it. In *The Concept of Anxiety* (1844), the pseudonymous author Vigilius Haufniensis likens superficial spiritual experiences to the twitching of "a galvanized [*galvaniseret*] frog,"[201] and a similar comparison is made in the *Postscript*, where Johannes Climacus argues that the authentic "religious speaker" must strive "to express in existence what he proclaims and not to electrify [*electrisere*] the congregation once a week and galvanically make them twitch."[202] A third reference is found in a version of the tortuously revised and posthumously issued *Book on Adler* (1872), in which Kierkegaard argues that only concrete ethical decisions can help the person who "stands still in fantasy and does not earnestly grasp any task for his life, and therefore he becomes like a galvanic frog that twitches for a moment."[203]

These passages not only locate Kierkegaard within an era of deepening knowledge of electricity, but they also demonstrate his attentiveness to electrical technology and experimentation. Moreover, even though these allusions do not give us a clear sense of his response to electrical research, they do seem to indicate an ongoing reserve vis-à-vis such developments. It is telling, for example, that each of Kierkegaard's references to galvanism associate it with spiritual despair, that is, with a mindless and indeed mechanical relation to reality. One might even see Kierkegaard as paralleling some of the insights of Mary Shelley's celebrated novel *Frankenstein; or, The Modern Prometheus* (1818). Shelley was, for all intents and purposes, a contemporary of Kierkegaard, and she too was familiar with the tests of Galvani, his nephew Giovanni Aldini (who even galvanized a human corpse), and their occasional scientific adversary Alessandro Volta.[204] Further, and also like Kierkegaard, Shelley articulated reservations about the rise of science, not only in terms of its promotion of scientific hubris (as represented by Victor Frankenstein),[205] but also in terms of its methodical yet rapacious attempt to dominate the acquiescent natural world. "Read in this way, science appears to be individualistic, egotistical and opposed to the feminine."[206]

Although Kierkegaard owned a book by Shelley's husband, the romantic poet Percy Bysshe Shelley,[207] he himself did not own *Frankenstein*. Moreover, there are no references to "Frankenstein" in Kierkegaard's authorship. So, rather than posit a direct relationship between him and Shelley's masterpiece, it would be more prudent to conclude that his views on electricity echo a general "Romantic hostility toward [the] seemingly 'inhuman' aspect of science."[208] For Kierkegaard, there is genuine power in electricity—power to shock and even to stir inanimate being—but this power is ultimately external to the person and thereby available for grotesque manipulation. Lasting and genuinely powerful change must come from within the person and be oriented toward the ethico-religious aspect of human life.

Telegraph. The word "telegraph" can be traced back to the Greek terms *tele-* ("far off") and *graphein* ("to write"). A telegraph, then, is a means of conveying textual or symbolic information from afar, and, understood as such, there are a variety of telegraphic methods, from smoke signals to blinking lights. Nevertheless, by the mid-eighteenth century, science's ever-deepening understanding of electricity encouraged the development of *electrical* telegraphy, chiefly "as a response to a general need for faster communication."[209] In fact, a decisive breakthrough for electrical telegraphy took place in Denmark, when Hans Christian Ørsted, motivated by theoretical rather than technical concerns, demonstrated the interaction of electrical and magnetic forces.[210] In turn, the telegraph would come to operate by way of an electromagnet, which, stimulated by external electric impulses, directed a writing utensil capable of recording messages.[211] Working electrical telegraphs began to appear in the 1830s, the most famous one owing to the American painter Samuel Morse, who exhibited his new invention before President Martin Van Buren and his administration in 1838.[212] A subsequent report to the House of Representatives claimed that Morse's telegraph "will amount to a revolution unsurpassed in moral grandeur by any discovery that has been made in the arts and sciences."[213] Morse himself did not deny the gravity of his work. Upon completion of the first telegraph line in the United States, which ran from Washington, D.C., to Baltimore, Morse's initial message was a quotation from Num. 23:23: "What hath God wrought?"[214]

Denmark soon established its own telegraphic networks,[215] and Kierkegaard quickly took notice of this new technology. He mentions the telegraph as early as 1835,[216] noting that modern long-distance communication has an analog in the Bible. Yet, over time, Kierkegaard's remarks about the telegraph became less casual and more critical. Two previously mentioned passages link the telegraph with distorting the way human beings conceive of God[217] and with fomenting "windbaggery"[218] in general. Other references level more substantive charges. As has been seen, the telegraph was developed explicitly to accelerate communication, particularly over significant distances. But what sort of information is most readily transmitted in this way? Already in 1854, Kierkegaard observed that telegraphic communication was being used chiefly to convey what has come to be known as "news." Thus his views on the telegraph are related to his views on the press, which will be discussed in the next chapter. But it is worth underlining here that, even as Kierkegaard concedes that the telegraph is quite capable of telling persons that there "is a war going on in Europe," thereby creating a demand for updates that arrive "every day [from] the telegraph dispatcher," he questions the utility of such information.[219] Like a mother trying to entertain a child, the news has the effect of distracting the individual from that which concerns her both in a personal and in an ultimate sense.[220] In short, the telegraph is another modern means of keeping people busy, and, in this way, "the millions live and the millions die; they are just statistics and the statistical is their horizon, their everything."[221]

Indeed, what especially disturbs Kierkegaard is that this sort of mass society has been baptized, as it were, by the Christian Church. He argues that the vices of mass society are as opposed to Christianity as the rapacity and violence of the Roman Empire. And yet, while the early Christians resisted and even died opposing the sins of Rome, their modern descendants not only support mass society but are impudent enough to call it "Christendom." At bottom, then, "the very atmosphere of this Christian world is a lie," and "the lie is so habitual, such a state of lying that thousands and thousands are bona fide thoughtlessly lost in a lie."[222] Still worse, technology has been developed to enable and to further the situation: "Rejoice, O human race, that you have invented the telegraph; be proud of your discovery which is so appropriate to the times, calculated to lie on the greatest possible scale. Just as the Romans branded slanderers with the letter C, so the telegraph is a brand upon the human race—you liars."[223] Kierkegaard's words are undoubtedly acerbic, but, in another sense, he is making an observation that has since become commonplace in the West—namely, that society has grown cynical, virtually nihilistic. "We regard lying as unavoidable," Kierkegaard laments, "and we admire the big lie."[224]

Previously it was mentioned that Morse regarded the single-wire telegraph as a kind of revelation, so much so that he cited the Bible when speaking of it. What he implied thereby was that technologies such as the telegraph indicated God's ongoing intervention in human affairs. Historical development, on this view, does not run counter to the divine plan but, on the contrary, evinces the progressive unfolding of God's purposes. Famously, Kierkegaard opposed a straightforward identification of history and progress, particularly in its Hegelian-cum-speculative iteration; however, his remarks about the telegraph demonstrate that he likewise objected to a different account of "progress," according to which technological advances beckon divine favor (however construed) and the ultimate arrival of a techno-utopia. On the contrary, Kierkegaard writes, "I wonder if this whole matter of world history, the four monarchies, Hegel, Grundtvig . . . the railways and telegraphs, is of any concern to God or pleases him more than all the noise and fun children can make in the playroom instead of sitting still and studying their lessons, which would please their parents."[225] Might it not even be the case, he continues, that the more human beings record every aspect of their lives, the more trivial history seems? There are so many events, so many ideas and persons, that nothing really stands out, that history becomes a "mass of information down to the most trivial about what triviality's mass has done for the mass of trivialities."[226] Thus "what once inspired men to want to become more significant now no longer inspires them," so that "indifference" comes to reign and "the concept of history is completely abolished."[227] Over a century before Francis Fukuyama popularized the phrase,[228] Kierkegaard was alluding to "the end of history."

These comments stem from an 1854 journal entry, and it is intriguing to ponder the extent to which Kierkegaard's "attack upon Christendom," launched around this time, was an attempt to "produce history,"[229] to stand out from the masses and to defend that which modern society had rendered negligible. Whatever the case, it is certain that Kierkegaard understood the telegraph as part of the problem, precisely because it facilitated a mode of communication whose profitability was matched only by its superficiality. Chapter 4 will detail how he came to level the same charge at the press, albeit with greater perspicuity and vigor.

Other Innovations. The preceding has made clear that, even if Kierkegaard never developed anything like a unified philosophy of technology, his comments on technologies such as the railroad and the telegraph add up to a significant body of thought. In other words, Kierkegaard dedicated enough time and space to these innovations that a Kierkegaardian critique of modern technology comes into view—a critique that doubtless centers on how modern technology expedites the West's transformation into a bourgeois, mass society. The Dane's references to other modern technologies are less frequent and typically less substantive, but, taken as a whole, they further indicate his interest in, and concerns about, the rise of a culture given over to technology.

A curious case is public lighting, especially as provided by gas lamps. Copenhagen itself did not have gas lighting during Kierkegaard's lifetime—the city's first gasworks opened in 1857—but Kierkegaard was familiar with this innovation from his visits to Berlin. Prior to gas lighting, city streets became dangerously dark at night, particularly when the moon was in a waning phase. Night watchmen were employed to cope with this problem, and they remained active in Copenhagen until the early 1860s, where they monitored public safety and, to that end, manually lit streetlamps.[230] Gas lighting not only streamlined this process, but it promised better illumination and thus safer streets—another example of the symbiotic relationship between urbanization and technology.

Kierkegaard scatters a few references to this development in his authorship, most of which jest at the notion that gas lighting will unequivocally improve the human situation. In fact, it is curious that Kierkegaard's motley crew of pseudonyms appear to agree on this point. The smarmy Johannes the Seducer notes that gas lighting would make it both easier and harder to reconnoiter potential lovers—easier because he could observe others more effectively, harder because he too could be spotted more readily.[231] The devout Christian Anti-Climacus concedes that gas lighting is useful for public safety, but, anticipating Max Weber[232] by more than half a century, he adds that the disenchantment of modern society stems from a bourgeois, technologically driven culture. With this in mind, he imagines a conversation between a youth who longs to live like a saint and a representative of "established Christendom" who advises him that there is no longer any need: "My young friend . . . you are not in the world of fairy tales but in the civilized and polished world . . . where you are living among cultured and well-educated people, and where, in addition, the police watch over your security and the clergy your morality, and gas lighting [*Gasbelysningen*] makes the night just as safe as day."[233] Likewise, in an 1854 journal note, Kierkegaard suggests that the benefits afforded by gas lighting pale in comparison with the benefits of candid self-knowledge. Just as thieves lurk in the shadows of an alleyway, so do persons tend to hide among the shadows of life, acting one way while thinking another, or maintaining a public façade that is readily cast off in private. The obverse of this state is "becoming a person," which Kierkegaard defines as being "so illuminated that [one] cannot hide from [oneself]."[234] He then continues: "The municipality is already of the opinion that gas-illumination at night helps to prevent a lot of crime because light frightens crime away. Consider, then, the piercing illumination of being personality, light everywhere."[235] There are, then, different orders of illumination, and it is as if they stand in inverse proportion to one another. As Kierkegaard notes in another 1854 passage, the nineteenth century has been dubbed "enlightened" (*oplyste*) due to technological inventions such as "gas lighting" (*Gasbelysningen*), but its lack of *spiritual* illumination is unparalleled.[236]

As discussed in Chapter 2, the daguerreotype was another key invention of Kierkegaard's era—one that, after developing into film photography, eventually revolutionized human art and culture. Thus, it is somewhat disappointing that Kierkegaard only makes one reference to the daguerreotype in his entire authorship; moreover, given that daguerreotypy arrived in Denmark in the early 1840s, it is curious that this reference did not come until 1854. That being said, the comment in question is pregnant with meaning, both in terms of its assessment of this technology and in terms of its place within Kierkegaard's authorship: "By means of the daguerreotype [*Daguereotypen*] it will be easy for everyone to have his portrait made—formerly only the distinguished were able to do this; and at the same time every effort is made to make us all look alike—therefore, only one single portrait is needed."[237] Kierkegaard is indeed right that the daguerreotype changed the way that people related to and thought about representation, personal or otherwise. In a quotation strikingly similar to Kierkegaard's, James Monaco explains, "The daguerreotype allowed thousands of ordinary people to achieve the kind of immortality that hid hitherto been reserved to an elite. The democratization of the image had begun. Within a few years, thousands of portrait galleries had come into being."[238] The development of photography, then, bears a paradox: photographic technology allows more and more persons to set themselves apart by way of pictorial reproduction; however, the more persons avail themselves of this opportunity, the more this very reproduction becomes ordinary and thus less and less distinguishing. All come to see themselves and the world through the same technology; all become the same in depicting their difference.

For Monaco, these developments mark a further and ineluctable step toward the desacralization of the artistic product, whereby it "can be seen as 'semifinished' material, to be *used* by the observer."[239] But Kierkegaard takes a wider perspective. For example, the journal entry that mentions the daguerreotype is entitled "*Double Leveling*. Or a Leveling that Thwarts Itself."[240] The word "leveling" (*Nivellering*) is more than a little significant, harking back to Kierkegaard's *A Literary Review*. Thus, it is a term often associated with Kierkegaard's analysis of the press, though the passage in question here demonstrates that Kierkegaard believed that other technologies fostered leveling—a social disorder that arises when individuals, lacking a common idea or purpose, relate to one another on the basis of the same superficial concerns.[241] More will be said about this phenomenon later, though, for now, it is worth noting that photography does indeed typify Kierkegaard's worries about leveling: its ubiquity establishes a set of crude habits and predilections, but these lack any determinate *Weltanschauung* and consequently nourish an underlying yet enervating interpersonal tension and envy. Kierkegaard, it is safe to say, would not at all be surprised by the body dysmorphia and social anxiety disorders stemming from our contemporary use of image-based media platforms such as Facebook and Instagram.[242]

Given that photography made it possible to produce and reproduce images en masse, it is worth closing this section with a few remarks about how Kierkegaard realized that other technologies were being developed to promote mass production and reproduction. One 1854 journal entry compares work in a "paper factory" (*Papir-Fabrikken*) to a society dominated by the press: the upshot, in both cases, is the reduction of individuals to a corporate end.[243] Another passage, written a decade earlier, observes that the utilitarian nature of factory work nourishes a sense of "meaninglessness" and that the goal, both in work and in life, is to "make all of temporality into a week of work without pay."[244] Kierkegaard almost sounds like a Marxist in such passages, but elsewhere he suggests that the mechanical uniformity of modern industry also characterizes modern politics. "I still hope that a reformation will come once again,"[245] he writes in an 1851 journal entry, though he immediately tempers this expectation by lamenting the procedures of liberal democracy. Whereas genuine reform comes through a personal encounter with "ideals,"[246] liberalism depersonalizes the political process by making truth a function of popularity. In order to do this, it requires a technology that can conduct a mass survey of the *vox populi*: "In place of 'the reformer,' and despite its apparent unsociability, people install a voting machine [*Balloteermaskine*]—a sociable something that is compliant in a quite different way."[247] What unites modern industry and modern politics, then, is their common desire to manufacture cheaply and efficiently (whether paper or popular opinion) and their respective use of machines to facilitate this process.

Cheap production and efficient reproduction—Kierkegaard sees these trends across all walks of modern life, and the machine is the instrument by which these goals are met.[248] Thus it is telling and perhaps even essential that Kierkegaard repeatedly compares Christendom itself to a "machine" (*Maskine*). As he writes in one 1854 journal entry:

> Just as production by machine is on a much larger scale and more accurate than by hand, so also generation after generation the state delivered an assortment of Christians, all with the factory stamp of the state, each Christian an accurate copy of the others, so accurate that the heart of every manager of a factory must leap to see what matchless heights of accuracy the art has attained.[249]

Another passage from the same period distinguishes between *Christianity*, which "concentrates everything on the quality," and *Christendom*, which seeks to furnish "millions and millions of Christians in every possible model."[250] This distinction sheds light on Kierkegaard's so-called "attack upon Christendom," which commenced around the same time. Much ink has been spilled as to the basis of Kierkegaard's late polemical writings against Denmark's state church, from his long-standing concerns about the Hegelianism[251] rampant among the Danish intelligentsia to his newfound interest in the ascetical pessimism of Arthur Schopenhauer.[252] The influence of modern technology, however, has been overlooked in this regard, even though Kierkegaard himself underlines its import: "Christendom can best be looked at as an enormous factory."[253]

The aim of this section has been to determine how Kierkegaard saw the form of modern life, paying special attention to his views on urbanization and instrumentalization. It is now clear that Kierkegaard thought a great deal about those developments and, indeed, that he was profoundly troubled by their influence on Western culture. What has emerged, then, is an early critique of modern technology—one that cut against the grain of nineteenth-century optimism and anticipated the views of figures such as Heidegger by several decades. This inquiry also has shed light on Kierkegaard's authorship itself, underscoring his frequent and sharp engagement with sociopolitical questions. More than just a critic of the print media, Kierkegaard understood that technology was becoming the medium through which persons relate to the world, to themselves, and even to God. Modern life, he was willing to concede, possesses certain advantages over that of preceding generations, but, in the end, it is arranged in such a way that humanity's most decisive and meaningful concerns are suppressed.

Kierkegaard on the content of modern life

The final section of this chapter moves from Kierkegaard's reflections on the technological phenomenality of modernity to the theoretical developments underlying it. In other words, this section represents a shift from "form" to "content." Given the overarching purpose of the present study—namely, to focus on how Kierkegaard himself addressed the so-called "question concerning technology"—the division between form and content is essentially heuristic and, for that reason, is not meant to indicate a robust independent analysis of whether or not scientific theory precedes technological implementation or vice versa. Furthermore, since the above discussion of "form" has been lengthy, this section will need to be more modest in its aims, restricting itself to an overview of Kierkegaard's response to scientific concepts and systems. Despite such limitations, however, it seems worthwhile to survey Kierkegaard's understanding of science, so as to gain a fuller picture of his response to modernity in general and technology in particular.

As discussed in Chapter 2, Kierkegaard was a contemporary of arguably the greatest of all Danish scientists, Hans Christian Ørsted, whose achievement was nothing short of revolutionary:

> When [Ørsted] matriculated in 1794, there was no degree in physics, chemistry, or any other individual scientific discipline on offer at the University of Copenhagen. By the time of his death [in 1851] the Polytechnic Institute as well as a Faculty of Science at the University had been established thanks to his efforts.[254]

To live during the time of Ørsted, then, was to live during the rise of modern science in Denmark. What is more, Kierkegaard knew Ørsted personally and seemed to appreciate his scientific accomplishments,[255] even as he was skeptical of his attempts to harmonize science and religion.[256] In fact, this concern permeates his response to scientific thinking in general, which, in his view, prioritized objectivity to the detriment of matters requiring subjective passion and responsibility. As Julia Watkin puts it, "[Kierkegaard] considers that science, since it is concerned only with what can be measured, cannot possibly explain the entire human person."[257]

For Kierkegaard, the epistemological approach of the sciences would not be problematic if it were merely one way among many. He argues, however, that modernity has enthroned scientific *Wissenschaft* as the only valid means of knowledge: "The natural sciences have conquered,"[258] he complains in an 1850 journal entry, adding elsewhere that, while scientists play the role of the underdog, "in fact natural science is dominant and theology was dethroned long ago."[259] In one sense, this change seems to represent the victory of modern scholarship over traditional belief, of disinterested knowledge over intimate concern. As Kierkegaard observes, "The scientist [*Videnskabsmanden*] and scholar has his personal life in categories quite different than his professional life."[260] This is a methodological commitment. Inasmuch as science brackets questions about the immaterial and the infinite, its "attention is incessantly being diverted by [the] intrinsically interesting knowledge of details."[261] Kierkegaard understands this diversion as the sea change of modern thinking. Whereas ancient philosophy treated the natural world as the *terminus a quo* for higher-order deliberation on the nature of the good life, modern philosophy has grown "tired" of such questions and instead swiftly "turn[s] to nature."[262]

This approach has been pitched to modern society as "progress,"[263] but Kierkegaard argues that it is more likely to signal "decline."[264] After all, science is preoccupied with data gleaned from empirical observation, and thus it is an "aesthetic" discipline in the strict sense of the word. Indeed, the term "aesthetics" comes from the Greek term *aisthanesthai* ("to perceive"), and so "aesthetics" broadly concerns the study of objects of perception. Of course, through Plato, Immanuel Kant, and others,[265] this study has come to be associated with perceptions that are particularly beautiful or sublime, and Kierkegaard famously devotes a portion of his authorship to the problem of "the aesthetic"—a existential sphere, contrasted with "the ethical" and "the religious," in which one orients one's life to what is immediate, especially to "the satisfaction of desires the person happens to have."[266] Yet, for Kierkegaard, the desire for immediate or sensory fulfillment is by no means monolithic but exists on a continuum. One person may have a coarse urge for a given material good (food, sex, etc.), while another may seek the same good in a sophisticated manner. The latter has a "well-schooled mind and well-developed imagination,"[267] but, just to the extent that she finds her life's purpose in aesthetic mastery, she remains within the aesthetic sphere. As C. Stephen Evans explains, "A certain kind of reflection and knowledge lends itself well to, or perhaps even requires, what we might call the stance of the spectator, who can 'make observations' about an issue without much in the way of personal involvement."[268] Such a person, then, is "well-developed intellectually but existentially not developed at all, and therefore still in one sense immediate."[269]

The trouble with this life-view, as Kierkegaard sees it, is that the aesthete never develops as an ethical and/or religious person and thereby fails to become a complete self. This analysis may seem almost obvious in relation to, say, a person who fritters his life away on wild parties and raunchy sensuality, but Kierkegaard thinks it no less true of an expert whose knowledge wins renown and procures material benefits but does not spur him, *qua* individual, to seek the good of others or to wrestle with the question of his ultimate end. And precisely because science deals with objective (or aesthetic) information, it is liable to inculcate such tendencies, not only in scientists themselves but also in a society determined by scientific epistemology. "Ethical reflection itself should be the first concern," Kierkegaard notes, whereas modern persons presuppose that "everyone, and thus also the scientist and the scholar, knows what he ought (ethically) to do in the world."[270] This presupposition makes it all too easy to prescind from questions pertaining to oneself—"What is the goal of *my* unique and unrepeatable existence?" "What am *I* to do about it?"— and to concentrate instead on abstract problems, that is to say, problems that are "drawn away" (*abstractus*) from the most intimate aspects of an individual's life. As Kierkegaard remarks in an 1849 journal entry, "Approaching something scientifically, esthetically, etc., how easily a person is led into the conceit that he really knows something for which he has the word. It is the concrete intuition which is so easily lost here."[271]

Yet, just as Kierkegaard would admit the aesthetic pleasure of good wine and fine tobacco,[272] he concedes that the aesthetic learning of science has its place. "The endeavor of science is established on the premise of making distinctions," Curtis L. Thompson writes, "so Kierkegaard clearly appreciated the world of science."[273] To be sure, Kierkegaard's pseudonymous treatise *The Concept of Anxiety* emphasizes that different concepts belong to different disciplines, and thus "every science must vigorously lay hold of its own beginning and not live in complicated relations with other sciences."[274] For instance, Christian dogmatics must not encroach upon the science of psychology, though the obligation runs the other way too: "[Psychology] is unwittingly in the service of another science that only waits for it to finish so that it can begin and assist psychology to the explanation. This science is not ethics . . . . This science is dogmatics."[275] Ideally, then, the different sciences complement one another, with psychology observing the possibility of sin[276] and dogmatics presupposing the actuality of sin "in order to raise it up into ideality."[277] The scientist who would violate such complementarity "thereby acquires the dubious perfectibility of being able to become anything and everything."[278] To "proceed in a scientific manner" is to take "care to see that the individual issues do not outrun one another, as if it were a matter of arriving first at the masquerade."[279]

In short, the knowledge attained in and through science is valuable as far as it goes, but it is necessarily limited by the methods and purposes underlying it. It can neither fully grasp the human self,[280] nor can it guide one through the deeply personal art of living well.[281] Moreover, if science were to forget or to discount these limitations, it could become positively dangerous. Indeed, Kierkegaard was concerned that science had become an end in itself in the modern world, thereby displacing the importance of ethics and religion. This has proven to be a perspicacious observation vis-à-vis the West's financial and intellectual commitment to scientific research, which continues to outpace the humanities by a wide margin.[282] Yet, for Kierkegaard, this may not even be the biggest danger. The disinterested standpoint of the sciences also fosters disinterest in ethical and religious issues, so that people no longer view these as self-implicating exigencies but, rather, as objects for scientific management and/or therapy. As it is put in *Fear and Trembling*, modernity is "an age that has crossed out passion [*Lidenskaben*] in order to serve science [*Videnskaben*]."[283]

In the end, then, Kierkegaard understood science to be the epistemological and methodological basis of modern secular society, which, in turn, is exemplified by "finite striving."[284] Grounded in empirical observation, science ipso facto assumes an aesthetic worldview, and thus it is the means by which "secular life goes on splendidly and mankind makes great strides in physical discoveries etc."[285] As has been detailed, Kierkegaard recognized that technological innovation was a decisive and alluring aspect of such "physical discoveries." Yet, as a dialectician, who was certain that modernity's "immanent frame"[286] was too reductive, he also saw the shadow side of this allurement. It leads to a "slackness and absence of spirit," which is but thinly disguised by "the most convenient religion possible," Christendom.[287] The ruse of Christendom is precisely that it "hypocritically" pays lip service to Christian truth but is really "about nothing at all or a divine strengthening of the pursuit of the finite."[288] It baptizes the techno-scientific order. Consequently, as Kierkegaard contends, the immanent frame of modernity is not so much a human achievement as a sign of divine abandonment—a notion that is ripe for dialogue with the later thinking of figures such as Nietzsche and Heidegger. As Kierkegaard concludes, "Now the most horrible punishment of all has come upon us . . . God ignores us entirely."[289]

Conclusion

This chapter has been lengthy, but it has established a number of key points. First, it has shown that, while Kierkegaard lacks the vocabulary and methodological distinctions made by later philosophers of technology, he nevertheless realized that his era was defined in large part by the conditions and developments of the modern, secular West. He also understood that technology and science play a decisive role in just these conditions and developments. This recognition has been demonstrated by his numerous observations on various innovations and trends, whether in transportation or in the physical sciences. And while such observations will not be mistaken for a systematic examination of the issue, they collectively establish Kierkegaard's fundamental response to modernity's technological imperative—namely, that it does not guarantee unambiguous progress, as so many gurus of modern culture have promised but that its advances are accompanied by significant losses. Broadly speaking, these losses might be described (albeit imperfectly) as "spiritual," since they largely involve those areas of human life that withstand quantification and replication, from ethical relations to divine worship.

These findings constitute the core of Kierkegaard's response to modern technology. But there is one technology that has yet to be explored—one that garnered the bulk of Kierkegaard's attention, namely, the printing press. Chapter 4 will take up this topic, showing that Kierkegaard's critique of "the press," while consistent with his concerns about other modern technologies, marks his most robust contribution to the philosophy of technology, particularly in light of the twenty-first century's rapid advances in so-called "information technology." It is to this subject, then, that this study now turns.

Kierkegaard's Analysis of Information Technology

The American philosopher Hubert L. Dreyfus has argued that the internet is not just a "technological innovation" but, rather, "one that brings out the very essence of technology."[1] By this he means that, inasmuch as "the essence of technology is to make *everything* accessible and optimizable, then the Internet is the perfect technological device."[2] The upshot is unparalleled freedom. Just as, say, the forklift enables a person to lift a weight that otherwise would be insuperable for human strength, so does the internet allow persons to transmute the limits imposed on human interaction by space and time. What a customer once had to buy in a local market and during a particular span of time can now be purchased online from anywhere in the world and at any time of day; what once had to be said in face-to-face conversation can now be communicated instantly online, even if the two interlocutors are separated by thousands of miles and multiple time zones. In short, the internet makes the information we hope to access and the commodities we hope to acquire available to us with minimal inconvenience.

Thus it is no wonder that people have sought "to digitalize and interconnect as much of reality as [they] can."[3] In doing so, they are able to transform our present world, which includes "all aspects of our finitude and vulnerability,"[4] into one in which these limits no longer obtain. According to "technolibertarian" activist John Perry Barlow, the internet is "a world that is both everywhere and nowhere, but it is not where bodies live."[5] And yet, is it a good thing to live as if without a body? On the one hand, if a person in Philadelphia were able to see and to speak to a loved one in London via an instant messaging app such as Skype, then the technological overcoming of the body would seem to be beneficial, for otherwise human finitude and vulnerability would render such a connection impossible. On the other hand, if a person were able to ridicule and to disparage a person or a group online without having to reveal his identity or to take responsibility for his comments, then the internet's disembodiment of human interaction would seem to be deleterious. In this case, the overcoming of human finitude and vulnerability are precisely the occasion for existential inauthenticity. For Dreyfus, this is ultimately the key dilemma presented by the rise of information technology in general and by the internet in particular: in these developments, human beings have acquired "a remarkable new freedom," even as that freedom leads to the diminishment of several "crucial capacities," from "our sense of the seriousness of success and failure that is necessary for learning" to "our ability to make maximally meaningful commitments."[6]

Dreyfus analyzes this quandary across several chapters, and, notably, one of his key interlocutors is Kierkegaard. Indeed, as he sees it, Kierkegaard's 1846 work *A Literary Review* provides a compelling and indeed prophetic analysis of one of the key problems presented by the internet—namely, the empowerment of a "desituated and anonymous" media by which "nihilistic leveling" comes to dominate society.[7] As Dreyfus goes on to explain:

> Kierkegaard would surely have seen in the Internet, with its Websites full of anonymous information from all over the world and its interest groups that anyone in the world can join without qualifications and where one can discuss any topic endlessly without consequences, the hi-tech synthesis of the worst features of the newspaper and the coffeehouse.[8]

Dreyfus is right that the news or, as Kierkegaard tended to put it, "the press" (*Pressen*) was a frequent object of Kierkegaard's criticism. Moreover, it is true that, in many ways, the internet is an extension or an intensification of the press-driven culture of Kierkegaard's day: "What Kierkegaard envisaged as a consequence of the press's indiscriminate and uncommitted coverage is now fully realized on the World Wide Web."[9] This is not to imply that print media and digital media are identical. Inasmuch as the internet is a computerized phenomenon, it is serving to push "the printing press and its products . . . from the center of our intellectual life to its edges."[10] At the same time, however, the "new world" of the computer remains "a literate world," in which the "technologized" word plays a decisive role.[11] As Walter J. Ong puts it, "Writing and print and the computer are all ways of technologizing the word."[12] Thus Dreyfus is right to underscore the fundamental continuity between Kierkegaard's nineteenth-century critique of the press and twentieth-century concerns about the internet.

Still, to note Dreyfus's interest in *A Literary Review* is not to analyze the text itself, nor is it to situate *A Literary Review* within Kierkegaard's wider authorship and its relation to technology. The goal of this chapter, then, is threefold. First, while Chapter 2 surveyed the rise of print technology in Denmark and its general effect on Danish culture, it remains crucial to examine Kierkegaard's participation in debates about the free press as a student. This appraisal will demonstrate that Kierkegaard's interest in and criticism of journalistic media effectively spans his career. Second, an examination of *A Literary Review* is necessary, both in terms of the context out of which the book emerged and in terms of its key concepts—indeed, the very concepts that Dreyfus draws upon in his critique of net-driven culture. Third, while the preceding reflections will establish Kierkegaard as a long-standing and pointed critic of the new media of his day, this chapter will conclude with an overview of his culminant "attack upon Christendom," which was carried on first through the liberal press and later through Kierkegaard's own periodical, *The Moment*. Was Kierkegaard, then, contradicting his prior indictment of journalism? Or was his use of the press tantamount to an ironic send-up of liberal Danish society—an attempt to destabilize further a "culture . . . seen as in decline,"[13] so as to prepare the way for something better? While there may be no definitive answer to such questions, it will be argued that Kierkegaard's foray into journalism is indeed best thought of in terms of irony, particularly the *Socratic* irony explored in his 1841 dissertation *The Concept of Irony*. Thus, Kierkegaard's final "attack upon Christendom" was a return to his intellectual roots and yet, in another sense, a final expression of his concerns regarding the influence of information technology on Western society.

Kierkegaard's early critique of journalism

Kierkegaard is considered one of the pioneering critics of mass culture, but, in truth, such critiques go back to the "reflections on modern life and leisure that began appearing in the sixteenth century during the demise of feudalism."[14] An outline of this development already has been sketched in the first two chapters of this study, which traced the gradual urbanization, industrialization, and democratization of Western society. The coalescence of these processes led to an evolution in societal expectations and habits, one of which was a newfound "need for diversion."[15] As Leo Lowenthal has shown, "the discussion of popular culture has a century-old tradition in modern history," with figures such as Michel de Montaigne, Blaise Pascal, and Johann Wolfgang von Goethe chiming in on the subject.[16] Indeed, by the turn of the nineteenth century, "Goethe and others noted that popular entertainment and journalism were serving as major means of diversion and escape."[17] Goethe, in particular, satirized the press, lyrically saluting its ability to manufacture consent:

> Come let us print it all
> And be busy everywhere;
> But no one should stir
> Who does not think like we.[18]

Of course, not all shared Goethe's skepticism regarding the rise of the press,[19] but it is clear that the proliferation of print media in the wake of the American and French Revolutions was a controversial topic. Hence, when the young Kierkegaard entered disputes about the free press in Denmark, he was entering disputes that were still very much alive.

Kierkegaard's first foray into media criticism came in November 1835, when he delivered a paper to the University Student Union entitled "Our Journalistic Literature." As mentioned in Chapter 2, this piece was a response to a paper given by Johannes Ostermann two weeks earlier. Whereas Ostermann's "lecture expressed the view that the press was responsible for inspiring current political initiatives,"[20] leading him to endorse liberal papers such as *The Copenhagen Post* (*Kjøbenhavnsposten*) and *The Fatherland* (*Fædrelandet*), Kierkegaard understood the expansion of press freedom in different terms. At the outset of the paper, Kierkegaard makes clear that his goal is to "embark upon investigation of only the factually given and to inspect it in the noonday light."[21] That is to say, he does not intend to present a partisan case—he even concedes that "Liberal newspapers . . . do more and better than the Conservative papers"[22]— but instead wants to encourage "the reflection" that "conditions new and vigorous activity."[23]

Kierkegaard begins with a historical overview of the press's influence in Denmark. Like Ostermann, he agrees that Matthias Winther's *The Rocket* (*Raketten*) jumpstarted Danish journalism in 1831, triggering the founding of several copycat papers. Unlike Ostermann, however, Kierkegaard is reluctant to credit such journals for promoting political change. "I look upon Liberal journalism," he opines, "as a new development that no doubt may have many connections with a previous one."[24] After all, press freedom in Denmark was first granted in 1770 during the Struensee regime, and, as Kierkegaard indicates, the Freedom of the Press Ordinance (*Trykkefrihedsforordningen*) of 1799, though often seen as an organ of censorship, actually made certain allowances for the press.[25] This line of reasoning—that the Danish press is more reactive than revolutionary—emerges as one of the central themes of Kierkegaard's talk, and he goes on to multiply examples. With regard to the consultative assemblies, which the Royal Council permitted in 1831, thereby allowing the enfranchisement of Danes meeting certain "property qualifications,"[26] Kierkegaard maintains that the Danish press did not demand the establishment of such representative bodies until *after* the government announced their founding. The royal "order was the sunshine that called forth the flowers of literature."[27] This pattern even postdates the acrimony between Frederik VI and the liberal press that erupted in late 1834, when the king threatened full censorship, resulting in the founding of the Society for the Proper Use of Freedom of the Press (*Selskabet for Trykkefrihedens rette Brug*) in March 1835. Thus, Kierkegaard concludes, "The relation between the government and journalistic literature on the whole can be described as follows: the government was active-passive (or affected through an activity); journalism was passive-active (or acting through a passivity)."[28]

With this point established, Kierkegaard seeks to "pay attention to the compass"[29] of *The Copenhagen Post*. If it is not driving political reform, what influence *is* it having on Danish culture? Kierkegaard's response to this question is dialectical. On the one hand, *The Copenhagen Post*, *qua* literary endeavor, is marked by "instability" and an absence of "unity."[30] It is like an interstellar cloud in which "the harmony of the forces has not taken place as yet, nor the rotation on the axis either."[31] This issue carries over to the hostility that characterizes *The Copenhagen Post*'s defense of liberalism. According to Kierkegaard, it is one thing to write acrimonious pieces that, even if wrong on certain points, are nevertheless sincere; it is something else to conceal one's criticisms "in notes and footnotes, in questions and exclamation marks,"[32] while remaining anonymous to boot. Thus, public accusations that *The Copenhagen Post* has been marred by "dishonesty and untruthfulness" are unsurprising, since "hardly anyone wants to appear before a secret court."[33]

On the surface, then, it would seem that papers such as *The Copenhagen Post* would be unable to guide or to mold society. And yet, as Kierkegaard sees it, an organ of instability and disunity can have a *negative* influence; that is to say, rather than bringing people together over a common goal or principle, it can disrupt them through commotion and distraction. Kierkegaard compares the activity of *The Copenhagen Post* to that of Don Quixote:

> There is always something Don Quixotic about such striving; one sounds the alarm every minute, gives Rosinante the spurs, and charges—at windmills; at the same time there is no lack of discernment to make one aware that some evil demon or other has changed the giants into windmills, although Sancho Panza most solemnly swears that they were, are, and will remain windmills.[34]

The result is an unsettled society, whose general "nervousness is something very harmful."[35] Incited by journalism, people are busier and more engaged than ever before, but they lack the "calm circumspection"[36] needed to live *well*. But such circumspection requires a determinative "idea" that gives order to society, whereas modern society is marked by a "formal striving" that lacks an idea.[37] Kierkegaard even suggests an additional yet more damning comparison between the violence of Robespierre's Reign of Terror and the "nitpicking irritation [*smaalig Irriteren*]" found in *The Copenhagen Post*.[38] In both cases, busyness and commotion are mistaken for progress, while, in reality, these qualities represent an "erratic groping [*ustadig Famlen*]."[39]

As will be seen, these last several insights anticipate *A Literary Review* in a number of ways, showing that Kierkegaard's views on the press were not merely formed in reaction to the so-called "*Corsair* Affair." On the contrary, they were taking shape during Kierkegaard's student years, just as the struggle for press freedom began. This point is borne out by a trio of short pieces that Kierkegaard published in 1836, each of which appeared in Johan Ludvig Heiberg's paper *Copenhagen's Flying Post* (*Kjøbenhavns flyvende Post*). Heiberg was a celebrated philosopher, playwright, and poet, who, despite the fact that his father had been "exiled in 1800 for a politically offensive publication," nevertheless adopted a "conservative stance" in relation to liberal reforms—a stance that "showed itself in his choice of theater material as well as in his political outlook."[40] Son of the venerable novelist Thomasine Gyllembourg and husband to Denmark's leading actress Johanne Luise Pätges, Heiberg's favor was desired "by writers and intellectuals of many stripes—by everyone who was anyone"[41] in the 1830s. Such indeed was the case with the young and ambitious Kierkegaard, who, like Heiberg, was skeptical of "the approach of modern mass society and democratic government."[42]

In the *Flying Post's* February 1836 issue, Kierkegaard published "The Morning Observations in *The Copenhagen Post* No. 43," albeit under the anonym "B." His decision to publish anonymously, while common at the time, was a curious one. After all, Kierkegaard had already come out against the journalistic tendency to shirk responsibility for controversial opinions. In fact, as Joseph Westfall notes, one of the distinguishing marks of B's point of view is that he not only debates press freedom in Denmark but takes on "the literary form of journalistic debate,"[43] particularly the role of anonymity in the media. For B, the trouble with *The Copenhagen Post* is that it will not "step forward so one can see with whom one has to do."[44] It is acceptable to pen a novel or a poem anonymously, and yet, insofar as *The Copenhagen Post* has styled itself as an agent of political change, which bitterly attacks its opponents, its anonymity is puerile and thus undermines its message: "There is certainly a noble heat in battle that can easily induce a writer to use a somewhat acrimonious expression. But one readily forgives him that. One tolerates a large dog barking, even in the wrong place, but these little dogs that always yap, and in the moment of danger creep into hiding . . . are intolerable."[45] Kierkegaard goes on to contrast *The Copenhagen Post*'s "anonymous reformers" with history's great figures, from Moses "through Luther to an O'Connell," each of whom refused to "stay in the background."[46] His point is clear: true reform happens when one is willing to venture one's life for the sake of a given cause. Hence, to the extent that *The Copenhagen Post* (and other papers like it) prefers to offer criticism behind a veil of anonymity, "it is rather a parody of the reforming endeavor."[47]

B's analysis gives no indication of being a blanket dismissal of the press. What he does maintain, however, is that the print media, no matter how modish or progressive, is vulnerable to a host of errors. Yes, it foments animosity, but, even worse, it does so with an absurd (and therefore dangerous) lack of sophistication. B jibes at *The Copenhagen Post*'s "swagger-booted, high-tragic posture,"[48] which slaps condescending labels on previous historical eras in order to cast the present in a more favorable light. But this tactic is fallacious, since the present cannot leave the past behind but, rather, must be committed to learn from it: "I certainly know that it goes with states as it does with individual people, and that an individual who has never been any good at anything is always in a terrible hurry to rush into the future."[49]

Underlying these concerns is a wider observation about print technology and the new sociopolitical era that it has instigated. Roughly a week before B's piece appeared, *The Copenhagen Post* published "Press Freedom Affair V," in which the author (most likely Orla Lehmann)[50] pleads for the public to be patient with the press's mistakes. The Danish press is not only "young and inexperienced," but it faces a spate of challenges, from governmental regulations to the public's "scrupulousness that often degenerates into ungratefulness and unfairness."[51] The latter is particularly troubling, since people hold the press to a higher standard than they do themselves: "God have mercy on every tongue in all the king's realms and dominions if it has to be answerable in this way for every single little word!"[52] Moreover, this meticulousness does not take into account the very nature of journalism, which is to circulate news quickly and widely: "If only one were to let every work, every little item of news, lie aside for three days in order to think carefully over every word, then one would hear a complaining."[53] The press, then, should not apologize for doing its job. The time will come when the press will gain "in vigor and activity but also in dignity and bearing,"[54] and, in the meantime, its mistakes should be viewed as part and parcel with other problems in a fallen world. "Here below where everything is imperfect," the author asks, "how could *this* alone be perfect?"[55]

According to B, this is a paltry defense. The issue, he contends, is not *that* the press makes mistakes but *how many* mistakes it makes. To be sure, as a technological medium, the press is managed by human beings and is ipso facto susceptible to human error, but "one must be very easy to satisfy if one will let oneself be fobbed off at all with the admission by *Kjøbenhavnsposten* that it is a human product."[56] No, the issue is not the nature of humanity but the nature of the press, that is to say, the press's predisposition to provoke discord, its preference for haste over sophistication, always moving to the next story at the expense of "retrospection."[57] Curiously, Westfall has argued that B "is an anonym with a point of view, albeit a point of view on little more than anonymity,"[58] but, in light of the above analysis, it actually appears that B identifies a number of serious concerns about the media—concerns that persist to the present day, when people often struggle to distinguish between "real" and "fake" news.

Kierkegaard would return to these questions in his next piece for the *Flying Post*, which came out roughly a month after "Morning Observations." This article resembled its predecessor in two formal ways: Kierkegaard again attributed it to B, and he again wrote it as a response—this time to an editorial that had denounced "Morning Observations" in *The Fatherland*. The latter was penned by Johannes Hage, coeditor of *The Fatherland* and a noted proponent of press freedom and representative government. In his paper for the Student Union, Kierkegaard had spoken highly of both *The Fatherland* and of Hage,[59] but Hage saw "Morning Observations" as part of a wider campaign by the *Flying Post* to undermine Danish liberalism and thus felt compelled to retort. The core of Hage's argument centers on the *Flying Post*'s general preference to "amuse its readers with witticisms without caring whether or not the truth suffers on that account,"[60] and he believes B's "Morning Observations" typifies this inclination. For example, B's ridicule of the editor of *The Copenhagen Post* fails to take into account just how difficult it is to edit a newspaper. After all, such an enterprise cannot "survive if the editor with great severity were to reject the contributions he receives."[61] The same is true with regard to journalistic accuracy: "If [the editor] accepted only those [contributions] of whose complete accuracy he was certain, the majority of contributions would have to be excluded, and then the paper would totally fail in its aim."[62] When mistakes occur, they can be corrected at a later date.[63] In the meantime, the task of the newspaper is to provide new content on a regular basis. Thus, B's complaint that *The Copenhagen Post* fails to attend to the past misses the point. It goes without saying that the past cannot be totally neglected, "but this must not . . . weaken the vigor with which [we] are going to meet the future, for, first and foremost, we have to do with this."[64] The very nature of journalism is to move forward; it could not endure otherwise.

B's reply to Hage, simply entitled "On the Polemic of *Fædrelandet*," begins by lamenting *The Fatherland*'s entry into what had been a row with *The Copenhagen Post*; he also reiterates that the *Flying Post*'s critique is directed at *The Copenhagen Post* first and foremost—a focus that he maintains is justified.[65] In fact, "On the Polemic of *Fædrelandet*" is basically a point-by-point riposte to Hage's piece, albeit a sarcastic one: "We owe it to the author in *Fædrelandet* to admit," B wryly concludes, "that of the two linguistic errors he has found in our piece, one is a linguistic error."[66] He even seems to regard this sort of trivial back-and-forth as a sign of the times. Whereas *The Copenhagen Post* had ridiculed the inadequacy of prior historical eras, B sees his own age as "drunk with the penny ale offered . . . by the journals."[67] In other words, the present age struts about "in fancied competence,"[68] congratulating itself for its alleged triumphs, though it too has its own failings and will one day be judged accordingly. "One age cannot do everything,"[69] B asserts. In a piece otherwise filled with gibes and quibbles, this seems to be the bottom line. Inasmuch as "every age has its own fundamental stamp, its character, from which all its expressions of life must take their color,"[70] so must the present age be careful not to allow its habits and tendencies to cloud both its evaluation of other epochs as well as its own self-understanding. And yet, that is precisely the danger, particularly in and for a journalistic era, which "has such a great lack of intelligence that it gives ear to [slanderous] invectives."[71]

In his next and final piece for the *Flying Post*, Kierkegaard does not use an anonym but writes in his own name. Moreover, he takes personal responsibility for his earlier articles in the *Flying Post*.[72] These changes signify that he had managed to shift the terms of debate with the liberal papers. As discussed, B had persistently criticized the shadowy nature of journalistic criticism, implying that its anonymity indicated a lack of integrity, especially for those claiming to be "reformers." Eventually, this line of reasoning prodded Orla Lehmann to offer a direct response in *The Copenhagen Post*. Published on March 31, 1836, Lehmann's account is marked by a "conciliatory tone."[73] He continues to assume the moral high ground, boasting that "the Liberals have been concerned with the country's political and economic conditions," but, on the other hand, he wishes "to terminate the polemical combat" with B.[74] Still, when Kierkegaard replied nearly two weeks later in the *Flying Post*, he made it clear that he could not be dismissed so easily.

Entitled "To Mr. Orla Lehmann," Kierkegaard's piece is indeed a direct jab at Lehmann and, to a lesser extent, Hage. According to Julia Watkin, Kierkegaard primarily wanted to insist "on the last word," thereby demonstrating his "literary and polemical abilities to the university and to Heiberg."[75] And yet, substantive points do turn up in the piece, particularly those centering on the relation between journalism and the truth. For example, Kierkegaard remains disappointed by the liberal press's treatment of the past. While Lehmann and Hage make sweeping assertions about prior generations in Denmark, charging them "with lack of competence on the whole," they nevertheless find it "very difficult to fix correctly the time when the weak condition began."[76] What characterizes their account, then, is not so much accuracy as expediency, comparing past and present in such a way that "the comparison redound[s] completely to the advantage of the present."[77] This approach is all the more galling given that Lehmann himself had admitted that "our political life and its reforming endeavor have not yet displayed any great vigor."[78] As Kierkegaard elaborates:

> A poor article in a paper that presents itself as reforming, a poor article that is itself a reforming attempt, is indeed *eo ipso* a poor reforming product. And moreover, since Mr. Lehmann can readily agree with me that our time's reformers lack vigor and manliness and *Kjøbenhavnsposten* forms a link in this chain . . . and that a reformer without vigor and manliness is really a nothing, a flower without color and scent, the parody of the true reformer, it seems to me that I have said with perfect justice that the conduct of *Kjøbenhavnsposten* was the parody of the reforming endeavor, for it relates to this as the Children's Crusade does to Gottfred of Bouillon's.[79]

Once more, the issue shifts to whether or not genuine reform (political or otherwise) can originate in the press. Newspapers can and do provide a forum in which reform can be debated, but Kierkegaard is reluctant to equate *talk* about reform with reform as such—a point that he will return to later in his authorship. As will be seen, he argues that the kind of talk fostered by the press actually hampers reform, because the press's advancement of public reflection leads to the attenuation of individual action.

Kierkegaard's writings for the *Flying Post* have not received a great deal of scholarly attention, especially in comparison with his great works of the 1840s. But it is clear that, in addition to establishing Kierkegaard's intellectual steeliness and rhetorical dexterity, this early period launched a number of themes that would come to characterize his authorship: (i) that a free press, just to the extent that it lacks a common idea or an underlying principle, is bound to bring about a society centered on denial or dissent; (ii) that a free press, since it provides a forum for anonymous opinions and caters to an abstract public, depersonalizes cultural life and thus leads to the diminution of individual accountability and action; and (iii) that a free press, *qua* popular medium, prioritizes flair and notoriety over depth and discretion. Viewed in these terms, it could be argued that Kierkegaard's *A Literary Review* is merely a refined treatment of the issues that first stirred him in 1835–36. Moreover, unlike that later work, which came out during a period of personal isolation and pain for Kierkegaard, his early writings for the *Flying Post* saw him emerge as an exciting new voice among Copenhagen's intelligentsia. As Peter Rørdam, then a local teacher and later a priest in various parishes around Zealand, wrote to his older brother Hans: "There has also been a change in the Student Union. Their chief and leader, Lehmann, has fallen, totally defeated . . . . With him has fallen *Kjøbenhavns-Posten*, for which he had recently been writing. And the victor is the younger Kierkegaard, who now writes in *Flyvende Post* under the pseudonym B."[80] A letter from Johan Hahn to Kierkegaard's brother Peter Christian corroborated Rørdam's account: "I hear from many quarters that your brother Søren has made a witty and powerful appearance in *Flyveposten*."[81] Of course, that it is not to imply that Kierkegaard's pieces for the *Flying Post* received unanimous acclaim—in fact, a trio of anonymous satirical articles appeared in May 1836, which took aim at Heiberg's circle in general and at Kierkegaard in particular[82]—but it is fair to say that Kierkegaard's first authorial efforts indicated that he would be a force to be reckoned with, both as a prose stylist and as a cultural critic.

Still, questions remain about the nature of Kierkegaard's early cultural criticism. Does it mark him as a champion for right-wing political interests? Or was he merely a freelancing satirist, exposing the weaknesses of the day's public figures, regardless of their political affiliation? Regarding the first question, Robert Perkins contends that Kierkegaard's critique of the liberal press hardly makes him "an apologist for the absolute monarchy."[83] It is true that Kierkegaard raises thorny "philosophic and methodological questions . . . about the examination of sources, truth, and the necessity of interrogating one's self-justifying and flattering assumptions,"[84] but these concerns transcend partisan politics. Besides, Perkins adds, "on all important matters regarding the freedom of the press, Kierkegaard sided with the liberals."[85] This fact is borne out by Kierkegaard's willingness to criticize the government's "repressive steps" in its struggle with the press, including (but not limited to) its "ban on publicizing the proceedings of the Provincial Consultative Assemblies."[86] If, Perkins reasons, Kierkegaard was willing to critique state censorship even in just a few cases, then *in principle* he must be open to a free press. Thus, Kierkegaard can in no way be thought of as a supporter of absolutism, however murky his views on liberal society remain. As Perkins concludes, "It is difficult to understand why Kierkegaard, though he was a conservative for most of his life, has ever been thought to be a defender of absolute monarchy."[87]

In one sense, it is difficult to gainsay this point. Kierkegaard never penned a treatise dedicated to the defense of absolutism, and, as noted, he did not have a blind allegiance to absolutist or conservative causes. This point is further corroborated by Kierkegaard's relationship with Christian VIII, king of Denmark from 1839 to 1848. Kierkegaard recounts that, even though Christian VIII sought him out as an intellectual companion, he preferred to keep his distance from the aging monarch.[88] This was not because he disliked Christian VIII, and, on one visit, he even presented the king with a copy of *Works of Love*.[89] Still, he could not help but observe Christian VIII's shortcomings, including a lack of "ethical backbone" and an overarching skittishness that made him vulnerable to "duplicity."[90] Hence, whatever defense Kierkegaard could offer on behalf of absolute monarchy would have to be based on principle and not on a personal association. As Kierkegaard remembers telling the king, "Everything is weakened when explained by mixed motives. The only way to remain unimpaired is to be a private citizen."[91]

This attempt to remain beyond the pale of partisanism is fairly typical of Kierkegaard's politics. Throughout his authorship, he refuses to identify himself with a particular coalition or program—a stance that he expressly articulates in "An Open Letter," which he published in *The Fatherland* in January 1851. According to Perkins, this posture is already evident in Kierkegaard's early writings for the *Flying Post*, and it indicates the idiosyncratic nature of Kierkegaard's critique of liberalism in general and of the press in particular:

> Kierkegaard's claim to be a *réflecteur* is more than a mere resignation from active political life. Positively, he has marked out the life of the mind as his form of life, though the full content of that form of life is still undetermined. From our vantage point we can recognize even in this first brush with the press the irony, humor, and intellectual penetration that characterize his authorship, the birth of his disdain for politics, his immense capacity for careful conceptual analysis, and his tenacity once he has decided that a stand must be taken.[92]

On this reading, Kierkegaard's censure of the free press was not motivated by political affiliation; rather, he wanted to raise crucial questions about the press's purpose and tendencies. For Perkins, then, Kierkegaard remains relevant for media studies, no matter where one falls on the political spectrum: "The issue of truth and myth making is still a subtle issue in dealing with the media," and Kierkegaard was ahead of his time in calling attention to the "inventions of cynical power brokers" and the promulgations "by a beguiled and beguiling media corps."[93]

Others paint a less noble picture of Kierkegaard's early writings. Teddy Petersen reduces Kierkegaard's early polemics to a pair of "chief aims" (*hovedformål*): "to win respect and admiration in the Student Association" and "to demonstrate his literary and polemical abilities to Heiberg."[94] Petersen argues that Kierkegaard's journals admit as much, and he highlights an 1836 passage in which Kierkegaard boasts that his work for the *Flying Post* has been a "success," so much so that some readers assumed that Heiberg himself was the author.[95] Joakim Garff offers a similar appraisal, claiming that Kierkegaard was "bewitched by the Heiberg cult"[96] at that time—a spell that would soon come to an end, when, as Garff sees it, Heiberg gravitated toward another young protégé, Hans Lassen Martensen.[97] This snub pushed Kierkegaard in a different direction, encouraging him to take on the identity of an "outsider" rather than that of an "insider," because insiders—like Heiberg, like Martensen—are happy to exploit the truth for personal gain, yet loath to be transformed by it.

In short, whereas Perkins sees a principled (if evolving) analysis of the press in Kierkegaard's early writings, Petersen and Garff see a scheming (if clever) attempt to curry favor with Copenhagen's cognoscenti. But is it necessary to see these options as mutually exclusive? After all, even if Kierkegaard's writings for the *Flying Post* were meant to appeal to the Heiberg circle, they also tackle issues and themes that would occupy Kierkegaard for the remainder of his career, indeed, well after he had fallen out with Heiberg. Thus, it is sensible to conclude that Kierkegaard had legitimate concerns about the advent of the liberal press and its impact on Western society, though, at this point in his life, he articulated these concerns in an impishly confrontational manner. As both Danish culture and his own thinking developed, he would come to adopt a darker, more ominous standpoint, which eventuated in the book that, at the beginning of the twenty-first century, Hubert Dreyfus deemed prescient in its understanding of the internet—*A Literary Review*.

The fruition of Kierkegaard's press criticism

Kierkegaard's final piece for the *Flying Post* appeared in April 1836, and he published *A Literary Review* in March 1846. The intervening years saw his life alter drastically. Not only did he finish his university studies, receiving his magister degree (the equivalent of today's PhD) in 1841, but his personal life underwent a series of upheavals, from the death of his father in 1838 to the end of his engagement with Regine Olsen in 1841. Moreover, Kierkegaard's career as an author began to take off, particularly with the publication of a series of pseudonymous works, beginning with *Either/Or* and culminating in *Concluding Unscientific Postscript*. In just a decade, Kierkegaard had gone from an ambitious yet inexperienced student to an accomplished yet world-weary thinker.

Given such changes, one might expect that his views on the press also evolved during this period, perhaps resulting in new essays or, at least, a number of journal entries on the subject. In truth, however, he tended to refrain from direct criticism of the press in the years leading up to his conflict with *The Corsair* (*Corsaren*)—a satirical

Danish periodical, issued by Meïr Aron Goldschmidt, which launched a series of attacks on Kierkegaard in January 1846. It was in the wake of the so-called "*Corsair* affair" that Kierkegaard renewed and intensified his polemics against the press, both in his published writings (*A Literary Review*) and especially in his unpublished journals, the latter of which index Kierkegaard's recurrent censures of and warnings about the press right up until he fell ill in the autumn of 1855.

So, then, there was only one period during Kierkegaard's authorship that his castigation of print technology seemed to abate—the stretch from his last student publication in the *Flying Post* until December 1845, when his row with *The Corsair* began. That this gap is remarkable shows how concerned Kierkegaard generally was about the press: the figure supposedly lost in the "lonely labyrinth"[98] of his own melancholy turns out to have been preoccupied with social issues for the better part of his career. Still, the question remains as to why Kierkegaard's criticism of the press subsided for a time, only to return with unappeasable ferocity.

This matter can be addressed on a personal and on a philosophical level. With regard to the former, the turbulence of Kierkegaard's life during this period was doubtless a factor. Not only did he face intimate challenges such as his breakup with Regine, but he also was busy preparing for various professional opportunities. Moreover, with the publication and subsequent success of *Either/Or* in 1843,[99] his literary activity accelerated. Kierkegaard soon issued three short articles in *The Fatherland* (two under a different moniker), seeking to stoke curiosity about who had authored *Either/Or*,[100] a tactic that Joakim Garff calls both a "marketing campaign" and a "giddy satire of his times."[101] Other and more significant projects would come thereafter.

This productivity gestures toward the philosophical issue: the period 1843–46 was arguably the busiest in Kierkegaard's authorship, especially in terms of pseudonymous writings. Yet, as Kierkegaard himself insisted, pseudonymous works such as *Fear and Trembling* were not expressions of his own views; indeed, they were not to be ascribed to him at all.[102] On the contrary, this phase of his authorship was conceived as a poetic reduplication of the modern world, which lives under the "illusion"[103] that it is progressive, fair, and even Christian but, in truth, is an aesthetically oriented age. Kierkegaard developed a distinctive philosophy of pedagogy in order to deal with this problem. Rather than carry out a "direct assault" on the era's mendacity, which would be antagonistic and thereby reinforce "a person in the illusion,"[104] he instead would assume a variety of aesthetic personae, exposing the errors and pitfalls of the present age from the inside: "To be a teacher is not to say: This is the way it is, nor is it to assign lessons and the like. No, to be a teacher is truly to be the learner. Instruction begins with this, that you, the teacher, learn from the learner, place yourself in what he has understood and how he has understood it."[105]

In short, Kierkegaard's period of silence regarding the press was also strategic. He refrained from condemning the press directly so as to hold up a looking glass to an age formed by the press. He was already playing with this idea in 1837, when he composed *The Battle between the Old and the New Soap-Cellars*—a satirical play that apes Copenhagen's intelligentsia with gleeful abandon. The play's titular "battle" is an allusion to the debates that had come to dominate modern intellectual life, characterized "not [by] genuinely differing positions, but rather argumentativeness and wrangling of the more meaningless sort."[106] Kierkegaard even floated the idea of calling the play "The All-Embracing Debate on Everything against Everything, or The Crazier the Better,"[107] and many of the characters are borrowed from Denmark's burgeoning newspaper scene: Mr. von Jumping-Jack is likely Heiberg, while Mr. Holla Hurrison, Mr. Phrase, and Mr. Ole Wadt resemble Lehmann, Martensen, and the journalist Jens Giødwad, respectively. Moreover, in an obvious nod toward Kierkegaard himself, the narrative centers on Willibald, "a young man" whose demanding studies collide with his equally demanding social calendar.

Weary of tea parties and sycophantic friends, Willibald drifts into fantasy, suddenly finding himself in the "prytaneum,"[108] a kind of intellectual utopia, where von Jumping-Jack, Phrase, and others are conversing. Phrase argues that the time has to come to provide "the great results of scholarship" for "the educated middle class, for wholesalers, polytechnic students, for capitalists," since "our time's development ought to gain in extensity what it loses in intensity."[109] Wadt adds that this is not a difficult goal, since one only needs to make "modern philosophy" more aesthetically pleasing: "Yes, the style, the style of writing, that is what counts."[110]

Initially, Willibald believes that he has been "transported to a region where wisdom must necessarily dwell,"[111] but difficulties emerge. Von Jumping-Jack launches into a speech about Descartes's founding of modern philosophy, only to be arrested when he refuses to stop talking. Phrase steps in, claiming that he himself has managed to advance the modern project: "Gentlemen, I have gone beyond Hegel; where to, I cannot yet say very precisely, but I have gone beyond him."[112] Unimpressed, Willibald is referred to the prytaneum's "*World-Historical College*," an institution boasting an atrium "so large that four professors lectured there simultaneously without disturbing one another," though "the audience could not even hear what the lecturers were expounding."[113] Then a meeting is called. Attended by the society's leaders, along with "Polytechnic Students" and "Philologists," the conference comically devolves into a shouting match, with Hurrison representing the position of activist journalism, von Jumping-Jack that of Hegelian speculative philosophy, and the philologists that of historical criticism.[114] Willibald even encounters a "fly [that] buzzes past him reciting some Hegelian propositions, and [a] horn can be heard sounding out some political axioms."[115] In turn, he succumbs to the sagacity of the prytaneum, recognizing that "world history is now over, for now nature itself can grasp the concept."[116] At last, as a gesture of goodwill, Willibald seeks to reconcile the prytaneum's members by giving "our Society a new name under which it will nevertheless remain the same."[117]

Joakim Garff notes that Willibald's conversion is surprising,[118] but it coincides with the play's larger point: just as Willibald wants to rename the prytaneum but can only come up with "prytaneum,"[119] so is Kierkegaard implying that modernity is marked by the repetition of the same under the illusion of difference. In the prytaneum, as in the present age, there is a profusion of information and a cadre of public voices, but nothing ever really changes. Discourse about action is mistaken for action itself; the appearance of reform is more important than actual reform. Moreover, certain persons, particularly those with access to organs of public opinion, benefit from just this situation.

That Kierkegaard packages these very real concerns in a work that is otherwise aesthetic anticipates his approach during the 1843–46 period. Works such as *Either/Or*, *Fear and Trembling*, and *Stages on Life's Way* do not attack the present age as such but, instead, tender the perspectives of fools, seducers, skeptics, and melancholics, among others. "Here the *beginning is made*," Kierkegaard explains, "*maieutically*, with a sensation, and with what belongs to it, the public, which always joins in where something is going on; and the movement was, *maieutically*, to shake off 'the crowd' in order to get hold of 'the single individual,' religiously understood."[120] In other words, aesthetic writings attract an aesthetic public, and, through the aesthetic, Kierkegaard sought to expose both the insufficiency of an aesthetic worldview and the religious desires latent therein. But this approach was not to last. In an 1851 text, Kierkegaard recalls that, upon the publication of *Concluding Unscientific Postscript*, "a pseudonym, most appropriately in a newspaper article, made the greatest possible effort to alienate the public and after that began the decisively religious production."[121] If, in fact, the immediate goal of this article was to provoke the public, Kierkegaard clarifies that it was also a "kindness" (*Velgjerning*),[122] intended to lay bare what he terms "the press of literary contemptibility."[123]

It is striking here that Kierkegaard equates the beginning of his so-called "second authorship"[124] with the resumption of his overt criticism of the press—in this case, an article attributed to Frater Taciturnus and published in *The Fatherland* in December 1845. This event marked the beginning of the "*Corsair* Affair," at which point Kierkegaard's concerns about information technology would again take center stage in his authorship.

The *Corsair* Affair

The story of the *Corsair* affair has been well covered in the secondary literature,[125] so there is no need to focus on minutiae in this setting. Of greater importance is how Kierkegaard's understanding of *The Corsair* encouraged him to question the very idea of the free press, that is, of the rapid and increasingly deregulated dissemination of information through technological means. For, as Kierkegaard saw it, the fact that a periodical such as *The Corsair* was able to attain a wide following revealed the underbelly of bourgeois society and, with it, of the liberal-technological experiment in general.

The Corsair was founded in 1840 by a group of left-wing writers, headed by Goldschmidt. It quickly gained notoriety for its "constant conflict with the censors,"[126] and Goldschmidt landed in jail for a time. Undeterred, he continued to publish and eventually achieved a print run extensive enough that *The Corsair* could be had "for only five marks every three months."[127] Thus it "was read by everyone, from plebeian to aristocrat,"[128] all attracted by its satirical attacks on public figures such as Heiberg and Hans Christian Andersen. Kierkegaard was on cordial terms with Goldschmidt, and, for a time, Kierkegaard's writings mostly received praise in *The Corsair*'s pages.

But their relationship soured when Goldschmidt allied himself with the writer and coxcomb P. L. Møller, whom Kierkegaard loathed to the same degree that Goldschmidt adored. In one encounter, Kierkegaard even suggested to Goldschmidt that *The Corsair* was a manifestation of his subservience to Møller's insolent swagger.[129]

This tension erupted into a full-blown conflict when, in December 1845, Møller published "A Visit to Sorø," a lengthy article in his own "aesthetic yearbook" *Gæa*.[130] "A Visit to Sorø" was styled as a conversation about the day's literary scene, and, in this fashion, Møller makes a number of observations about Kierkegaard's pseudonymous works, frequently speculating on what sprawling, multivalent tomes such as *Either/ Or* and *Stages on Life's Way* imply about their author. Of course, Møller (and much of his audience) knew very well who had written those texts, and so his comments were thinly veiled assessments of Kierkegaard's person. In many cases, these remarks were not only unflattering but downright acerbic. The lowest blow came when Møller suggested that parts of *Stages on Life's Way* reveal a personality "dissolved in dialectic, in a barren dialectic,"[131] so much so that the author callously exploits others in his quest for intellectual experimentation—an allusion to Kierkegaard's breakup with Regine.

Kierkegaard responded less than a week later with the article mentioned above, namely, "The Activity of a Traveling Esthetician and How He Still Happened to Pay for the Dinner," attributed to Frater Taciturnus. Though replete with wry references to Møller's money troubles and superficiality, this piece also seeks to identify a red thread linking Møller, *The Corsair*, and the problem of journalism writ large. Taciturnus argues that the existentially wrenching literature found in *Stages on Life's Way* is the sort of work that "cannot be dealt with in a newspaper."[132] He contrasts this with Møller's writing, which is not "dialectically difficult" and, for that reason, "has an advantage when the matter is . . . taken to the public at large."[133] An author who wants to challenge and to edify "is contented with a few readers, with one," whereas Møller concentrates on what his "powers of comprehension" allow—"the trip to Sorø, the stagecoach, the driver, the meals and the drinks, the pack-asses."[134] Taciturnus concludes by underlining that papers such as *The Corsair* "are not part of my environment," and he calls attention to Møller's association with "obtrusive and rude" journalism: "Therefore our vagabond quite properly ends his 'Visit to Sorø' with one of those loathsome *Corsair* attacks on peaceable, respectable men."[135] Indeed, he adds, it is a lamentable aspect of modern life that persons who dedicate themselves to the service of others can be damaged by "people who by having something printed are also authors."[136]

In identifying Møller with a tabloid like *The Corsair*, Kierkegaard effectively destroyed Møller's chances of ever receiving a serious academic appointment. Moreover, he encouraged Goldschmidt to enter the fray. The next issue of *The Corsair* mocked Kierkegaard as "Denmark's greatest mind, the author of Denmark's thickest books,"[137] and the derision intensified and became more personal in the ensuing weeks. Kierkegaard's appearance and eccentricity emerged as popular topics, mocked in words and in cartoons. Only once did Kierkegaard directly address these attacks in public, namely, in "The Dialectical Result of a Literary Police Action," which appeared in a January 1846 issue of *The Fatherland*. Again ascribed to Taciturnus, this short article begins by asserting that *The Corsair* is a base and trifling literary endeavor. The reading public already grasps this point, because no one would dare cite *The Corsair* as a source of legitimate information.[138] To read it is a kind of guilty pleasure, which people only do to get the latest dirt about public figures and to laugh at their expense. Indeed, this is the paper's raison d'être: "So *The Corsair* can be hired to abuse just as a hand organ can be hired to make music."[139] Consequently, the paper is a public menace, fueled by "producers and peddlers of pandering witticisms," and it "must and should be ignored literarily just as public prostitutes should be ignored civically."[140]

In order to facilitate such a downfall, Taciturnus developed a dialectical strategy: since no wants to be ridiculed by *The Corsair*, and since just this fear gives it power over others, he would "make application to be abused by the same paper."[141] The irony of *wanting* to be abused would render *The Corsair* impotent, because it would show that the paper's attacks are nothing to dread. In fact, inasmuch as *The Corsair* does not serve the good, to suffer at its hands is a compliment and to be praised by it, an insult. In making this point clear, Taciturnus aims to free others from the tabloid's tyranny: "I cannot do any more for others than to request to be abused myself."[142]

Taciturnus elucidates this situation with a story. There once was a tailor, he begins, who hoped and prayed for more business. The tailor longed to become rich and powerful, but, when he suddenly received so many orders that he could not keep up, he collapsed from exhaustion—his wish having become his ruin.[143] So it is with *The Corsair*. It too practices a "trade," namely, to engage in "literary polemic by . . . contemptibleness."[144] It is always looking for "more and more people to vilify," delighting in the "delusion" that "it is dreadful to be the object of [its] abuse."[145] What, then, will *The Corsair* do when a notable person, whom the paper once "praised and immortalized,"[146] now demands to be derided by it? Like the tailor, it will be undermined by its own greed. In heaping abuse on such a person, *The Corsair*'s business will flourish, but its fearsome reputation will diminish. Moreover, as other persons in society follow suit, the paper will receive "the judgment of decent literature," harsher than any governmental censorship: "[*The Corsair*] is to be permitted to continue its trade of attacking and vilifying at will, but if it has the nerve to praise, it must on this occasion encounter the brief protest: May I ask to be abused—the personal injury of being immortalized . . . is just too much."[147]

In short, Kierkegaard dared *The Corsair* to continue its polemics. And continue it did. *The Corsair*'s final disparagement of Kierkegaard came in July 1846, close to seven months after the row began. By the time the dust had settled, Kierkegaard had published two of his most enduring works (*Concluding Unscientific Postscript* and *A Literary Review*) and reoriented his authorship, now focusing more on explicitly Christian themes and on how these clashed with the mores of the modern bourgeoisie. But whatever advances he made came at a price. *The Corsair* had rendered Kierkegaard an "object of scorn"[148] in society—a person seen as a caricature rather than as a champion of truth. Even worse, he soon realized that the guardians of "decent literature," whom he had assumed would take his side against sensationalist journalism, were not "the least bit tempted to launch any torpedoes at the nuisance represented by *The Corsair*."[149] Kierkegaard was on his own.

As has been detailed, Kierkegaard was already troubled about the press prior to the *Corsair* affair. Thus, the events of the first half of 1846 did not so much elicit a new concern as compel him to crystallize his thinking about an old one. Indeed, from the perspective of this study, it is irrelevant whether or not Kierkegaard *should* have taken the *Corsair* affair so seriously—a question that Garff believes ought to be answered in the negative.[150] What matters is that his analysis of information technology was broadened and deepened by this public feud.

This point is evinced by journal entries stemming from 1846. One extensive entry, entitled "Some Instructive Comments on *The Corsair's* Drastic Errors," indicates a shift from personal enmity toward Goldschmidt and Møller to wider reflections "in a more social and political vein on journalism."[151] Kierkegaard begins with an observation: modern bourgeois society is characterized by public "protest," and people are quick to complain when "the drinking water in the city is polluted or the baker uses contaminated flour, or even when the streetlights do not burn."[152] Such commercial and technological matters are taken seriously, and civic officials respond with "rules and regulations and preventive measures."[153] Kierkegaard does not condemn this trend in and of itself; what disturbs him is that such material concerns have eclipsed those of an ethico-religious nature. In other words, the one who sells a faulty product is indictable but the one who sells literary spite is not: "In everyday life, when suddenly there is too much fresh fish on the market, the police ban it; but when tainted wit is offered for sale in such a mass that even the rare good witticism is spoiled by the encompassing mass . . . then nothing happens."[154]

This contradiction is one of many problems. It is not just that *The Corsair* is *allowed* to distribute its brand of literature; it is that the public patronizes "a paper that lives on daring to say and do anything, a paper devoid of ideas, that caters to the passions and is out for profit," so much so that "few civil employees, even in the higher positions, and no artists and scholars in Denmark are paid on the same scale."[155] *The Corsair's* popularity is attributed to its attacks on Danish cultural elites—attacks that "the working class and the ordinary middle class"[156] view as justified. But this perception is wrong for two reasons. First, *The Corsair's* content is often gathered "by way of anonymous letters" and frequently concerns "the most private information."[157] Thus its sources are dubious at best, fake at worst, and its subject matter lacks public utility. Second, *The Corsair* opposes society's power brokers but, in doing so, sets itself up as the powerful arbiter of justice and truth: "In Denmark one dares to speak freely about the king and the authorities, but beware of speaking freely about *The Corsair!*"[158]

In this sense, Kierkegaard indicates that *The Corsair* represents a new "phenomenon,"[159] namely, the conversion of information (much of it spurious) into a popular and lucrative commodity. Whereas before "scholars and scientists [argued] in big books that few read," or an occasional periodical in "dedication to the service of honor and responsibility [insisted] on knowing what it writes and does," now "the most widely read paper in the country" exploits progressively lax press restrictions in order to pander cynicism and gossip: "*The Corsair* wheels and deals in people, holds their honor and serene private lives in its hands as if they were trifles."[160] Thus literary culture in Europe has begun to decline, and it poses a threat to the very fabric of society. As Kierkegaard goes on: "If I paid no attention . . . I would have to be completely devoid of sympathy for my fellow men, for the beautiful aspects of private life, for the quiet intimacy of marriage, for the shielding of children's upbringing, and for many other relations that have been injured."[161] In defense of these goods, Kierkegaard willingly subjected himself to *The Corsair*'s abuse, and, at the time of writing this entry, he was optimistic about his ability to bring about an "elevating reconciliation": "I am positive that I can have some effect on *The Corsair* as a literary phenomenon," despite the fact that "passion and commercial interest" jeopardize his efforts.[162]

On the far side of the internet and smartphone, Kierkegaard's solemnity on this matter can seem precious, even sanctimonious. Suffused as our culture is with websites such as *Breitbart*, *Gawker*, and *TMZ*, all trading in salacious gossip and sardonic takes on the day's hottest stories, it is easy to grow numb to their implications and influence. But this is precisely why Kierkegaard's critique is relevant, since he encountered this "phenomenon" before it became an ordinary aspect of Western culture. His dismay and shock, then, are immediate responses, and his journals betray an exasperated attempt to gain philosophical clarity on the issue. An 1846 entry shows him almost doodling about *The Corsair* in various dicta: "*The Corsair*'s position / *Leveling* / good-natured envy (its elevating quality) / contemptible envy / A desire to tear down the great—with the help of a contemptible person so that there is nothing left."[163] Another sketch indicates a sense of powerlessness over against the press: "No recourse against *The Corsair*'s attacks / (1) not in court / (2) not with a witty polemic—for there is no honor to win this way / (3) not by showing that it is a contemptible paper—for then everybody will say: We knew that."[164] A subsequent passage argues that this is a uniquely modern problem. The printing press has depersonalized communication, fostering a culture in which violence is carried out through a literary medium for the sake of public entertainment. At least in the ancient world the abuser and those titillated by the spectacle of abuse "had to appear in person in the square"; moreover, "when the attack itself was over, it was forgotten."[165] In an era of mass media, however, "these things drag on a long time," and the hostility circulates beyond a proximate environment to the general population.[166]

For Kierkegaard, such discrepancies undercut the prevailing narrative about modern progress, namely, "that the world has the equilibrium and balanced distribution that make it the best of all worlds that the liberals and optimists assume it to be."[167] As he sees it, modernity's celebration of reason, science, and technology is not in service to truth but to personal gain; consequently, the one who seeks truth is set up to fail: "He who aspires to honor, status, and money acquires these goods with the help of his unsound views; he who aspires to a sound point of view must purchase it with financial loss and the disdain of all."[168] That a person such as Goldschmidt, who is "intelligent and not without a certain talent,"[169] has succumbed to this twisted calculus indicates its seductiveness. Even more concerning is the fact that, if this logic were to pervade society, it would skew people's aesthetic and ethical judgment:

> It [is] necessary to treat *The* Corsair at this time . . . with a decisively ethical assurance. It may already be difficult for unstable people to distinguish between talent and misuse of talent, to champion ethical judgment against mercenary

prostitution of talent, but if sympathy is to be gained, then it almost takes ethical elevation to see which is which, and this cannot be presupposed at all in the average individual.[170]

Kierkegaard illustrates this concern with a pair of vivid examples from his personal life. First, he mentions the night watchman on his street, who views Kierkegaard as a "quiet, industrious, student-type" and who therefore is angry about the way that *The Corsair* has treated him: "If I were to drop a hint to my watchman about going and beating up the newspaper writer, I believe that he would do it for free, simply because the whole affair makes him sorry for me."[171] Kierkegaard appreciates the loyalty of the watchman but regrets that he cannot perceive the larger point—that Goldschmidt is not as powerful as he seems and that Kierkegaard is stronger than *The Corsair*, precisely because he is on the side of what is right and good. In contrast to the watchman is the local "alehouse keeper," who "believes that what appears in the newspapers is public opinion, the voice of the people and of truth."[172] Hence, in reading *The Corsair* and in seeing Kierkegaard disparaged in its pages, the alehouse keeper assumes that Kierkegaard is no longer a person with whom he should associate—something that Kierkegaard has noticed, inasmuch as the man now tries to dodge him in public and will only greet him if they are in close proximity.[173] As Kierkegaard adds:

> Our alehouse keeper assumes that people can make mistakes . . . a king, a court, even the supreme court, but anything that appears in print he regards as infallible. He says, "Is it possible that anything can be a lie which is printed in countless copies, is read all over the country, and, from what I hear, no one yet has ventured to refute!" This explains his altered opinion of me.[174]

In short, the popular press has become the medium through which people view not only Kierkegaard and his work but also other persons and issues. And what authority underlies this mediating power? The answer lies neither in philosophical expertise nor in religious wisdom, still less does it lie in moral integrity. No, its authority is technologically determined and politically tolerated: it comes from the wide public circulation afforded to journalism—a historically contingent circumstance consequent upon the ongoing development of the printing press and the subsequent rise of liberal political culture. Essentially, then, the *Corsair* affair (as well as other controversies like it) is not a referendum on truth and goodness but on whose opinions are most widely distributed and most shrewdly marketed.

And yet, for Kierkegaard, the ease with which *The Corsair* reaches people should not be confused with a desire to offer a variety of perspectives or to present an impartial selection of news reports. Rather, the paper is meant "for private circulation among friends."[175] That is to say, *The Corsair*'s subject matter is basically "town gossip and rumor and scandal."[176] The upshot is a kind of "inverse situation,"[177] whereby a newspaper attains a mass audience by salaciously highlighting the affairs of a few. Its circulation, then, is not essential but "incidental"; it is printed just because it can be, like a fortune cookie or a menu.[178]

In a later journal entry, Kierkegaard predicts that such gratuitous attention to trivialities will be the undoing of society: "With the press as degenerate as it is, human beings eventually will surely be transformed into clods [*Fæ*]."[179] Indeed, *The Corsair*'s content proves that this process is already underway. If a "certain well-known person (mentioned by name) wears an embroidered shirt," it becomes "the most widely read of everything read" in society.[180] Notably, Kierkegaard does not treat this as a *moral* problem above all. In other words, he does not simply assign blame to a few "bad" people who are misusing an otherwise benign instrument. Rather, he believes that the problem is ultimately technological. Yes, human beings themselves are lamentably "immediate and momentary," but the modern printing press magnifies the "scale" of these flaws to untold proportions: "to use the circulation of the press to discuss for half a year something which, after all, the most addlebrained person ought to be sufficiently human not to talk about for more than five minutes—it can only lead to idiocy [*Fæiskhed*]."[181]

Kierkegaard again contrasts the culture of mass media with the book culture that preceded it. Whereas books emerge after a "laborious process of study and development and after painstaking effort continued over a long period," newspaper articles are written by "half-witted but sly, reprehensible fellows called journalists, busily operating, and their cogitations are read by all."[182] Kierkegaard likens this situation to a "cook's mate" who has procured a megaphone in order to communicate with his fellow sailors. Eventually, even the ship's captain has to convey orders through the cook's mate, despite the fact that these messages are "completely garbled in going through the cook's mate and his megaphone."[183] What, then, is the source of the cook's mate power? It is neither his experience nor his training but simply his access to technology: "Finally the cook's mate gets control, because he has the megaphone."[184]

Kierkegaard would continue to analyze the origins and the implications of the press for the rest of his authorship. And yet, while most of his reflections on this subject are confined to his journals, there is one significant exception—*A Literary Review*. It was in this text that Kierkegaard schematized his analysis of the mass media and, as Dreyfus would later contend, established an enduring critique of information technology.

A Literary Review

It has now been seen that, in a variety of settings and in a variety of voices, Kierkegaard had long expressed reservations about Europe's embrace of liberal journalism. What he had yet to do was provide a cohesive, conceptual analysis of this phenomenon, and therein lies the achievement of *A Literary Review*. Kierkegaard uses Thomasine Gyllembourg's novel *Two Ages* (*To Tidsaldre*, 1845) as the occasion for *A Literary Review*. The novel chronicles a pair of historical time periods—the revolutionary, passionate 1790s and the banal, calculative 1840s, the latter of which is typified by bourgeois liberalism.[185] Kierkegaard began reviewing *Two Ages* in December 1845 and intensified his efforts in the wake of *The Corsair*'s first attacks in January 1846. The aptly named *A Literary Review* appeared in March of the same year.

Much of *A Literary Review* is, indeed, a literary review—that is to say, a close reading of Gyllembourg's novel. But the third and final part of the book is an "ethical-philosophical evaluation"[186] entitled "The Results of Observing the Two Ages." It is here that Kierkegaard's critique of information technology appears, though his stated goal is to contrast the two historical periods featured in *Two Ages*. On the one hand stands the "age of revolution," which "is essentially passionate [*lidenskabelig*], and therefore it essentially has *form*."[187] For Kierkegaard, passion and form go together. To be passionate involves suffering (*lidende*) or submitting to some object. Accordingly, the revolutionary age's "form" is the active expression of the idea to which it is attracted and by which it is shaped. That is precisely why the age of revolution is potentially dangerous: it can be so committed to a certain viewpoint that it turns "ruthless toward everything but its idea."[188] Here "individuals relate to an idea merely *en masse* (consequently without the individual separation of inwardness)," and the result, as in the French Revolution, is "anarchy, riotousness."[189]

This danger haunts the age of revolution, but it is not a fait accompli. If an era were to support the right idea, and if that era were to relate to the right idea properly, then its revolution would be a good and beneficial one:

> When individuals (each one individually) are essentially and passionately related to an idea and together are essentially related to the same idea, the relation is optimal and normative. Individually the relation separates them (each one has himself for himself), and ideally it unites them. Where there is essentially inwardness, there is a decent modesty between man and man that prevents crude aggressiveness; in the relation of unanimity to the idea there is the elevation that again in consideration of the whole forgets the accidentality of details. Thus the individuals never come too close to each other in the herd sense, simply because they are united on the basis of an ideal distance. The unanimity of separation is indeed fully orchestrated music.[190]

Just as members of a musical ensemble play the same song (say, "Hey Jude") but each in a unique way (Paul on piano, John on guitar, and so on), so is an "optimal" society one in which each person relates to the same idea but in such a way that her or his individual capacities are elicited rather than suppressed.

And yet, when this "harmony of the singled out" (*Udsondringens Samdrægtighed*)[191] is lacking, problems ensue. As noted, the revolutionary age's passion for the idea is liable to evacuate individual responsibility, as when an angry mob goes about marauding and slaughtering in the name of "justice." Such violence is the outcome of a provisional and reactive idea being elevated to absolute status: "Simply as reaction [the revolutionary age] can be transformed by one single deviation into untruth, which in an accidental way accentuates the polemical."[192] On the other hand, what if a given age were to lack a unifying idea altogether? That is to say, what if the trouble were not a dearth of "singling out" but an absence of "harmony"? What if persons were hostile to or irresolute toward the idea to which they are to relate? In that case, according to Kierkegaard, a different society would emerge—one differentiated by its "crudeness" or, more specifically, by "an uncomfortable lack of specific quality."[193] It is this kind of society that characterizes "the present age" (*Nutiden*), which Kierkegaard equates with the second age treated in Gyllembourg's novel.

Kierkegaard defines the present age as a "*sensible, reflecting age, devoid of passion, flaring up in superficial, short-lived enthusiasm and prudentially relaxing in indolence.*"[194] His analysis of the present age takes a variety of rhetorical strategies, alternating between philosophy, satire, and even parable. What is crucial here, however, is Kierkegaard's understanding of *how* the present age came to be. As he sees it, the present age does not represent the essential progress of world history but is contingent upon the political-cum-technological conditions of bourgeois society. These conditions have already been outlined in the first few chapters of this study; they involve the West's gradual industrialization, mercantilization, and urbanization, leading eventually to its political liberalization. In *A Literary Review*, Kierkegaard argues that the popular press dangerously accelerates and intensifies this modern transformation.

So, then, how does the press give rise to an apathetic, frivolous, and utilitarian era? This question must be answered in relation to Kierkegaard's sociological theory, outlined above. Recall that he sees social harmony occurring when individuals, precisely as singular and inward-looking persons, passionately dedicate themselves to a common idea. The popular press, however, occludes this process: "The abstraction of the press (for a periodical [*Blad*], a newspaper [*Avis*] is no civic concretion and an individual only in an abstract sense) combined with the age's lack of passion and reflectiveness gives rise to the phantom of the abstraction—the public [*Publikum*], which is the actual leveler [*Nivellerende*]."[195] This sentence needs unpacking. First, there is the claim that the press is an *Abstraktion*. The terms "abstraction" and "abstract" are derived from the Latin verb *abstrahere*, which can be translated as "to draw away" or "to detach." Thus to say that the press is an abstraction is to say that it is disconnected from actual social relations: there is not a flesh-and-blood person named "The Press" with whom one can converse or to whom one can give something. That is why the views espoused in the press are deceptive. Though they may be attributed to a person, they are not, *sensu stricto*, the views of a concrete individual. The medium of the printed word, disseminated impersonally and vastly, stands between person and person and thereby supersedes face-to-face interaction. Communication happens, but it is essentially and necessarily a *detached* form of communication.

Hence, if the press were to become a decisive means of human discourse, the results would be grievous. It would indeed lead to the kind of reflective ennui characteristic of the present age. There are two reasons for this outcome. First, whereas Kierkegaard's optimal society features concrete individuals, each ardently engaged in actualizing his or her own relation to a formative idea, a press-driven society lacks concrete individuality precisely in and through its dedication to a technologically mediated interpersonal communication—a phenomenon that Kierkegaard concisely terms "the public" but describes as "a monstrous abstraction, an all-encompassing something that is nothing, a mirage."[196] Kierkegaard insists that the *Publikum* is a product of the press: "Only in a passionless but reflective age can this phantom develop with the aid of the press, when the press itself becomes a phantom."[197] Moreover, this situation is unique to modern society:

> The public is a concept that simply could not have appeared in antiquity, because the people were obliged to come forward *en masse in corpore* [as a whole] in the situation of action, were obliged to bear the responsibility for what was done by individuals in their midst, while in turn the individual was obliged to be present in person as the one specifically involved and had to submit to the summary court for approval or disapproval. Only when there is no strong communal life to give substance to the concretion will the press create this abstraction "the public," made up of unsubstantial individuals who are never united or never can be united in the simultaneity of any situation or organization and yet are claimed to be a whole.[198]

"Only when there is no strong communal life": this phrase implies—quite rightly, as has been seen—that the press emerged out of a much larger social and technological shift in the modern West, whereby industrialization, mercantilism, and urbanization slowly but surely dissolved the bonds of medieval culture, eventually leading to the foundation of a liberal political order centered on individual freedom and rights. It is in this context that the influence of the press and public becomes so dangerous, because individuals now develop their personal ideals and mores in accordance with what the *Publikum* supposedly thinks or wants, and yet the "public is not a people, not a generation, not one's age not a congregation, not an association, not some particular persons."[199] To join the public is to join nothing and thus to be nothing or nobody: "Not a single one of these who belong to a public is essentially engaged in any way. For a few hours of the day he perhaps is part of the public, that is, during the hours when he is a nobody, because during the hours in which he is the specific person he is, he does not belong to the public."[200] Kierkegaard observes that, ironically, there is comfort in seeking an alliance with the *Publikum*. As an individual human being, one may feel insignificant, even meaningless, but the sense of being associated with the public can be intoxicating: "The public is the fairytale of an age of prudence, leading individuals to fancy themselves greater than kings,"[201] he adds.

In addition, the press fosters a culture of reflective ennui by its occlusion of a unifying idea. For Kierkegaard, such an idea is necessary if society is to flourish, but the press presents so much information and does so with such rapidity that a unifying idea cannot take root. As a result, the present age is a *"dialectical tour de force,"* which *"lets everything remain but subtly drains the meaning out of it."*[202] Rather than foster commitment to ideals or movements, this tendency *"exhausts the inner actuality of relations in a tension of reflection that . . . has transformed the whole of existence into an equivocation."*[203] Indeed, just as the press dispassionately tenders stories about good and evil, so is the present age morally indifferent:

> No one is carried away to great exploits by the good, no one is rushed into outrageous sin by evil, the one is just as good as the other, and yet for that very reason there is all the more to gossip about, for ambiguity and equivocation are

stimulating and have many more words than are possessed by joy over the good and the loathing of evil.[204]

In this way, people begin to approach issues and even "life-relationships" as bystanders: "The citizen does not relate himself in the relation but is a spectator computing the problem."[205] The upshot is not a bloody revolution but "a tension that enervates life";[206] the social order is debated and doubted but never overthrown.

Eventually, as the press becomes a cultural presupposition, this "tension of reflection establishes itself as a principle, and . . . so *envy* becomes the *negatively unifying principle* in a passionless and very reflective age."[207] This means that people are brought "together on the basis of what they are against rather than what they are for."[208] Envy, then, indicates the absence of a determinative idea. It counteracts a sense of common purpose and undermines those persons (say, political or religious leaders) who would promote such a purpose: "The age of heroes is past."[209] Kierkegaard terms this process "leveling," and it fully emerges when envy "no longer has the character to come to a self-awareness of its own significance."[210] In other words, leveling occurs when envy suffuses society, thereby serving "to degrade [excellence], minimize it, until it actually is no longer excellence."[211] This is true both of the excellence "which *is* [and] that which *is to come*."[212]

Again, the techno-cosmopolitan conditions of modernity underlie this situation. Whereas the "dialectic of antiquity was oriented to the eminent," the "dialectic of the present age is oriented to equality, and its most logical implementation, albeit abortive, is leveling."[213] In this vacuum of individual excellence, the *Publikum* becomes the new standard of right and wrong. That is why "we compute numbers . . . in connection with the most trivial things," and this numerical verdict is treated as sacrosanct since "the individual fears . . . reflection's judgment upon him."[214] In turn, a new form of subjugation has appeared. The aristocracy has been overthrown, but the public has taken its place: "The individual does not belong to God, to himself, to the beloved, to his art, to his scholarship; no, just as a serf belongs to an estate, so the individual realizes that in every respect he belongs to an abstraction in which reflection subordinates him."[215]

It is indeed significant that Kierkegaard compares the public to "one of the Roman emperors, an imposing, well-fed figure suffering from boredom and therefore craving only the sensate titillation of laughter."[216] Like a Nero[217] or an Elagabalus, the public requires something to while away the time, and so it "keeps a dog for its amusement. This dog is the contemptible part of the literary world,"[218] in short, the press. Through the press, the public exposes and undercuts persons of distinction and excellence:

> The superior one, the stronger one, has been mistreated—and the dog, well, it remains a dog that even the public holds in contempt. In this way the leveling has been done by a third party; the public of nothingness has leveled through a third party that in and through its contemptibleness was already more than leveled and less than nothing. And the public is unrepentant, for after all it was not the public—in fact, it was the dog, just as one tells children: It was the cat that did it.[219]

Crucially, Kierkegaard is talking about more than the press's defiance of the "powers that be." He is "not a pure, 'party-line' conservative mainstreamer or a dogmatic Hegelian."[220] In other words, he recognizes that the diminishment of, say, the absolute monarchy is but a symptom of a wider problem—namely, the diminishment of individual excellence tout court.

This expansive understanding of leveling can be seen in Kierkegaard's parable of the jewel. Imagine, he begins, an enthralling treasure positioned far out on a thin sheet of ice. In a passionate age, the courageous person who dared to retrieve the jewel would be hailed as a hero, as a "superior one," because her gamble would entail genuine risk and thus exceptional bravery. In a reflective age, however, no one would actually venture onto the thin ice. Instead, people would employ a trained skater, who would approach the danger zone yet turn away at the last moment. The onlookers would celebrate the skater's intrepidity, but, Kierkegaard adds, the habits of the reflective age—superficiality, envy, leveling, and so on—would undermine her accomplishment:

> At the banquet in the evening, the admiration would resound. But whereas what usually happens where admiration is authentic is that the admirer is inspired by the thought of being a man just like the distinguished person . . . here again practical common sense would alter the pattern of admiration. Even at the giddy height of the fanfare and the volley of hurrahs, the celebrators at the banquet would have a shrewd and practical understanding that their hero's exploit was not all that good, that . . . any one of the participants could have done almost the same thing with some practice in tricky turns.[221]

This, indeed, is what happens in the present age: people want the appearance of courage without actually exhibiting courage; they venerate exceptionality even as they have rendered it meaningless.

It would seem that this state of affairs is unpalatable, but Kierkegaard insists that it is amusing, even exciting. Here, again, the print media plays a role: "The present age is an age of publicity, the age of miscellaneous announcements: nothing happens but still there is instant publicity."[222] Publicity keeps life interesting in the present age, giving people the opportunity to *pretend* that something is going to change, even if they know otherwise. "The age of great and good actions is past," Kierkegaard states, "the present age is the age of anticipation."[223] Anticipation encourages public debate but requires no action. All are given an opportunity to talk, but such talk is an end in itself, void of individual distinction and thus with "no assets of feeling in the erotic, no assets of enthusiasm and inwardness in politics and religion, no assets of domesticity, piety, and appreciation in daily life and social life."[224] In short, leveling razes far more than the absolute monarchy; it actually threatens to raze the very meaning of life.

But that is not to imply that leveling is good for nothing. In fact, according to Kierkegaard, it is good for business: "An age without passion possesses no assets; everything becomes, as it were, transactions in *paper money*."[225] Kierkegaard cites comedy as a case in point. People in the present age want to enjoy the comic, but, since there is not "consistent and well-grounded ethical view" (as in, say, the comedies of

Aristophanes), this desire does not point to anything essential but is simply a matter of amusement, "like selling one's trousers and buying a wig."[226] In this situation, humor is converted into a commodity—"a profitable industry" that turns authentic wit into "its most trite and hackneyed opposite."[227] Since the significance of art now lies in how much money it can make, it too has exchanged passion for "an abstraction."[228] Something of no intrinsic value (paper currency) has become that which motivates and governs human behavior:

> A young man today would scarcely envy another his capacities or his skill or the love of a beautiful girl or his fame, no, but he would envy him his money. Give me money, the young man will say, and I will be all right. . . . He will die in the illusion that if he had had money, then he would have lived, then he certainly would have done something great.[229]

These comments recall Kierkegaard's concern that technology—including the increasingly lucrative print media—is fundamentally in service to financial gain. Not only is the industrial-cum-urban landscape of the modern West oriented toward commerce, but, with the demolition of high ideals, the abstraction of monetary wealth is now the last remaining "excellence."[230]

The present age, then, manifests a symbiosis of forces. Let loose by political and technological reform, the print media propels the leveling process, fashioning an abstract civic space in which the pursuit of individual distinction is subordinated to public opinion. As a result, society is preoccupied with reflection—with discussing what the *Publikum* wants—and this concern drives the public's interest in the press, not to mention the press's frequent need to keep the public interested. Reflection begets reflection; it is a cycle of pragmatic tedium made acceptable by advertisements, banquets, gadgetry, gossip, and other forms of entertainment. This form of social organization has its benefits (diminished threat of violent upheaval, greater freedom of expression, etc.), but it also bears an immense danger—that persons will mindlessly follow the crowd, relishing the age's material comforts while forgetting the singular importance of their own lives and of human life writ large. "This is why," Kierkegaard concludes, "eventually not even a very gifted person is able to liberate himself from reflection, for he soon realizes he is merely a fraction in something utterly trivial."[231]

Kierkegaard's analysis is sobering, and doubtless he is critical of the present age in general and of the influence of mass technology in particular. Yet, as *A Literary Review* draws to a close, he again shows why he is not an apologist for political conservatism, still less an advocate for a fascistic counterrevolution. For one thing, *A Literary Review* exhibits a profound sense of resignation, as if the present age represents the proverbial "end of history": "The abstraction of leveling . . . will stay with us, as they say of a tradewind that consumes everything."[232] It is a "negatively superior force," which cannot be resisted by a great leader, an "assemblage" (*Congregation*), or even patriotic nationalism (*Nationaliteternes Individualitet*).[233] Second, Kierkegaard insists that the perils of the present age are educative. If one will attend to the phenomenon itself, rather than participate in or flail against it, one will secure a "severe taskmaster who takes on the task of educating."[234] Leveling is a teacher in that it strips away illusions of being "the man of distinction, the outstanding hero," and, seen properly, it convinces one to become "an essentially human being in the full sense of equality."[235] To understand leveling is to understand that the sort of greatness that has guided and molded human history for eons is gone. But just this realization can put one's life on an alternate course, which does not consist in power but in service: "Through the leap out into the depths one learns to help himself, learns to love all others as much as himself."[236]

In this sense, the "deathly stillness"[237] of leveling points the way toward the resurrection of authentic religion: "By means of [leveling] every individual, each one separately, may in turn be religiously educated."[238] Since I have dealt with this issue elsewhere,[239] I will not dwell on it here. Still, it is worth underlining that, while Kierkegaard continues to assert that "leveling is what the selfish individual and the selfish generation meant for evil," he also believes that it "can be the point of departure for the highest life."[240] This is because "the eternal life-view of the essentially religious it cannot buy,"[241] and consequently only religion can deliver persons from the bilious envy of the present age.[242] Kierkegaard makes this case by examining the concept of "equality" (*Ligelighed*). As notions of authority and excellence recede into the past, "equality" has emerged as present age's watchword.[243] In fact, the leveling activity of press and *Publikum* seeks a kind of equality—that of reducing all distinction and truth to a mere matter of opinion—though it is won at the expense of virtue. But equality without virtue is despair: "The terrible thing is . . . the thought of the many human lives that are squandered or may easily be squandered," whether by playing "the role of the dog for money" or by getting "no deeper impression of life than this foolish grinning."[244] Even those who share in the leveling process for ostensibly good reasons—say, out of "sympathy for the victims of the attack"—fail to realize that in such a situation "the victims are always the strongest."[245] Equality won through leveling, no matter how well-intentioned, always reproduces the mechanism of leveling.

Thus a different form of equality is needed, whereby people live in accordance with "the universal in equality before God, because of their acceptance of the responsibility for this at all times."[246] This is "the full sense of equality" that constitutes the very "idea of religiousness,"[247] and, since leveling obviates a return to authority, this religious equality stands as the lone egress from the "diabolical principle of the leveling process."[248] Those who choose the path of religiousness understand the nature of leveling and, in a sense, are prompted *by* leveling to heed God's eschatological call:

> Then it will be said: "Look, everything is ready; look, the cruelty of abstraction exposes the vanity of the finite in itself; look, the abyss of the infinite is opening up; look, the sharp scythe of leveling permits all, every single one, to leap over the blade—look, God is waiting! Leap, then, into the embrace of God."[249]

To make this leap, however, is to leap into a hidden life, "unrecognizable (without authority)."[250] Kierkegaard refers to such persons as "the unrecognizables," and they have learned that leveling cannot be defeated openly but only "in suffering."[251] This type of servanthood "is not to reign, to control, to lead, but in suffering to serve, to help indirectly."[252]

Such words suggest a repudiation of public activity, and, as Kierkegaard finished *A Literary Review*, he was indeed thinking about retiring as an author and assuming a rural pastorate.[253] However, he soon scrapped this plan and instead elected to reorient his authorship: now he would focus more explicitly on religious topics and would tender increasingly direct criticism of the Danish state church. In the end, and with a measure of irony, this polemical dénouement meant that Kierkegaard was heading toward one last major encounter with the press—one that complicates and arguably even contradicts his earlier critique of information technology.

Kierkegaard's later use of the press: Journalist or Ironist?

As with the *Corsair* affair, Kierkegaard's so-called "attack upon Christendom" is a complicated and controversial historical occurrence. Not only does it involve a number of important figures in Danish history, each with a peculiar connection to the events in question, but it compresses and, in substance, amplifies many of Kierkegaard's philosophical and theological ideas. Given this complexity,[254] I will not be able to discuss Kierkegaard's "attack" in great detail here. Rather, after an inventory of the case's basic facts, I will attend to the ways in which it impinges on Kierkegaard's relation to information technology. More specifically, I will argue that, even though Kierkegaard used the press to disseminate his criticism of the Danish state church, this should not be confused with an endorsement of journalism per se. As Kierkegaard explains in his doctoral dissertation *The Concept of Irony* (1841), the ironist sometimes must destroy "actuality by means of actuality itself."[255] In this sense, Kierkegaard's "attack" was as Socratic as it was Christian: alienated from the warp and woof of bourgeois modernity, Kierkegaard sought to use society's essential technological instrument— the popular media—against society itself. And, *qua* ironist, he was willing to bear with the paradoxicalness of this endeavor: "Only history can judge whether the irony is justified or not."[256]

After releasing *For Self-Examination* in September 1851, Kierkegaard did not publish again until December 1854. His return to public activity was prompted by the death of Jacob Peter Mynster—bishop of Zealand and one of the leading civic figures of the day. Mynster was succeeded by Hans Lassen Martensen, an accomplished yet career-minded churchman, whose funeral eulogy hailed Mynster as a "witness of the truth" (*Sandhedsvidne*). This description enraged Kierkegaard, who could not stomach the incongruity of one bourgeois dignitary identifying another with the apostles and martyrs of Christian history. Eventually, Kierkegaard would issue a diatribe against Mynster and Martensen in *The Fatherland*. His polemics caused a scandal, and, sensing an opportunity, Kierkegaard pressed his case in additional articles, haranguing the Danish state church and indeed the very idea of Christendom. In May 1855, he even began publishing his own paper, *The Moment* (*Øieblikket*), which had a print run of nine issues before Kierkegaard fell ill in September of the same year. He died less than two months later and, controversially, received a full funeral at Vor Frue Kirke, the cathedral of Copenhagen.

That Kierkegaard's life ended in this way is curious, perhaps even shocking. It is true that his criticism of Denmark's state church had intensified in the years after the *Corsair* affair, but his thorough and uncompromising assault against the Danish establishment seemed to contradict the overarching thrust of his politics. Moreover, that he conducted this assault by way of the print media was virtually unthinkable. How could Kierkegaard, who had publicly criticized the press since his student years, have not only taken a regular column in a liberal paper but even started his *own* paper? Had he changed his mind about this new technology? Was Kierkegaard now in favor of journalism and, with it, the dissemination of information and opinions by way of mass technology?

However one chooses to answer these questions, one thing is absolutely certain: Kierkegaard's journals register disdain for the popular media both in the years immediately preceding his "attack upon Christendom" and *during* the attack itself. That is, even as Kierkegaard was using the press to level Christendom, he continued to be critical of journalism and of those who promoted it. As one 1854 journal entry explains:

> When one can get men as individuals, there is much about them that is lovable; but as soon as they become the public, the crowd etc., all the detestable features appear. "The journalist" is really the corrupter; he (worse than any brothel keeper [*Bordelvært*] living off men's debauchery) lives off promotion of the evil principle in man: the numerical.[257]

Another passage from the same period clarifies this point. Modernity, says Kierkegaard, is stained by a "sophistry" that determines the legitimacy of a deed or an idea by how many people approve of it.[258] Thus "everything is relative, numbers decide the outcome."[259] Though people have wrestled with the question of relativism for centuries, technological development has made it "the real sovereign" in human affairs: "This matter of the press is the deepest degradation of the human race, for it encourages revolt from below; a monstrous weapon has been invented that is designed and intended to kill everything that amounts to something."[260]

Kierkegaard also sought to put his concerns in conversation with other thinkers. Subsequent 1854 journal entries note that he has recently begun reading Arthur Schopenhauer[261] and that the two agree on a number of issues, including the press. In particular, Kierkegaard appreciated Schopenhauer's comparison of journalism to costume rental stores: the journalist supplies the public with ideas that are neither original nor essential, just as the costume rental store loans out used clothing and sham accessories.[262] The only difference is that, whereas "in the outer world the majority would be ashamed to go around in a hat, coat, etc. that someone had discarded, this is not at all the case in matters of the mind. There everybody goes around in discarded clothing."[263] The journalist, then, "live[s] by renting opinions"; "first he drills it into [the public] with all his might that it is necessary for every man to have an opinion—and then, then he recommends his own assortment."[264]

A later passage—dated September 24, 1855, roughly a week before Kierkegaard was admitted to Frederik's Hospital with what turned out to be a terminal illness—extends this insight. Great thinkers, Kierkegaard laments, are unable to achieve anything in the world, because "their words are drowned in the babbling of the age."[265] That is, once the great thinker's ideas are "printed," they become fodder for journalists, pastors, and professors, who convert them into a respectable source of income.[266] Journalism, in particular, demonstrates this point, since it merely reifies the "chitchat" (*Snak*) of the public and yet is considered a valid profession: "If the barbers made a living by carrying on town-gossip instead of sustaining themselves in another way . . . their status would also rise."[267] In contrast, the great thinker must be content with the "immortality" attendant upon dedication "to carrying the idea."[268]

It is plain, then, that Kierkegaard's critique of the print media did not abate in the last years of his life—if anything, it strengthened. So, why did he carry out his "attack upon Christendom" by way of the press? First, it is worth underlining that Kierkegaard himself was cognizant of this ostensible contradiction. In "Why I Have Used This Newspaper," a journal entry dated April 8, 1855, Kierkegaard contends that Christian communication should not be reserved for "quiet places and quiet hours," since this assumption "represents a changing (an altering) of Christianity by placing it at an artistic distance from actuality."[269] "Therefore," he avers, "preaching should not be done in churches but in the street, right in the middle of life, the actuality of ordinary, daily life."[270] Since he did not feel physically up to this task (likely his health was already deteriorating), he "decided to use this newspaper" in order to "achieve an approximation of preaching in the streets."[271] This is a type of apology: Kierkegaard concedes that utilizing the press is not ideal, but the medium's popularity makes it a good substitute for public speaking. Second, Kierkegaard claims that, insofar as he publishing in *The Fatherland*, "a political paper" that "has completely different interests," he is not entangling himself in party politics.[272] He is but "a tenant," speaking as himself and for himself, and consequently he is not treating the press as "a sensate power itself," nor is he using it "anonymously."[273] Thus he concludes: "I . . . succeeded in using the daily press without contradicting my own views of the press."[274]

This appears to be a straightforward account of Kierkegaard's position, but, in fact, he was already plotting another step—namely, to cease publishing with *The Fatherland* and to start his own paper. As early as March 1855, Kierkegaard began to ponder a "flysheet" or a "pamphlet" entitled *The Moment*, "to which subscriptions can be made at the bookstores."[275] The first edition of this paper was issued on May 24, 1855, and it consisted of four short articles, plus an "Addendum." In the latter section, Kierkegaard explains that hitherto he has avoided a deep relationship with the modern world: "I have been at a distance from the present age, even very distant, and close only insofar as this distance was well calculated and full of purpose."[276] But now the time has come when the eternal ideality of the New Testament, "which exercises great power over me,"[277] must be put in contact with the present age. This intersection of eternality and temporality is "the moment" (*Øieblikket*).[278] Hence, if Kierkegaard's task is to relate to the temporal sphere in full, he must avail himself of its media: "I cannot do without an organ by which I can instantaneously address my contemporaries,"[279] though this organ, however modish, is also a receptacle of timeless ideals. Indeed, for that reason, he has decided to name his endeavor *Øieblikket*.

The unique coincidence of eternal and temporal, Kierkegaard adds, is precisely what distinguishes his project from that of a regular paper. Yes, people can subscribe to *The Moment*, but the paper is being published neither for profit nor for the sake of entertaining an audience: "I reserve for myself in *every* regard the *most unconditional* freedom; otherwise I cannot do it."[280] Unlike most publishers, who promote their product and seek to entice prospective readers, Kierkegaard thus does the opposite: "I do not urge anyone to subscribe; I rather ask everyone at least to think twice before he does it."[281] After all, to read *The Moment* is not a means of passing the time or of getting cheap amusement; in fact, it will make one uneasy and quite possibly unhappy. Yet, if it were to reach the right reader, "eternally he will not regret heeding my words."[282]

Of course, one might wonder whether or not this is the shrewdest form of advertisement—to bait the reader with a "hot take" (to use contemporary parlance) that provides not only earthly diversion but, indeed, the possibility of an eternal one. On this reading, Kierkegaard's *Moment* verges uncomfortably close to subsequent applications of popular media in religion (televangelism, online scams, etc.). Still, there is a Socratic component to Kierkegaard's last foray into journalism that undermines such a perspective. In the tenth edition of *The Moment*, published posthumously but completed in September 1855, Kierkegaard compares his mission not to a Christian apologist or martyr but, rather, to "antiquity's noble simple soul . . . the only *human being* I admiringly acknowledge as a thinker."[283] As he explains: "The only analogy I have before me is Socrates; my task is a Socratic task, to audit the definition of what it is to be a Christian—I do not call myself a Christian (keeping the ideal free), but I can make it manifest that the others are even less."[284] Moreover, in this very enterprise, Kierkegaard does not expect immediate reward but derision and suffering: "O Socrates! . . . [T]he same thing has happened to me that happened to you . . . namely, that you thereby made many enemies for yourself by making it manifest that they were ignorant."[285] So thorough is Kierkegaard's negation of Christian definitions that he refuses to call himself a Christian.[286] The purpose of *The Moment*, then, is not to build up an alternative church community or to frame a neoteric teaching; it is to tear down prevailing assumptions about Christianity (and about Western culture writ large) so that something new might emerge. That is precisely why his task is less conservative than distinctive: "In Christendom's eighteen hundred years there is absolutely nothing comparable, no analogy to my task; it is the first time in 'Christendom.'"[287]

Kierkegaard's affinity for Socratic apophasis, for dialectic rather than system, is well known in philosophical and theological circles. But his invocation of Socrates in *The Moment* also sheds light on his late appropriation of the popular media—a point elucidated by returning to the origins of Kierkegaard's authorship. In his doctoral thesis *The Concept of Irony, with Continual Reference to Socrates* (1841), Kierkegaard analyzes the major sources of Socrates's life and teaching (especially Aristophanes, Plato, and Xenophon) and, in turn, investigates the concept of irony as such. With the latter task in mind, Kierkegaard returns to the ironic "position that appeared to have been characteristic of Socrates."[288] But what, exactly, is the nature of this position?

Kierkegaard defines it as "infinite absolute negativity" (*uendelige absolute Negativitet*), inasmuch as it exclusively seeks to nullify the present age for the sake of a "higher something that still is not."[289] As such, irony is a "divine madness that rages like a Tamerlane and does not leave one stone upon another," and it tends to appear at "every world-historical turning point."[290] Hence, just as the conqueror demolishes the society that he has infiltrated, the ironist is not bound to a given "historical actuality"[291] but instead "is negatively free and as such is suspended, because there is nothing that holds him."[292]

Hence, detached from present considerations yet powerless to establish something new, the ironist "destroys the given actuality by the given actuality," realizing that "every particular historical actuality" bears "within itself the seeds of its own downfall."[293] What appears to be complacency, then, is actually a form of sabotage: "[The ironist] permits the established to remain, but for him it has no validity; meanwhile, he pretends as if it did have validity for him, and under this mask leads it to its certain downfall."[294] Socrates's clash with the Athenian establishment exemplifies this form of irony; "he used irony as he destroyed Greek culture,"[295] not in the role of a sociopolitical revolutionary, but as an individual loosed from the bonds of a corrupt society. As Kierkegaard clarifies in a lengthy passage:

> The whole substantial life of Greek culture had lost its validity for [Socrates], which means that to him the established actuality was unactual, not in this or that particular aspect but in its totality as such; that with regard to this invalid actuality he let the established order of things appear to remain established and thereby brought about its downfall; that in the process Socrates became lighter and lighter, more and more negatively free; consequently, that we do indeed perceive that according to what is set forth here Socrates's position was, as infinite absolute negativity, irony. But it was not actuality in general that he negated; it was the given actuality at a particular time, the substantial actuality as it was in Greece, and what his irony was demanding was the actuality of subjectivity, of ideality.[296]

Thus Socrates's "sacrifice" is "world-historically justified"[297] and, as such, is distinct from the irony characteristic of romanticism, in which irony does not seek a "given actuality that must be negated and superseded by a new element" but instead annihilates "*all* of historical actuality . . . in order to make room for a self-created actuality."[298] In other words, whereas Socrates employs irony as the means by which sophistic culture is overturned for the sake of the truth, romantic figures such as Friedrich Schlegel and Ludwig Tieck promote an "exaggerated subjectivity" that draws on the "Fichtean principle that subjectivity, the *I*, has constitutive validity, is the sole omnipotence."[299] Theirs is an irony of radical individual self-determination, rather than ethico-religious revitalization.

In light of this analysis, Kierkegaard's later use of the print media comes into focus. Inasmuch as the "attack upon Christendom" was a Socratic endeavor—and Kierkegaard himself accentuates precisely this point—it is clear that *The Moment* (not to mention Kierkegaard's other forays into journalism) cannot be seen as a straightforward embrace of the press. Rather, in the manner of Socratic irony, these efforts use a given historical actuality (the bourgeois liberal order) against itself, since the establishment bears the seeds of its own downfall (the free press). Just as the culture hastened by the printing press slowly but surely erased the ancien régime, so must this new order be erased. Those who live by the media must die by the media; the levelers, too, must be leveled.

Kierkegaard had already teased out this logic in *A Literary Review*, and, as his final literary gesture, *The Moment* seeks to enact it. After all, Socrates confronted his Athenian interlocutors in the Agora, where the era's leaders gathered and discussed philosophical, political, and religious questions. With *The Moment*, Kierkegaard does something similar: he enters the print media's agora of ideas, not so that he might personally profit but so that he might undermine those who dominate it. He does not oppose the press directly and, in fact, acts as if it were valid. Yet, by foregrounding questions of "ideality," of what it means to be a true Christian, he demands of bourgeois sophistry what it cannot and will not deliver. In doing so, judgment is brought down upon the establishment—namely, that it conceals rather than reveals the truth, that it prioritizes trivial matters over existential authenticity, that it benefits a few at the expense of many, that it deifies the temporal order while obfuscating the eternal one. Kierkegaard knew that his views would not persuade, or even be comprehensible, to everyone. Yet, in the manner of Socrates, he understood himself as a necessary sacrifice, who, in turn, might precipitate the demise of his age. He could not prophesy what would come next, but, as described in *A Literary Review*, he was ready to detach himself from "the vanity of the finite" and to leap "into the embrace of God."[300]

In his 2005 book *The Philosophy of Kierkegaard*, George Pattison observes that, prima facie, Kierkegaard's union of Socratic irony and Christian piety is curious: "The Christian communicator who seeks to take Socrates as a model must, after all, confront the fact that he lives in a situation very different from that of Socrates."[301] It is not that human nature has changed; rather, "there are cultural changes that would make a modern Socrates very different in a number of respects from the historical original."[302] Though Pattison does not specify the development of information technology, he makes clear that Kierkegaard's attempt to replicate Socratic dialogue in print is as bold as it is questionable: "Can *writing* ever be Socratic?"[303]

Kierkegaard certainly thought so, and he was aware that others had already attempted similar projects.[304] As Pattison sees it, then, Kierkegaard's oeuvre balances a "constructive" theological anthropology with an "analytical" or Socratic component that evinces a "passion for tricking, teasing or arguing his readers into thinking for themselves about the values, relationships and goals that govern their lives, and, in doing so, to strip them of the self-flattering illusions to which both the age and their own inclinations made them prone."[305] This is true as far as it goes. However, to the extent that *The Moment* exemplifies Socratic irony (as Pattison indicates and as I have argued above), Kierkegaard's ultimate trick is to give the impression that the press is a legitimate form of communication when, for him, it is actually "the deepest degradation of the human race."[306] Herein lies Socratic irony at its highest pitch: it becomes what it hates for the sake of something greater; it dies so that life may go on.

Moreover, on this point, the Christian and Socratic features of Kierkegaard's task come together at last. As Pattison puts it, "The dissimilarity between faith and philosophy consists precisely in their similarity."[307]

Conclusion

As with Chapter 3, the task of the present chapter has been to examine Kierkegaard's response to developments in modern technology. Yet, whereas the previous chapter focused on a variety of technologies (railroad, telegraph, etc.), this unit has been limited to information technology. This division corresponds to the singular importance Kierkegaard assigns to the popular press—a technology that, in summoning the *Publikum*, leads to a swarm of societal ills.

Still, Kierkegaard's approach to the print media is dialectical. He appropriates what he condemns, not out of absentmindedness or incoherence but out of a devotion to the example of Socrates, who ironically used the Athenian establishment against itself. In a number of ways, Kierkegaard too prefers to lean into the dynamics of modern Western culture. The age of leveling is inevitable, and, if it is to be resisted, it first must be seen for what it is. Of course, cultural elites (ecclesiastics, the intelligentsia, politicians, and so on) endure by suggesting otherwise, but, Kierkegaard argues, they are concealing the truth. The individual's choice to live for God and neighbor can only come into focus when the crisis of the present age—a crisis initiated and hastened by information technology—is encountered.

Now that Kierkegaard's own response to technological development has been surveyed, it is time to *apply* his thought to contemporary questions in the philosophy of technology. After all, it is one thing to learn what Kierkegaard thought of omnibuses and various nineteenth-century periodicals but something else to consider how his philosophy might address the culture of thermonuclear weapons and the iPhone. Two chapters will be dedicated to these sorts of questions—one that fleshes out a Kierkegaardian critique of Google (with particular focus on its eponymous web search engine), another that seeks to determine Kierkegaard's influence on twentieth-century philosophy of technology and, in turn, to identify where he might be situated in current debates about technology. Due to the wide-ranging subject matter, these chapters will hardly be exhaustive. However, if they stimulate further thinking on and research into this topic, their goal will be accomplished.

From Hegel to Google: Kierkegaard and the Perils of "the System"

The name "internet" first achieved currency in the mid-1980s. A shorter, more graceful version of the term "internetwork," it came to be applied to the medium by which computers from around the world are connected. Thus, the internet is, by definition, a *global* instrument, facilitating the exchange of information between computer systems and those who use them. At first, this exchange was as clumsy as it was limited; however, technological advancement has increased its accessibility and its rapidity. No enterprise better represents this development than Google.

Google is a multinational corporation, whose eponymous search engine has revolutionized the way in which internet users seek and process information. According to its company homepage, "Google's mission is to organize the world's information and make it universally accessible and useful."[1] But is this goal *actually* desirable? Indeed, might it be dangerous?

If, as this book has argued, Kierkegaard ought to be considered a contributor to the philosophy of technology, it stands to reason that his thinking can be applied to contemporary technological questions. This chapter aims to make such an applicative move, paying particular attention to the issues raised by Google. It will proceed in two main ways. First, it will sketch how the question concerning Google harks back to the kind of questions Kierkegaard raised about Hegelianism in his day. In turn, it will analyze Google's mission (or business model) and show how it recalls what Kierkegaard saw as the trouble with Hegelian thinking—namely, a tendency toward speculation that encourages an abstract relation to existence and, with it, a diminished interest in ethico-religious engagement. The claim here, then, is *not* that Google was founded on Hegelian principles per se; still less is it a straightforward identification of the two. Rather, the point is that, from a Kierkegaardian perspective, Hegel and Google stand in an analogous relation to one another: both promote the systematic collection and distribution of knowledge at the expense of concrete human flourishing.

Second, it will argue that Kierkegaard's brush with Hegelianism disposed him to extol and to foster a different way of thinking—*Betragtning* or "contemplation," which centers the existing person and so is propaedeutic to an earnest engagement with reality. If Google harvests information at a rate heretofore unseen, Kierkegaard suggests that one should not conflate its task with thinking as such. In the end, then, to read Kierkegaard is a kind of *therapy*, not only redressing philosophy's tendency toward abstraction but also anticipating the same (and more pervasive) propensity in technology.

The rise of Google

In his 2008 book *Against the Machine: Being Human in the Age of the Electronic Mob*, Lee Siegel quips that "popularity is Web culture's Holy Grail."[2] His complaint, in particular, is directed at the internet's prioritization of popularity over expertise—a tendency that he likens to a high-school "class clown," who "[transforms] his very self . . . into a product that [fits] the needs of others."[3] What he fails to note is that this is precisely what the founders of Google, Larry Page and Sergey Brin, foresaw when they started the company in 1998. Recognizing the staggering proliferation of sites on the Web, they sought a means to "evaluate and rank the value of all the pages on the Web."[4] The result was a new search engine, which, today, has become the chief mediator of data on the internet.

As a search engine, Google is designed to receive requests for information and, in seconds, to return with pertinent results. With informational pages on the internet numbering in the billions, this is no easy task. Google copes by indexing the frequency with which a search result is recognized (or "clicked"), providing, in turn, an unparalleled ability to manage "a seemingly infinite amount of information."[5] The more clicks, the higher a given page is ranked—and the more Google collects in advertising fees.

It is, doubtless, a shrewd money-making program, garnering the company assets in the vicinity of 100 billion dollars. Yet, Google insists that it is a force for the common good. A few reasons account for this fact. First, Google has imposed order on that which was once thought "ungoverned and ungovernable,"[6] namely, the internet. Siva Vaidhyanathan even compares the search engine to Julius Caesar, whose Roman dictatorship was a welcome change to the "state of chaos and civil war"[7] that preceded it. Second, by collecting hard data about user preferences and by conducting psychological research,[8] Google has become adept at *directing* the way individuals interface with the Web. As Eric Schmidt, then CEO of Google, put it in 2010, "[People] want Google to tell them what they should be doing next . . . .We know roughly who you are, roughly what you care about, roughly who your friends are."[9] Like a trusty guide, Google knows how to get people where they want (or think they want) to go. Third, and following on from the previous point, Google styles itself as a progressive, democratic institution, which puts science in service to human productivity—an approach that recalls many of the great inventions of the Industrial Revolution, only now the product is *knowledge*. "In Google's view, information is a kind of . . . utilitarian resource,"[10] whose excavation and efficient distribution is the foundation of constructive thinking.

But what effect does Google and its services have on its customers, that is to say, on the millions of persons (including this one) who use it everyday? It is at this point that Kierkegaard's critique of Hegelianism—limited here to his 1846 text, *Concluding Unscientific Postscript to Philosophical Fragments*—is worth remembering. After all, in this critique, Kierkegaard not only questions but even warns against a number of features that would come to characterize Google over a century later, from the prioritization of objective knowledge to the construction of a "system" to which all knowledge is subordinated. Of course, this critique cannot be taken as an indictment of Google per se; indeed, some commentators have even wondered if it is a fair critique of Hegel himself.[11] At the same time, however, the lack of a clear-cut historical referent should not discredit the position sketched in the *Postscript*, for, as will be seen, the book's concerns about Hegelianism anticipate the era of Google in striking fashion. One might even wonder if Google does not epitomize the "system" and its dangers better than Hegel (or, for that matter, nineteenth-century Danish Hegelianism) ever could.

Johannes Climacus and the perils of the system

Before discussing the *Postscript* and its critique of Hegelianism, it is worth surveying G. W. F. Hegel and how his thinking relates to the rise of modern technology. Hegel is typically regarded as one of the leading figures of absolute idealism—a post-Kantian movement in philosophy, which sought "to penetrate existence to find the rational, conceptual truth, which is its core or kernel."[12] This ambitious task is already manifest in the extensity of Hegel's philosophical output; he composed treatises on logic, nature, and spirit (*Geist*), among others. Just as the young Hegel admired Napoléon—whom he called a "world-soul," unafraid of "reaching across the world and ruling it"[13]—so did he seek to master the history and scope of the philosophical enterprise. That this objective would come to overlap with the rise of modern technology may seem surprising. However, as will be seen, Hegel himself realized that the development and application of technology goes hand in hand with the progress of philosophy.

Hegel, technology, and the "Systematic Exposition of Philosophy"

In his well-known work, *The Technological Society* (1964), Jacques Ellul claims that one of the defining traits of the modern West is a "clear technical intention," that is to say, "a mass intention, clearly understood and deliberately guiding the whole society in a technical direction."[14] For Ellul, this phenomenon arose by "historical coincidence."[15] On the one hand, a variety of special interests, each pursuing the most efficient way to accomplish its objectives, collectively rendered technology dominant in Western society; these interested parties included industrial capitalists, the state, and the bourgeoisie. On the other hand, there was a philosophical or theoretical impetus behind this change. Here, according to Ellul, a number of figures and issues might be named, but Hegel garners explicit mention as one who "reinforced" this technical intention.[16]

Precisely how Hegel reinforces the dominance of technology in the West is not addressed in *The Technological Society*, though it is clear that, for Ellul, Hegel's importance lies in his connection to Karl Marx. It was Marx, he notes, who argued that technology's influence must proceed according to Hegelian dialectic. Whereas the proletariat had once endured "the hardships of technical advance without sharing in the triumphs," Marx predicted that the ongoing development of technology "would automatically bring about the collapse of the *bourgeoisie* and of capitalism."[17] In this way, thesis would yield to antithesis, and, following Hegel, a synthesis would emerge— namely, a society lacking in class and wealth distinctions.

And yet, Marx's appropriation of Hegelian dialectic notwithstanding, there is actually a significant difference between the two thinkers on technology. As Stephen Houlgate argues, Marx understands "technological change, change in the material forces of production, as the primary determining factor in history."[18] In other words, for Marx, a given culture's intellectual, political, and religious life ultimately stems from its technological development and skill. But Hegel takes just the opposite approach. On his reading, "what is primary in a society is its general character of 'spirit,' and the development of the technological power of a culture or society itself stems from the kind of character the society has."[19] Hence, for Hegel, society's *Geist* orders its technology, not the other way around. The value (or lack thereof) of an innovation or a tool is established by the way that it is seen or understood in a civilization.

Hegel illustrates this point in *The Philosophy of History*. In discussing the development of the "Oriental World," he notes:

> [The Chinese] knew many things at a time when Europeans had not discovered them, but they have not understood how to apply their knowledge: as *e.g.* the Magnet, and the Art of Printing. But they have made no advance in the application of these discoveries. In the latter, for instance, they continue to engrave the letters in wooden blocks and then print them off: they know nothing of movable types. Gunpowder, too, they pretended to have invented before the Europeans; but the Jesuits were obliged to found their first cannon. As to Mathematics, they understand well enough how to reckon, but the higher aspect of the science is unknown.[20]

In contrast, Hegel sees the "German World"—whose "Spirit is the Spirit of the new World"[21]—as one developing "in the direction of *Science*."[22] By "science" he does not merely mean the investigation of the natural world through empirical research; rather, he is referring to something more encompassing, namely, "development of Thought—the abstractly Universal."[23] In other words, the modern Germanic world is no longer content to think along the lines of "that elder scholastic theology"—namely, in focusing on "the doctrine of the Church"—but, instead, unfolds toward an ever-expanding "Universality."[24] Reason has become conscious of itself as universal, as that which is "immanent within the world and so . . . genuinely objective."[25]

In this scenario, writes Hegel, an "interest in the contemplation and comprehension of the present world" becomes paramount.[26] The world appears to reason as knowable, as *searchable*: "that which is diverse from [the pure Ego], sensuous or spiritual, no longer presents an object of dread, for in contemplating such diversity it is inwardly free and can freely confront it."[27] Human thinking stands confident before the world of knowledge, "challenging the external world to exhibit the same Reason which Subject [the Ego] possesses."[28] Here, indeed, empirical science emerges as "the science of the World," inasmuch as its commitment to view phenomena in terms of "Sorts, Genera, Power, Gravitation, etc." comes to characterize the relation of the human subject to the external object.[29] The goal is now to understand the world as a "system of known and recognized Laws," wherein "that only passes for truth in which [Man] finds himself at home."[30] This is as true for "the Spiritual side of things" as it is for the physical;[31] even "man's eternal destiny [his spiritual and moral position] must be wrought out *in himself* [cannot be an *opus operatum*, a work performed *for him*]."[32] In modernity, human knowledge and human autonomy have come to reinforce one another, and that is precisely why, for Hegel, the Germanic world stands as an advance over previous civilizations. As Houlgate puts it, "Hegel understands human beings to be *essentially* self-determining."[33]

This turn to the abstractly universal forms the basis of Hegel's own well-known "System" (*Das System*). In his first major work, *Phenomenology of Spirit* (1807), Hegel writes that his aim is to make philosophy scientific—that is to say, systematic. As he explains:

> The true shape in which truth exists can only be the scientific system of such truth. To help bring philosophy closer to the form of Science, to the goal where it can lay aside the title "*love* of knowing" and be *actual* knowing—that is what I have set myself to do. The inner necessity that knowing should be Science lies in its nature, and only the systematic exposition of philosophy itself provides it.[34]

This search for actual or absolute knowledge means that truth cannot just be sought here and there; rather, it "involves grasping the way [the truth's] various components contribute not only toward constituting the whole but each other as well."[35] In other words, the true philosophy is the one that, quite literally, *comprehends* the historically evolving consciousness of truth, thereby becoming a "single unity-in-diversity, a single dialectical system, which will constitute a 'systematic science.'"[36]

This is, doubtless, an ambitious task. Yet, for Hegel, it is an ambition consonant with its place in history, and so it should not frighten but inspire. In his inaugural lecture in Berlin, Hegel speaks of the need to pursue knowledge with boldness, even to pry open the very mystery of the universe:

> The courage of truth, faith in the power of mind is the first condition of philosophical studies; we should honor ourselves and hold ourselves worthy of the highest. We cannot think highly enough of the greatness and power of mind; the hidden essence of the universe possesses no power in itself to resist the courage of knowledge; it must open itself to us, placing its riches and depth before our eyes for our enjoyment.[37]

According to Merold Westphal, this passage epitomizes the "spirit" of Western philosophy, which, since the time of Plato, has stressed a "technical interpretation of thinking."[38] Such, indeed, was the reading of Martin Heidegger, whose 1957 seminar[39] on Hegel's *Science of Logic* identified Hegel as a "prime instance of onto-theological thinking" and therefore of the "rationalist demand for total intelligibility."[40] Yet, for Heidegger, it is just this kind of thinking that undergirds modern technology. As Westphal adds, "What Heidegger calls calculative thinking (and the Frankfurt school calls instrumental reason) is thought in the service of technology."[41] To be sure, there is a line from metaphysics to science to technology—a line that, as has been seen, Hegel himself recognized. And this point leads to a key conclusion: modern technology is not a historical accident but, rather, the fruit of (Western) philosophical *development*.

Of course, in recent decades, Heidegger's "The Question Concerning Technology"[42] has become almost obligatory reading in the philosophy of technology. However, long before Heidegger's critique of Western metaphysics, there was Kierkegaard's own multifaceted response to modernity, which raised a number of concerns about Hegel's role in the formation of Western thinking. As noted above, these concerns are found throughout Kierkegaard's authorship, though they receive particular (and pointed) emphasis in *Concluding Unscientific Postscript*.

Climacus against the system

Attributed to the pseudonym, Johannes Climacus, the *Postscript* takes aim not only at Hegel's "System" but, indeed, at the very notion of philosophy as *Wissenschaft*. As Climacus sees it, Hegel's attempt to comprehend existence systematically is speculative and, therefore, problematic on a number of fronts. For one thing, the System fails to distinguish between thinking *about* existence and existence as such. The former may strive for philosophical closure—for a totalizing grasp of knowledge—but the latter rules out this possibility in advance. After all, the one who is existing cannot transcend that which is still unfolding, namely, one's existence: "Whoever is himself existing cannot gain . . . conclusiveness outside existence, a conclusiveness that corresponds to . . . eternity."[43] To think otherwise, Climacus jokes, is not only "a false presupposition but a comic presupposition, occasioned by . . . a kind of world-historical absentmindedness [of] what it means to be a human being."[44] It follows that truly systematic thinking requires a being who "in his eternity is forever concluded and yet includes existence within himself,"[45] and only a deity could be described in such terms. Thus, self-deification emerges as the gravest danger facing not only Hegelian philosophy but all who crave systematic clarity and total knowledge. As Westphal notes, it "is as producers and consumers of the system that Hegelian humanity takes itself to be divine."[46]

Of course, it would be one thing if such ambition promoted human flourishing; however, Climacus "sees it as pure loss, the loss of our humanity, our true self."[47] Indeed, herein lies the second overarching problem with the System: it mistakes the accumulation of knowledge with human well-being, which, in truth, is always bound up with particular concerns and needs. In other words, even if one were able to systematize all knowledge, the complete *application* of that knowledge would remain an unattainable horizon, ever frustrating the System's pretensions of closure. With this in mind, Climacus makes note of the irony that "through Hegel a system, the absolute system, was brought to completion—without having an ethics."[48] Climacus does not attribute this absence to an oversight on Hegel's part. Rather, it is a consequence of his project as such, which prescinds from the concrete and, thereby, adopts a disembodied vantage point:

> This objective thinking has no relation to the existing subjectivity, and while the difficult question always remains—namely, how the existing subject gains entrance into this objectivity in which subjectivity is pure abstract subjectivity (which again is an objective qualification and does not signify any existing human being)—it is certain that the existing subjectivity evaporates more and more.[49]

All of the information in the world, if it is abstracted from actual existence, amounts to nothing, and so the thinker disposed to objective knowledge "becomes something infinitely great and nothing at all."[50] She has an untold expanse of data but no concrete life in which to make it meaningful. Of course, one may object that such data is fascinating, *intéressant*. Climacus would even grant the point.[51] But life, he insists, is far more than amusement: "To be simply and solely a human being means something more than playing party games this way."[52]

This problem only deepens when the possibility of transcendence is introduced. After all, no matter how glittering its results, the system is framed by human knowledge, and, precisely for that reason, it is discontinuous with transcendence. In contrast, as Climacus points out, "Christianity wants to give the single individual an eternal happiness," and this hope "wants to intensify passion to its highest, but passion is subjectivity and objectively it does not exist at all."[53] Thus human beings nurtured on the system will lack passion precisely to the extent that they are preoccupied with immanent objectivity. They "have" the truth but relate to it the wrong way or, even worse, fail to relate to it at all. That is why Climacus eulogizes the epistemological humility of Gotthold Lessing, who contended that relating to the truth is as much about the *how* as the *what*: "Lessing speaks of a striving for truth; and he uses a peculiar phrase regarding this urge for truth: *den einzigen immer regen Trieb* [the one and only ever-striving drive]."[54] And yet, if the pursuit of truth is *immer regen*, then the very notion of an objective system falls into contradiction, though Climacus quips that there nevertheless may be good reasons for calling it such: "Perhaps the systematician thinks this way: If on the title page or in the newspaper I call my production a continued striving for the truth, alas, who will buy it or admire me; but if I call it the system, the absolute system, everyone will buy the system."[55] This is particularly relevant passage, for it implies that information, when packaged a certain way, can be commodified. Indeed, as Climacus sees it, Hegel's system is a prime example of how information can be sold, bought, and finally consumed in order to "*demonstrate, rationally*, the superiority of [a given] system and to demand everybody's support."[56] This is what Ellul calls *propaganda*.[57]

Of course, by now, Climacus's reproach of Hegel has become part of philosophical lore, and, to put it in broader terms, the Hegel-Kierkegaard divide has emerged as one of the great fault lines in modern ideas. As Jon Stewart puts it, scholars "seem to assign the two thinkers to opposite ends of the philosophical spectrum."[58] And yet, as is often the case, the notoriety of such a dispute belies its ongoing importance. Even if, following Stewart,[59] Kierkegaard's relation to Hegel is more complicated than often assumed, their respective philosophical approaches have significance well beyond the history of ideas. At stake here is a timeless (and therefore all too timely) question about how persons ought to interact with human knowledge, which never emerges *ex nihilo* but, rather, bears a number of presuppositions and implications, whether anthropological, sociological, or theological. That Kierkegaard recognized this fact distinguished his response to Hegel. Moreover, it renders his views germane when considering what may be the greatest information system ever devised—Google.

A Kierkegaardian critique of Google

Earlier in this chapter, it was noted that Google "rose to the top of the technological heap by tackling the challenge of the era—too much information."[60] However, to note this fact is to say nothing about the significance of a surfeit of information. What end, if any, does it serve? And how does Google's systematic mastery of so much knowledge affect our perception of the company? After all, if Google is able to encompass our relation to virtually all extant knowledge, then is it not, in Hegelian terms, the apex of all intellectual enterprise—the technological embodiment of what Hegel calls "the courage of knowledge"?

That such questions can be asked of Google is, in one sense, ironic. Brin and Page hardly set out to exemplify the Hegelian system; they simply wanted to facilitate the finding of information on the internet.[61] Theirs was not a mission of authority but of service—an objective that, quite literally, received mathematical expression in an algorithm designed "to recognize the sources and pages that informed what was popular [on the Web]."[62]

And yet, it is just here that a Kierkegaardian critique of Google might begin, for Brin and Page *assume* that more information distributed to more people is more useful. Peter Barron, Google's head of communications for Europe, the Middle East, and Africa, puts it like this: "Google starts from a position that we seek to make information available to the widest number of people. Google is built on free expression."[63] To use Google, then, is to tap into the values hailed by Hegel as hallmarks of the Germanic world—namely, reason and freedom. Google expresses reason's consciousness of its own utility, of its ability to transform the world by answering the questions (however trivial, however profound) that beguile us. What is more, this ability is no longer confined to the ideas or innovations of a particular thinker but, rather, is mediated digitally as a kind of collective genius, unfettered by the limitations intrinsic to a given person's intellect. Through Google, notes Vaidhyanathan, "I have access to more information that I could ever know what to do with. So it feels somewhat liberating that I don't have to remember very much."[64]

Still, in the *Postscript*, Climacus cautions against such assumptions. First, he points out that information, in and of itself, is not a good. That is to say, it always already arrives conditioned by extrinsic factors. For example, the vehicle for a piece of information influences the way in which one receives it. Climacus makes this point clear in his critique of Hegel's system. Hegel implies that his thought, *qua* system, is "positive," possessing a secure basis in "sensate certainty, historical knowledge, [and] speculative result."[65] And yet, snaps Climacus, "all of this positive fails to express the state of the knowing subject in existence; hence it pertains to a fictive objective subject."[66] Thus the *form* of Hegel's system belies its *content*. That which is presented as objective is, in truth, an "approximation-knowledge,"[67] since its positivity is abstracted from the existing subject, who, in turn, "comes to know much about the world, nothing about himself."[68] The upshot is an "illusion"[69] wherein the person perceives that she knows more even as she really knows less.

Something very similar could be said of Google. It does not just deliver information but also shapes the way persons relate to it; it is a medium that, as Marshall McLuhan famously observed,[70] becomes the message. Recall that Google responds to queries in two main ways: (i) by determining how often search results are clicked and (ii) by ranking these results from most to least popular. What the user receives, then, is not necessarily the best piece of information, still less something akin to wisdom. It is simply what is popular or "trending," filtered, moreover, according to "the identity, history, and location of the user."[71] This *modus operandi* is no secret, but Google's reputation for scientific rigor, not to mention financial heft, lends it an air of authority. The reality, however, is that Google only provides what Climacus calls "approximation-knowledge," not just in terms of the veracity (or lack thereof) of the information it locates but also inasmuch as its provision of objective information "pertains to a fictive objective subject, and to mistake oneself for such a subject is to be fooled and to remain fooled."[72] In other words, Google may strive to resolve our questions, but, for Climacus, this ambition itself is problematic: there are no final answers in human existence—for at the core of human existence is a contradiction, namely, that the self is a "synthesis" of the eternal and the temporal and therefore finds rest in neither alone[73]—and so the true teacher "keeps open the wound of negativity" and indicates that genuine learning consists of "continually striving."[74] This is a far cry from Google's unqualified language of "search results" and "useful" information.

Thus Google, as an efficient digital system designed to distribute putatively objective information to existing subjects, is based on a flawed premise that has the potential to mislead persons about the nature of knowledge and its relation to human existence. But this concern only involves the systematic propagation of information as such. There is also a concern about how *much* information Google mediates to us. As Vaidhyanathan puts it, "Google puts previously unimaginable resources at our fingertips—huge libraries, archives, warehouses of government records, troves of goods, the comings and goings of whole swaths of humanity."[75] In this way, Google is a virtual apotheosis of Enlightenment thinking, positioning every aspect of human life under the watchful eye of impersonal reason. The step from Hegelian *Vernunft*[76] to the "Googlization of 'everything'"[77] is surprisingly short.

But herein lies a problem. As Climacus sees it, "the very home of existence" does not lie in thought but in ethics, not in the accumulation of knowledge but in a "continued striving" by which the "existing individual . . . directs all his attention to the actuality that *he* is existing."[78] But one can only enter into actuality when abstract reflection stops; otherwise one will end up like Trop—a character in J. L. Heiberg's 1826 vaudeville, *The Critic and the Beast* (*Recensenten og Dyret*), who brags that his studies have led him to *almost* take the bar exam on numerous occasions.[79] "Everyone laughs at this," notes Climacus, "but when one chatters speculatively in the same manner in the realm of truth, in the shrine of science and scholarship, then it is good philosophy—genuine speculative philosophy."[80] The joke, then, is on those who prioritize reflection over action. But if one wants to break the cycle of reflection—and, for Climacus, this move is necessary if one is to flourish as a human being—then reflection *must* come to a stop. But how? Objective data itself cannot halt reflection. The opposite is rather the case: the more information, the more reflection. Part of Climacus's critique of Hegel is that *das System* does not adequately address this problem and, instead, relies on glib obfuscations such as "in logic . . . reflection is stopped by itself and . . . doubting everything flips over into its opposite by itself."[81]

Yet, if Hegelianism fails on this point, one can be sure that Google, whose raison d'être is to disseminate information, does so as well. After all, the company's profitability is tied to an oversupply of data, since its search results always include advertisements, thereby making Google the world's "most efficient (and valuable) advertising delivery service."[82] It would be bad business, then, for Google to restrict the flow of information, regardless of the effect on the user. To be sure, popular lingo suggests that people "surf" the internet, but, in truth, they face a "sheer avalanche of choices [that] can inhibit [them] from taking action."[83] Moreover, and perhaps just as dangerously, too much information renders the acquisition of knowledge routine, even uninspiring. As David Shenk puts it, "Information, once rare and cherished like caviar, is now plentiful and taken for granted like potatoes."[84] When information arrives disconnected from one's concrete existence, it becomes superfluous—a mere matter of course or, at best, an idle curiosity, which may help pass the time but neglects to encourage a transition to the ethical life.[85]

With this sort of scenario in mind, Climacus insists that the only solution lies with the single individual, who must refuse to participate in an otherwise interminable flirtation with objective data. As he goes on to explain:

> If the individual does not stop reflection, he will be infinitized in reflection, that is, no decision is made. By thus going astray in reflection, the individual really becomes objective; more and more he loses the decision of subjectivity and the return into himself. Yet it is assumed that reflection can stop itself objectively, whereas it is just the other way around; reflection cannot be stopped objectively, and when it is stopped subjectively, it does not stop of its own accord, but it is the subject who stops it.[86]

Within the context of the *Postscript*, these comments are directed toward the would-be philosopher, who does "not want to become a ludicrous creature by being transmogrified—*eins, zwei, drei, kokolorum* [one, two, three, hocus pocus]—into speculative thought."[87] Otherwise, he will see neither himself nor his interlocutors as human beings, flesh and bone; otherwise, philosophy will become a mere game in which parties "make sport of each other."[88]

However, as discussed in Chapter 2, Kierkegaard would expand on these insights in his next work, *A Literary Review*. There he argues that, via the print media, this philosophical problem has reached sociocultural proportions. In turn, he abandons Climacus's humor and adopts a far more austere tone: "the present age" *in toto* has embraced reflection and, with it, a skeptical relation to authority, tradition, and ultimately God himself. In this context, utility trumps truth, and so the arbiters of utility—from the inventors of technological devices to the shapers of public opinion— are confused with the truth. They have become what, in an older theological parlance, are termed *idols*.

There is a connection, then, between systematic thinking and deification. According to Climacus, it follows from the notion of system itself. Whereas concrete human existence is limited, often messy, and constantly subject to change, the system is ostensibly abstracted from these conditions, providing access to objective knowledge. Such knowledge is thought to be clear, reliable, and therefore conclusive, even as human existence is anything but that. Indeed, if there *were* an existing being whose knowing is transparently and steadfastly conclusive, it would have to be a divine one. As Climacus argues:

> Whoever is himself existing cannot gain this conclusiveness outside existence, a conclusiveness that corresponds to the eternity into which the past has entered. . . . [T]hat he himself is existing implies the claim of existence upon him and that his existence, yes, if he is a great individual, that his existence at the present time may, as past, in turn have the validity of conclusiveness for a systematic thinker. But who, then, is this systematic thinker? Well, it is he who himself is outside existence and yet in existence, who in his eternity is forever concluded and yet includes existence within himself—it is God.[89]

Of course, Climacus's point here is that, to the extent that Hegelian thinking is understood as system, it is confused with divine thinking. This confusion forgets that, like all human thinking, the Hegelian system was developed *in* time and consequently bears the limitations of temporality. To neglect this fact is comical at best, perilous at worst. It renders Hegel either a "ludicrous" creature, who thinks that he is something he is not, or "the good Lord" himself, in which case his thinking is taken as the *summum bonum*.[90]

This line of reasoning shifts the focus back to Google, for, as Nicholas Carr writes, Google has emerged as "the Internet's high church," which has a "messianic" sense of purpose.[91] Vaidhyanathan agrees, adding that "Google's appeal is almost divine," enrapturing its votaries with apparent "miracles" while concealing "the ways in which [it] exerts control over its domain."[92] Yet, in the wake of Kierkegaard's insights, this should come as no surprise. Google's goal is to organize—indeed, to systematize—

human knowledge. It is an ambitious objective, so much so that "Page and Brin put forth ten commandments to guide Google's ethos."[93] The wisdom once received in the cloud on Mount Sinai (Exod. 24:15-18) is now promulgated from the glass-encased buildings of the Silicon Valley.

Of course, Google's use of a decalogue[94] might be seen as little more than an ironic twist on the vision statements often issued by corporations. And yet, at the very least, the similarity does suggest that the founders of Google grasp the precariousness of their project, that the very attempt to order human knowledge is a risk of, quite literally, biblical proportions. As one Google employee has remarked, "We try really hard not to be evil. But if we wanted to, man, could we ever."[95] Part of this power derives from the confidence, or faith, that people invest in knowledge brokers—a point that Climacus raises vis-à-vis the Hegelian system and one that Detweiler reiterates in relation to Google:

> Our faith in Google's answers is nearly absolute. We rarely question their algorithmic authority. In fact, we imbue it with an almost mystical power. Type a few letters into its search engine, and Google will fill in the blanks, anticipating our intentions. It autocompletes us—in almost any language. With the rise of personalized search, Google seems to do more than half the thinking for us. So how should we think about Google? Have we defaulted to blind faith in the wisdom of their engine?[96]

As Climacus long ago realized, the underlying question here is that of authority. On what grounds does a human-engineered system merit our faith? Does the matter of existence not throw a spanner in the works of systematic projects, no matter their relative value? Nevertheless, with Google's influence (and revenue) increasing at almost exponential rates,[97] consumers are apparently ignoring these questions and, in effect, deifying Google. As Detweiler quips, "'I saw it on Google' [has] become a twenty-first equivalent to 'God said it, I believe it.'"[98] Googling, one might very well conclude, is the new praying.[99]

If such concerns seem removed from the conscious experience of most users of Google, there are more mundane problems as well. Clinical studies have now confirmed that using Google alters brain functioning.[100] It presents persons with a glut of information and, in neurological terms, overloads the working memory, making it "harder to distinguish relevant information from irrelevant information, signal from noise."[101] As a result, attention is divided and meaningful activity hindered.[102] It is the extensity of information, rather than the intensity of thought, that now characterizes our intellectual *habitus*. As Carr puts it, "We are evolving from being cultivators of personal knowledge to being hunters and gatherers in the electronic data forest."[103] But that is not Google's problem. The more information it provides, the more it fulfills its mission. Indeed, if "the medium is the message," Google conveys that knowledge is there to be sold, bought, and consumed. "The last thing it wants is to encourage leisurely reading or slow, concentrated thought. Google is, quite literally, in the *business of distraction*."[104]

Here, again, Carr effectively reiterates Climacus's concerns about system building and, in turn, traces a Kierkegaardian critique of Google. As with previous systems, Google cannot help but divert persons from ethico-spiritual exigencies. It does not orient learning toward wisdom about oneself but, instead, treats it as a means to an external end, whether the rapid assimilation of knowledge for the sake of social productivity or the simple satisfaction of idle chatter. In short, Google molds its users into fetishizers of information, who prefer to browse and to manipulate data rather than to apply it.[105]

What, then, are persons to do? Certainly many answers might be ventured here. Consideration, however, will be given to Kierkegaard, who strives to counteract systematic thinking with a marked emphasis on *Betragtning* or "contemplation." As will be seen, where Google ties one up in the abstract assessment of information, Kierkegaard promotes a way of thinking that centers the existing person.

Betragtning as therapy in the age of Google

The word *Betragtning* appears, in one variation or another, over 1,000 times in Kierkegaard's authorship. Similar to the German *Betrachtung*, it can be translated in a number of ways, including "consideration," "meditation," and "contemplation." The latter seems particularly apt, as the verb *betragte* means "to look at" or "to regard." This optical connotation dovetails nicely with the typical English usage of "contemplation," defined as "thinking in a concentrated manner about something." People often speak of contemplating a beautiful landscape or a religious icon. Thus, it is a matter of attending to, but never dominating, a given object.

In Kierkegaard's authorship, the meaning of *Betragtning* becomes clearer when it is contrasted with two other terms that turn up in his writings—*Spekulation* and *Reflexion*. The former, naturally, is translated as "speculation," and, though it too bears visual connotations, it tends to imply a disconnection from what is at hand. To speculate, as Webster's defines it, is to "review something idly and inconclusively." In the *Postscript*, Climacus's frequent criticisms of *Spekulation* echo this meaning, since, as has been seen, the trouble with the System is precisely that it weakens an earnest engagement with reality.

Reflexion is a more ambiguous term. Although a topic that outstrips the present discussion, Kierkegaard's use of the term varies across contexts. Importantly, however, his most famous utilization of *Reflexion* comes in *A Literary Review*, which lambasts the reflection of the present age for imprisoning persons in a state of ethical lassitude, wherein the good is pondered but not acted upon.[106] This application of the term is etymologically correct, for the Latin cognate literally means "to bend back." *Reflexion*, then, suspends the individual in thought. It is a necessary exercise at times, but, for Kierkegaard, it is "not the kind [of thinking] that springs from and reinforces any deep, demanding commitments on the part of the individual."[107]

In contrast, Kierkegaard treats *Betragtning* as a mode of thought that grounds the existing person. To contemplate is to focus on those questions that underpin human life.

Who am I? Why am I here? Why is anything here? What is the good life? What happens after death? Who (or what) is God? How can I relate to God? Thus contemplation correlates with "earnestness" (*Alvor*), which Kierkegaard defines as "the relationship to the eternal."[108] Together they are essential precursors to existential growth.

This link between contemplation, earnestness, and self-development is, perhaps, best seen in Kierkegaard's various upbuilding discourses—a series of writings that foster *Betragtning* in two main ways. First, Kierkegaard's upbuilding discourses implore the reader to practice contemplation. Indeed, it is noteworthy that *Two Upbuilding Discourses* of 1843—the collection that inaugurates Kierkegaard's cycle of upbuilding writings—begins by recommending contemplative practice. As he writes in the opening prayer of "The Expectancy of Faith," the book's first discourse:

> When in mournful moments we want to strengthen and encourage our minds by contemplating those great men, your chosen instruments, who in severe spiritual trials and anxieties of heart kept their minds free, their courage uncrushed, and heaven open, we, too, wish to add our witness to theirs in the assurance that even if our courage compared with theirs is only discouragement, our power powerlessness, you, however, are still the same, the same mighty God.[109]

Kierkegaard does not use *betragte* here but, rather, the more informal phrase, "by the thought of" (*ved Tanken om*). Nevertheless, the Hongs rightly translate it as "contemplating," since that term more fully conveys Kierkegaard's meaning. After all, he is extolling an earnest consideration of these biblical icons, not a fleeting or frivolous thought. In doing so, he also implies that his own authorship is a means to that end—a place where such figures can be encountered and pondered.[110]

Unsurprisingly, then, contemplation surfaces elsewhere in his upbuilding writings. In 1847's "What We Learn from the Lilies in the Field and from the Birds of the Air," Kierkegaard urges the reader to contemplate nature for the sake of spiritual growth. In fact, as he sees it, created things such as flowers and birds are ideal for contemplative practice. While human teachers instruct with words and stand over against their interlocutors, the lilies and the birds are silent, beckoning. In this way, they function in the manner of icons. As Kierkegaard explains:

> Out where the lily blooms so beautifully, in the field, up there where the bird is freely at home, in the heavens, if comfort is being sought—there is unbroken silence; no one is present there, and everything is sheer persuasion.
>   Yet this is so only if the person . . . actually gives his attention to the lilies and the birds and their life and forgets himself in contemplation of them and their life, while in his absorption in them he, unnoticed, by himself learns something about himself—unnoticed, since there is indeed sheer silence, no one present. The . . . person is free of any and all co-knowledge, except God's, his own—and the lilies.[111]

This call to contemplation, Kierkegaard adds, is implicit in Jesus's own words: "*Look at [Betragter] the lilies in the field,*" look at [*betragt*] them—that is, pay close attention to them, make them the object—not of a fleeting glimpse in passing but of your contemplation [*Betragtning*]."[112] Thus Kierkegaard suggests that his discourse is a contemplative aid: it is tendered for "properly looking at"[113] the lilies and the birds.

And yet, Kierkegaard does more than *exhort* the reader to practice contemplation. Rather, as George Pattison has argued, his use of language epitomizes as well as induces something akin to contemplation. In particular, the rhetoric employed in Kierkegaard's upbuilding literature seeks "to construct an ethical and religious appeal to the reader," albeit in such a way that one is persuaded, rather than pressured, to adopt a "determinate response."[114] By addressing the reader in conversational, inquisitive fashion and by presenting "an array of personified subjunctive possibilities," the discourses commend not only values such as love and patience but, in Pattison's words, "the inner dialogue of the self with itself."[115]

Thus Pattison reinforces the notion that Kierkegaard does not merely endorse *Betragtning* but, quite literally, fosters it. The upbuilding discourses require the reader to slow down, to concentrate, and to open himself or herself up to the presence of the eternal, both in the world and in the self. In this way, they become occasions for self-actualization and, hopefully, for a relationship with the divine—a relationship that is irreducibly mysterious, always grounded in the here and now (what Kierkegaard refers to as *Øieblikket* or "the moment"),[116] and, therefore, qualitatively different than the abstracted information tendered by Google.

Intriguingly, Carr himself suggests that a return to such a way of thinking is critical if human beings are to avoid losing "our humanness . . . the very qualities that separate us from machines."[117] But this resistance cannot be done *for* human beings. It is not a matter of finding the right piece of information, still less of downloading an app for enhanced productivity. Rather, it involves the cultivation of alternative habits and practices. Carr mentions "self-awareness" and "courage,"[118] and Neil Postman urges that persons must become more "conscious" of their interaction with media, lest the "spiritual devastation" of "the age of advanced technology" catch them unawares.[119] Persons may be willing to fight physical oppressors but, Postman goes on, "what if there are no cries of anguish to be heard? Who is prepared to take arms against a sea of amusements?"[120]

This is a decisive question, because it hits on the fact that the struggle against technology—against the instrumentalizing frame of the system—is ultimately an internal struggle. After all, even if persons *wanted* to eliminate modern technology, technology would be required in order to carry out the task: "De-technologizing would paradoxically confront us with one of the greatest technological challenges of all."[121] What is needed, then, is a spiritual revolution, yet it is precisely here that Postman despairs: "I fear that our philosophers have given us no guidance in this matter."[122] Indeed, while intellectual attention is diverted to either abstract problematics or overt threats, "public consciousness has not yet assimilated the point that technology is ideology," since "no *Mein Kampf* or *Communist Manifesto* announced its coming."[123]

On this point, however, Postman is not exactly right. It is true, of course, that modern technology has not arrived with the thunderous menace of a Hitler or a Stalin, but, then, it is doubtful whether such a comparison is even apt. For that reason, it may very well be that the best responses to technology will not come from tracts seeking to "overcome" its threat but, rather, from those that cultivate a different way of thinking about and participating in reality. Put in concrete terms, having a conversation, taking a walk in the woods, or spending time in prayer may very well be more important in this area than any particular philosophical or sociological retort. And it is just here that Kierkegaard's authorship stands out. For Kierkegaard did not only realize this point but, rather, made it central to his literary task.

Conclusion

Google has come to rule the internet because it organizes data at a rate heretofore unseen. Yet, as a manifestation of the human desire to create an absolute system of knowledge, it is hardly the first of its kind. The Googles of the world will always be with us.

However, precisely for that reason, Kierkegaard remains (and will remain) an important figure. A self-styled "corrective," he stands as a reminder that the glittering results of Google ought not be confused with thinking itself. Moreover, his upbuilding writings serve as apertures for contemplation—a mode of thought that centers the existing person and, in turn, prepares the way for an earnest engagement with the whole of reality. Perhaps *that* is why Heidegger, himself concerned with the obtrusive nature of technical thinking, once famously observed, "There is more to be learned philosophically from [Kierkegaard's] 'edifying' writings, than from his theoretical ones."[124]

And yet, if that is true, then what is Kierkegaard's legacy as a thinker confronting the question concerning technology? On the one hand, it has been shown throughout this study that Kierkegaard engages many of the problems associated with modern technology, from the rise of a media-dominated culture to the ongoing quest for systematic knowledge. On the other hand—and as Heidegger suggests—it appears that Kierkegaard can only be called a "philosopher of technology" with a degree of imprecision. He does not so much provide abstract analyses of the nature and purpose of technology as seek to tease out its existential implications. What this particular emphasis means for the reception of Kierkegaard's thinking about technology is the business of this book's sixth, and final, chapter—a chapter that will center on Kierkegaard's influence on subsequent philosophers and theologians who asked the question concerning technology.

The Question Concerning Technology: Searching for Answers with Kierkegaard

In considering a thinker's position on a given issue, one obviously must attend to what he or she wrote about it. Moreover, it is critical to study the context in which he or she lived and worked, since, to quote Hans-Georg Gadamer, "the self-awareness of the individual is only a flickering in the closed circuits of historical life."[1] This book has followed these two basic principles, not only showing that Kierkegaard had much to say about the encroaching dominance of modern technology but also situating his ideas in the industrializing culture of nineteenth-century Denmark. In and of itself, this might be enough to show that Kierkegaard's thinking ought to be viewed in light of the question concerning technology. However, as will be seen, there are other ways in which we might consider Kierkegaard's relation to technology—namely, his association with later thinkers.

Indeed, there is a sense in which this approach is especially appropriate with regard to Kierkegaard. Unlike a Hegel or a Barth, Kierkegaard was not considered an "essential" thinker in his day, not even in Denmark. The Danish literary critic and philosopher Georg Brandes published the first monograph about Kierkegaard, and it was intended "to free Danes from [Kierkegaard's] influence."[2] Other Danish commentators followed suit. Harald Høffding, while appreciative of Kierkegaard's talents, nevertheless criticized Kierkegaard's tendencies toward disunity, equivocation, and polemics.[3] Likewise, Troels Frederik Troels-Lund—a distinguished Danish historian, and himself a relative of Kierkegaard—concluded that "Kierkegaard was little better than an eccentric, though obviously one of genius."[4]

Thus it was outside of Denmark—first in Germany and then elsewhere in Europe—that Kierkegaard would come to fame. But here another problem turned up. For a variety reasons, ranging from translation issues to the character of the *Zeitgeist*,[5] Kierkegaard's writings arrived piecemeal, their contents often misrepresented, misunderstood, or even just misappropriated. As Roger Poole notes, "Kierkegaard's communication, which he insisted upon calling 'indirect,' has most often been indirect in its effect and, quite often too, only indirectly alluded to, even by those who have fallen heavily under its influence."[6] For Poole, this tendency to manipulate or to borrow from Kierkegaard can be found in a variety of authors. For example, Kafka's diary suggests that he drew on Kierkegaard for inspiration; Jaspers's turn from psychiatry to philosophy is permeated by a Kierkegaardian emphasis on *Existenz*; and in Sartre's magnum opus, *Being and*

Nothingness (*L'Être et le Néant*, 1943), "Kierkegaard's influence is everywhere though his name is unspoken."[7] And this is to say nothing of Martin Heidegger, in whom "the affliction Harold Bloom calls 'The Anxiety of Influence' is particularly marked"[8]—a topic to which this chapter shall return.

It stands to reason, then, that Kierkegaard's relation to the philosophy of technology, particularly as it emerged in the twentieth century, will often be more implicit than explicit. Put differently, several of the figures who have come to be associated with the rise of the philosophy of technology—for example, Herbert Marcuse, Gabriel Marcel, Jacques Ellul, and, above all, Heidegger—have significant connections to Kierkegaard's authorship, even as Kierkegaard's influence on their analyses of technology remains underexplored. A key goal of this chapter is to redress this problem. In particular, it will contend that Kierkegaard's role in the development of the philosophy of technology is palpable, if not always obvious. This case will be made in two overarching ways: (i) by surveying Kierkegaard's reception among thinkers concerned with question of technology and (ii) by noting parallels, as well as differences, between Kierkegaard and his inheritors on this issue. The outcome will be partly philological, partly speculative. That is to say, while a kind of *Familienähnlichkeit* (in the Wittgensteinian sense) between Kierkegaard and later thinkers on technology will be apparent, it will also be clear that aspects of Kierkegaard's thinking were disregarded, frequently without explanation. Here, then, there will be speculation as to why Kierkegaard's response to technology was not fully embraced—a point worth considering, given the frequent exclusion of Kierkegaard from the ranks of "philosophers of technology."

Yet, before beginning, a few qualifications are in order. First, it must be stressed that not every twentieth-century thinker dealing with technology can be discussed in this chapter. Such an approach would require a monograph unto itself and, even then, would likely prove unwieldy. As a result, I will restrict my focus to a few notable figures, each of whom has significant connections to Kierkegaard. Inevitably, the question of omissions will arise: no Nikolai Berdyaev? no Jacques Maritain? Again, though, the goal is not to provide a comprehensive assessment of the reception of Kierkegaard's thinking among those concerned with technology. It is simply to establish Kierkegaard's importance for this conversation and, in turn, to encourage further work on the subject.

Second, despite its title, this chapter will not limit itself to what is typically considered the "philosophy of technology." In other words, it will attend to *theology* as well as to philosophy. Of course, the distinction between these two fields is itself a question, as witnessed in analyses of figures such as Thomas Aquinas and Martin Heidegger.[9] Even a thinker like Thomas Merton—himself squarely situated in the tradition of Christian spirituality—has noted points of overlap between existentialist themes and "the climate in which monastic prayer flourished."[10] So, to whatever extent there is a "philosophy of technology," it would not at all be surprising if its interests were to intersect with those of theology or, so to speak, a "theology of technology."

But that is not the only reason to consider theology here. As will be seen, Kierkegaard's thinking on technology had a conspicuous influence on a number of twentieth-century theologians. Indeed, it may even be the case that, given its

Christological and eschatological undertones, Kierkegaard's response to technology is more suited to a theological reception, though, intriguingly, Kierkegaard proved exacting even for ascetics such as Merton. Hence, in the end, it is not unreasonable to wonder if Kierkegaard is to thinking about technology as the Desert Fathers are to dogmatic theology—not so much an opponent as a thorn in the flesh, whose value lies in keeping open the "wound of negativity."[11]

Kierkegaard's relation to philosophical responses to technology

This chapter aims to explore Kierkegaard's relation to twentieth-century responses to technology, but what, exactly, does it mean to *relate* to something? The word itself can be traced to the Latin *referre*, which means "to carry back" or "to refer." Hence, strictly speaking, "to relate" is to carry something from one place to another, though this meaning has evolved into the current definition of the term—namely, "to have or to establish a connection between things." Sometimes such a connection is direct, but it need not be. For example, a father and a son are related, but we also say that third cousins are related. In the latter case, we do not use the word "related" improperly, even if the connection between third cousins is more indirect than that of father and son. Things, then, are said to be "related" in a plethora of ways, and so the word's plurivocity makes it crucial to focus on *how*, and *to what degree*, they are related.

These points, however general, are worth bearing in mind with regard to Kierkegaard's relation to the philosophy of technology. For, as will be seen, it is not possible to speak of Kierkegaard's relation to the field and its representatives in univocal fashion. Put in more concrete terms, while Kierkegaard's connection to someone like Heidegger is well established, his relation to an Ellul or to a Merton is less obvious. And even this fact is not as straightforward as it may seem. After all, Heidegger was notoriously reticent to acknowledge Kierkegaard's otherwise palpable encouragement to his thinking, while other authors draw on Kierkegaard far more sparingly and yet do so in clearer fashion.

Is, then, the present exercise so imprecise as to render it futile? Two reasons suggest not. First, while some ambiguity is inevitable, it is still possible to discern Kierkegaard's general impact on twentieth-century thinking about technology. In other words, this chapter should make clear that Kierkegaard was an interlocutor with a number of the figures who are considered pioneers in the philosophy of technology. From this point follows a second: in terms of the history of ideas, this chapter should encourage the expansion of our understanding of nineteenth-century responses to the technological condition. After all, a well-regarded anthology on the topic begins with a section entitled "The Historical Background"—a section that runs from Plato all the way to Karl Marx and Friedrich Engels, only then to move on to Heidegger and to other twentieth-century authors.[12] Alas, Kierkegaard is not mentioned in this context. It is hoped that this chapter will prevent future omissions.

Walter Benjamin

Walter Benjamin, one of the leading figures associated with the so-called "Frankfurt School," grew up in *fin de siècle* Berlin—a "city deeply marked by the rampant growth of German industry in the last quarter of the nineteenth century."[13] A literary critic by trade, Benjamin became involved with "avant-garde artists, architects, and filmmakers"[14] in the 1920s, including film theorist Siegfried Kracauer, philosopher Theodor Adorno, and Dadaist painter Hans Richter. This group "focused on the possibilities that new technologies and industrial practices were opening up for cultural production," and Benjamin himself was intrigued by the "relationships among technology, media, and the human sensory apparatus," particularly the way in which various technological instruments "*mediate* the complex processes by which we perceive, act upon, and function within that world."[15] Yet, Benjamin was not just a theorist but also a kind of historian. Similar to Kierkegaard, who identified the press as essential to the rise of bourgeois modernity, Benjamin's *Arcades Project* (*Das Passagen-Werk*) saw the *passages couverts* of nineteenth-century Paris as an "organizing metaphor" for the West's shift to a culture of urban capitalism.[16]

Indeed, as Rainer Nägele notes, it may be that Kierkegaard plays a "discreet but decisive role in Benjamin's thought in general."[17] Benjamin did pen a "sustained examination"[18] of Kierkegaard's thought—albeit in a review of a book by Adorno[19]— and direct and indirect references to Kierkegaard are scattered throughout his writings. Moreover, the bulk of these references are found in the posthumously published *Arcades Project*, which, as noted, resembles Kierkegaard's own interest in modern culture. In this way, "basic themes"[20] linking the two thinkers emerge, a few of which concern the topic of this study.

First, Benjamin repeatedly calls attention to Kierkegaard's aesthetic stage.[21] Like Adorno, he is critical of Kierkegaard's emphasis on an "inward spirituality"[22] ostensibly prescinded from material conditions, and he applies this reproach to Kierkegaard's rendering of the aesthetic, especially as found in the first volume of *Either/Or*. The Kierkegaardian aesthete, Benjamin goes on to argue, is destined to suffer as one who has lost connection to the real world and who, therefore, is preoccupied with simulacra. "Melancholy, pride, and images"[23] are Benjamin's words for this kind of existence, but that should not imply that Benjamin fails to see the peculiar potency of the aesthetic. Just as Charles Baudelaire, the great poet of modern Paris and the object of much of Benjamin's attention in *The Arcades Project*, possessed an ability "to live in the heart of unreality (semblance)," so does Kierkegaard's aesthete bear the same "signature of heroism."[24] Put differently, Kierkegaard's pseudonyms such as Johannes the Seducer and Constantin Constantius are literary types of a real-life flâneurs such as Baudelaire and Arthur Rimbaud.

Hence, even if "Benjamin must be read as a critic of Kierkegaard,"[25] it is also true that his critique of modern Western society is informed by Kierkegaard's representation of the aesthetic. The word "representation" here is crucial, because Benjamin did not have extensive knowledge of Kierkegaard's authorship.[26] Consequently, his criticism of "Kierkegaard" is actually criticism of Kierkegaardian personae that the Dane himself tendered as critiques of certain existential possibilities, particularly those that thrive in the modern world.

It stands to reason, then, that Kierkegaard and Benjamin *share* concerns about techno-cosmopolitan modernity. According to Marcia Morgan, Benjamin and Kierkegaard draw on a common "literary-philosophical spirit"[27] by which the reader is persuaded and provoked rather than ordered and propitiated. They both complain that the conditions of modern life have enervated the ability of people to make decisions: "Benjamin and Kierkegaard lament the fall of decisiveness into melancholic contemplation or, taking Kierkegaard's term, reflection."[28] Whereas persons once were willing to struggle for the good (however conceived), they now respond to it with "meaningless resignation."[29] Max Pensky summarizes Benjamin's analysis in a manner that evokes Kierkegaard too: "Melancholy infects any political cause that it seeks to support, for the melancholic's support (of anything) is always tinged with the atmosphere of meaninglessness. Politically, meaninglessness translates into resignation, the precise negation of decisiveness."[30] For Benjamin, the demise of decisiveness is felt most acutely in political life, whereas for Kierkegaard it is in religious life. Still, the task of each thinker is to break the spell of melancholic reflection by way of a critical-dialectical project that plumbs "the very bottom of the well of subjective inwardness."[31]

This exploration is, for both thinkers, inseparable from an exploration of modernity as a technological age. *Pace* Adorno, who viewed Kierkegaard as a type of bourgeois intellectual, "living on private income, shut in on himself,"[32] this study has demonstrated that Kierkegaard was keenly aware of the self's interchange with society in general and with technology in particular. To recap two broad examples, Kierkegaard emphasized that the urban-cum-industrial character of modern life—whereby human beings are clustered in cities, linked by communications and transportation technologies, and marshaled for business—is the sine qua non for the creation of a mass society. Second, he claimed that the print media amplifies this very social order, inasmuch as the press fosters the superficial reflection needed to facilitate compliance with bourgeois culture. Benjamin has been described in similar terms: "Everything that Benjamin brings together in *The Arcades Project* is based on the moments of the beginning and creation of the modernist city in 1841–46 (the peak years of Kierkegaard's pseudonymous authorship), through train travel, photography, steam power and gas lighting industrialisation."[33] Thus Benjamin was one "equally fascinated and repelled by the emergence of the city."[34]

Still, if it is clear that the modern city, with all of its infrastructure and quotidian rhythms, "provides the landscape for both [Kierkegaard and Benjamin] to work and deviate in order to articulate indirect politics,"[35] to what extent can their views on a given technology be put in conversation? Here a range of possibilities emerge, but I will restrict myself to two—one that is palpably relevant (journalistic media), another that is more speculative (cinema). As with Kierkegaard, Benjamin's writings probe the rise and influence of information technology. In June 1927, Benjamin published a piece entitled "Journalism." Penned in the wake of Charles Lindbergh's pioneering nonstop flight from Long Island to Paris, Benjamin complains that the "Paris evening papers" have been "exposed"[36] by the hullabaloo surrounding Lindbergh's feat. First, they have revealed a tendency toward "regrettable frivolity,"[37] stirring up expectations that have no basis in reality. Indeed, less than two weeks earlier, the papers had reported that Frenchmen Charles Nungesser and François Coli were the first aviators to cross the Atlantic Ocean, when, in truth, their plane disappeared en route and was never found. Second, "all the papers"[38] in Paris falsely claimed that Lindbergh once had been a student at L'École normale. Thus, Benjamin observes:

> Among the medieval Scholastics, there was a school that described God's omnipotence by saying: He could alter even the past, unmake what had really happened, and make real what had never happened. As we can see, in the case of enlightened newspaper editors, God is not needed for this task; a bureaucrat is all that is required.[39]

Like Kierkegaard, then, Benjamin anticipates the problem of "fake news." That is to say, both thinkers recognize that print technology gives those who control it the power to sway public opinion by disseminating misinformation. Moreover, both understand this power as an annexation of the truth itself—a technological claim to divinity, thereby rendering the Christian God superfluous.

Also like the Dane, Benjamin draws attention to the fact that the press does not just tender information disinterestedly but, rather, belongs to a wider economic network. "How much capital," he wonders, "has migrated into publishing from the banking, textile, coal, steel, and printing industries?"[40] Whereas most persons take an "abstract view of publishing," assuming that literary success resembles a "lottery," Benjamin aspires to embark on a "sociological study" of *who* is actually issuing printed material and *why* they are doing so.[41] Of course, Benjamin's desire to research these questions is quite different than Kierkegaard's polemical response to the print media. Still, the same insight underlies works such as *A Literary Review* as it does Benjamin's Marxist exploration of the publishing industry—namely, that publications require more than a prima facie analysis, since, in addition to being "funny," "interesting," "provocative," and so on, they also bear a "social function."[42] To uncover this function—and in highlighting the Danish press's tendency toward leveling, Kierkegaard attempts to do just that—is to reveal what Benjamin terms "the spiritual currents of the nation."[43]

So, if the texts that people read divulge their spiritual disposition, what does that say about a culture dedicated to the rapid dissemination of information? Benjamin addresses this question in a 1934 piece called "The Newspaper." He states that "impatience is the state of mind of the newspaper reader," yet, in qualifying this claim, he arrives at a Kierkegaardian insight: "This impatience is not just that of the politician expecting information, or of the speculator looking for a stock tip; behind it smolders the impatience of people who are excluded and who think they have the right to see their own interests expressed."[44] Just as Kierkegaard compares the press to a dog kept by the public, so does Benjamin observe that the newspaper is an instrument for the ostensive empowerment of its readers, "who are instantly elevated to collaborators."[45] Both thinkers, then, perceive the dialectical relationship between press and public, and both would agree that the newspaper constitutes "the limitless debasement of the word."[46] At the same time, however, Benjamin closes with a Marxist optimism[47] foreign to Kierkegaard's writings. He declares that, in dissolving the associations between "literary competence" and "specialized training," the modern newspaper is preparing the way for a different and potentially salvific form of literature, whereby what once was the province of a few is now "public property."[48]

A similar tension is evident in Benjamin's writings on cinema, perhaps especially in his celebrated treatise "The Work of Art in the Age of Its Technological Reproducibility" (*Das Kunstwerk im Zeitalter seiner technischen Reproduzierbarkeit*, 1935). On the one hand, "The Work of Art" bears Kierkegaard's intuition that, in modernity, arts and letters have become increasingly subject to efficient and mass reproduction. Kierkegaard largely focuses on the daily press's influence on literature, but analogies to other aesthetic media are not hard to find—for example, the difference between an original Rembrandt portrait and a modern photograph. While the latter accelerates "the process of pictorial reproduction," the former is essentially a one-off, expressing what Benjamin calls "the here and now of the work of art—its unique existence in a particular place."[49] For that reason, one can speak of an "authentic Rembrandt" and, indeed, observe firsthand the Dutch master's *Self-Portrait* (1660) in New York City's Metropolitan Museum of Art. With technological reproduction, however, artwork is now made *for* reproducibility, whereby "*a mass existence*" is substituted for "*a unique existence*" so that "*the reproduction* [can] *reach the recipient in his or her own situation.*"[50] Again, then, something once reserved for cultural elites (a symphony by Mozart, performed live in a palazzo) is now available to masses (at home or the gym via a Spotify account), and, even though this "may leave the artwork's other properties untouched," these changes "certainly devalue the here and now of the artwork."[51]

For Benjamin, as for Kierkegaard, this "massive upheaval" is "related to the mass movements of our day."[52] Hence, as George Pattison puts it, "It is clear that [Benjamin's] analysis can lend itself to . . . complaints about the leveling tendencies of modern society."[53] At the same time, however, Benjamin is more sanguine than Kierkegaard about art's politicization. In a society where "literary competence is no longer founded on specialized higher education but on polytechnic training," and where "the newsreel demonstrates unequivocally that any individual can be in a position to be filmed," an environment "from which all customary behavior toward works of art is today emerging newborn."[54] Benjamin is particularly optimistic about cinema, which not only "furthers insight into the necessities governing our lives . . . by its exploration of commonplace milieux through the ingenious guidance of the camera," but promises "*to establish equilibrium between human beings and the apparatus.*"[55] That is not to suggest that Benjamin fails to see the danger of the "technologization" of art: it has indeed contributed to "the present crisis" in Western society and has been exploited by National Socialism, which seeks to "*aestheticize politics*"[56] and to harness the "proletarianized masses while leaving intact the property relations which they strive to abolish."[57] Still, Benjamin retains a confidence that the people ultimately will evince a "*progressive reaction*"[58] to reproducible artwork. The "capacity for improvement"[59] inherent in a technological medium such as cinema means that art is becoming akin to history itself.

In a recent text, Eric Ziolkowski concedes that "Kierkegaard would supposedly have been wary of the association Walter Benjamin perceived between the cinematic medium and the increasingly emergent 'masses.'"[60] Thus he reasons that Kierkegaard's influence "seems not to have extended to that German thinker's pioneering theory of film."[61] This may be true, sensu stricto. And yet, this section has shown that the two have much in common, including a notable interest in how technology has shaped mass society. They both write in the midst of the modern West, while, in some sense, pointing beyond it. They are both, in the end, "urban vagabonds."[62]

Martin Heidegger

No twentieth-century interpreter of Kierkegaard is more important than the German philosopher Martin Heidegger. And yet, as has been noted, Heidegger's reading of Kierkegaard is notoriously ambiguous, exhibiting a plain debt to the Dane's thought but either reappropriating it or leaving it unacknowledged. For some, in fact, it is not a stretch to say that Heidegger is untruthful about his indebtedness to Kierkegaard. As John Caputo writes:

> Heidegger not only understates his dependence on Kierkegaard, he misstates it. Heidegger differs from Kierkegaard, not as an ontological thinker from an ontic, as he likes to make out, but principally in terms of the degree to which Heidegger has formalized and articulated Kierkegaard's ontology in a more systematic, professorial manner.[63]

Caputo's claim here is not an example of revisionist history. As early as 1920, Heidegger himself noted that he had been "misinterpreted" as a disciple of Kierkegaard.[64] A few years later, Heidegger would admit that he received "impulses" from Kierkegaard, though he quickly added that it was Edmund Husserl, and not Kierkegaard, who "gave me my eyes."[65] Indeed, by 1943, Heidegger was almost flippant about Kierkegaard's influence on his philosophy, even writing that "Kierkegaard is not a thinker but a religious writer"[66]—a claim that is not only misleading with regard to Heidegger's appropriation of Kierkegaard but also patently confused in its understanding of Kierkegaard's project. For Kierkegaard *was* interested in exploring genuine philosophical problems, despite (or even because of) his religious predilections. As Caputo puts it, "Both Kierkegaard and Heidegger were drawn to the Aristotelian critique of Platonic intellectualism. Contrary to Heidegger's view of the matter, Kierkegaard pressed a strictly ontological issue."[67]

Whatever the case—and, indeed, the larger question of Heidegger's intellectual development is far too complex to delve into here—this brief sketch shows that Heidegger's relation to Kierkegaard cannot be sought in candid autobiographical statements. Nor can it be found in his comments on the Dane's oeuvre, since, in truth, Heidegger's writings seldom refer to Kierkegaard. Even if readers of the two thinkers "come away feeling certain that Kierkegaard has been a significant influence on Heidegger's thought," it is nevertheless the case that "Heidegger never explicitly acknowledges a direct or significant Kierkegaardian influence on *Being and Time*, and he is grudging, at best, in crediting Kierkegaard with a role in his intellectual development."[68] And if this problem is true of *Being and Time*, long considered one of existentialism's *loci classici* due to its phenomenological analysis of Dasein,[69] how much more true must it be of Heidegger's output after *Being and Time*, when Heidegger seems to turn "in focus from Dasein to Being."[70]

Notably, it is the so-called "later Heidegger" who devotes sustained attention to technology. This fact would seem to mitigate the possibility of Kierkegaard's influence, but, before reaching this conclusion, it makes sense to survey Heidegger's understanding of technology. As early as *Being and Time*, Heidegger had been critical of what he saw as the Cartesian basis of the modern world. While Descartes understood the *cogito* as a private entity—a subject set in opposition to objects—Heidegger argues that the human being stands open to existence in such a way that inner-outer, subjective-objective distinctions do not obtain.[71] In other words, we "always depend on a pre-established network of purposes that draws on the established traditions of our community and shows us things . . . as genuinely meaningful within our world."[72] Dasein never simply wills that a given thing be used in this or that fashion; rather, Dasein receives a way of looking at and responding to what is found in the world.[73]

For Heidegger, this is precisely why the culture of modern technology is so important—and perilous. In his posthumously published *Contributions to Philosophy* (*of the Event*) (*Beiträge zur Philosophie* (*Vom Ereignis*)), written roughly a decade after *Being and Time*, Heidegger begins to focus on how the "technological understanding of our existence" constitutes "the degenerate condition of the modern world."[74] Modernity has been hailed as an epoch of enlightenment, as a time "that has *dispelled* all bewitchery," but "it is just the reverse."[75] What Heidegger calls "machination" (*Machenschaft*) has attained "ultimate dominance," thereby directing "everything toward calculation, utility, breeding, manageability, and regulation."[76] It is important to underline that, for Heidegger, "machination" does not merely pertain to technological devices or to scientific pursuits. It is, rather, a "*revelation of beings as a whole* as exploitable and manipulable objects."[77] This way of looking at the world certainly owes much to Descartes, but, according to Heidegger, it actually dominates "the history of being in the previous Western philosophy, from Plato to Nietzsche."[78] In fact, so pervasive is machination that it is no longer perceived as such; it is simply the way the world appears to modern people.[79] The upshot is "the rejection of genuine knowledge," "the dread of questioning," and, at last, "the foundering of the West; the absconding of the gods; the death of the moral, Christian God."[80] On a practical level, moreover, it means that human life tends toward "lived experience" (*Erlebnis*), that is, toward a "superficial stimulus" whereby "we consume neverending quantities of entertainment and information."[81]

In subsequent decades, Heidegger would expand on these themes. In 1949, he delivered a series of talks broadly dealing with technology. One of these, "The Enframing" (*Das Gestell*), was later revised as "The Question Concerning Technology" (*Die Frage nach der Technik*) and presented to the Bavarian Academy in 1953. It has since become a seminal text in the philosophy of technology, even if it was the "locus of the question of being in the late-modern age,"[82] rather than technology per se, that prompted Heidegger to write the piece. In other words, Heidegger's principal interest is rooted in the history of metaphysics, which, as he sees it, is responsible for modernity's "nihilistic 'technological' understanding of the being of entities and its devastating historical consequences."[83]

"The Question Concerning Technology" is indeed precisely that—Heidegger's attempt to think through the meaning of technology, in terms of both its origins and its role in modern society. Through this questioning, he aims "to prepare a free relationship to [technology]," whereby human beings can perceive "the essence of technology" and, in turn, "be able to experience the technological within its own bounds."[84] This goal, however, bears a conundrum: "The essence of technology," Heidegger writes, "is by no means anything technological."[85] Most people assume that they understand what technology is—namely, "a means to an end,"[86] as a knife is to cutting or an airplane to transport—and this is correct as far as it goes. But recognizing the instrumentality of technology does not disclose the essence of instrumentality: "We must ask: What is the instrumental itself? Within what do such things as means and end belong?"[87]

Heidegger answers that instrumentality is a mode of "bringing-forth"[88] or, in the parlance of antiquity, *poiēsis*. It is by no means the only such mode. There is the work of "the crafts and the arts," in which the artisan provides "the irruption belonging to bringing-forth."[89] There is also *phýsis*, "the arising of something from out itself,"[90] as when a bud comes to bloom in the natural world. In each case, *poiēsis* brings something "out of concealment into unconcealment" and thus is a kind of "revealing."[91] Famously, Heidegger notes that the Greek word for "truth" is *alētheia*, which literally means "unconcealment." This insight prompted his conclusion that truth "presupposes a clearing or opening in which entities can be unconcealed."[92] Consequently, the essence of technological bringing-forth, of instrumentality, is not some sort of permanent trait but the way that entities come to presence in and through technology. As Iain Thomson puts it, "The referent of Heidegger's phrase 'the essence of technology' is our current constellation of historical intelligibility . . . [it is] an historical 'mode of revealing.'"[93]

What, then, is shown by the bringing-forth that characterizes technology? Heidegger seems to struggle to find the right words. First, he clarifies that it is "challenging" [(*Herausfordern*)], insofar as technology, especially modern technology, which makes demands of the natural world, forcing it to "supply energy which can be extracted and stored as such."[94] Then he calls it a "setting-upon" (*Stellen*), which further underlines the calculated temerity of modern technology. Heidegger provides an example: "The hydroelectric plant is set [*gestellt*] into the current of the Rhine. It sets [*stellt*] the Rhine to supplying its hydraulic pressure, which then sets the turbine turning. This turning sets those machines in motion whose thrust sets going the electric current for which the long-distance power station and its network of cables are set up [*bestellt*] to dispatch electricity."[95] Heidegger's repetitive use of the verb *stellen* and its variants is significant, for he ultimately identifies the essence of modern technology as "enframing" (*Gestell*). In the mode of *Gestell*, "everything is ordered to stand by, to be immediately on hand, indeed to stand there just so that it may be on call for a further ordering."[96] To see the world in the mode of *Gestell*, then, is to see it as "standing-reserve" (*Bestand*),[97] a term that "designates nothing less than the way in which everything presences that is wrought upon by the revealing that challenges."[98]

In one sense, the claim that things now appear as standing-reserve seems almost obvious, and Heidegger has no trouble finding examples—dams, wind farms, mines, agribusiness, machinery, the lumber industry, journalism, and even the HR (human resources) departments that have become ubiquitous in Western institutions.[99] In another sense, however, Heidegger is talking about a fundamentally mysterious process, since enframing is a *response* to "unconcealment itself, in which at any given time the actual shows itself or withdraws."[100] In other words, while human beings cooperate with the challenging-forth of *Gestell*, they can only do so as those "claimed by a way of revealing that challenges [them] to approach nature as an object of research, until even the object disappears into the objectlessness of standing-reserve."[101] As Heidegger sums up, "Modern technology, as a revealing that orders, is thus no mere human doing."[102] Indeed, he later will add that human beings have been sent or destined to see the world from the perspective of modern technology: "Enframing is an ordaining of destining [*Geschick*], as is every way of revealing."[103]

What, then, can be done? Is this "destining" not "a fate that compels"?[104] For most people—and here Heidegger harks back to his Kierkegaard-inflected analysis of "the they" (*das Man*) in *Being and Time*—enframing is inseparable from everyday life in the modern world and thus has become the de facto lens through which being is understood. This is precisely why Heidegger was so alarmed by modern technology: "As this historical transformation of beings into intrinsically meaningless resources becomes more pervasive, it comes ever more to elude our critical gaze; indeed, we late moderns come to treat even ourselves in the nihilistic terms that underlie our technological refashioning of the world."[105] At the same time, however, Heidegger insists that he is not a technological determinist. The era of technological nihilism, like any other era, is given as a field for the enactment of human freedom, but this enactment requires attention, lest people "misconstrue the unconcealed and misinterpret it."[106] Hence, when the human being "becomes one who listens, though not one who simply obeys,"[107] then she is free. This freedom is twofold, consisting positively in the person's actualization of the essence of what it means to be human—a being open to the truth of being—and consisting negatively in the person's resistance to the dominance of *Gestell*. For "where this ordering holds sway," Heidegger notes, "it drives out every other possibility of revealing. Above all, enframing conceals that revealing which, in the sense of *poiēsis*, lets what presences come forth into appearance."[108]

The free person, then, is one who is not blinded by the radiance of enframing—the "machines and apparatus of technology"[109]—and instead attends to the essence of technology. Only in this way is salvation made possible. Thus, Heidegger quotes his muse, the romantic poet Friedrich Hölderlin: "But where danger is, grows / The saving power also."[110] Enframing is "the extreme danger,"[111] since it treats "our worlds and ourselves as resources to be optimized" to such an extent that "we could lose the very sense that anything is lost with such a self-understanding."[112] That is why Heidegger's task first and foremost lies in asking the *question* concerning technology. In a theme that resurfaces in subsequent writings such as "Memorial Address"—a 1955 talk that criticizes modern society's preference for "calculative thinking" over "meditative thinking"[113]—Heidegger concludes by calling for a return to questioning: "The closer we come to the danger, the more brightly do the ways into the saving power begin to shine and the more questioning we become. For questioning is the piety [*Frömmigkeit*] of thought."[114]

This is, of course, only a sketch of Heidegger's analysis of modern technology, but it is sufficient to begin to ponder how Heidegger and Kierkegaard might be related in this area. Since Heidegger himself is not forthcoming on this question, this comparison will require a measure of speculation. The goal, however, is not to provide a definitive examination of Heidegger's relation to Kierkegaard (something not possible in this context anyway) but to demonstrate that Kierkegaard's thought is pertinent to the philosophy of technology—a field with which Heidegger is associated, despite the primacy of his larger philosophical project. In order to meet this task, it will be important to open with a few general observations, followed by a closer look at the problem of technology per se.

First, Heidegger assumes that "the question of technology is a species of the general question of how things show up for Dasein."[115] Consequently, Heidegger's later writings on technology build on, rather than break from, the existential phenomenology delineated in *Being and Time*. This point implies that the valence of Heidegger's critique of technology in some sense hinges on the valence of his study of Dasein—a study that has strong resonances with Kierkegaard's thought. For example, as David Lewin puts it, the process of "questioning technology goes hand in hand with the questioning of objectivity and subjectivity."[116] According to Heidegger, the objectivity with which the sciences look at, say, a plant or a planet is but the flipside of the establishment of a certain kind of subject:

> Insofar as being appears in the objectness of the object, it surrenders its determinability to cognition understood in the sense of reflective representation which renders beings to cognition as objects. . . . And with this one has, for the first time, the possibility of what we call the modern natural sciences and modern technology.[117]

Yet, in contrast to this subject-object opposition, so typical of Enlightenment thinking, Heidegger insists that human beings already find themselves *in* the world rather than *over against* it. This is *Dasein's* "thrownness" (*Geworfenheit*). Always already, then, "we live within a world of things that concern us"[118] and Heidegger describes this way of being with things as "care" (*Sorge*). As *Dasein's* "being-ahead-of-itself in its always already being involved in something,"[119] care precedes other types of human activities and concerns, including that of ostensibly neutral or objective thinking. But herein lies the peril of modernity's focus on technology: it designates an abstraction "to represent the model of how knowledge for the most part is,"[120] whereas human life is actually a "complex phenomenon," involving "the forward thrust of the existent into his possibilities in tension with the factical conditions and limitations that he already brings with him."[121]

John Macquarrie has noted that there is a "close kinship"[122] between Kierkegaard and Heidegger (not to mention other existentialist thinkers) regarding this approach to human nature. Indeed, Kierkegaard was among the pioneers (along with figures such as Blaise Pascal and Johann Georg Hamann) of this critical response to post-Cartesian foundationalism. If, for the foundationalist, true knowledge is "certain and indubitable,"[123] and if, in turn, the means of acquiring true knowledge is to abstract from personal feelings and perspectives, then it might rightly be said that one of Kierkegaard's great intellectual tasks was to refute foundationalism. In anticipation of Heidegger, Kierkegaard's pseudonym Johannes Climacus insists that human finitude ipso facto excludes the possibility of a complete system of knowledge: "In [such] a logical system, nothing may be incorporated that has a relation to existence, that is not indifferent to existence."[124] This requirement, however, is patently absurd, since even the thinker who tries to develop such a system has to start it *herself*—that is, as a human being "thrown" (to use Heidegger's terminology) into a world of concerns and interests. There is, in other words, no pure "objectness of the object": "The systematic idea is subject-object, is the unity of thinking and being; existence, on the other hand, is precisely the separation."[125] It is a "deception," moreover, to believe that this primordial truth of existence has been overcome by modern progress: existence has "the very same claim upon the existing individual that it has always had."[126]

While Climacus's polemics in *Concluding Unscientific Postscript* primarily are directed at Hegelianism, he elsewhere addresses Descartes's role in modern foundationalism. The posthumously published *Johannes Climacus, or De Omnibus Dubitandum Est: A Narrative* serves as both Climacus's mock autobiography and a philosophical exploration of the problem of doubt. In an 1842 journal entry, Kierkegaard pithily indicates the book's approach: "Descartes has to a great extent laid down his system in the first six meditations. One does not need, then, to always write systems."[127] Indeed, the task of *Johannes Climacus* is to "strike a blow"[128] at Cartesian foundationalism by highlighting the incongruity between Descartes's methodological skepticism (doubt as means of securing objective knowledge) and a life *actually* engaged in such skepticism. Whereas Descartes coolly uses doubt to arrive at philosophical certainty, *Johannes Climacus* implies that this is only possible in the abstract. As Climacus comes to learn, doubting everything is a spiritual undertaking that, if taken to its logical conclusion, leads to a sense of meaninglessness.[129] The most essential human knowledge—the knowledge needed in order to lead a full and meaningful life—is that which also engages qualitative human experience, since human freedom is always exercised in conjunction with anxieties, emotions, and passions.

In light of this common (if not identical) understanding of human nature, it is hardly surprising that both Kierkegaard and Heidegger were critical of the modern West's tendency toward mechanistic reductionism. The former's critique of mass media and mass transport has been explored in depth—a critique that Heidegger's notions of "enframing" and "standing-reserve," sketched above, serve to clarify and to expound. For example, Heidegger sees modern technology as a mode of revealing: the techno-scientific order shows entities to Dasein as things to be consumed and utilized. The world appears *as* standing-reserve. Here Heidegger converts Kierkegaard's insights into a philosophical register. Recall that Johannes Climacus characterizes modernity as "the age that travels by railroad," thereby encouraging it to see history as a "systematic world-historical railroad."[130] An even more salient passage, given the Heideggerian emphasis on "seeing as," comes from *The Moment*, wherein Kierkegaard observes that modern transport cannot help but transform the way human beings experience the world: what once was an arduous journey is now borne while "sitting and smoking a cigar in the cozy dining car"; what was once the "frightful Wolf Ravine" is now part of the tourist trade; what was once a source of "fear and trembling" (the New Testament) is now an occasion for idle and spurious speculation.[131] Of course, Kierkegaard seems to sidestep what Heidegger would call the *ontologisch* analysis of these problems. Nevertheless, the phenomenon that Kierkegaard is describing is strikingly similar— namely, the revealing of entities as "controlled" and "ready for use."[132] For both thinkers, "technology" does not just refer to certain kinds of applications and devices but to a *Weltbild* that ranges across human activity.

It seems fair to say, then, that Kierkegaard and Heidegger have a similar understanding of both the origins and the significance of modern technology. One might even reason, to put it in more provocative terms, that Heidegger's analysis of modern technology is predicated on (if not identical with) Kierkegaard's exploration of the subject. The preceding sketches of the thinkers' respective positions already educe the contours of this relationship, and more narrow studies draw similar implications. Alastair Hannay demonstrates that Heidegger's concept of "leveling" (*Einebnung*) is dependent on Kierkegaard's *A Literary Review* and other writings by the Dane.[133] Just as Kierkegaard critiques modernity's elevation of "human numbers," whereby "animal-man has courage to do the most frightening things as long as he . . . knows that others are doing the same thing,"[134] so does Heidegger discuss the "leveling and the disappearance of Dasein in the Anyone," whereby the individual is "covered up by the public and everyday character of the Anyone."[135] David Dwan maintains that Heidegger's "critique of a media-saturated age"[136] smacks of Nietzsche's influence, though he concedes (perhaps a bit too reluctantly) that Kierkegaard also stands behind Heidegger's concern with mass communication:

> Heidegger derived his term "idle talk" or chatter from Kierkegaard who in *The Present Age* spoke of the devastation wrought on social intercourse by media, advertising and publicity. Everydayness, which Heidegger defines as "averageness, levelling down, publicness, the disburdening of one's Being and accommodation," were all key features of the Kierkegaardian critique of the modern age.[137]

Dwan adds that, for Heidegger, existential inauthenticity occurs whenever Dasein understands its own possibilities in terms of the disclosure of *das Man*—a mode of interpretation that Heidegger calls "publicness" (*Öffentlichkeit*). The chitchat and novelty of publicness are connected to information technology, but they also extend to other modern technological means such as mass transport.[138] Sounding more than a little like his Danish predecessor, Heidegger puts it this way: "In utilizing public means of transport and in making use of information services such as the newspaper, every Other is like the next. This Being-with-one-another dissolves one's own Dasein completely into the kind of Being of 'the Others.'"[139] But it is not only the "existentialistic" Heidegger who resembles Kierkegaard. Clare Carlisle argues that, while the Heidegger of *Being and Time* draws on "immediately recognizable Kierkegaardian concepts and categories," the thought of the later Heidegger expands "to encompass the structures of the Christian life that he had hitherto overlooked"— namely, that "the proper relationship between Being and (human) beings is one of giving and receiving: the movement of a gift."[140] In this way, Heidegger's indebtedness to Christian thinkers in general, and to Kierkegaard in particular, becomes clearer. For the later Heidegger, the true thinker is characterized by the heart's openness to the "unconcealment of being itself, which bestows itself in pure bounty as a gift,"[141] much as Kierkegaard understands the "process through which the existing individual relates herself to the truth" as a "'taking to heart' (*Inderliggjørelse*), a passionate 'making inward.'"[142] Carlisle does not connect this insight to technology per se, but points of correspondence are evident. As has been seen, both Kierkegaard and Heidegger warn that, for all of its practical benefits, the technologically influenced pace and structure of modern life threaten to sunder human beings from questions of ultimate significance.

There is scope for concluding, then, that Heidegger inherited Kierkegaard's anthropology and critique of mass culture, even if he wove these components into a larger—and less obviously Kierkegaardian—project of effecting a formal phenomenology of Being. On this reading, Kierkegaard's insights into the question concerning technology complement but hardly transcend those of Heidegger. But is it possible that Kierkegaard's response to modern technology actually surpasses that of Heidegger? Andrew Komasinski has recently argued that Kierkegaard's most robust critique of technology is found in *The Sickness unto Death*, which reveals "that the solution that Heidegger recommended [regarding technology] turns out to be a form of despair as well."[143] According to Komasinski, Anti-Climacus, the pseudonym to whom Kierkegaard attributes *The Sickness unto Death*, develops a notion of "despair" (*Fortvivlelse*) that anticipates Heidegger's "inauthenticity" (*Uneigentlichkeit*). That is to say, for both Anti-Climacus and Heidegger, the self determined by technology, whether unconsciously or consciously, is one who has failed to attain "the optimal human condition [of] self-completion."[144] However, whereas Anti-Climacus "presents a timeless solution to a timely problem" by urging the self to recognize its "eternal nature" and to refuse to be "defined merely by technology," Heidegger insists that "*Dasein* itself is temporal" and is thus always already being-toward-death.[145] Hence, on a Kierkegaardian reading, even Heidegger's authentic individual is desperately bound to her own finitude and, consequently, cannot overcome the finite world, including the reductionism of technological enframing: "Anti-Climacus's account has the interesting effect of redeeming technology for the self in a way that an authentic orientation towards death cannot."[146]

Of course, Komasinski's claims are arguable. The point, however, is that it is worth pondering whether or not Kierkegaard's thought on technology actually surpasses that of Heidegger. For Komasinski, this possibility lies in the spiritual-cum-theological dimension of Kierkegaard's thought. Others agree. Liselotte Richter, who studied with Heidegger early in her career, gave an overview of Kierkegaard's response to the "age of technocracy" in a 1955 article, not long after the appearance of Heidegger's "The Question Concerning Technology." Her conclusion resembles that of Komasinski: "Faith alone opens the self-understanding of the human being as spirit before God, in contrast to disorientation through the mechanical-quantitative, the numerical."[147]

Such readings, admittedly, tend to conflate Heidegger's thought in general with *Being and Time* in particular, while, as Carlisle suggests, the later Heidegger may prove a better dialogue partner with Kierkegaard. Still, what seems clear is that the two thinkers *should* be put in dialogue—and not just over, say, the history of existentialism. Kierkegaard, no less than Heidegger, was confronted by the question concerning technology, and, though differences can be found, the two thinkers' responses possess a notable degree of continuity. Indeed, at the most fundamental level, both saw questioning itself as a key response to modern technology. When Heidegger claims that "questioning is the piety of thought," it sounds remarkably similar to Kierkegaard's career-long commendation of "Socratic questioning" (*socratiske Spørgen*).[148] In an age of positivism, both show that what falls outside the control of modern technology is just as important, or even more important, than what lies within.

Other philosophers

The above sections on Walter Benjamin and Martin Heidegger represent an attempt to demonstrate, however pithily, that Kierkegaard stands as an interlocutor with two of the twentieth century's preeminent philosophers of technology. In contrast, the subsections that follow are meant to be more like "snapshots," that is to say, glimpses into how Kierkegaard might be linked to others in the field. This intention should not imply that longer studies are unfeasible. On the contrary, it is hoped that these snapshots will illuminate how more robust projects might proceed. Nor should it imply that a Benjamin is of greater importance than a Jacques Ellul. Rather, it is assumed that each of these thinkers is worthy of consideration, not least because of their respective connections to Kierkegaard.

Thus the reason for these shorter sections is pragmatic. Having devoted substantial attention to Benjamin and especially to Heidegger, there is simply not enough space to do the same below. Nevertheless, these snapshots serve a crucial purpose: they trace the extensity of Kierkegaard's influence on the contemporary philosophy of technology.

Herbert Marcuse

Like Walter Benjamin, Herbert Marcuse was associated with Goethe University Frankfurt's Institute for Social Research—the so-called *Frankfurter Schule*. He joined the institute after studying at the University of Freiburg under Edmund Husserl and Martin Heidegger, the latter of which directed Marcuse's *Habilitationsschrift* on Hegel. Heidegger's philosophical interests, including his concern with the essence of technology, remained with his pupil. Still, Marcuse took a "materialist turn" in Frankfurt, advancing an "immanent critique" of modern Western society.[149] The word "immanent" here refers to the attempt to identify contradictions or tensions internal to a given object of study. Consequently, this type of critique seeks to reveal both "the oppressive and the libratory potentials"[150] opened up in modernity, especially through scientific and technological development.

As has been seen, the same dialectic is present in Benjamin's thought. Furthermore, Marcuse's ostensibly cool reception of Kierkegaard echoes Benjamin. In *Reason and Revolution* (1941), which focuses on Hegel's connection to modern social theory, Marcuse provides a brief assessment of Kierkegaard in a chapter entitled "The Foundations of the Dialectical Theory of Society." According to Marcuse, Kierkegaard's social thought centers on the individual, who "is essentially unique" and thus is "isolated from all others."[151] While this tendency concretizes Kierkegaard's philosophy, obviating the possibility that "reason or mankind or the state" can secure existential truth, it also "turns into the most emphatic absolutism."[152] For Kierkegaard, there "is only one truth, eternal happiness in Christ,"[153] and its attainment is to be pursued at the exclusion of sociopolitical considerations. But here, Marcuse concludes, is precisely where Kierkegaard founders. For the real "core of religion" lies in the "concrete struggle for social liberation," and thus Kierkegaard divorces truth from "the social and political vortex in which it belongs."[154]

Though perceptive in places, Marcuse's critique is hardly well rounded, betraying limited familiarity with Kierkegaard's authorship, not to mention the Frankfurt School's general bias against thinkers associated with existentialism.[155] Yet, if one looks beyond *Reason and Revolution*, it becomes clear that Marcuse does bear a resemblance to Kierkegaard, particularly with regard to their thinking on technology. For example, in *One-Dimensional Man* (1964), Marcuse assesses what he sees as the simplistic calculus of the modern West, namely, a techno-logic that has come to dominate society by ostensibly "satisfying the needs of [its] individuals" while, at the same time, subordinating them to "more effective, more productive corporations."[156] The upshot, as Marcuse famously puts it, is a "comfortable, smooth, reasonable, democratic unfreedom."[157]

For Marcuse, to be "unfree" is to exchange certain liberties—say, intellectual and political autonomy—for the sake of material comfort. No matter how diverse and enlightened modern society appears, it is predicated on a "non-terroristic economic-technical coordination which operates through the manipulation of needs by vested interests."[158] In this context, individuals are so thoroughly indoctrinated into the rationale of capitalism that they are bereft of the "consciousness of servitude."[159] "The people recognize themselves," Marcuse explains, "in their commodities; they find their soul in their automobile, hi-fi set, split-level home, kitchen equipment."[160] Thus a consumerist ideology has become conflated with reality itself, leaving "only one dimension, and it is everywhere and in all forms."[161] Here "technological rationality" exhibits sociopolitical repercussions: the institutions and methods of modern Western society produce goods and services that shackle people to those same institutions and methods.[162] As Marcuse continues:

> The means of mass transportation and communication, the commodities of lodging, food, and clothing, the irresistible output of the entertainment and

information industry carry with them prescribed attitudes and habits, certain intellectual and emotional reactions which bind the consumers more or less pleasantly to the producers and, through the latter, to the whole. The products indoctrinate and manipulate; they promote a false consciousness which is immune against its falsehood. And as these beneficial products become available to more individuals in more social classes . . . it becomes a way of life.[163]

Assured of superficial choices and placated by the promise of ever-improving technological amenities, people rarely muster the energy to oppose this societal arrangement. Moreover, when they do, "the modes of protest against this uniformity that surface are quickly or immediately appropriated by the social system."[164] In other words, countercultural modalities of expression—as by athletes, celebrities, and political commentators—are ultimately "sanitised, optimized and consumable"[165] themselves.

Even religion fails to provide a dimension of otherness. The "makers of politics and their purveyors of mass information" have learned to enclose the spiritual life within the system and to use it to augment the established order:

There is a great deal of "Worship together this week," "Why not try God," Zen, existentialism, and beat ways of life, etc. But such modes of protest and transcendence are no longer contradictory to the status quo and no longer negative. They are rather the ceremonial part of practical behaviorism, its harmless negation, and are quickly digested by the status quo as part of its healthy diet.[166]

Just as "operationalism" dominates the physical sciences, whereby the meaning of a thing is reduced to a set of empirical figures, so does "behaviorism" reign in the soft sciences, whereby the "denial of the transcending elements of Reason" begets new habits of thinking that disqualify non-empirical explanations of human action.[167] In this context, religion is approached as a mere aspect of human culture, rather than as a conduit for the supernatural; thus it may have psychological or social utility, but it can never be true or salvific in the highest sense. Technological society "bars a whole type of oppositional operations and behavior; consequently, the concepts pertaining to them are rendered illusory or meaningless."[168]

Marcuse's critique of the modern West harks back to Heidegger[169] and, in turn, to Kierkegaard. Certainly Marcuse's analyses of systematic objectivity, bourgeois indulgence, and religious servility invoke different sides of Kierkegaard's authorship, a number of which have been discussed in this study. Furthermore, he appears to subscribe to Kierkegaard's interpretation of information technology and its role in underpinning the hegemonies of modernity. In *A Literary Review*, Kierkegaard reasons that the power of the *Publikum* lies precisely in its mystery. Conjured by the press, the public enforces the status quo by being everywhere and nowhere at once—a kind of phantom that keeps people in line by making them afraid to be different. Thus, the basis of mass society is, paradoxically, something woolly and fantastical; that is why Kierkegaard must rely on metaphors to describe it, from monsters to profligate Roman emperors. Marcuse offers a similar notion: "The tolerance of positive thinking is enforced tolerance—enforced not by any terroristic agency but by the overwhelming, anonymous power and efficiency of the technological society. As such it permeates the general consciousness."[170] So comprehensive is the techno-logic of modern society that even its failures are viewed as accidents of a larger curve of "growth and progress."[171] As a result, the critic of this order, of "the present age," is sucked into the machinery of leveling. Her jabs become fodder for interesting debate in the media and, as such, participate in and lend credence to the status quo. But real change is unattainable.

Kierkegaard puts forward the "unrecognizability" of humble Christian service as the ideal way of countering this state of affairs, whereas Marcuse, like Heidegger, prefers art as a means "to challenge, oppose or contradict social norms."[172] To what extent this difference is substantive is worth pondering, as is the fact that religion and art frequently underwrite, rather than undermine, the one-dimensionality that Kierkegaard and Marcuse lament.[173] In short, the possibilities for dialogue between the two thinkers are significant, even more so now than in Marcuse's day, when Kierkegaard's individualism was crudely thought to be indifferent to social concerns.

Gabriel Marcel

Often labeled a "Christian existentialist," the French philosopher and playwright Gabriel Marcel favored the term *néo-Socratisme* when describing his literary project.[174] This distinction can be understood against the backdrop of Marcel's feud with Jean-Paul Sartre. It was, after all, Sartre who neatly distinguished between "two kinds of existentialist."[175] As he goes to explain: "First, [there are] those who are Christian, among whom I would include Jaspers and Gabriel Marcel, both Catholic; and on the other hand the atheistic existentialists, among whom I would class Heidegger, and then the French existentialists and myself."[176] Not only did Marcel oppose such simplistic characterizations, but he objected to what he saw as the *terminus ad quem* of Sartre's atheism. The latter's insistence that "man is nothing else but what he makes of himself"[177] seemed to manifest itself in the trials of alleged Nazi collaborators in postwar France. While Marcel worried that these tribunals were often biased and thus unjust, Sartre was willing to defy "traditional principles of fairness and impartiality"[178] under the circumstances. The rift occasioned by these debates proved irreparable, and "the two men remained estranged for the rest of their lives."[179]

At odds, then, with the atheistic existentialism of his day, and identifying his project with the figure of Socrates, Marcel would seem to have a natural affinity for Kierkegaard—a Christian thinker who, following a notable line of like-minded authors,[180] also identified his project as "Socratic." Curiously, however, Marcel claimed to have "developed his philosophy of existence independently of any direct influence ... from Kierkegaard."[181] His professed inspirations were the Frenchmen Blaise Pascal,[182] Maurice Blondel, and Henri Bergson, while "Kierkegaard's influence on his thinking seemed to him to be 'practically nonexistent.'"[183] This, however, may be an exaggeration or, at any rate, a matter of semantics. Marcel had read both *Philosophical Fragments* and *Concluding Unscientific Postscript* prior to the Second World War, the latter on the recommendation of the Jesuit theologian Henri de Lubac.[184] Moreover, Marcel scatters references to Kierkegaard throughout his authorship—for example, in the second volume of *The Mystery of Being* (*Le Mystère de l'être*, 1951) and in *The Problematic Man* (*L'homme problématique*, 1955)—and he was a reader of several authors who "themselves were more or less inspired by Kierkegaard,"[185] both philosophers (Jacques Maritain) and poets (Rainer Maria Rilke). These points of overlap serve to illuminate Jean Wahl's otherwise peculiar summation: "Gabriel Marcel was not particularly influenced by Kierkegaard, although in certain respects his position has paralleled Kierkegaard's."[186]

Wahl does not address the question of technology per se, but he hints at how it might be a concern that bonds the two thinkers. Like Kierkegaard, Marcel aims "to arrive at a domain that he calls the domain of *mystery* in contradistinction to the domain of *problems*."[187] When one becomes aware of mystery, one begins to understand, albeit imperfectly, "the inexhaustible, the non-objectifiable which encompasses us and transcends us, *which we have not invented but recognize*."[188] The tension between that which exceeds human measure and that which is subordinate to it appears in the critiques of mass society offered by Kierkegaard and Marcel. The latter gathers his thoughts on this issue in his 1951 text *Man against Mass Society* (*Les Hommes contre l'humain*). According to Marcel, while technology can "rightly astonish us," there is an "infrangible sphere of being to which techniques are never able to gain access."[189] This sphere entails that which is incalculable and sublime—indeed, mysterious. Here Marcel highlights human reflection, since it involves the always provisional and necessarily self-reflexive task of pondering the origins and ends of one's life. But it is just this sort of thinking that is flagging amid modern technology: "The more techniques advance, the more reflection is thrust into the background."[190]

For Marcel, then, the one who wants to affirm "*metatechnical*" realities such as "mind" or "love" has to become a critic of technological society, for the thinking typical of this "mass world" is reducible to "*training*."[191] It involves mobilizing vast numbers of persons for a given socioeconomic end, while dismissing personal growth (or, as Kierkegaard might put it, upbuilding) as trivial, perhaps even dangerous. As Marcel explains:

> The masses exist and develop (following laws which are fundamentally purely mechanical) only at a level far below that at which intelligence and love are possible. Why should this be so? Because the masses partake of the human only in a degraded state, they are themselves a degraded state of the human. Do not let us seek to persuade ourselves that an education of the masses is possible: that is a contradiction in terms. What is educable is only an individual, or more exactly a person.[192]

As with Kierkegaard, Marcel's "individualism" is by no means indifferent to the political or social sphere, nor is it an uncritical embrace of the *liberum arbitrium*. Rather, it is meant to combat a perversion of the social to which modernity is especially prone, namely, that of "mass impulses to violence."[193] As Marcel continues, "The masses are of their very essence—I repeat, *of their very essence*—the stuff of which fanaticism is made: propaganda has on them the convulsive effect of an electric shock."[194]

Marcel's comments clearly evoke the first half of the twentieth century—the advance of industrialization, the ghosts of trench warfare, labor camps, gas chambers, and nuclear bombs. But they also strongly resonate with Kierkegaard's prior critiques of mass society. In this connection, Marcel's reflections on "techniques of degradation"[195] and on how they make mass society possible are especially important. Citing the memoirs of survivors of Auschwitz and Ravensbrück, Marcel contends that a "utilitarian explanation"[196] is unable to account for such horrors. In other words, the Nazi treatment of prisoners was not a mere expediency; it was a vivid manifestation of a new way in which ideas are received and processed. The task of the philosopher, then, is to tease out the nature of this change.

With this in mind, Marcel turns to propaganda, which he defines as the "manipulation of opinion."[197] Here the trouble is twofold. First, opinion as such "can never serve as a solid foundation for any social or political system," since opinion is "what *people* think, not . . . what *you* or *I* think; in so far as it seems to be something that floats from mind to mind like a murky cloud."[198] And yet, in modernity, it is precisely "as governments of opinion" that tyrannies originate, until they slowly but surely refuse "to recognize the competence of individual opinion."[199] This leads to the second problem: "technical progress in recent years has favoured this manipulation of opinion."[200] Marcel sees propaganda as a corollary to the rise of modern information technology, though his analysis demonstrates that Kierkegaard's concerns about print media are applicable to newer technical innovations. Indeed, Marcel centers his critique on the radio, which "is one of the palpable factors making for our present spiritual degradation."[201] Just as the printing press makes it possible to widely disseminate and empower the viewpoints of an author, no matter how erroneous or glib, so does the radio seem to imbue its operator with supernatural power: "A Hitler or a Mussolini, speaking into the microphone, could really seem invested with the divine privilege of being everywhere at once."[202] Furthermore, this license comes cheap in an era in which radios are mass produced and made available to everyone—a "mechanical method of diffusing thought"[203] that prioritizes circulation over coherence. "How can we allow," Marcel wonders, "that it is quite safe for any individual, whoever he is, to be granted the gift of being everywhere at once in return for the payment of an annual rent for radio time?"[204]

Indeed, that which characterizes the radio—an immense power placed at expeditious disposal—seems to characterize "every kind of technical progress."[205] A thing arrived at through years of difficulty is now usurped "*without having had any share in the effort.*"[206] In *The Mystery of Being*, Marcel expands on this concern. If a scientist or technician achieves a desired result—say, a new drug or a better mobile phone—then this achievement will come to "have a separate existence"[207] from its inventor. In turn, a consumer can take advantage of this innovation without understanding where it came from, how it works, or who invented it: "From the strictly technical point of view all that background is, obviously and inevitably, something to be abstracted from."[208] With this in mind, Marcel offers an analogy. The accidents of a technological discovery—say, that its inventor was poor or wealthy or that there was political unrest at the time of its conception—are ultimately like "useless roundabout routes taken by a raw tourist in a country with which he has not yet made himself familiar."[209] Eventually, they will be forgotten, because the result alone matters.

This state of affairs has become the norm in modern society, so much so that, for Marcel, it has led to a "certain degradation at the spiritual level."[210] At the very least, it fosters an attitude of casual self-indulgence: "In our modern world, because of its extreme technical complication, we are, in fact, condemned to take for granted a great many results achieved through long research and laborious calculations."[211] At worst, it represents "a genuine intellectual conquest," whereby "satisfaction at a material level" is exchanged for "spiritual joy" and a "widely diffused pessimism" preferred to the earnest thought that life is "a divine gift."[212] As Marcel continues:

> In our contemporary world it may be said that the more a man becomes dependent on the gadgets whose smooth functioning assures him a tolerable life at the material level, the more estranged he becomes from an awareness of his inner reality. I should be tempted to say that the centre of gravity of such a man and his balancing point tend to become external to himself: that he projects himself more and more into objects, into the various pieces of apparatus on which he depends for his existence. It would be no exaggeration to say that the more progress "humanity" as an abstraction makes towards the mastery of nature, the more actual individual men tend to become slaves of this very conquest.[213]

The antidote to this development is, in a word, "philosophy." That is not to suggest that Marcel would dismiss the importance of, say, art and religion, but those domains are also "philosophical" in Marcel's broad sense of the term. For Marcel, one of the hallmarks of philosophy is that it refuses to sever means from ends;[214] one cannot use philosophy like a car or a laptop, enjoying the result without participating in the means. Rather, the individual herself is always caught up in a philosophical question, the meaning of which is inseparable from the circumstances of her life. In contrast, "the technician" deals with objects or operations that "anybody could carry out in his place."[215]

Marcel takes pains to stress that both modes of thinking—the philosophical and the technological—are valuable in and of themselves. The problem is that, in modern society, "technical progress is tending to emancipate itself more and more from speculative knowledge," so that "the place of contemplation" is abandoned for a "philosophy which is not so much a *love of wisdom* as a *hatred of wisdom.*"[216] Even worse, as this trend accelerates and as people increasingly fall under the sway of mass thinking and "its ancillary operations at the level of publicity or pseudo-art," the "very bases of discussion" are eroded and "the fine shades of truth, so inseparable from the sense of truth itself, [are] being literally stifled by partisan passions."[217] There is, in fact, a "reciprocal solidarity" among technology, propaganda, and partisanism, and people exhibit a "spirit of complicity" in relation to it.[218] "To dispose of your opponent," Marcel laments, "it is enough, in France to-day, to stick an obnoxious label on him and then fling in his face, as one might a bottle of acid, some gross accusation to which it is impossible for him to reply."[219]

Marcel's observations seem almost prophetic in the internet era. In particular, his concerns about a technologically mediated propaganda anticipate today's "fake news" and the attendant problem of a "post-truth" political culture.[220] Of course, as has been seen, Kierkegaard raised related concerns about information technology, starting in the 1830s and culminating with *A Literary Review*. Given Marcel's limited familiarity with Kierkegaard's writings, it is not surprising that he fails to recognize how much he resembles the Dane on the interchange between technological development and the formation of mass society. What *is* surprising, however, is that the broad theme of "technology" does not figure prominently in research on Kierkegaard's influence on subsequent philosophy. To wit, a recent and otherwise excellent work on Kierkegaard and the existentialist tradition does not even list "technology" in the index and only references *A Literary Review* three times across more than 400 pages of text.[221] Minimally, then, there is room to consider how Kierkegaard's groundbreaking critique of mass culture seeped into the thought of figures such as Heidegger and Marcel, particularly as regards technology.

At the same time, however, it is doubtful that either Kierkegaard or Marcel would identify themselves as "philosophers of technology." Their real concern lies in human existence, which always eludes technological mastery. As they see it, to disregard this basic existential factum is to fall into hopelessness: "If the pursuit for technological gain—rather than a pursuit for the betterment of the world—occurs, the *only* result Marcel foresees is a world of despair."[222] This is because the core aspects of human life—especially freedom, love, and happiness—are finally nontechnical. Whether directly or indirectly, Kierkegaard highlights this point throughout his authorship, from his polemical articles on journalism to his Socratic use of pseudonymity, where figures such as Johannes Climacus argue that, even if technology has made modern life easier, real questions remain about human destiny, if one will only dare to ask them. Marcel, for his part, was up to that task: "To the question: what can man achieve? we continue to reply: He can achieve as much as his technics; yet we are obliged to admit that these technics are unable *to save man himself.*"[223]

Jacques Ellul

Over two decades younger than Marcel, Jacques Ellul exhibited a different relationship to Kierkegaard's writings than his French compatriot. Whereas Marcel seemed to have only a cursory understanding of Kierkegaard's thought, Ellul held Kierkegaard in great esteem, so much so that Patrick Troude-Chastenet considers Ellul "not merely Kierkegaard's spiritual heir but his kindred spirit."[224] Indeed, while Ellul's own thinking reveals a "clear indebtedness to Kierkegaard,"[225] he saw the Dane as a confidante above all: "When I read Kierkegaard, I feel the ground floor. A man speaks to me. When I read most of the commentators, I am perplexed, because I do not recognize anything in the Kierkegaard that I think I have met."[226]

At first glance, this sense of "brotherhood"[227] appears essentially religious. Ellul was a lay leader in the Église Réformée de France, and he identified with Kierkegaard's own lay theological endeavors, especially "the radical nature of his approach to theology."[228] Whereas modern thinkers tend to focus on an external system, whether as an object of critique or of promise, Kierkegaard asks the individual to confront herself. As Ellul puts it, "I face a truth that I cannot prove, but only live."[229] This was a dynamic that Ellul himself sought to imitate. In books such as *Living Faith: Belief and Doubt in a Perilous World* (*La foi au prix du doute: "Encore quarante jours . . . ,"* 1980) and *The Subversion of Christianity* (*La subversion du christianisme*, 1984), Ellul juxtaposes the "fear and trembling" of genuine Abrahamic faith with the pat and mollifying answers of sociopolitical parties and ecclesiastical leaders. The latter revel in "the lore of Christmas" and recommend that one's "religious needs [be] met by the church," but to attain true faith is "to receive the shock of revelation, to discover the Unique One, and to enter into the dark night of the soul."[230]

On the surface, such comments appear unrelated to Ellul's interests in philosophy and sociology. While Ellul's religious writings are provocative, his scholarly reputation lies largely outside of theology. For nearly forty years, he served (among other things) as Professor of the History and Sociology of Institutions in the Faculty of Law at the University of Bordeaux, and the principal branch of his authorship has been termed "social theoretical."[231] In this vein, he penned a number of "major sociological works," including *The Technological Society* (*La technique ou l'enjeu du siècle*, 1954), *Propaganda: The Formation of Men's Attitudes* (*Propagandes*, 1962), and *The Technological System* (*Le Système technician*, 1977), for which he became known "chiefly as a critic of technology," perhaps even "a Luddite crank."[232] To be sure, Ellul was deeply suspicious of the modern West's prioritization of "artifice over nature and necessity over freedom."[233] He sums up this situation with a single word—"technique," defined as "*the totality of methods rationally arrived at and having absolute efficiency . . . in every* field of human activity."[234] For Ellul, "technology" refers to a mechanical thing (say, an airplane or an elevator), but "technique" is "a sociological phenomenon" that has come to pervade "every factor in the life of modern man."[235] In fact, what technique does is transform "everything it touches into a machine," insofar as the machine is "pure technique" and thus "represents the ideal toward which technique strives."[236] This transformation is problematic because, however useful a particular machine is (for flying or sewing or whatever), the very concept of machinery is "inhuman."[237] To be *inhumanus* is, quite literally, to be "not human," and that is precisely why the rise of technique threatens the *humanum*: "The machine took its place in a social milieu that was not made for it, and for that reason created the inhuman society in which we live."[238]

This inhumanity, continues Ellul, is manifold. For centuries, technique had existed alongside the traditions of human culture, but, in modernity, technique "has become autonomous."[239] Put differently, technique has become *the* tradition of the modern West, to which all other traditions are subordinated. There is even a sense in which technique is a kind of religion, inasmuch as it bears a series of determinative habits and practices: "Primitive man . . . was, of course, socially determined. But it is an illusion—unfortunately very widespread—to think that because we have broken through the prohibitions, taboos, and rites that bound primitive man, we have become free. We are conditioned by something new: technological civilization."[240] Ingredient in this habituation is a "tacit optimism, a need to hold that technical progress is unconditionally valid."[241] If, as Voltaire famously lampooned,[242] trust in divine providence can easily lapse into a gullible saccharinity, so does Ellul complain that modern people emphasize "the most positive aspect of technical progress, as though it were its only one."[243] When technique disappoints or fails, its inadequacies are regarded "as a realm of pseudo-problems, or simply as non-existent."[244]

These supposed pseudo-problems are "ends."[245] Ends such as interpersonal relationships and reverence for the created world are not "reducible to numbers," whereas "technique is nothing more than *means* and the *ensemble of means*."[246] But it is the latter that has come to dominate. As Ellul explains, "Our civilization is first and foremost a civilization of means; in the reality of modern life, the means, it would seem, are more important than the ends."[247] Once this shift occurs, there is a "clear, voluntary, and reasoned"[248] effort to determine the most efficient means for any given activity. This "phenomenon is the main preoccupation of our time."[249] More specifically, the quest for increasingly efficient means is manifest in three sectors of modern society: *the economic*, which seeks increased productivity on both micro and macro levels; *the organizational*, which aims to find ways to better administer law and warfare; and *the human*, which acclimates persons to this state of affairs through a range of techniques, from pharmaceuticals to propaganda. So pervasive are these sectors that "the social order is everywhere essentially identical."[250] Even an individual's private, nontechnical initiatives are bound to conflict with technological society. Ellul gives the example of an outdoorsman, who leaves the city in order to escape "his technical fate" but finds that even nature has been conquered by technique:

> Suppose he disturbs the "paying" guests? or trespasses on private property and hunting preserves? The public interest is then involved and technique intervenes, as it invariably does where large numbers of men are concerned. (Inversely, technique is creating a culture in which if large numbers are not involved, there is nothing at all.) Intervention then takes the form of an administrative police technique. Obligatory camp sites are established, complete with regulations. The camper is forced to carry a license, and the erstwhile act of free individual decision becomes a purely technical matter.[251]

This situation has a parallel in the "subjection of mankind's new religious life to technique."[252] One might expect that "technique and religion were in opposition and represented two totally different dispensations," but, Ellul contends, technique urges artistic-cum-spiritual expression in exchange for subservience. "Revolt is necessary to make a technical society,"[253] precisely because the technological demonstration of countercultural impulses is preferable to their nontechnical repression. Consider the "radical" literature disseminated through mass media: it may cause a ripple of sociopolitical activity but little more. For the reader is so saturated with publications that he "becomes a butterfly dipping into whatever flower he chooses."[254] In an especially prescient passage, Ellul puts it like this: "Technique erects a screen between the author and his readers. Miniature fireworks issue from the magic bottle, but not revolt. A few printed pages out of the deluge of printed matter will never make the butterfly a revolutionary."[255]

Of course, Kierkegaard was making similar observations about the print media of his day, but, aside from a general resemblance, is it possible to connect Ellul's critique of technological society to Kierkegaard's influence? Ellul himself provides a starting point:

> In the middle of the nineteenth century, when technique had hardly begun to develop, [a] voice was raised in prophetic warning against it. The voice was Kierkegaard's. But his warnings, solidly thought out though they were, and in the strongest sense of the word prophetic, were not heeded—for very different reasons. They were too close to the truth.[256]

Curiously, however, this is the only reference to Kierkegaard in *The Technological Society*. Though Ellul cites Kierkegaard as a visionary, who accurately predicted the dangers of modern technology, he fails to specify the nature of the Dane's warnings and/or why they were ignored. Even in a work such as *Propaganda*, which argues that "the media of mass communication" situates "the individual where he is most easily reached by propaganda,"[257] Kierkegaard's name is not mentioned. This lack of detail is likely one reason why, "despite the numerous references to Kierkegaard in Ellul's *corpus*, there are very few articles, written either in English or French, on the subject of Kierkegaard's influence on Ellul."[258]

Still, it is by no means a stretch to connect Kierkegaard and Ellul on the question of technology. One can begin by noting the dialectical *form* of their respective authorships. As Frédéric Rognon explains:

> For Kierkegaard, this [dialectic] was between an aesthetic pole that seeks to attract the reader and a religious pole that seeks to edify him. For Ellul, it was between a pole of sociological critique and a counterpoint that is biblical, theological, and ethical, even confessional. But in both cases, the normative pole was Christianity.[259]

Both thinkers juxtapose the ineluctable advance of a culture devoid of God with the enduring possibility of Christian redemption, whether on an individual level or on an eschatological one. Rognon here draws a slight distinction between Kierkegaard's polemics against "so-called Christian culture" and Ellul's critique of "technical and modern culture,"[260] but, as this study has shown, Kierkegaard's social criticism was as extensive (if not as intensive) as Ellul's. In other words, the Dane's "attack upon Christendom" is inseparable from his assessment of technologically determined mass society. It will not do to see the former as an essential component of Kierkegaard's legacy but the latter as a mere sidebar, since, for Kierkegaard, Christendom represents the translation of Christianity into a "historical sociopolitical institution,"[261] especially one that mirrors the tendencies of modern bourgeois consumerism.

Other commentators clarify how Kierkegaard's condemnation of Christendom might be linked to an Ellulian critique of modern technology. According to David Lovekin, Ellul inherited Kierkegaard's insistence that God is the Wholly Other, "always beyond systemic understanding and inclusion and, thus, in a value always beyond the *hic et nunc.*"[262] With this in mind, it would be idolatrous to conflate the "here and now" with the divine, but for Ellul, as for Kierkegaard, this is precisely the error of modernity. God has been subjugated to historical necessity, whether in terms of the primacy of Christendom or the incontrovertible logic of *la technique*. But this coup means that something finite and limited (a historically accidental establishment, a constellation of means and processes) now marks the limits of possibility, "which is never more than the technically possible."[263] Thus the meaning of human life is bound up with whatever technique can accomplish—a sacrilege from a Christian point of view and, following Kierkegaard's analysis of the self in *The Sickness unto Death*, a counsel of despair. As Anti-Climacus explains, "The philistine-bourgeois mentality is spiritlessness . . . but spiritlessness is also despair."[264] One with such an outlook "is like that king who starved to death because all his food was changed to gold."[265]

Lawrence Terlizzese expands on these insights. "It appears clear," he observes, "that Ellul followed Kierkegaard in his understanding of freedom and limit."[266] Just to the extent that modern technology insists upon its own necessity, it has led to a sinister paradox—a comfortable prison or an imprisoning comfort. As Terlizzese goes on:

> What method works best? Moral lapses are excused because it was necessary. Publishing houses must publish only what will turn a profit. The government must use propaganda and espionage and must spread misinformation. The corporation must use sexually oriented advertisements. All takes place under the justification that this is the way the world works. "It is necessary!"[267]

Ironically, this sort of determinism ultimately intersects with a fantasy, namely, that technology is without limits. Better communication, faster transport, more economical and effectual warfare, pharmacological enhancement, biogenetic progress, even unto immortality—these become the sole objects of human hope.[268] "There Is No Finish Line," reads one of Nike's slogans. Apple's tagline is "Think Different." Both promote perpetual development, the never-ending pursuit of the new and improved. Yet, as Terlizzese remarks, Kierkegaard and Ellul maintain that such a *need* for technological change unmoors the self from its creaturely status and, in turn, casts it adrift on a sea of *potential*: "We lose ourselves in the pursuit of more and more possibilities; always striving but never reaching the goal; always wanting more but never satisfied with what we have already attained."[269] Here, again, it is *The Sickness unto Death* that seems to point the way forward, inasmuch as it reasons that infinity and finitude, possibility and necessity, must be set in balance. "The self," writes Anti-Climacus, "is the conscious synthesis of infinitude and finitude that relates itself to itself, whose task is to become itself . . . . To become oneself is to become concrete. But to become concrete is neither to become finite nor to become infinite, for that which is to become concrete is indeed a synthesis."[270]

The respective analyses of Lovekin and Terlizzese imply that Kierkegaard's spiritual-cum-theological concerns provide the theoretical framework for Ellul's sociology. As Terlizzese puts it, "Ellul fleshed out in the concrete reality of technique what Kierkegaard argued for abstractly."[271] This may be true as far as it goes, but it overlooks the fact that Kierkegaard himself had an interest in technology on the ground—an issue that this study has addressed, indexing Kierkegaard's encounters with and reflections on the day's technological developments. And yet, to see that Kierkegaard was a kind of philosopher of technology, whose thought may even anticipate that of Ellul, raises a key question: *is that a good thing?* Ellul, after all, is typically regarded as a technological pessimist, whose *Technological Society* was of "special significance"[272] to Ted Kaczynski, the so-called "Unabomber." That is not to insinuate that Ellul can or should be held responsible for Kaczynski's brand of eco-terrorism, though it is fair to wonder if Ellul's picture of a monolithic and totalizing technological order does not beg for a radical response.

Such a question, it seems, might be asked of Kierkegaard as well. After all, Ellul presents (albeit cryptically) *The Technological Society* as an extended postscript to Kierkegaard's prior analyses of technique, and Kierkegaard did indeed offer substantial criticisms of many of the core instances of modern technology—mass media, public transport, aesthetic reproduction, and so on. Moreover, one could argue that they are united in their views on modern urbanity. George Pattison finds that both authors fall into a biblically based "typological reading of the modern city," whereby today's "technopolis" is understood to be a repetition of ancient Babylon, in contrast to "God's own 'Jerusalem.'"[273] For example, in *The Meaning of City* (*Sans feu ni lieu: signification biblique de la Grande Ville*, 1970), Ellul performs a canonical exegesis of "the city" in Scripture. As he sees it, the Bible offers insights into the nature of urban life that cannot be found in political or sociological works. "We are in no way putting the city on trial," Ellul avows, "or making an apology for the country. Our only intention is to discover what the Bible reveals concerning the city."[274] But this, as it turns out, is a vision of the city as a site of spiritual trial, where human beings face a fundamental either/or—the choice between God or mammon, between the heavenly city of Jerusalem or the cursed city of Babylon. Pattison sees a similar thrust in Kierkegaard's authorship,[275] even as he locates greater nuance in Kierkegaard's life and authorship. "One of modernity's great urban strollers, who combined something both of the flâneur and of the empathetic wanderer,"[276] Kierkegaard sees the city with a kind of "double-vision": "As a Christian critic of the modern city, he is with Ellul: but as an urban writer he is with Baudelaire."[277] Put differently, Kierkegaard's theological criticism of the city does not assume that the city simply can be left behind. For him, modernity is "precisely an urban moment," and, since the human being always lives *in concreto* and not *in abstracto*, "it would be a mistake to hear Kierkegaard as calling on us simply to abandon the call and care of the social moment."[278]

To be fair, one may say something similar about Ellul, whose own thought was not bereft of "hope."[279] As he puts in *The Technological Bluff* (*Le bluff technologique*, 1988), "Following Hegel, Marx, and Kierkegaard, I have often said that we show our freedom by recognizing our nonfreedom . . . it is by being able to criticize that we show our freedom."[280] Certainly both Kierkegaard and Ellul were first-rate critics, so much so that one can hardly help feeling that "the fulfillment of hope" is "not as certain"[281] as the counterfeit freedom reigning in technological society. Nevertheless, in a later section, I will propose that, at least as far as Kierkegaard is concerned, this sense of hopelessness paradoxically constitutes the greatest source of hope.

Changing scene, perennial questions

Heidegger, Marcuse, Ellul—these thinkers, just to name a few, have become seminal in the philosophy of technology. Needless to say, one may object to certain or, indeed, to many aspects of their thought. But their influence is undeniable, forming, both in a positive and in a negative sense, an entire generation of philosophers, from Albert Borgmann to Andrew Feenberg to Carl Mitcham, among others. And this legacy continues on, albeit in an increasingly empirical and/or postphenomenological vein,[282] in the work of persons such as Peter Kroes and Peter-Paul Verbeek. The philosophy of technology, then, is an evolving field, and yet, no matter how much it changes, it cannot finally escape the perennial philosophical questions that underlie it, whether in ethics, metaphysics, or politics. This is a point that twenty-first-century philosophers of technology are not only willing to concede but also ready to engage. As Philip Brey insists, "Many more studies are needed of the implications of particular technologies and technological products for different dimensions of [human] well-being."[283]

If this is true—and how could it not be, since even the most positivistic philosopher finds himself amid ongoing human cares and questions—then Kierkegaard would seem to merit inclusion among the field's touchstones. Not only did he develop a critique of modern technology well before his twentieth-century inheritors, but his thought on the matter proved simultaneously controversial and influential. Simply put, the history of the philosophy of technology would not look the same without him, and one might even wonder if his oeuvre was a necessary ingredient in the field's development: *Si Kierkegaard n'existait pas, il faudrait l'inventer.*[284]

At the same time, however, Kierkegaard's marginalization in the philosophy of technology is significant in its own right. That is to say, it does not simply indicate how Kierkegaard was received by later thinkers but, indeed, discloses that his intellectual legacy extends well beyond philosophy, so much so that some might even consider his thought, well, unphilosophical. Whether or not that charge is true—I, for one, do not think so—is a question far too labyrinthine to delve into here. The salient point is that Kierkegaard's critique of technology was not confined to philosophy departments in places such as Freiburg and Paris. On the contrary, it seeped into the field of theology and, finally, into the Church. This fact, in and of itself, hardly makes Kierkegaard unphilosophical, but it does mean that his thought on technology must also be studied in terms of its *theological* influence.

Kierkegaard's influence on theological responses to technology

Kierkegaard's impact on twentieth-century theology was as extensive as it was intensive. As Jon Stewart summarizes, "Kierkegaard has . . . very often been understood primarily as a theologian or religious thinker. In this capacity he has exercised a significant influence on different religious traditions and denominations."[285] Thus it goes without saying that, as in philosophy, it will be impossible to detail each and every theologian that Kierkegaard kindled on the question concerning technology. Instead, the task is to provide a representative survey of the topic, so as to stimulate further inquiry and interest. As will be seen, Kierkegaard's reflections on technology exercised considerable influence on some of the most important thinkers in modern Christianity, both Protestant (Paul Tillich) and Catholic (Romano Guardini and Thomas Merton). And yet, it is equally notable that, in the end, the Dane's eschatological bent distinguished his approach from that of his theological inheritors.

Romano Guardini

The son of an Italian diplomat, Romano Guardini grew up in Mainz, Germany, and elected to become a German citizen in 1911—a decision that would divide him from his family when the First World War broke out a few years later.[286] In a sense, however, Guardini's change of citizenship was symptomatic of a prior estrangement. His upbringing in the Catholic Church was rote at best, and his "conversion to a deeper Catholicism was along a very personal road."[287] Against his family's wishes, he entered seminary in 1908 and developed a particular interest in Benedictine spirituality, Platonism, and the then relatively new philosophical school known as phenomenology.[288] This combination of influences is notable, because it suggests Guardini's desire to relate traditional Christian thought to "other modes of knowing than the dogmatic"[289] and to attend to "real world" philosophical problems. Aidan Nichols, in fact, terms Guardini's philosophical interest "*das Lebendige-Konkrete*, the 'vitally concrete,'" which moves from "the phenomenon to the wider conceptual picture."[290] That he ultimately would allot a portion of his authorship to the modern situation in general, and to technology in particular, is thus consonant with his larger intellectual program.

Something similar might be said of Guardini's affinity for Kierkegaard. When, in the early 1920s, he began teaching at Friedrich Wilhelm University (today Humboldt University) in Berlin, he did not limit himself to Catholic doctrine and/or persons but preferred to focus "on a variety of epistemological, moral, axiological, pedagogical, and ecclesiological topics, combining these with profiles of inspirational personalities of mostly Christian philosophy and literature."[291] One of these figures was Kierkegaard, to whom Guardini would devote a number of writings as the decade progressed. His efforts were very much du jour. The author and critic Theodor Haecker—who, notably, converted to Catholicism in 1921—had popularized Kierkegaard among the Germanophone intelligentsia, both by translating several of the Dane's works and by issuing the monograph *Kierkegaard and the Philosophy of Inwardness* (*Kierkegaard und die Philosophie der Innerlichkeit*, 1913). Guardini ran in the same circles as Haecker and, with him, became involved in a group of Catholic intellectuals who regularly contributed to *Highland* (*Hochland*), a monthly magazine dedicated to art and religion. Guardini also assumed the editorship of *Comrades of the Shield* (*Die Schildgenossen*), another journal of the era, this one serving the Catholic youth movement. Amid these activities, Guardini published two treatises on Kierkegaard's thought—"The Starting Point of Søren Kierkegaard's Movement of Thought" ("Der Ausgangspunkt der Denkbewegung Søren Kierkegaards," 1927) and "On the Meaning of Melancholy"

("Vom Sinn der Schwermut," 1928). It is for these reasons that Peter Šajda has called Guardini "a key figure in the inter-war wave of Catholic Kierkegaard reception in Germany."[292]

And yet, at first glance, one might question the extent to which Kierkegaard shaped Guardini's views on technology. Guardini's writings tend to focus on Kierkegaard's anthropology, and, accordingly, there "were undoubtedly three works from which he seems to have derived his fundamental convictions about Kierkegaard's philosophical position: *The Sickness unto Death*, *The Concept of Anxiety*, and *Philosophical Fragments*."[293] As has been seen, Kierkegaard's reflections on technological modernity are clustered in *A Literary Review*, albeit with crucial references scattered throughout his oeuvre. Notably, however, Guardini did not keep a copy of *A Literary Review* in his personal library.[294] It is not surprising, then, that Kierkegaard's influence on Guardini's social criticism has received little mind.[295]

That is not to suggest, however, that such an influence is lacking. Indeed, Guardini seems to have been familiar with *A Literary Review*, perhaps from discussions and lectures but certainly from secondary literature. In his library was Olaf P. Monrad's *Søren Kierkegaard: His Life and His Works* (*Søren Kierkegaard: Sein Leben und seine Werke*, 1909)—a text that provides a pithy yet germane overview of *A Literary Review*. According to Monrad, *A Literary Review* stands as Kierkegaard's "piercing sketch of [the modern] condition."[296] It is a work that identifies "the daily press" as the creator of "the public" and, with it, the ethico-religious inertia of contemporary society.[297] As Monrad explains, "A lack of responsibility [according to Kierkegaard] increasingly appeared to be the characteristic sign of the times," resulting in the "idolization of leveled mediocrity."[298] Crucially, these same themes would turn up in *Letters from Lake Como* (*Briefe vom Comersee*, 1927), Guardini's own "general critique of technology as a civilisational epoch."[299]

Written and published during the same period as Guardini's other treatises on Kierkegaard, *Letters from Lake Como* certainly expresses *A Literary Review*'s concern about technological progress. Guardini begins by noting that the industrialized culture of northern Europe entails a pervasive sense of loss: gone is a culture in which humans dwelt alongside nature, replaced by factories, machines, and their implications of "grim seriousness, violent power."[300] Not only, then, is the natural world at risk but humanity as well: "A world is developing . . . that is in some way nonhuman."[301] The problem, however, goes much deeper than mechanical development. Like Kierkegaard, Guardini seeks to identify the *spiritual* malaise underlying technical change. Where cultural artifacts once stood in "vital relation"[302] to those who produced them, now there is a tendency toward abstraction. This situation stems from an alteration in human consciousness. Human knowledge has become so expansive that immediate relations have been rendered obsolete. Guardini traces this development in the growing fields of anthropology and psychology. He also sees it in literature, especially in the impersonal "language of newspapers."[303] As he explains:

Newspapers are a technique of developing awareness. By them we today become aware of what is going on around us and to us and in us. Reporters are present at events to describe and integrate them. Cameras take pictures of them. Nothing happens anymore without being noticed. The decisive point is that we accept all this as normal.[304]

Thus established, this sort of consciousness cripples meaningful activity: "Our action is constantly interrupted by reflection on it."[305] Guardini likens the situation to a plant that has been ripped from the soil. Although totally exposed to the light, it will die because its roots have been severed from the nourishment of the soil.[306]

Guardini's concerns about reflection lead to other Kierkegaardian themes. For instance, he argues that this new distribution of information begets a culture of mastery, whereby knowledge "unpacks, tears apart, arranges in compartments, takes over and rules."[307] Again, newspapers accomplish in the social sphere what scientists do in laboratories: they harness and shape raw material ("public opinion") according to their own ends.[308] Thus "a technique of controlling" permeates "every sphere of human existence and creativity,"[309] even as it is passed off as a form of liberation. This process terminates in mass society—a world in which the content of social life is sacrificed on the altar of efficiency and entertainment. Envy and leveling thrive in this environment: "Nothing commands respect, and nothing is inviolable. We lay hands on everything."[310] People "speak about lofty things, religious and philosophical, but they do so mistakenly in a way that is journalistic. They criticize, but they do not ask with what validity they do."[311] This is a world made in the image of the press.

Louis Dupré once dubbed *Letters from Lake Como* "the jewel in the crown of Guardini's writings," adding that it predated Martin Heidegger's far more celebrated exploration of "the dominance of technology."[312] Similarly, Oliver O'Donovan calls the *Letters* "the earliest attempt I know of to sketch"[313] such a critique of technology. It is true, of course, that Guardini's *Letters* served as a prelude to the more robustly philosophical accounts of Heidegger, Marcuse, and others. At the same time, however, it is wrong to view Guardini as an innovator on this matter, since the *Letters'* most piercing criticism of technological society is derived from Kierkegaard. But why, then, has Kierkegaard's influence on the *Letters* been forgotten? Though doubtless a thorny question, one likely answer has to do with Guardini's break from Kierkegaard on how to *correct* the technological order—a pattern that has already emerged in the Dane's reception by the *Frankfurter Schule*.

Indeed, from a certain perspective, *A Literary Review*'s "answer" to the problem of technology appears to suffer from what Andrew Feenberg has termed "substantivism."[314] "Substantive critique," argues Feenberg, assumes "that technology is inherently biased toward domination" and that this will-to-power "unfolds autonomously once technology is released from the restraints that surround it in premodern societies."[315] To be a substantivist, then, is to be a kind of fatalist, who believes that modern technology lies outside of human control. Feenberg attributes this position to Heidegger and Ellul (among others),[316] but surely he would say the same of Kierkegaard. After all, Kierkegaard's turn to "the unrecognizables" at the end of *A Literary Review* implies that the powers of information technology and leveling have outstripped sociopolitical restraint. Kierkegaard acknowledges that such a response is distasteful. The natural reaction would be to attempt to resist leveling and the media, either through the leadership of a great person or through the support of strong community.[317] The trouble, however, is that the press cannot be overcome in that way, since it simply draws all opposition into the complex of leveling. Only the public, which feeds off such reflection, wins.

In this development Kierkegaard sees what amounts to the end of history. Drawing on eschatological imagery, he compares the modern situation to a panorama of "air and sea" with no points of orientation—a dizzying scene, exposing the relativity and vanity of earthly existence.[318] Yet, realizing that nothing can be done to *stop* leveling, some will choose to *bear* it. These are the people that Kierkegaard deems "unrecognizables," for their suffering is to let go of the reins of history, to refuse "to rule, to guide, [and] to lead."[319] Thus they seem to vanish from the contemporary milieu, even as, like "secret agents,"[320] they serve the good behind the scenes. In short, they renounce what the world has become, while continuing to work for its God-given integrity. Perhaps characteristically, Kierkegaard pictures this decision as a *leap*: "Look, God is waiting! Leap, then, into the embrace of God."[321]

Guardini shares Kierkegaard's suggestion that only a turn to the religious life can stem the encroachment of technology, but, along the lines of Feenberg, Guardini rejects any hint of fatalistic passivity. For Guardini, the challenges of the technological age must be met with a "yes to what is happening historically."[322] This affirmation requires an ever-deepening consideration of technology, because "if we are thoughtless, we relate to it thoughtlessly."[323] Part of this process involves recognizing that "Christianity . . . has made possible science and technology" and, therefore, has the resources "to gain mastery over it."[324] The answer, then, is not to abandon technological development; it is to invest more heavily in it. As Guardini puts it, "What we need is not less technology but more."[325] This development must proceed from a "new, free, strong, and well-formed humanity."[326] With a better form of education—one that will treat scientific knowledge as a single aspect of a larger spiritual matrix—it is possible that "the technological will be not merely adorned but truly expressed and molded."[327]

Here Guardini might be likened to another important Catholic commentator on modern technology, namely, Pierre Teilhard de Chardin. A notoriously complex figure, whose writings blend his training in geology, paleontology, and theology, Teilhard takes a "fundamentally positive view . . . of modern technology."[328] In that sense, he is different than Guardini, though the two nevertheless wind up in a similar place. According to Teilhard, the unfolding of history—including the development of modern technology—is simply a part of the evolution, which "is a light illuminating all facts, a curve that all lines must follow."[329] Teilhard's understanding of evolution, however, is quite different than that articulated by evolutionary biologists such as Ernst Mayr.[330] For Teilhard, evolution is at once a material and spiritual process, occurring on the ground, as it were but also directed from on high: "The future depends not only upon worldly actuality as it pushes towards the future, but upon God who pulls it towards its completion."[331] Thus the constant state of flux found in the cosmos and in human history is not haphazard but is advancing "toward a particular end."[332]

Despite his Kierkegaardian critique of the press, Guardini reasons along the same lines. He suggests that, rather than abandon technological development, people need to embrace its material *and* spiritual aspects—indeed, to see it as an extension of God's providential action in the world. The real danger, then, is pitting technology against religion, which cuts the former off from its raison d'être and excludes the latter from society's divinely ordained present. On this view, which risks being "over-optimistic, even naïve,"[333] Kierkegaard's sense of sociohistorical decline would be not only untenable but perhaps blasphemous. On the other hand, it is intriguing that Guardini explicitly references Kierkegaard when discussing God's providence: "We must yield ourselves continually to God's mysterious guidance, and 'practice self-surrender,' as Kierkegaard said. . . . One must practice one's faith in strict obedience and loyalty, and refuse to be misled by such terms as 'necessity.'"[334] Perhaps—and this is a pregnant "perhaps"—Guardini and Kierkegaard were not so different after all.

Paul Tillich

Born in 1886 in the small German village of Starzeddel (today Starosiedle, Poland), Paul Tillich was the only son of the Reverend Johannes Tillich—a "traditionalist Lutheran of decided views."[335] His early years were "quiet, simple,"[336] often spent playing outside with his two younger sisters and other local children. Yet, as his father ascended the church hierarchy, his family relocated—first to Königsberg in der Neumark (today Chojna, Poland) and then to Berlin. It is notable that, in retrospect, Tillich did not lament leaving the pastoral landscapes of his birthplace for life in the city:

> I was saved from romantic enmity against technical civilizations and was taught to appreciate the importance of the big city for the critical side of intellectual and artistic life. Later there was added to this . . . an esthetic appreciation of the internal and external immensity of the metropolis; and finally I gained personal experience of the political and social movements that are concentrated in the capital.[337]

In the years preceding the First World War, Tillich was occupied with his studies, finishing a doctorate in philosophy in 1910 and a licentiate in theology in 1912, the same year he was ordained.

A stable career as a scholar and churchman seemed to await Tillich, but, over the next few decades, his life would mirror the turmoil into which Europe had been thrown. In 1914, he entered the Imperial German Army as a chaplain during the Great War, even seeing action at the devastating Battle of Verdun (1916). Disheartened and fearful, Tillich began to read deeply in the writings of Friedrich Nietzsche and Rudolf Otto, craving the former's "joyful vitalism" and the latter's "experience of the numinous."[338] In turn, Tillich's social and political views began to shift, abandoning the staid conventionality of his upbringing and instead identifying with the emerging avant-garde left wing. Already familiar with Kierkegaard through his study of German idealism, Tillich began to appreciate the Dane's social criticism, especially "his rejection of bourgeois values and the facile assimilation of Christianity to societal certitudes."[339] Intriguingly, it was around this time that Tillich began to write on technology, for example, in *The Religious Situation of the Present* (*Die religiöse Lage der Gegenwart*, 1926) and in "The Logos and Mythos of Technology" ("Logos und Mythos der Technik," 1927). These newfound interests also may be attributed to Tillich's association with Martin Heidegger—a colleague at the University of Marburg in the mid-1920s—though Tillich himself understood that Heidegger's thought owed much to Kierkegaard.[340]

In 1929, Tillich accepted a professorship in philosophy and theology at Frankfurt. He became involved with the *Frankfurter Schule* and spoke out against the looming threat of National Socialism. After Adolf Hitler came to power, Tillich was suspended from the academy and soon emigrated to America, where he would teach at a number of prominent institutions. Ironically, it was during these years that Tillich's thought received wide recognition, even celebrity: "During the late 1950s and early 1960s he attained something like cult status on American campuses, preaching and lecturing with great intensity and was lionized wherever he went."[341] This new, "American" Tillich somewhat muted his Marxist sympathies, but he continued to confront social and political questions. In fact, the bulk of Tillich's writings on technology postdate his move to the United States.

That Tillich would develop his thinking on technology over the course of the twentieth century is not surprising. In his view, theology has to be done in context, and thus in modernity it has to be done with an eye to "the structure and meaning of science, technology, and capitalism."[342] Indeed, since Tillich takes it as axiomatic that culture (in this case, technological culture) constitutes the form of religion, just as religion comprises the content of culture, modern theology simply is not possible without accounting for technology.[343] This form-content dialectic is "among the most central, if not also the most obscure"[344] in Tillich's intellectual project. The essential point here is that, in keeping with Tillich's "method of correlation," the questions raised by the technological order receive answers in Christianity: "The Christian message provides the answers to the questions implied in human existence."[345] As a result, the task of the modern theologian is to attend to the question concerning technology and to the answers tendered by Christian faith.

One might assume that Tillich's interest in Kierkegaard is bound up with the latter subject. Tillich's theological dissertation on Friedrich Schelling betrays an interest in Kierkegaard's "dialectical psychology," namely, the Christian-inflected pseudonymous works *The Concept of Anxiety* and *The Sickness unto Death*.[346] Similarly, *Philosophical Fragments* and *Concluding Unscientific Postscript*, both bearing deep theological import, also belonged to "the enduring core of [Tillich's] Kierkegaardian canon."[347] Finally, he had a familiarity with the secondary literature on Kierkegaard, singling out works by theologians Walter Lowrie and Eduard Geismar.[348] Thus it was only natural that, as a Christian theologian steeped in philosophy, Tillich would be drawn to Kierkegaard. As Tillich himself put it, "[Kierkegaard's] importance for the German post-war theology and philosophy can hardly be overestimated."[349]

Despite this indebtedness, "Tillich seldom drew upon Kierkegaard's descriptions of the Christian life of love," and, in turn, he tended to focus on "the negative moment" of the Dane's thinking.[350] This response would surface in Tillich's writings on technology, in which his critical and indeed Kierkegaardian analyses of technological society ultimately would yield to constructive proposals. In "The World Situation" (1945), Tillich offers a history of modern thought, tracing the rise of "autonomous reason" through the protests of existentialism in the mid to late nineteenth century.[351] According to Tillich, once philosophy wrenched itself free from theology in the eighteenth century, it became possible to reduce knowledge "to what is natural and reasonable" and, eventually, to view the natural sciences as "the pattern for all knowledge."[352] Ironically, this change made philosophy subservient to "technical science":

> Philosophy was largely restricted to epistemology. It became the servant of technical progress, its scientific foundations and its economic control. Following the breakdown of belief in rational truth as the determining factor in life, "technical reason"—not aspiring to provide truth but merely to furnish means toward the realization of ends determined by instincts and will—became decisive throughout the world.[353]

The goal of technical reason was to manipulate things at will, beginning with external objects and then moving to the human self as such: "Man had become a part of the abstract mechanism he himself had created for purposes of control. He had become a part of the machine."[354] The upshot was a contradiction—a society of unprecedented technological and economic productivity in which human "spontaneity" and "creativity" were increasingly deficient.[355]

Of course, not all benefited from this social order, and protests soon arose, first in the arts and then in philosophy. It is in this connection that Tillich mentions Kierkegaard, who was a pioneer of the philosophical opposition to "the imperious reign of technical reason."[356] For Kierkegaard, as for Marx and Nietzsche after him, knowledge and truth were "a matter of fate and decision, not of detached observation or of ultimate rational principles."[357] And yet, says Tillich, herein lies the danger of existentialist thinking: it undermines the validity of objective knowledge while nevertheless viewing technology as an inevitable (though useful) matter of fact. Such, indeed, was the dangerous formula of the Nazis and Soviets: "Technical reason is employed to execute the commands of an existential decision above which there is no rational criterion."[358] Tillich does not link Kierkegaard to either of these totalitarian movements, but, later in "The World Situation," he does suggest that Kierkegaard's "negative resistance" to modernity has proven ineffectual.[359] At best, it has issued in the rhetorically powerful, yet practically impotent, orthodoxy of Karl Barth.[360] Hence, while this Kierkegaardian school is neither fundamentalist nor accommodationist, its dialectic fails to be dynamic: "When this type of theological thinking tried to become constructive, it simply relapsed into the mere reiteration of tradition. It became 'neoorthodoxy.'"[361]

Tillich registers a similar complaint in his 1953 essay "The Person in a Technical Society." He identifies Kierkegaard as a key representative of existentialist philosophy, which "rebels in the name of personality against the depersonalizing forces of technical society."[362] From the outset, Tillich declares that he sees his own project as "a continuation of this tradition," albeit "under new conditions and with new means."[363] This point leads to his assessment of Kierkegaard, who, he says, takes up and validates the concerns of prior critics of modernity such as Blaise Pascal. Intriguingly, Tillich views the core of Kierkegaard's authorship as pertaining to technological society: "[Kierkegaard sought] to resist a world in which everything was transformed into a thing, a means, an object of scientific calculation, psychological and political management."[364] In fact, Kierkegaard's opposition to Hegelian thought is an extension of this concern: "Kierkegaard saw that, in spite of many romantic elements in Hegel and in spite of his doctrine of freedom as the purpose of history, *this* was the meaning of his attempt to subject all reality to a system of logical forms: the existing individual was swallowed; the deciding personality was eliminated."[365] Yet, while Tillich sympathizes with Kierkegaard's criticism of modernity, he once again finds Kierkegaard's solution ineffective. If Hegel "makes classical Protestantism a useful element within the frame of technical society," Kierkegaard "asks the individual to break away from this society in order to save his existence as a person."[366] This rupture is Kierkegaard's so-called "leap," which, in the context of Christian faith, entails one's acceptance that God, as the infinitely qualitative Other, cannot be instrumentalized by human reason. Tillich's concern is that the Kierkegaardian leap displaces one form of heteronomous authority (the modern technological order) only to reinscribe another (Protestant orthodoxy): "The leap liberates, but does it not enslave again?"[367]

Such criticisms notwithstanding, Tillich could not help but borrow from Kierkegaard's insights into the modern condition. In "The Lost Dimension in Religion" (1958), Tillich laments how modern technology has deprived the world of a "dimension of depth."[368] Published on the cusp of the Space Age, this essay describes the flattening out of "the relation of man to his world and to himself."[369] As Tillich explains, "Life in the dimension of depth is replaced by life in the horizontal dimension. The driving forces of the industrial society of which we are part go ahead horizontally and not vertically."[370] Such a notion is conspicuously similar to Kierkegaard's concept of "leveling," and, indeed, Tillich goes on to update, as it were, the Dane's analysis of "the present age." What Kierkegaard experienced in its nascent form, with the press and rail travel, has come to permeate society:

> Our daily life in office and home, in cars and airplanes, at parties and conferences, reading magazines and watching television, while looking at advertisements and hearing radio, are in themselves continuous examples of a life that has lost the dimension of depth. It runs ahead; every moment is filled with something that must be done or seen or said or planned.[371]

Also like Kierkegaard, Tillich expresses doubt about whether or not this societal transformation can be halted. Modern culture constantly promotes "phrases like 'better and better,' 'bigger and bigger,' 'more and more,'" but this pressure overwhelms life's most meaningful questions: "As long as the preliminary, transitory concerns are not silenced, no matter how interesting and valuable and important they may be, the voice of the ultimate concern cannot be heard."[372] The loss of depth, then, cannot be curtailed from the outside, only from within: "No one can experience depth without stopping and becoming aware of himself. Only if he has moments in which he does not care about what comes next can he experience the meaning of this moment here and now and ask himself about the meaning of his life."[373] Leveling cannot drive out leveling; only the individual, committed to work in quiet humility, can do so.

In the end, then, Tillich sees Kierkegaard's strength also as a weakness. Kierkegaard is adept at diagnosing what is *wrong* with the modern condition, and this is an invaluable service: "Only if we face realistically this situation can we realize the seriousness of the problem: 'The person in a technical society.'"[374] At the same time, however, Tillich argues that Kierkegaard fails to extricate himself from a nostalgic negation of modernity. Kierkegaard knows how to critique but not to construct. That is why Tillich could link his project with that of Kierkegaard while seeking to "go beyond" him.

Whether or not Tillich succeeds in this attempt is another question. It is true that an activist current runs through his writings, particularly as regards the Church's role in society. In "The Person in a Technical Society," Tillich advocates for an "attack on the technical society and its power of depersonalization," adding that it "is the task of active groups within and on the boundary line of the church to show the possibilities of attack, to participate in it wherever it is made, and to be ready to lead it if necessary."[375] He goes on to identify various fronts for "a Christian action today,"[376] including tasks intellectual (apologetics) and political (peace and justice movements). Such recommendations certainly appear more progressive than Kierkegaard's ironic disavowal of modern Western conventionality.

And yet, Tillich never fully divests himself of Kierkegaard's influence. "The technical development is irreversible," Tillich confesses, "and adjustment is necessary in every society, especially in a mass society."[377] Such acquiescence may seem (and likely is) more accommodationist than anything proposed by Kierkegaard, but Tillich retains a Kierkegaardian sense of detachment from political compromises and macro solutions. The problems presented by technological society, which as such cannot be solved by a social order permeated by technology, must be faced by the individual. As Tillich puts it, "The person as person can preserve himself only by a *partial nonparticipation in* the objectifying structures of technical society. But he can withdraw even partially only if he has a place to which to withdraw."[378] Calling on theologians "to describe the place of withdrawal,"[379] Tillich invokes the "place . . . that transcends every place," the "New Reality that is manifest in Christ."[380] This transcendent space could be interpreted in various ways, and, given Tillich's activism, it would be a stretch to equate it with Kierkegaard's suggestion of an "unrecognizable" Christianity. Nevertheless, it is part of Kierkegaard's legacy that, over against the question concerning technology, an answer is found in an existential transformation—a deeper realization of the Christian life— and not in ecclesial or political power.

Thomas Merton

Though a priest and a cloistered monk, Thomas Merton has been referred to as "the quintessential American outsider."[381] This may seem like a contradiction, but

Merton's path to religion—and, indeed, his life *as* an ecclesiastic—was by no means conventional. Born in southern France to a pair of expatriate artists, Merton had an itinerant childhood, alternating between schools in the United States, France, and the United Kingdom. The instability of his upbringing would soon be heightened. Merton lost both of his parents to cancer before his sixteenth birthday and, as a young man, fell into a dissolute lifestyle. In 1933, he entered Clare College, Cambridge but was forced to leave after a series of personal scandals.[382] He returned to New York City, where he enrolled at Columbia University in Manhattan. Here, slowly but surely, Merton developed into an outstanding student, focusing on literature, the arts, and reading "so deeply in the Western spiritual tradition that he was transformed from the inside out."[383] In 1938, he was received into the Catholic Church and, after a period of discernment, was accepted as a postulant at the Cistercian Abbey of Gethsemani in central Kentucky. This would be Merton's home until his death in 1968.

Merton's decision to become a Trappist monk was inseparable from a profound dissatisfaction with the modern world. As Robert Inchausti puts it: "[Merton's] reasoning was really very simple: If bourgeois civilization was failing, then leave it; if the West had become blind to its spiritual heritage, then reclaim it; and if poverty and obscurity were the price one had to pay to live a life in accord with conscience, then wholeheartedly embrace them and don't look back."[384] There is, doubtless, a Kierkegaardian tenor to this description, further underscored by Merton's disappointment in "the artistic counterculture and political radicalism that pretended to scorn"[385] the modern world. And yet, as with Tillich, Merton's similarities to the Dane would be offset by a prominent politically tinged activism. After publishing his best-selling autobiography *The Seven Storey Mountain* (1948), Merton became involved with Dorothy Day's Catholic Worker Movement and Martin Luther King's nonviolent protests against racial injustice. In turn, his "reflections on the spiritual poverty of contemporary life began to take on a new social relevance,"[386] and, seemingly against all odds, he emerged as a favorite of avant-garde figures such as the comedian Lenny Bruce and Black Power leader Eldridge Cleaver.[387]

Merton's cross-cultural appeal is attributable to his ability to synthesize diverse interests. On the one hand, he was well schooled in poetry, Christian theology, and various spiritual traditions, especially those of Christianity and Buddhism. Indeed, in the wake of *The Seven Storey Mountain*, his writings on contemplative prayer garnered a significant following; these include *Seeds of Contemplation* (1949), *The Silent Life* (1957), and *New Seeds of Contemplation* (1961). On the other hand, he was familiar with current trends in philosophy, politics, and popular culture, reading in existentialism, postcolonial theory, Marxism, and the philosophy of technology, including Marcuse's *One-Dimensional Man* and Ellul's *The Technological Society*.[388]

It is by no means surprising, then, that Merton studied Kierkegaard, whom he once called "one of the great religious geniuses of an irreligious century."[389] Merton was acquainted with Kierkegaard as early as 1940, when, in a journal entry, he "discusses Kierkegaard's treatment of the faith of Abraham in *Fear and Trembling* at length in relation to Saint John of the Cross."[390] This passage would later be issued in *The Secular Journal* (1959).[391] Thus Merton was aware of the existential-cum-spiritual dimension of Kierkegaard's authorship, but he was also attentive to the Dane's social criticism. In July 1968, just a few months before his death, Merton had begun to study Kierkegaard's "attack upon Christendom," referring to its critique of the Christian establishment as "fascinating and deeply disturbing" and, later, as "incontrovertibly *true*."[392] Similarly, in the posthumously published *Contemplation in a World of Action* (1971), Merton urges Catholic leaders to be "concerned with twentieth-century man, with technological man" and, in turn, recommends that they ponder thinkers such as Kierkegaard, who call attention to the fact that the structures of modern life stand "between man and reality, as veils and deceptions."[393]

Still, the "backbone"[394] of Merton's appropriation of Kierkegaard's thinking is found in the lengthy essay "The Other Side of Despair: Notes on Christian Existentialism" (1961), in which Merton draws explicitly on *A Literary Review* as a critique of "technological society."[395] According to Merton, Kierkegaard's great insight was that modernity issues in leveling, which Merton defines as "that by which the individual person loses himself in the vast emptiness of a public mind."[396] The "public mind" is a danger because it is a "pure abstraction": to identify with it is to forfeit one's own selfhood.[397] But this forfeiture is precisely what is seductive, since it unmoors the self from the burden of responsibility. As a member of the public, the individual can desire or think anything, even "the most shameful of deeds," since the public can "contradict itself and remain consistent with itself."[398] The "self-abandonment" of leveling entails a subjection of the individual to "the common endeavor of technological society."[399]

Moreover, Merton agrees with Kierkegaard that the instrument of this conformity is the mass media. Through newspapers and (by Merton's day) television, the media manages to make even the individual's private life a venue for "the public image and the public voice."[400] As he goes on to explain in *Conjectures of a Guilty Bystander* (1966):

> This is one of the few real pleasures left to modern man: this illusion that he is thinking for himself when, in fact, someone else is doing his thinking for him. And this someone is not a personal authority, the great mind of a genial thinker, it is the mass mind, the general "they," the anonymous whole. One is left, therefore, not only with the sense that one has thought things out for himself, but that he has also reached the correct answer without difficulty—the answer which is shown to be correct because it is the answer of everybody. Since it is at once my answer and the answer of everybody, how should I resist it?[401]

Hence, for Merton, to label Kierkegaard and his successors as "individualists" is to miss the point. In their rebellion against mass society, they are trying to preserve the possibility of free thought and of genuine interpersonal *relationships*. Kierkegaard's condemnation of modern "progress" and the tepidity of bourgeois Christianity is hardly a nihilistic attack; it is a recognition that "the 'goodness' of the good may in fact be the greatest religious disaster for a society."[402]

All in all, there are references to Kierkegaard in over a dozen of Merton's works,[403] and these citations are almost uniformly appreciative. And yet, Kierkegaard's influence on Merton tends to be neglected by Merton scholars. For example, Phillip Thompson argues that Merton's censure of technological progressivism owed primarily to his reading of Ellul's *The Technological Society*. However, he does not mention Kierkegaard, despite acknowledging Merton's concerns about the mass media.[404] Similarly, Paul R. Dekar omits Kierkegaard when discussing Merton's worries over a "more and more collectivist, cybernated mass culture."[405] Dekar goes on to explain that, for Merton, one of the chief threats of technology is that it "prevents our discovering of our truest selfhood," particularly insofar as "political demagogues and . . . modern mass media" now manipulate human consciousness.[406] But nowhere does Dekar cite Kierkegaard in connection with Merton's insights, even though Merton himself clearly did so.

This oversight is significant, because Merton's sympathy for Kierkegaard helps explain why his distrust of modern technology was deeper than that of Guardini and, above all, of Teilhard.[407] Indeed, while finding value in Teilhard's work, Merton worries that it has spawned a false optimism detached from "Christian hope, hope in the Cross and Victory of Christ."[408] Thus he prefers to "go along with Kierkegaard, [and] Guardini,"[409] among others. Doubtless part of Merton's bleakness has to do with chronology: Merton's writings on technology postdate the Shoah and the atomic bombings of Hiroshima and Nagasaki. But there is a philosophical undercurrent at work too. Following Kierkegaard, Heidegger, and others, Merton harbored doubts about whether or not human beings can control over modern technology. Moreover, and in the manner of Kierkegaard's polemics against the Danish state church, Merton does not absolve Christianity from its role in these developments. He chastises Western Christians for facilitating a "spiritually and mentally insolvent society," adding that "though we have no good motive for hoping for a special and divine protection, that is about all we can look for."[410] Here Merton echoes the Christian eschatology of Kierkegaard's *A Literary Review*, not to mention Heidegger's famous formulation: *Nur noch ein Gott kann uns retten*.[411]

But how committed was Merton to such observations? As the 1960s progressed, he became increasingly involved in the political movements of the day, even as technology remained a pressing question for him. These tendencies eventually converged. In 1964, Merton hosted a retreat at the Abbey of Our Lady of Gethsemani in Kentucky. The idea was to gather a group of religious leaders for the sake of discussing and answering the problem of technology—a move that suggests a break from Kierkegaard. For the Dane, programmatic "answers" to technological society remain within its epistemological framework; they mistake the poison for the medicine. In contrast, Merton puts forward a number of potential solutions. He recommends a return to nature, since the natural world "is the privileged locus of a secret and eternal love."[412] Moreover, he seeks to emphasize the difference between the "collectivity" of technological society and the promise of genuine "community," wherein human dignity, fragility, and spirituality are preserved. Only in a communal context, according to Merton, can technology be "changed from the ruler to a servant of contemporary life."[413]

In the end, then, Merton does not decisively break from his Catholic predecessors. As with Guardini, Merton channels his Kierkegaardian criticisms of technological society into proposals for a humane and, in a sense, ecclesiastical appropriation of technology. It is through an intentional and public return to religious praxis that persons are situated in a proper relation to technology. Moreover, and perhaps most tellingly, Merton dedicated personal time and energy to promoting this message, whether in literary works, church involvement, or social activism. Whether or not Merton was right to take such an approach is an open question. The point here is that he did not press his Kierkegaardian sympathies to their utmost conclusion—a common refrain in the theological reception of Kierkegaard's critique of technological society.

By way of conclusion: Kierkegaard, technology, and the wisdom of the Desert

In surveying the responses of Guardini, Tillich, and Merton to Kierkegaard's social criticism, a few key themes have emerged. First, each of these major figures in twentieth-century Christian theology was conversant with and indebted to Kierkegaard's analysis of "the present age." Second, each of them understood Kierkegaard as a progenitor of existentialism—a philosophical movement with which they were generally sympathetic and out of which related critiques of modern technology had emerged. In and of itself, then, Kierkegaard's critique of modernity was not seen as singular, though his roots in the Christian tradition lent special credence to his concerns. Third, and despite these positive evaluations, each of these theological thinkers at last break, whether explicitly or implicitly, from the ostensibly relentless negativity of Kierkegaard's condemnation of technological society. It is one thing, they suggest, for Christians to refuse to be *of* the world, but, as the Body of Christ, the Church must remain *in* the world and seek to transform it. Kierkegaard, on the view, is insufficiently constructive and, *eo ipso*, insufficiently ecclesial.

Similar charges have been leveled (rightly or wrongly) at thinkers such as Heidegger and Ellul. But the militant irony of Kierkegaard's final attack on Western bourgeois culture, including established Christianity, seems to distinguish the Dane from his successors. Here, it seems, is a thinker who evanesced into his deconstructive project, whose contributions are ultimately exhausted by his polemics. After all, Kierkegaard dismisses his *own* call for "unrecognizability" as "tomfoolery"![414] But this claim is consistent with his logic. For Kierkegaard a "solution" to the present age cannot be sponsored without triggering the mechanism of leveling and, therefore, perpetuating the problem. That is why *A Literary Review* does not adopt the hopefulness of a Guardini or the balance of a Merton. The only option is to forsake the machinating calculus of technological society; it is to abandon oneself *wholly* to the will of God.

But what would that even look like? Is there a model to which Kierkegaard's suggestion can be compared? One might address these questions in various ways, and, in the present context, there is not scope for a complete answer. But I would like to venture a potential line of reasoning that might be expanded elsewhere. In short, Kierkegaard's thought evokes the example and insights of earlier Christians who refused to participate in common society—for example, the Desert Fathers, who fled to the wilds of Syria and Egypt once the Christian Church was recognized as a legal institution in the Roman Empire in the fourth century.[415] Whereas the church fathers (such as Augustine of Hippo) sought to integrate Christianity into normal Roman society, the Desert Fathers (such as Anthony the Great) lived in an "eschatological dimension," detaching from public life in order to contemplate "the source of sin in the human heart."[416] In this way, their testimony hit a different register than that of their patristic peers. From the desert they came "to be regarded as intercessors for all humanity,"[417] rather than representatives of a theological position or a political faction. Like Kierkegaard's unrecognizables, they worked by not working; they saved by not trying to save.

If other thinkers offer more immediate answers to the question concerning technology, Kierkegaard's call for "unrecognizability" suggests that the best solution is to *wait* for God amid much anxiety and turmoil. This proposal is inadequately constructive from a certain point of view. However, that does not mean it is necessarily pessimistic. Indeed, Kierkegaard's approach may be likened to the parable of a desert monk. Confronted by robbers, the monk let them take all he had. Moreover, when the robbers began to leave, the hermit produced a sack that they had overlooked and gave it to them. On the face of it, this act of total self-dispossession is impotent, even foolish. But the parable ends in startling fashion: "[The robbers] were amazed at his patience and restored everything, and did penance."[418]

Concluding (Untechnological?) Postscript

One of the most celebrated works in Kierkegaard's authorship is *Concluding Unscientific Postscript* (1846)—the sequel to *Philosophical Fragments* (1844). Both texts are credited to Johannes Climacus, who aims to probe Christianity's claim that one's eternal happiness is dependent on historical events. Such a weighty topic would seem to be fodder for logicians and systematic theologians, but Climacus argues otherwise. As he sees it, the one who views Christianity from the disinterested standpoint of *Wissenschaft* risks confusing a fundamentally ethico-spiritual matter with an aesthetic amusement. That is why his concluding postscript to the *Philosophical Fragments* is called "unscientific" (*uvidenskabelig*). Climacus's task is to encourage persons to become subjective—"a purgative badly needed by an age that has seriously overindulged in a debilitating diet of world-historical objectivity."[1]

The notion that modernity is in need of a "purgative," while hardly new, seems to be gathering momentum in the twenty-first century. Such outcries traverse contemporary culture, raising, among other things, a host of concerns that involve modern technology. From fake news to global warming to screen time, debates about technological society have erupted on school boards and political committees, in popular media and academic seminars. Opinions vary, of course, and it is not an exaggeration to say that much public discourse on the subject is inconsistent, verging on incoherent. To cite but one example: while some school districts embrace "the Googlification of the classroom," providing students with discounted Chromebooks and encouraging skills like "teamwork and problem-solving,"[2] others argue that electronic devices in the classroom (including laptops) actually hinder academic performance[3] and that Google is using the educational sector to reel in new (and younger) customers.[4] Faced with such incongruous reports, it is no wonder that many people simply shrug their shoulders, resigned to whatever fate society has in store for them—an outcome that would come as no surprise to someone like Ellul.

Can Kierkegaard, then, offer anything to this situation? Can his authorship help persons navigate a society dominated by technology? The overarching aim of this study has been to demonstrate that the answer to these questions is "yes." I have shown that Kierkegaard ought to be seen as a key representative of the humanities philosophy of technology. As a son of the nineteenth century, he came of age during an era of rapid technological progress, not only globally but also in his native Denmark, where his daily affairs forced him to confront and to use a number of innovative technologies. Moreover, he keenly observed this development, taking time to reflect on it in his published and unpublished writings. Some of these reflections are extemporaneous and inchoate, while others, such as *A Literary Review*, denote profound and sustained attention. In both cases, however, Kierkegaard proved to be a perspicacious commentator on the rise of modern technology. For that reason, his thinking stands the test of time. Kierkegaard's ideas can be applied to the contemporary milieu of digital information, just as his influence can be detected in subsequent philosophers and theologians of technology. If, prior to this project, Kierkegaard's relevance to the philosophy of technology was underappreciated, overlooked, or even excluded, I hope that he now is seen as a noteworthy contributor and as a voice who, if not always right, remains thought-provoking and occasionally inspiring.

At the same time, however, this project is fundamentally a point of departure. It opens up possibilities but is hardly comprehensive. I would indeed be gratified if it encouraged scholars to investigate related areas or figures of interest. For when it comes to the question concerning technology, one thing is certain: we will continue to ask it. But whether or not we ponder the question aright depends, significantly, on the quality of our interlocutors.

Notes

Abbreviations

1 See the Works Cited section for complete details.
2 With the exception of *Søren Kierkegaard's Journals and Papers* and *Kierkegaard's Journals and Notebooks*, all abbreviations in this list correspond to editions of *Kierkegaard's Writings*, edited by Howard and Edna Hong. Again, see Works Cited for more information.

Preface

1 Carl Mitcham, *Thinking through Technology: The Path between Engineering and Philosophy* (Chicago, IL: The University of Chicago Press, 1994), 19.
2 Ibid., 20.
3 Ibid., 29.
4 Ibid., 33.
5 Don Ihde, *Heidegger's Technologies: Postphenomenological Perspectives* (New York: Fordham University Press, 2010), 23.
6 Ibid., 25.
7 Hans Achterhuis, *American Philosophy of Technology: The Empirical Turn*, trans. Robert Crease (Bloomington: Indiana University Press, 2001), 6–8.
8 Ihde, *Heidegger's Technologies*, 26.
9 Ibid.
10 Ibid., 115.
11 Ibid., 136.
12 Ibid., 139.
13 Mitcham, *Thinking through Technology*, 17.
14 Ibid.
15 Ibid.
16 Ibid., 26.
17 Ibid., 17.
18 Ibid., 39.
19 Ibid.
20 Ibid.
21 George Pattison, *Thinking about God in an Age of Technology* (Oxford: Oxford University Press, 2005), 100.
22 Ibid., 106–07.
23 See Martin Heidegger, "The Question Concerning Technology," *Basic Writings*, ed. David Farrell Krell (London: Routledge, 1978), 321.

24   See, for example, Herbert Marcuse, *Philosophy, Psychoanalysis and Emancipation:*
     Herbert Marcuse Collected Papers, vol. 5, ed. Douglas Kellner and Clayton Pierce
     (London: Routledge, 2011), 132ff.
25   Martin Heidegger, *Gelassenheit* (Pfullingen: Günther Neske Verlag, 1959). It should
     be noted that the texts comprising this book predate its publication. For example,
     the book's first part, "Die Rede gehalten am 30. Oktober 1955 in Messkirch," was
     originally a speech delivered at a celebration of the German composer Conradin
     Kreutzer (1780–1849), while its second part "Zur Erörterung der Gelassenheit. Aus
     einem Feldweggespräch über das Denken" stems from the mid-1940s.
26   Martin Heidegger, *Discourse on Thinking: A Translation of Gelassenheit*, trans. John
     M. Anderson and E. Hans Freund (New York: Harper Perennial, 1966), 46.
27   Ibid.
28   Ibid.
29   Ibid., 50.
30   Quoted in Ibid., 52.
31   Ibid.
32   Ibid., 46.
33   Ibid.
34   Ibid., 47. Also see Ibid., 56.
35   Ibid.
36   Ibid., 47–48.
37   Ibid., 55.
38   Ibid., 54.
39   Ibid.
40   Ibid., 54, 57.
41   Richard Rojcewicz, *The Gods and Technology: A Reading of Heidegger* (Albany: State
     University of New York Press, 2006), 13.
42   SKS 21, NB 6:93 / JP 3, 3704.
43   Of course, that is not at all to conflate the two thinkers. Heidegger explicitly
     distinguished his "ontological" (*ontologisch*) project from Kierkegaard's "ontic"
     (*ontisch*) focus. In other words, whereas Heidegger viewed himself as concerned with
     the being of entities—with the essence of things—he read Kierkegaard as attending
     to entities in their existential particularity. To what extent Heidegger is right about
     this distinction is another question. As one commentator has put it, "An ontology is
     quite clearly discernible in Kierkegaard," even though "Kierkegaard's challenge was
     essentially other than ontological" (Michael Wyschogrod, *Kierkegaard and Heidegger:*
     The Ontology of Existence [New York: The Humanities Press, Inc., 1954], vii).
44   Of course, just where philosophy ends and theology begins is a famously contentious
     question. This study presupposes that philosophy is concerned with human wisdom
     (*sophia*) about the basic principles of reality, while theology involves a methodical
     and rational attempt to understand God (*theos*), particularly through divine
     revelation. Yet, while these definitions afford a schematic distinction between the
     two "schools," a closer look reveals a number of overlapping points, whether in
     rational means, in methodological approaches, or even in the object of knowledge
     itself, insofar as various philosophical subdisciplines (philosophy of religion,
     philosophical theology, etc.) confront the status of religious claims and experience.
     Indeed, with regard to this study, it is notable that a figure such as Ellul—not to
     mention Kierkegaard—evinces a noticeable and frequently simultaneous interest in

both philosophy and theology. Thus, delineating respective sections on philosophy and theology is, admittedly, imperfect. At the same time, however, this demarcation is not done with pretensions of solving the wider debate but, rather, for the sake of clarity and organization. Moreover, it is meant to reflect prevailing attitudes about the thinkers in question: for example, Heidegger and Ellul, despite their theological proclivities, are typically grouped among philosophers, while Guardini and Tillich are often thought of as theologians, despite their attention to philosophy.

References to Kierkegaard's Works

1 Full citations list the text in question, the volume number (when apt) and the page number(s): for example, SKS 7, 41 / CUP1, 34.
2 Volume number, journal designation, and journal entry number are provided for SKS, while volume number and entry number are supplied from the Hong edition: for example, SKS 17, AA:13 / JP 3, 3245. When KJN are used, only the volume number is added, so as to avoid redundancy with the SKS (after which the KJN is modeled): for example, SKS 17 / KJN 1, AA:10.
3 These citations will be formatted as follows: *Pap.* V B 227 / JP 2, 2114.

Chapter 1

1 Otto Andersen, "Denmark," *European Population: I. Country Analysis*, ed. Jean-Louis Rallu and Alain Blum (Paris: John Libbey Eurotext, 1991), 114.
2 Michael E. Rose, "Society: The Emergence of Urban Britain," *The Cambridge Historical Encyclopedia of Great Britain and Ireland*, ed. Christopher Haigh (Cambridge: Cambridge University Press, 1985), 276.
3 D. B. Grigg, *Population Growth and Agrarian Change: An Historical Perspective* (Cambridge: Cambridge University Press, 1980), 191.
4 Bruce H. Kirmmse, "Kierkegaard and the End of the Danish Golden Age," *The Oxford Handbook of Kierkegaard*, ed. John Lippitt and George Pattison (Oxford: Oxford University Press, 2013), 28. It should be added that these percentages nevertheless indicate a relatively advanced level of urbanization: only Great Britain and the Netherlands were more urbanized at the start of the nineteenth century, and Jan Elvind Myhre even refers to Denmark as "a fundamentally urban nation" (Jan Elvind Myhre, "The Nordic Countries," *European Urban History: Prospect and Retrospect*, ed. Richard Rodger [Leicester: Leicester University Press, 1993], 171).
5 Kirmmse, "Kierkegaard and the End of the Danish Golden Age," 28.
6 Michael Ball and David Sunderland, *An Economic History of London, 1800–1914* (London: Routledge, 2001), 42.
7 Karl Marx, *The Poverty of Philosophy: Answer to the Philosophy of Poverty by M. Proudhon* (Moscow: Progress Publishers, 1955), 49.
8 Peter F. Drucker, *The Age of Discontinuity: Guidelines to Our Changing Society* (London: Heinemann, 1969), 247–48.
9 John Dyer, *From the Garden to the City: The Redeeming and Corrupting Power of Technology* (Grand Rapids, MI: Kregel Publications, 2011), 71–72.

10 Richard Rudgley, *The Lost Civilizations of the Stone Age* (New York: Touchstone, 1999), 10.

11 Francesca Bray, "Chinese Technology," *A Companion to the Philosophy of Technology*, ed. Jan Kyrre Berg Olsen, Stig Andur Pedersen, and Vincent F. Hendricks (Oxford: Wiley-Blackwell, 2009), 28.

12 Thomas F. Glick, "Islamic Technology," *A Companion to the Philosophy of Technology*, ed. Jan Kyrre Berg Olsen, Stig Andur Pedersen, and Vincent F. Hendricks (Oxford: Wiley-Blackwell, 2009), 34.

13 Ibid.

14 Keld Nielson, "Western Technology," *A Companion to the Philosophy of Technology*, ed. Jan Kyrre Berg Olsen, Stig Andur Pedersen, and Vincent F. Hendricks (Oxford: Wiley-Blackwell, 2009), 23.

15 Ibid., 24.

16 Henri Pirenne, *Medieval Cities: Their Origins and the Revival of Trade*, trans. Frank D. Halsey (Princeton, NJ: Princeton University Press, 1980), 16.

17 Ibid., 17.

18 Ibid., 45.

19 Nielson, "Western Technology," 24.

20 Ibid.

21 Ibid.

22 David C. Thorns, *The Transformation of Cities: Urban Theory and Urban Life* (Basingstoke: Palgrave Macmillan, 2002), 14.

23 Sam Bass Warner, Jr., "When Urban History Is at the Center of the Curriculum," *Journal of Urban History* 18 (1991), 3.

24 Richard Rodger, "Theory, Practice and European Urban History," *European Urban History: Prospect and Retrospect*, ed. Richard Rodger (Leicester: Leicester University Press, 1993), 1.

25 Ibid., 18.

26 Andrew Lees and Lynn Hollen Lees, *Cities and the Making of Modern Europe, 1750–1914* (Cambridge: Cambridge University Press, 2007), 1.

27 Robert Vaughan, *The Age of Great Cities: Or, Modern Society Viewed in Its Relation to Intelligence, Morals, and Religion* (London: Jackson and Walford, 1843), 1.

28 Lees and Lees, *Cities*, 1. The other "revolution" was that of "democratization" (ibid.), and it is noteworthy that Kierkegaard, too, saw the connection between industrialization and democratization—an issue that will be addressed in the following chapter.

29 Ibid., 21–22.

30 Ibid., 22.

31 Ibid., 44.

32 Ibid.

33 Ibid., 44–45.

34 Ibid., 45.

35 Ibid., 46.

36 Ibid.

37 Philip Sheldrake, *Spirituality: A Brief History* (Oxford: Wiley-Blackwell, 2013), 50–56.

38 Ibid., 57.

39 Ibid., 58–59.

40 Benedict of Nursia, *The Rule of Saint Benedict*, trans. Abbot Parry, OSB (Leominster: Gracewing, 1990), 1.

41 Lynn White, Jr., "Cultural Climates and Technological Advance in the Middle Ages," *Philosophy of Technology: The Technological Condition: An Anthology*, ed. Robert C. Scharff and Val Dusek (Oxford: Wiley-Blackwell, 2014), 514–15.

42 Ibid., 515.

43 Ibid., 516.

44 Hugh of St. Victor, *The Didascalicon of Hugh of St. Victor: A Medieval Guide to the Arts*, trans. Jerome Taylor (New York: Columbia University Press, 1991), 60.

45 Ibid., 74.

46 Ibid., 55.

47 Ibid., 56.

48 White, Jr., "Technological Advance," 516–17.

49 Nielson, "Western Technology," 24.

50 White, Jr., "Technological Advance," 517.

51 Nielson, "Western Technology," 25.

52 Ibid.

53 Ibid.

54 Ibid.

55 Ibid.

56 Ibid., 26.

57 Ibid.

58 Ibid.

59 Ibid. As will be seen, this trend was actually spearheaded by the Danish brewing magnate, J. C. Jacobsen, who founded the Carlsberg Laboratory in 1875.

60 Ibid.

61 Ibid., 27.

62 See, for example, Charles Taylor, *A Secular Age* (Cambridge, MA: The Belknap Press, 2007), 773–77.

63 Nicholas Carr, *The Shallows: What the Internet Is Doing to Our Brains* (New York: W.W. Norton & Company, Inc., 2011), 58.

64 Ibid., 59.

65 Ibid.

66 Ibid., 60.

67 Ibid.

68 Ibid., 67.

69 Ibid.

70 Lewis Mumford, *Technics and Civilization* (Chicago, IL: The University of Chicago Press, 2010), 109.

71 Ibid., 112.

72 Ibid., 134.

73 Quoted in ibid. Also see Thomas F. Carter, *The Invention of Printing in China and Its Spread Westward* (New York: Columbia University Press, 1931).

74 Quoted in ibid., 135.

75 Stephan Füssel, *Gutenberg and the Impact of Printing* (Aldershot: Ashgate, 2005), 8.

76 Ibid., 9.

77 Ibid., 15.

78 Ibid., 28.

79 Mumford, *Technics and Civilization*, 135.

80 Neil Rhodes and Jonathan Sawday, "Introduction: Paperworlds: Imagining the Renaissance Computer," *The Renaissance Computer: Knowledge Technology in the First Age of Print*, ed. Neil Rhodes and Jonathan Sawday (London: Routledge, 2000), 1.

81 Ibid., 6.

82 Daniel Roche, "Censorship and the Publishing Industry," *Revolution in Print: The Press in France 1775–1800*, ed. Robert Darnton and Daniel Roche (Berkeley: University of California Press, 1989), 5.

83 Raymond Birn, "Malesherbes and the Call for a Free Press," *Revolution in Print: The Press in France 1775–1800*, ed. Robert Darnton and Daniel Roche (Berkeley: University of California Press, 1989), 50.

84 Robert Darnton, "Introduction," *Revolution in Print: The Press in France 1775–1800*, ed. Robert Darnton and Daniel Roche (Berkeley: University of California Press, 1989), xiv.

85 Johanna Neuman argues otherwise, insisting that, while revolutionaries certainly had access to printing presses, so did absolutist regimes. Thus, the fight for public opinion, and the concomitant rise of Western liberalism, was hardly a fait accompli. See Johanna Neuman, *Lights, Camera, War: Is Media Technology Driving International Politics* (New York: St. Martin's Press, 1996), 34–37. Of course, Neuman is right that political change is not reducible to a single factor—even one as significant as the printing press—and yet she fails to pay sufficient attention to the fact that technologies such as the printing press are never just "neutral" tools in the hands of human beings. Rather, to paraphrase Marshall McLuhan, they come to mold the way that human beings think about and interact with reality. Indeed, that both revolutionaries and monarchists used the printing press is precisely the point— the instrument itself *implies* debate and diffusion, values that are always already allied to the liberal project. As will be seen, Kierkegaard himself will make a similar case in his reflections on the press.

86 Marshall McLuhan, *The Gutenberg Galaxy: The Making of Typographic Man* (Toronto: University of Toronto Press, 2011), 307.

87 Ibid., 144.

88 See, in particular, György Kepes, *Language of Vision* (New York: Dover Publications, Inc., 1995).

89 McLuhan, *The Gutenberg Galaxy*, 145.

90 Ibid.

91 Ibid., 146.

92 Ibid., 185.

93 See, for example, Marshall McLuhan, *Understanding Media: The Extensions of Man* (Corte Madera, CA: Gingko Press, 1994), 5. The original edition, it is worth adding, was published in 1964. Also see Marshall McLuhan, *The Medium Is the Massage* (London: Penguin Books, 1967).

94 McLuhan, *Understanding Media*, 30–31.

95 Carr, *The Shallows*, 75.

96 Ibid.

97 Ibid., 76.

98 Walter J. Ong, *Orality and Literacy* (New York: Routledge, 2002), 80.

99 Carr, *The Shallows*, 77.

100 The nineteenth-century English philosopher and scientist Charles Babbage is credited with inventing the first mechanical computer (the so-called "difference engine"). However, the advent of modern computing is typically dated to inventions such as Alan Turing's universal machine in 1936–37 and the establishment of Hewlett-Packard in 1939. Kierkegaard died in 1855, and so his era was, as a matter of fact, on the cusp of electronic and digital technology. For more on the history of the computer, see, for example, *Computer: A History of the Information Machine*, ed. Martin Campbell-Kelly, William Aspray, Nathan Ensmenger, and Jeffrey R. Yost (Boulder, CO: Westview Press, 2014).

Chapter 2

1 This is a label that Kierkegaard himself applied to Copenhagen on a number of occasions. For example, in an 1847 journal entry, Kierkegaard complains that his peers in Copenhagen fail to understand the "scale" of his authorship. Thus, he adds, "Oh, what a fate to be something out of the ordinary in a market town [*Kjøbstad*]!" See SKS 20, NB:194 / JP 5, 5997.

2 George Pattison, "Kierkegaard and Copenhagen," *The Oxford Handbook of Kierkegaard*, ed. John Lippitt and George Pattison (Oxford: Oxford University Press, 2013), 46.

3 Asa Briggs, "Changing Values in Art and Society," *The Nineteenth Century: The Contradictions of Progress*, ed. Asa Briggs (New York: Bonanza Books, 1985), 29.

4 Ibid.

5 Alfred Russel Wallace, *The Wonderful Century: Its Successes and Its Failures* (New York: Dodd, Mead and Company, 1899), vii.

6 Jacob Burckhardt, *Judgments on History and Historians* (New York: Routledge, 2007), 254.

7 Briggs, "Changing Values in Art and Society," 29.

8 Wallace, *The Wonderful Century*, 150.

9 Ibid., 150–51.

10 Ibid., 152–53.

11 Ibid., 153–54.

12 Ibid., 156.

13 Briggs, "Changing Values in Art and Society," 31.

14 Ibid.

15 Alexis de Tocqueville, *Journeys to England and Ireland*, ed. J. P. Mayer (London: Transaction Publishers, 2003), 107.

16 Ibid., 108.

17 Briggs, "Changing Values in Art and Society," 33.

18 Ibid.

19 Ibid.

20 Harold H. Schobert, *Energy and Society: An Introduction*, 2nd edition (Boca Raton, FL: CRC Press, 2014), 211–12.

21 Ibid.

22 Miriam R. Levin, "Dynamic Triad: City, Exposition, and Museum in Industrial Society," *Urban Modernity: Cultural Innovation in the Second Industrial Revolution*,

ed. Miriam R. Levin, Sophie Forgan, Martina Hessler, Robert H. Kargon, and Morris Low (Cambridge, MA: The MIT Press, 2010), 2.

23 Bruce H. Kirmmse, *Kierkegaard in Golden Age Denmark* (Bloomington: Indiana University Press, 1990), 9.

24 Ibid.

25 Ibid.

26 Ibid., 16.

27 Ibid., 17.

28 Ibid.

29 Ibid., 19.

30 Ibid., 20. Indeed, compared to countries such as Germany and Great Britain, "industrialisation came rather late to Denmark and the move from being an agricultural country to an industrial nation was slow and gradual" (Knud J. V. Jespersen, *A History of Denmark*, trans. Ivan Hill [Basingstoke: Palgrave Macmillan, 2004], 158). Still, this "gradual" process unfolded during Kierkegaard's lifetime, so that, less than two decades after his death, the "first real organised labour movement" commenced in Denmark, even if its activist beginnings soon gave way to a "peaceful, reformist approach" (ibid.).

31 See Thorkild Andersen, "Kierkegaard-Slægten og Sædding," *Hardsyssels Aarbog* 27 (1933), 26–40.

32 Peter Tudvad, *Kierkegaards København* (Copenhagen: Politikens Forlag, 2003), 338.

33 Joakim Garff, *Søren Kierkegaard: A Biography*, trans. Bruce H. Kirmmse (Princeton, NJ: Princeton University Press, 2005), 8.

34 Jørgen Bukdahl, *Søren Kierkegaard and the Common Man*, trans. Bruce H. Kirmmse (Grand Rapids, MI: Eerdmans, 2001), 35.

35 For more on this topic, see my *Kierkegaard, Pietism and Holiness* (Farnham: Ashgate, 2011), including Chapter Two, "Pietism in the Danish Context: From Its Beginning to the Family Kierkegaard."

36 Quoted in Garff, *Kierkegaard*, 159.

37 Garff, *Kierkegaard*, 155–59.

38 Ibid., 161.

39 Gordon Woodward, "Hjorth, Soren," *Biographical Dictionary of the History of Technology*, ed. Lance Day and Ian McNeil (London: Routledge, 1996), 598.

40 Ibid.

41 Garff, *Kierkegaard*, 463.

42 Ibid.

43 Norman Berdichevsky, *An Introduction to Danish Culture* (Jefferson, NC: McFarland & Co., 2011), 6.

44 Ibid.

45 Ibid.

46 Ibid., 7.

47 Garff, *Kierkegaard*, 199, 212. Kierkegaard would ultimately travel to Berlin four times in his life. See Ibid., 229, 333, 475. These journeys represented his farthest trips abroad—a point that hints at Kierkegaard's uneasiness with travel, perhaps especially with modern forms of travel. This issue will turn up again in Chapter 3.

48 Ibid., 229.

49 Ibid., 478.

50   Gunnar M. Idorn, *Concrete Progress: From Antiquity to the Third Millennium* (London: Thomas Telford Publishing, 1997), 24–25.

51   See, for example, Curtis L. Thompson and Joyce M. Cuff, *God and Nature: A Theologian and a Scientist Conversing on the Divine Promise of Possibility* (New York: Continuum, 2012), 15–16. Perhaps surprisingly, *The Spirit in Nature* was translated into English almost immediately. See Hans Christian Oersted, *The Soul in Nature, with Supplementary Contributions*, trans. Leonora and Joanna B. Horner (London: Bohn, 1852).

52   SKS 17, AA:12 / JP 5, 5092, my translation. Notably, these words were recorded in an 1835 letter to Professor Peter Wilhelm Lund—a Danish scientist and distant relative of the Kierkegaard family, who, during the 1830s, became a pioneer of paleontological and zoological study in Brazil. Kierkegaard claims that Lund had inspired his own love of nature and the "natural sciences" (ibid.), though Kierkegaard was to develop this interest in a different vein. For more on this topic, see my *From Despair to Faith: The Spirituality of Søren Kierkegaard* (Minneapolis, MN: Fortress, 2014), especially Chapter Four, "Icons of Faith: The Natural World."

53   Ibid., 25.

54   Ibid.

55   Ibid.

56   Garff, *Kierkegaard*, 463.

57   Ibid.

58   James D. Iversen, "The History of Wind Technology in Denmark," *Danish Culture, Past and Present: The Last Two Hundred Years*, ed. Linda M. Chementi and Birgit Flemming Larsen (Ames, IA: The Danish American Heritage Society, 2006), 154–57.

59   For more on the concept of "cultural technology," see, for example, Göran Bolin, "Introduction: Cultural Technologies in Cultures of Technology," *Cultural Technologies: The Shaping of Culture in Media and Society*, ed. Göran Bolin (New York: Routledge, 2012), 9–10.

60   M. Susan Barger and William B. White, *The Daguerreotype: Nineteenth-Century Technology and Modern Science* (Baltimore, MD: Johns Hopkins University Press, 1991), 1.

61   Ibid., 2. Indeed, daguerreotypes require a number of steps and are dependent on not only certain instruments (e.g., a camera) but also the availability of halides—binary compounds that were generally not discovered until the late eighteenth and early nineteenth centuries.

62   For more on the daguerreotype of Thorvaldsen, notable not only because the sculptor "had been the first Dane to have himself immortalized in this manner," but also because the picture shows him "making a pair of horns with the little and index fingers of his life hand in order to ward off the camera's evil eye" (ibid.), see Marie Louise Berner, *Bertel Thorvaldsen: A Daguerreotype Portrait from 1840* (Copenhagen: Museum Tusculanum Press, 2005).

63   Garff, Kierkegaard, 464.

64   Ibid.

65   Carlsberg Group, "1811-1870: Founding Carlsberg," *carlsberggroup.com*, accessed July 8, 2016, http://www.carlsberggroup.com/Company/heritage/Pages/FoundingCarlsberg.aspx.

66   Ibid.

67   Anders Brinch Kissmeyer, "Carlsberg Group," *The Oxford Companion to Beer*, ed. Garrett Oliver (Oxford: Oxford University Press, 2012), 224.

68   Ibid. It was, in fact, in such subtle yet significant ways that Denmark would come to influence Western industry. Due to a "lack of native raw materials like coal and iron," Danish industry was limited to a handful of "large-scale enterprises" such as "brewing, shipbuilding, tobacco production and sugar refining" (Stewart P. Oakley, "Industrialization," *Historical Dictionary of Denmark*, ed. Alastair H. Thomas and Stewart P. Oakley [Lanham, MD: The Scarecrow Press, Inc., 1998], 231). Yet, as has been seen, these industries sought to grow through science and technology, for example, through the application of "new electrical goods and chemicals" (ibid., 231).

69   Intriguingly, the relation between Carlsberg and Tivoli has long been more than coincidental: "Carlsberg started acquiring shares in Tivoli . . . in the late 19th century, when tough competition among Danish brewers made them invest in the entertainment business, restaurants and hotels to ensure distribution of their products" (Jan M. Olsen, "For Brewery Giant Carlsberg, It's Back to Basics," *latimes. com*, accessed July 20, 2016, http://articles.latimes.com/2001/mar/15/business/f i-38042). However, Carlsberg sold its shares in Tivoli in the early 2000s (ibid.), and the two Danish institutions have recently separated to an even greater degree. See RB-Børsen, "Tivoli dropper Carlsberg og Tuborg," *business.dk*, accessed July 20, 2016, http://www.business.dk/foedevarer/tivoli-dropper-carlsberg-og-tuborg.

70   George Pattison, *"Poor Paris!": Kierkegaard's Critique of the Spectacular City* (Berlin: Walter de Gruyter, 1999), 21.

71   Ibid., 22.

72   Ibid., 23.

73   Ibid.

74   Ibid.

75   See Peter Nicolai Jørgensen, *Bonden i Tivoli: En Historie* (Copenhagen: A. F. Høst, 1844).

76   Kirmmse, *Kierkegaard in Golden Age Denmark*, 21.

77   Garff, *Kierkegaard*, 60.

78   Kirmmse, *Kierkegaard in Golden Age Denmark*, 36.

79   Garff, *Kierkegaard*, 60–61.

80   Hans Vammen, "No One Other Than Ourselves? A Character Sketch of Frederik VI and His Régime," *The Golden Age Revisited: Art and Culture in Denmark 1800-1850*, ed. Bente Scavenius (Copenhagen: Gyldendal, 1996), 48–49.

81   Ibid., 50.

82   Quoted in Ibid., 52.

83   Ibid.

84   Garff, *Kierkegaard*, 61.

85   Johannes Ostermann, "Our Latest Journalistic Literature," *Early Polemical Writings: Kierkegaard's Writings I*, ed. and trans. Julia Watkin (Princeton, NJ: Princeton University Press, 1990), 189.

86   Ibid.

87   Ibid., 199.

88   Ibid.

89   Kirmmse, *Kierkegaard in Golden Age Denmark*, 49.

90   For more on the subject of Kierkegaard and nationalism, see, for example, Stephen Backhouse, *Kierkegaard's Critique of Christian Nationalism* (Oxford: Oxford University Press, 2011), though it is curious that Backhouse does not discuss a figure as prominent as Lehmann.

91   Ibid., 50.

92   Ibid., 52.

93   Wolfgang Undorf, *From Gutenberg to Luther: Transnational Print Cultures in Scandinavia 1450-1525* (Leiden: Brill, 2014), 13. Also see L. C. Nielsen, *Fra Johann Snell til vore Dage: Skildringer af Bogtrykkerkunstens Histoire i Odense* (Odense: Milo'ske Boghandels Forlag, 1908), 7ff.

94   Ibid.

95   Ibid., 14.

96   Ibid., 15.

97   Ibid., 15–16.

98   Ibid.

99   Ibid., 18–19.

100 Oscar Bandle (ed.), *The Nordic Languages: An International Handbook of the History of the North Germanic Languages*, vol. 2 (Berlin: de Gruyter, 2005), 1247.

101 Ibid.

102 Ibid., 1247–48.

103 Ibid., 1251–52.

104 Lisbeth Worsøe-Schmidt, "Spectators in Denmark," *Enlightened Networking: Import and Export of Enlightenment in 18th Century Denmark*, ed. Thomas Bredsdorff and Anne-Marie Mai (Odense: University Press of Southern Denmark, 2004), 23–24.

105 Ibid., 24.

106 Ibid., 25.

107 Quoted in Ibid., 32.

108 Henrik Horstbøll, "The Politics of Publishing: Freedom of the Press in Denmark, 1770-1773," *Scandinavia in the Age of Revolution: Nordic Political Cultures, 1740-1820*, ed. Pasi Ihalainen, Karin Sennefelt, Michael Bregnsbo and Patrik Winton (Farnham: Ashgate, 2011), 146.

109 Ibid.

110 Ibid., 149.

111 Ibid., 151. For more on Struensee and the circumstances surrounding his rise and fall, see Michael Bregnsbo, "Struensee and the Political Culture of Absolutism," *Scandinavia in the Age of Revolution: Nordic Political Cultures, 1740-1820*, ed. Pasi Ihalainen, Karin Sennefelt, Michael Bregnsbo and Patrik Winton (Farnham: Ashgate, 2011), 55–65.

112 Horstbøll, "The Politics of Publishing," 145.

113 Ibid., 147.

114 Ibid., 155.

115 Ibid.

116 As Christopher Dornan puts it, "It is not simply that a democratic society tolerates a free press, but that a free press makes for a democratic society" (Christopher Dornan, "Sounding the Alarm," *Media and Democracy*, ed. Everette Eugene Dennis and Robert W. Snyder [New Brunswick, NJ: Transaction Publishers, 1998], 184). Also see Elizabeth L. Eisenstein, *The Printing Press as an Agent of Change* (Cambridge: Cambridge University Press, 1979). Eisenstein's classic study does not treat democratic society per se, but she does show that several of the basic features of representative democracy—for example, an emphasis on individual rights and viewpoints, along with governmental statutes designed to protect them—emerge out of print culture.

117   Alastair H. Thomas, "Press," *Historical Dictionary of Denmark*, ed. Alastair H.
        Thomas and Stewart P. Oakley (Lanham, MD: The Scarecrow Press, Inc., 1998), 339.
118   Ibid., 339.
119   That is not to imply, however, that they were of equal importance to Kierkegaard. For
        example, Kierkegaard published a number of writings in *Fædrelandet*—including,
        most famously, several late diatribes against the Danish state church—while he just
        barely mentions a paper such as *Aftenposten*. See SKS 17, BB:43 / JP 5, 5206.
120   Jespersen, *A History of Denmark*, 61.
121   Ibid.
122   Ibid., 62.
123   Indeed, this "mark" may very well exceed voting rights and the like. It has been argued
        that the triumph of republicanism in Denmark actually brought the nation's celebrated
        "Golden Age" to a close: "After 1848, bare politics and democratic participation replaced
        philosophical/cultural debate as the engine of Danish society. It was democracy that
        killed the Golden Age. The socio-cultural stratification that fed the ability of the upper
        crust to creatively heal its internal rifts collapsed into a far more egalitarian social
        arrangement" (Thomas Gilbert, "Why a Danish Golden Age?: Structural Holes in
        19th Century Copenhagen," *Kierkegaard Studies: Yearbook 2013*, ed. Heiko Schulz, Jon
        Stewart and Karl Verstrynge [Berlin: de Gruyter, 2013], 430). There is not scope in the
        present work to investigate this thesis, but it is worth noting—and more than a little
        intriguing—that Kierkegaard's concept of "leveling" attributes just such a transition to
        the undertow of print technology. This issue will resurface in subsequent chapters.
124   Pattison, "Kierkegaard and Copenhagen," 60–61.
125   Here Pattison and Jon Stewart are salient examples. See, for example, George
        Pattison, *Kierkegaard, Religion and the Nineteenth-Century Crisis of Culture*
        (Cambridge: Cambridge University Press, 2002) and Jon Stewart, *Søren Kierkegaard:
        Subjectivity, Irony, and the Crisis of Modernity* (Oxford: Oxford University Press,
        2015). However, since neither of these authors foreground technology in their
        efforts to contextualize Kierkegaard's thinking, it is my hope that the present study
        will complement their respective contributions.

Chapter 3

1   Friedrich Ast, *Grundlinien der Grammatik, Hermeneutik und Kritik* (Landshut:
      Thomann, 1808), 179ff.
2   Richard N. Soulen and R. Kendall Soulen, *Handbook of Biblical Criticism*, 3rd edition
      (Louisville, KY: Westminster John Knox Press, 2001), 74.
3   See Heidegger, "The Question Concerning Technology," 326–27. At the same time,
      however, Heidegger maintains that technology is *ontologically* prior to modern
      science, since technology's essence as "enframing" (*Gestell*) views the world as
      "standing-reserve" (*Bestand*) in advance of the calculations of modern science. In other
      words, science has to see the world in a certain way—that is, as resource—before its
      calculations can begin. Whether or not these two positions on the relation between
      science and technology can be reconciled is another question. See, for example, Ihde,
      Heidegger's Technologies, 35ff. Also see Trish Glazebrook, *Heidegger's Philosophy of
      Science* (New York: Fordham University Press, 2000).

4 SKS 1, 25 / EPW, 69, my translation. Kierkegaard has capitalized *Teknik* here in accordance with the conventions of nineteenth-century Danish, which, like contemporary German, featured the standard capitalization of nouns. It is also worth adding that Blicher was a clergyman and author from the Jutland, whose poems were marked by a deep affection for nature. Kierkegaard even refers to him as a "voice in the wilderness" (SKS 1, 24 / EPW, 69). The author of *A Story of Everyday Life* (*En Hverdags-Historie*) was Thomasine Gyllembourg, who began publishing stories anonymously in the 1820s. Her last novel was *Two Ages* (*To Tidsaldre*), which, after appearing 1845, occasioned Kierkegaard's 1846 treatise *A Literary Review*—a work that will be discussed in detail later.

5 Heidegger, "The Question Concerning Technology," 318.

6 SKS 25, NB 30:67 / JP 4, 5044.

7 SKS 25, NB 30:67 / JP 4, 5044.

8 SKS 25, NB 30:67 / JP 4, 5044.

9 SKS 25, NB 30:67 / JP 4, 5044, my emphasis.

10 SKS 24, NB 22:128 / JP 2, 1891.

11 SKS 24, NB 22:128 / JP 2, 1891.

12 SKS 24, NB 22:128 / JP 2, 1891.

13 Strictly speaking, the Hongs did not compile this index, but, since the copyright is ascribed to Howard Hong, it is reasonable to assume that the couple oversaw its preparation. See Nathaniel J. Hong and Charles M. Barker (eds.), *Søren Kierkegaard's Journals and Papers: Volume 7, Index and Composite Collation* (Bloomington: Indiana University Press, 1978). It is worth adding (and is rather curious) that the collective index to Kierkegaard's published and posthumously published writings does *not* have an entry for "technology." See Nathaniel J. Hong, Kathryn Hong, and Regine Prenzel-Guthrie (eds.), *Cumulative Index to Kierkegaard's Writings* (Princeton, NJ: Princeton University Press, 2000).

14 SKS 20, NB:86 / JP 3, 2819.

15 SKS 20, NB: 86 / JP 3, 2819.

16 SKS 20, NB:86 / JP 3, 2819.

17 SKS 20, NB:86 / JP 3, 2819.

18 SKS 20, NB:86 / JP 3, 2819.

19 SKS 20, NB:86 / JP 3, 2819.

20 SKS 9, 281 / WL, 283.

21 SKS 9, 281 / WL, 283.

22 SKS 9, 282 / WL, 284.

23 SKS 9, 282 / WL, 284.

24 SKS 9, 282 / WL, 284. Intriguingly, the word translated here as "divulge" is *forraade*, which can also be translated as "sell." Thus Kierkegaard suggests that stories about human vice are stories that *sell*—an insight that almost seems clairvoyant regarding current trends in media. See, for example, Cees J. Hamelink, *Media and Conflict: Escalating Violence* (New York: Routledge, 2011). Even Alain de Botton, whose opinion of the media is considerably more hopeful than Kierkegaard's, is compelled to admit: "Journalism's own distinctive instrument [is]: humiliation. It shows reliable levels of enthusiasm for sarcastic stories, doorstep interviews, secret photographs and leaked correspondence. Flawed types must be turned *into* news and will then face the disgust of the moral-minded majority. The implicit idea is that society will be reformed through reputational ruin and public opprobrium. But . . . [do] people

grow better through being belittled? Does fear educate?" See Alain de Botton, *The News: A User's Manual* (New York: Pantheon Books, 2014), 64.

25 SKS 9, 283 / WL, 285.

26 Here Kierkegaard seems to have in mind 1 Cor. 14:20: "Brethren, be not children in understanding: howbeit in malice be ye children." This English translation from the Bible—and all others from this point forward, unless noted otherwise—is taken from *The Bible: Authorized King James Version*, Oxford World's Classics (Oxford: Oxford University Press, 1997).

27 SKS 9, 283 / WL, 285.

28 On this topic, see, for example, Joseph Owens, *Cognition: An Epistemological Inquiry* (South Bend, IN: University of Notre Dame Press, 1992).

29 SKS 9, 284 / WL, 286.

30 SKS 9, 284 / WL, 286.

31 Famously, the great Russian writer, Fyodor Dostoevsky, developed this point in a number of his novels, perhaps especially *The Idiot* (1868–69).

32 SKS 9, 285 / WL, 287.

33 SKS 24, NB25:23 / JP 4, 4217.

34 SKS 26, NB32:9 / JP 4, 4233.

35 See, for example, Plato, *The Republic*, trans. Desmond Lee (London: Penguin Books, 1987), 314ff.

36 SKS 26, NB32:9 / JP 4, 4233, my translation.

37 SKS 2, 408 / EO1, 421.

38 SKS 10, 246 / CD, 239.

39 Edward F. Mooney, "Pseudonyms and 'Style,'" *The Oxford Handbook of Kierkegaard*, ed. John Lippitt and George Pattison (Oxford: Oxford University Press, 2013), 209.

40 Datablog, "Percentage of Global Population Living in Cities, By Continent," *The Guardian*, accessed January 1, 2017, https://www.theguardian.com/news/datablog/ 2009/aug/18/percentage-population-living-cities.

41 Ibid.

42 Ibid.

43 The United States Environmental Protection Agency, "Heat Island Effect," accessed January 3, 2017, https://www.epa.gov/heat-islands.

44 For more on the significance of this letter, see Christopher B. Barnett, *From Despair to Faith: The Spirituality of Søren Kierkegaard* (Minneapolis, MN: Fortress Press, 2014), 90–92.

45 SKS 17, AA:12 / JP 5, 5092. Strandveien or "The Seaside Road" runs north out of Copenhagen along the Øresund strait. It is just under ten miles from the center of Copenhagen to Dyrehavsbakken and thus, in Kierkegaard's day, a roughly ninety-minute trip on horseback.

46 SKS 17, AA:12 / JP 5, 5093.

47 See, for example, Pattison, *"Poor Paris!,"* 98–107. Perhaps Kierkegaard's most significant series of reflections on Dyrehavsbakken is found in SKS 7, 428–48 / CUP1, 472–95. It is, to be sure, a discussion directly relevant to life among Copenhagen's bourgeoisie: "Our religious person is an independent and prosperous man who himself owns a horse and carriage. For that matter, he has both the time and the means to go out to the amusement park every day if he so pleases" (SKS 7, 448 / CUP1, 495).

48 SKS 18, FF:17 / JP 1, 217.

49 See, for example, Thomas Hall, *Planning Europe's Capital Cities: Aspects of Nineteenth Century Urban Development* (London: E & FN Spon, 1997), 327–28. Hall notes, to cite an example, that during "the second half of the nineteenth century it became increasingly urgent to improve the hygiene standards in the towns," due to the "accelerating growth and increasing density of the urban population" (ibid.). For more on the situation in Copenhagen in particular, see Henriette Steiner, *The Emergence of a Modern City: Golden Age Copenhagen 1800–1850* (Farnham: Ashgate, 2014), especially pp. 65–115.

50 SKS 17, DD:32 / JP 1, 220.

51 SKS 17, DD:32 / JP 1, 221.

52 C. Stephen Evans and Robert C. Roberts, "Ethics," *The Oxford Handbook of Kierkegaard*, ed. John Lippitt and George Pattison (Oxford: Oxford University Press, 2013), 213.

53 See Karl Marx and Friedrich Engels, *Manifesto of the Communist Party*, trans. Samuel Moore (Chicago, IL: Charles H. Kerr & Co., 1906): "[The bourgeoisie] has left remaining no other nexus between man and man than naked self-interest, than callous 'cash payment'" (Ibid., 16).

54 SKS 21, NB8:108 / JP 1, 224.

55 SKS 21, NB8:108 / JP 1, 224.

56 Julia Watkin, "Historical Introduction," *Early Polemical Writings: Kierkegaard's Writings I*, ed. and trans. Julia Watkin (Princeton, NJ: Princeton University Press, 1990), xviii. It should be noted that Kierkegaard's paper was a response to a previous talk given by Johannes Ostermann—a topic discussed in Chapter 2.

57 SKS 27, Papir 254 / EPW, 49.

58 SKS 27, Papir 254 / EPW, 48.

59 SKS 27, Papir 254 / EPW, 47. The term *stundesløs* is commonly defined as "restless," but, more specifically, it refers to continuous activity that nevertheless achieves little.

60 SKS 27, Papir 254 / EPW, 48.

61 SKS 28, Brev 27 / LD, 280.

62 SKS 28, Brev 27 / LD, 281.

63 SKS 8, 174–76 / UDVS, 66–68.

64 SKS 8, 176 / UDVS, 68.

65 SKS 25, NB30:70 / JP 4, 5045.

66 See, for example, Howard N. Tuttle, *The Crowd Is Untruth: The Existential Critique of Mass Society in the Thought of Kierkegaard, Nietzsche, Heidegger, and Ortega y Gasset* (New York: Peter Lang, 1996) and George Pattison, *Kierkegaard, Religion and the Nineteenth-Century Crisis of Culture* (Cambridge: Cambridge University Press, 2002).

67 Tuttle, *The Crowd Is Untruth*, 17.

68 Ibid., 20.

69 Ibid., 21.

70 Ibid., 160.

71 SKS 20, NB4:57 / JP 3, 2933.

72 SKS 26, NB34:26 / JP 3, 2999.

73 SKS 24, NB25:59 / JP 3, 2853. Kierkegaard is alluding to the words of Jesus: "Are not two sparrows sold for a farthing? and one of them shall not fall on the ground without your Father" (Matt 10:29).

74 SKS 24, NB25:59 / JP 3, 2853.

75 SKS 24, NB25:59 / JP 3, 2853.

76   SKS 24, NB25:59 / JP 3, 2853. In this passage, the Hongs have translated the Danish term *Stæder* as "centers," but it would be more accurately rendered as "cities." Indeed, at second glance, it seems likely that his reference to "cultural" here is not chiefly an allusion to the culture found *in* a city (e.g., shops, theaters, haute cuisine, and whatnot) but, rather, an acknowledgment that "great cities" (*store Stæder*) are constitutive "of cultural life" (*Culturlivets*) in modern Europe—a subtle but not insignificant difference, which gives his observation broader cogency.

77   See, for example, Lucien Goldmann, *The Philosophy of the Enlightenment: The Christian Burgess and the Enlightenment*, Routledge Revivals (New York: Routledge, 2010), 42ff. For a more contemporary work, which would make for an interesting juxtaposition with Kierkegaard's thought, see Deirdre N. McCloskey, *The Bourgeois Virtues: Ethics for an Age of Commerce* (Chicago, IL: The University of Chicago Press, 2006).

78   SKS 21, NB7:97 / JP 2, 2010.

79   SKS 21, NB7:97 / JP 2, 2010, my translation.

80   SKS 8, 261 / UDVS, 161.

81   SKS 8, 283 / UDVS, 186.

82   SKS 8, 282 / UDVS, 184.

83   SKS 8, 262 / UDVS, 162. I have treated these themes more fully elsewhere; see, that is, Barnett, *From Despair to Faith*, 100–16.

84   SKS 8, 276 / UDVS, 177.

85   SKS 8, 277 / UDVS, 179.

86   SKS 8, 287 / UDVS, 189.

87   SKS 8, 288 / UDVS, 190.

88   Stewart P. Oakley, "Absolute Monarchy or Absolutism," *Historical Dictionary of Denmark* , ed. Alastair H. Thomas (Lanham, MD: The Scarecrow Press, Inc., 1998), 26.

89   Stewart P. Oakley, "Consultative Assemblies," *Historical Dictionary of Denmark*, ed. Alastair H. Thomas (Lanham, MD: The Scarecrow Press, Inc., 1998), 106.

90   Michael Plekon, "Towards Apocalypse: Kierkegaard's *Two Ages* in Golden Age Denmark," *International Kierkegaard Commentary: Two Ages*, ed. Robert L. Perkins (Macon, GA: Mercer University Press, 1984), 47.

91   Bruce H. Kirmmse, "Biographical Introduction to the English Language Edition," *Søren Kierkegaard & the Common Man*, ed. and trans. Bruce H. Kirmmse (Grand Rapids, MI: Eerdmans Publishing Company, 2001), xviii.

92   SKS 16, 119, 121 / PV, 137, 140.

93   SKS 14, 111 / COR, 52.

94   SKS 14, 113 / COR, 54.

95   SKS 14, 112 / COR, 54.

96   SKS 14, 114 / COR, 56–57.

97   SKS 14, 114 / COR, 56.

98   SKS 14, 113 / COR, 55.

99   SKS 14, 113 / COR, 55.

100 SKS 23, NB15:54 / JP 3, 2951.

101 SKS 24, NB25:104 / JP 3, 2966.

102 SKS 24, NB25:104 / JP 3, 2966.

103 SKS 26, NB32:14 / JP 3, 2980.

104 SKS 26, NB32:14.b / JP 3, 2982.

105   SKS 26, NB34:26 / JP 3, 2999.

106   As Richard Kraut says of Aristotle's political theory: "The one end for the whole
      city is of course happiness—a life of virtuous activity sufficiently equipped with
      resources" (Aristotle, *Political Philosophy* [Oxford: Oxford University Press, 2002],
      207). But the provision of these resources is not the responsibility of the masses,
      nor is it decided by the popular vote. Indeed, Aristotle argues that, since happiness
      "cannot exist without virtue," government should fall on those "who are absolutely
      and not merely relatively just" (Aristotle, *Politics*, trans. Benjamin Jowett [New York:
      Cosimo, Inc., 2008], 274). The point here is not that Kierkegaard himself adhered to
      Aristotle's political science; it is simply to note that Kierkegaard's concerns about the
      rule of *Mængden* are hardly unprecedented.

107   SKS 26, NB33:15 / JP 3, 2986.

108   SKS 20, NB4:125 / JP 3, 2936.

109   SKS 20, NB4:125 / JP 3, 2936.

110   See, for example, Jacob and Wilhelm Grimm, *Grimm's Complete Fairy Tales* (New
      York: Barnes and Noble Books, 1993), 373ff.

111   SKS 18, EE:96.a / JP 4, 4094.

112   See, for example, Barnett, *Kierkegaard, Pietism and Holiness*; Backhouse,
      Kierkegaard's Critique of Christian Nationalism; Robert L. Perkins (ed.), *The Moment
      and Late Writings*, International Kierkegaard Commentary, vol. 23 (Macon, GA:
      Mercer University Press, 2009); Kirmmse, *Kierkegaard in Golden Age Denmark*; and
      Gregor Malantschuk and N. H. Søe, *Kierkegaards Kamp mod Kirken* (Copenhagen:
      Munksgaard, 1956).

113   SKS 26, NB33:51 / JP 3, 2993.

114   SKS 26, NB33:51 / JP 3, 2993.

115   See, for example, Garff, *Søren Kierkegaard*, 604ff.

116   SKS 22, NB12:141 / JP 4, 4166.

117   See, for example, Garff, *Kierkegaard*, 308ff.

118   SKS 25, NB28:71 / JP 3, 2968.

119   In addition to his walks, which made him a regular sight on Copenhagen's streets,
      Kierkegaard witnessed to his condemnation of the Danish state church in other
      ways. According to a pair of contemporary accounts, Kierkegaard began to spend
      "the church hour" in a prominent Copenhagen library known as the Athenæum
      (Bruce H. Kirmmse (ed.), *Encounters with Kierkegaard: A Life as Seen by His
      Contemporaries*, trans. Bruce H. Kirmmse and Virginia R. Laursen [Princeton,
      NJ: Princeton University Press, 1996], 115, 247). It was even said, not always
      benevolently, that "S.K. wanted to make people notice that he did not go to church"
      (ibid., 247).

120   SKS 22, NB12:141 / JP 4, 4166.

121   Pattison, *"Poor Paris!,"* 1.

122   Ibid.

123   Simon Webb, *Commuters: The History of a British Way of Life* (Barnsley: Pen and
      Sword Books, 2016), 39.

124   Ibid.

125   Ibid., 40.

126   Vukan R. Vuchic, *Urban Transit: Systems and Technology* (Hoboken, NJ: John Wiley
      and Sons, 2007), 9.

127   Webb, *Commuters*, 40.

128 Garff, *Kierkegaard*, 463.
129 J. Ewing Ritchie, "Copenhagen as It Was," *The Metropolitan Magazine* 49 (1847), 228.
130 Ibid., 229.
131 Ibid.
132 Ibid., 130.
133 C. Stephen Evans, *Kierkegaard: An Introduction* (Cambridge: Cambridge University Press, 2009), 68.
134 SKS 6, 65 / SLW, 64.
135 SKS 6, 65 / SLW, 65.
136 SKS 6, 65 / SLW, 65.
137 SKS 6, 66 / SLW, 65.
138 SKS 7, 25 / CUP1, 15.
139 SKS 7, 171 / CUP1, 185.
140 SKS 7, 170 / CUP1, 185.
141 SKS 7, 170 / CUP1, 185.
142 SKS 7, 171 / CUP1, 185.
143 SKS 7, 171 / CUP1, 186.
144 SKS 7, 172 / CUP1, 186.
145 SKS 7, 172 / CUP1, 187.
146 SKS 7, 172 / CUP1, 187.
147 For more on Nielsen, who was smitten with Kierkegaard's work for a time, so much so that the latter suspected him of plagiarism, see Garff, *Kierkegaard*, 582–89.
148 SKS 4, 104 / FT, 8.
149 SKS 28, Brev 286 / LD, 298–99. The Latin phrase *de omnibus dubitandum* is often associated with René Descartes, arguably the founder of modern philosophy, whose *Meditations on First Philosophy* begins with a reflection on the dubiousness of human knowledge. Seeking to attain a truly foundational certainty, Descartes turns to the self's status as a "thinking thing," an approach summed up in the famous phrase: "I think, therefore I am" (*Cogito ergo sum*). His argument is laid out in Meditation Two: see René Descartes, *Meditations on First Philosophy*, trans. Donald A. Cress (Indianapolis, IN: Hackett Publishing Company, 1993), 17–24. Not only was Kierkegaard suspicious of Descartes's method, but he felt that, by the nineteenth century, "doubt" had become little more than a philosophical cliché, parroted without attention to its veracity. The Dane addresses this issue in the pseudonymous text, *Johannes Climacus or De Omnibus Dubitandum Est: A Narrative*, composed around 1843 but not published until after his death.
150 SKS 26, NB31:13 / JP 3, 3221.
151 SKS 23, NB15:91 / JP 2, 1614.
152 Webb, *Commuters*, 39–41.
153 SKS 23, NB15:91 / JP 2, 1614. More will be said about the potential connection between Hegelian thought and technology in Chapter 5.
154 SKS 3, 17 / EO2, 7.
155 SKS 7, 69 / CUP1, 67–68.
156 SKS 7, 69 / CUP1, 68.
157 SKS 10, 82 / CD, 73.
158 SKS 10, 83 / CD, 74.
159 SKS 10, 80 / CD, 71.

160 SKS 10, 79 / CD, 70.

161 SKS 13, 165 / M, 123.

162 Garff, *Kierkegaard*, 229.

163 Ibid., 229–30.

164 See, for example, Matthew 7:13–14: "Enter ye in at the strait gate: for wide *is* the gate, and broad *is* the way, that leadeth to destruction, and many there be which go in thereat: Because strait *is* the gate, and narrow *is* the way, which leadeth unto life, and few there be that find it."

165 SKS 25, NB26:105 / JP 1, 540.

166 SKS 25, NB26:105 / JP 1, 540. Intriguingly, in a subsequent journal passage, Kierkegaard inverts the comparison: Christendom, he says, is like a "long railway train" (*uhyre Jernbane-Tog*) that has become unhinged from its "locomotive," namely, Christ himself (SKS 26, NB31:65 / JP 2, 1933). For Kierkegaard, then, true locomotion is provided by Christ, while Christendom, no matter how technologically oriented, "does not move from the spot" (SKS 26, NB31:65 / JP 2, 1933).

167 SKS 26, NB32:84 / JP 2, 1443.

168 Plato attributes this phrase to Protagoras, an ancient sophist and predecessor of Socrates. See, for example, Myles Burnyeat (ed.), *The Theaetetus of Plato*, trans. M. J. Levett (Indianapolis, IN: Hackett Publishing Company, 1990), 251ff. Of course, Kierkegaard's criticism of anthropocentrism extends well beyond Protagoras, from the biblical story of the Tower of Babel (Gen 11:1–9) to the modern philosophy of Hegel.

169 SKS 23, NB16:29 / JP 4, 4179.

170 SKS 26, NB33:33 / JP 3, 3224.

171 Juvenal, *Satires I, III, X* (Bristol, UK: Bristol Classical Press, 1982), 27.

172 SKS 26, NB33:33 / JP 3, 3224.

173 See, for example, B. E. G. Clark, *Steamboat Evolution: A Short History* (Raleigh, NC: Lulu Press, Inc., 2010), 19ff.

174 See, for example, Edgar C. Smith, *A Short History of Naval and Marine Engineering* (Cambridge: Cambridge University Press, 1938), 97ff.

175 SKS 7, 404 / CUP1, 445. Curiously, this passage is prefigured in a May 1844 letter from Kierkegaard to his brother, Peter Christian (SKS 28, Brev 11 / LD, 170); moreover, it is a near-direct quotation from an 1845 journal entry, in which Kierkegaard complains of an overwhelming "physical exhaustion" seemingly brought on by intellectual and spiritual strain (SKS 18, JJ:375 / JP 5, 5840). But to return to the passage in the *Postscript*: it is perhaps most intriguing that Climacus *dismisses* the severity of the poet's suffering, since it is merely "accidental" and thus lacks the "essential continuance" implicit in religious suffering (SKS 7, 404 / CUP1, 445).

176 SKS 27, Papir 589 / JP 6, 6967, my translation. Here the Hongs translate *Dampskib* simply as "boat," which fails to highlight its connection to modern technology and, in any case, is the less accurate rendering. *Dampskib* is literally a conjunction of steam- (*Damp-*) and -ship (*-skib*).

177 SKS 27, Papir 589 / JP 6, 6967.

178 SKS 20, NB4:32.

179 SKS 20, NB4:32.

180 The English engineer George Cayley is often credited with pioneering modern aviation in the late eighteenth century, and aeronautical societies began to appear in the mid-nineteenth century. Indeed, the first helicopter took flight in 1863, less than a decade after Kierkegaard's death. See, for example, Tom D. Crouch, *Wings: A History of Aviation from Kites to the Space Age* (New York: W.W. Norton & Company, 2003), 35ff.

181 See, for example, Garff, *Kierkegaard*, 161, 206, 212, 232, 333. Kierkegaard visited Berlin four times in total, traveling by steamship on each occasion. Also see SKS 20, NB2:132 / JP 5, 6041.

182 SKS 28, Brev 265 / LD, 257.

183 SKS 28, Brev 265 / LD, 257. The German word *Errungeschaften* can be translated as "achievements" and is derived from the verb *erringen*, which means "to achieve" or "to gain."

184 SKS 28, Brev 265 / LD, 257.

185 SKS 28, Brev 266 / LD, 259.

186 SKS 28, Brev 266 / LD, 260.

187 SKS 28, Brev 266 / LD, 260–61.

188 SKS 28, Brev 266 / LD, 262.

189 SKS 28, Brev 266 / LD, 263.

190 SKS 28, Brev 266 / LD, 263.

191 SKS 28, Brev 266 / LD, 262.

192 SKS 28, Brev 266 / LD, 262.

193 SKS 28, Brev 266 / LD, 262.

194 Robert Millward, *Private and Public Enterprise in Europe: Energy, Telecommunications and Transport, 1830–1990* (Cambridge: Cambridge University Press, 2005), 76–77.

195 Ibid., 82.

196 SKS 6, 259 / SLW, 278.

197 SKS 26, NB33:57 / JP 2, 2081. The Hongs translate *Elektriseermaskine* simply as "generator," which I have modified here.

198 Brian Scott Baigrie, *Electricity and Magnetism: A Historical Perspective* (Westport, CT: Greenwood Press, 2007), 30–32.

199 Ibid.

200 Ibid., 50.

201 SKS 4, 398 / CA, 95.

202 SKS 7, 423 / CUP1, 466.

203 SKS 15, 237 / BA, 290–91.

204 Andrew Smith, "Scientific Contexts," *The Cambridge Companion to Frankenstein*, ed. Andrew Smith (Cambridge: Cambridge University Press, 2016), 71–72.

205 Ibid., 77.

206 Ibid., 78. Also see Anne K. Mellor, "*Frankenstein*: A Feminist Critique of Science," *One Culture: Essays in Science and Literature*, ed. George Levine (Madison: University of Wisconsin Press, 1987), 287–312.

207 In particular, Kierkegaard owned *Percy Bysshe Shelley's poetische Werke in Einem Bande*, trans. Julius Seybt (Leipzig: Wilhelm Engelmann, 1844). See Katalin Nun, Gerhard Schreiber, and Jon Stewart (eds), *The Auction Catalog of Kierkegaard's Library* (New York: Routledge, 2015), 93.

208 Jonathan Smith, *Fact and Feeling: Baconian Science and the Nineteenth-Century Literary Imagination* (Madison: The University of Wisconsin Press, 1994), 90. According to Smith, "inspired" scientists such as Albert Einstein are "the exception that proves the rule" of an assumed division between poet and scientist (ibid.). David Knight concedes that this cultural assumption perdures, though he underlines that nineteenth-century romanticism tended to be open to science just to the extent that science celebrated "the organic rather than the mechanical" (David Knight, "Romanticism and the Sciences," *Romanticism and the Sciences*, ed. Andrew Cunningham and Nicholas Jardine [Cambridge: Cambridge University Press, 1990], 22).

209 Annteresa Lubrano, *The Telegraph: How Technology Innovation Caused Social Change* (New York: Garland Publishing, Inc., 1997), 37.

210 Dan Charly Christensen, *Hans Christian Ørsted: Reading Nature's Mind* (Oxford: Oxford University Press, 2013), 339ff.

211 Harry Henderson, *Communications and Broadcasting: From Wired Words to Wireless Web* (New York: Chelsea House, 2007), 5–6.

212 Lubrano, *The Telegraph*, 38.

213 Quoted in ibid.

214 Ibid.

215 Indeed, with the founding of the Great Northern Telegraph Company in 1869, Denmark would become a major player in international telecommunications. See Kurt Jacobsen, "The Great Northern Telegraph Company and the British Empire 1869–1945," *Britain and Denmark: Political, Economic and Cultural Relations in the 19th and 20th Centuries*, ed. Jørgen Sevaldsen (Copenhagen: Museum Tusculanum Press, 2003), 199.

216 SKS 27, Papir 74 / JP 1, 581. He makes a similar point in an 1840 passage (SKS 19, Not 6:13 / JP 1, 1027). Moreover, a letter to Regine Olsen from the same period refers to a "divine telegraph" (SKS 28, Brev 129 / LD, 63). Another early entry (dated 1838) playfully speaks of "telegraph ripples" (*Telegrapheringer*): see SKS 27, Papir 259:1 / JP 3, 3266. Also see SKS 21, NB10:37 / JP 6, 6345 and SKS 21, NB10:38 / JP 6, 6346.

217 SKS 26, NB32:84 / JP 2, 1443.

218 SKS 26, NB32:9 / JP 4, 4233.

219 SKS 25, NB29:11 / JP 2, 2049.

220 SKS 25, NB29:11 / JP 2, 2049.

221 SKS 25, NB29:11 / JP 2, 2049.

222 SKS 26, NB32:47 / JP 6, 6911.

223 SKS 26, NB32:47 / JP 6, 6911.

224 SKS 26, NB32:47 / JP 6, 6911.

225 SKS 26, NB35:15 / JP 4, 5035.

226 SKS 26, NB35:15 / JP 4, 5035.

227 SKS 26, NB35:15 / JP 4, 5035.

228 See, for example, Francis Fukuyama, *The End of History and the Last Man* (New York: Free Press, 1992). Of course, to see an analogy between Kierkegaard's ideas and those of Fukuyama is not at all to say that their views on history are identical.

229 SKS 26, NB35:15 / JP 4, 5035.

230 Garff, *Kierkegaard*, 301. Incidentally, there is a reference to night watchmen in Kierkegaard's authorship: SKS 6, 196–97 / SLW, 210. Moreover, the author of *The*

Concept of Anxiety is identified by the Latin name Vigilius Haufniensis, which can be translated as "The Watchman of Copenhagen."

231 SKS / EO1, 320.
232 See, above all, Weber's landmark sociological analysis of the modern West: *Die protestantische Ethik und der Geist des Kapitalismus* (Tübingen, 1904).
233 SKS 12, 214 / PC, 218.
234 SKS 26, NB33:33 / JP 3, 3224.
235 SKS 26, NB33:33 / JP 3, 3224. Also see SKS 24, NB23:36 / JP 6, 6728, which indirectly notes that municipal deliberations about gas lighting were taking place in the early 1850s.
236 SKS 26, NB34:42. Also SKS 26, NB35:11 / JP 4, 4357.
237 SKS 25, NB29:69 / JP, 4230.
238 James Monaco, *How to Read a Film: Movies, Media, and Beyond* (Oxford: Oxford University Press, 2009), 46.
239 Ibid., 42.
240 SKS 25, NB29:69 / JP, 4230, my translation.
241 See, for example, SKS 8, 77ff. / TA, 80ff.
242 See, for example, Sherry Turkle, *Alone Together: Why We Expect More from Technology and Less from Each Other* (New York: Basic Books, 2011), and Mary Aiken, *The Cyber Effect: A Pioneering Cyberpsychologist Explains How Human Behavior Changes Online* (New York: Spiegel & Grau, 2016).
243 SKS 26, NB33:15 / JP 3, 2986.
244 SKS 18, JJ:182 / JP 1, 911.
245 SKS 24, NB23:37 / JP 3, 3732.
246 SKS 24, NB23:37 / JP 3, 3732.
247 SKS 24, NB23:37 / JP 3, 3732, my translation.
248 Also see SKS 28, Brev 262 / LD, 247.
249 SKS 26, NB33:37a / JP 4, 4502.
250 SKS 26, NB35:43 / JP 4, 4493.
251 See, above all, Jon Stewart's numerous writings on this subject. For an accessible overview, see Jon Stewart, "Kierkegaard's View of Hegel, His Followers and Critics," *A Companion to Kierkegaard*, ed. Jon Stewart (Oxford: Wiley-Blackwell, 2015), 50–65.
252 See, for example, George Pattison, *Kierkegaard and the Theology of the Nineteenth Century: The Paradox and the "Point of Contact"* (Cambridge: Cambridge University Press, 2012), 206–11.
253 SKS 26, NB35:43 / JP 4, 4493. For more comparisons of Christendom to a machine, see SKS 25, NB26:24 / JP 1, 1001; SKS 26, NB33:32 / JP 4, 4056; *Pap.* XI 3 B 126 / JP 4, 4242.
254 Christensen, *Hans Christian Ørsted*, 3–4.
255 SKS 17, AA:12 / JP 5, 5092.
256 SKS 22, NB14:124 / JP 6, 6564.
257 Julia Watkin, *Historical Dictionary of Kierkegaard's Philosophy* (Lanham, MD: The Scarecrow Press, Inc., 2001), 230.
258 SKS 23, NB15:62 / JP 1, 820.
259 SKS 23, NB15:65 / JP 4, 4174.
260 SKS 18, JJ:437 / JP 1, 928.
261 SKS 26, NB33:42 / JP 4, 3870.

262 SKS 24, NB24:70 / JP 4, 4284. Also see SKS 20, NB:80 / JP 4, 4267.

263 Another example of Kierkegaard's concern about the language of "progress" is found in his unpublished satirical play, *The Battle between the Old and the New Soap-Cellars* (1838). In it, one of the characters compares the efforts of "the modern period to emancipate the sciences and scholarship and macadamize them" to "the solemn break of day . . . [to] the sun's struggle with the final efforts of darkness" (SKS 17, 293 / EPW, 120). In contrast, the play's protagonist is an "existential doubter," who nevertheless allows himself to be seduced by such talk rather than "go home and face up to himself" (Watkin, *Historical Dictionary*, 28).

264 SKS 26, NB33:42 / JP 4, 3870.

265 See, for example, Jerrold Levinson (ed.), *The Oxford Handbook of Aesthetics* (Oxford: Oxford University Press, 2003).

266 Evans, *Kierkegaard*, 73.

267 Ibid.

268 Ibid., 73–74.

269 Ibid., 74.

270 SKS 18, JJ:437 / JP 1, 928.

271 SKS 22, NB14:61 / JP 3, 2324.

272 See, for example, Garff, *Kierkegaard*, 102, 517.

273 Curtis L. Thompson, "Speculation/Science/Scholarship," *Kierkegaard's Concepts: Tome VI: Salvation to Writing*, ed. Steven M. Emmanuel, William McDonald, and Jon Stewart (Farnham: Ashgate, 2015), 69.

274 SKS 4, 363 / CA, 58.

275 SKS 4, 330 / CA, 23.

276 SKS 4, 330 / CA, 23.

277 SKS 4, 326 / CA, 19.

278 SKS 4, 317 / CA, 9.

279 SKS 4, 317 / CA, 9.

280 SKS 4, 382–83 / CA, 78–79.

281 Thompson, "Speculation/Science/Scholarship, 70–71.

282 See, for example, Ella Delany, "Humanities Studies under Strain around the Globe," *New York Times*, December 1, 2013. One of the most intriguing examples in Delany's article is the fact that the state of Florida has considered monetarily penalizing students who study the liberal arts, since these have been deemed "'nonstrategic disciplines'" (ibid.). Kierkegaard would find this logic as predictable as it is ominous.

283 SKS 4, 103 / FT, 7.

284 SKS 25, NB28:91 / JP 3, 2563.

285 SKS 25, NB28:91 / JP 3, 2563.

286 This phrase is Charles Taylor's and is thus anachronistically applied to Kierkegaard. Still, I think Taylor's definition of "immanent frame" accords quite nicely with what Kierkegaard observed about Western society in the nineteenth century—that it had come to understand human life "as taking place within a self-sufficient immanent order; or better, a constellation of orders, cosmic, social and moral . . . orders [that] are understood as impersonal" (Taylor, *A Secular Age*, 543).

287 SKS 25, NB28:91 / JP 3, 2563.

288 SKS 25, NB28:91 / JP 3, 2563.

289 SKS 25, NB28:91 / JP 3, 2563.

Chapter 4

1   Hubert L. Dreyfus, *On the Internet*, 2nd edition (London: Routledge, 2009), 1.
2   Ibid., 1–2.
3   Ibid., 2.
4   Ibid., 4.
5   John Perry Barlow, "A Declaration of the Independence of Cyberspace," *eff.org*, accessed June 11, 2017, https://www.eff.org/cyberspace-independence.
6   Dreyfus, *On the Internet*, 6–7.
7   Ibid., 77.
8   Ibid.
9   Ibid., 78.
10 Carr, *The Shallows*, 77.
11 Ibid.
12 Ong, *Orality and Literacy*, 79.
13 Watkin, *Kierkegaard's Philosophy*, 132.
14 Steven Best and Douglas Keller, "Modernity, Mass Society, and the Media: Reflections on the *Corsair* Affair," *International Kierkegaard Commentary: The Corsair Affair*, ed. Robert L. Perkins (Macon, GA: Mercer University Press, 1990), 24.
15 Ibid.
16 Leo Lowenthal, *Literature, Popular Culture and Society* (Englewood Cliffs, NJ: Prentice-Hall, 1961), 15ff.
17 Best and Keller, "Modernity, Mass Society, and the Media," 25.
18 Quoted in Lowenthal, *Literature, Popular Culture and Society*, 8.
19 Best and Keller, "Modernity, Mass Society, and the Media," 26.
20 Watkin, *Kierkegaard's Philosophy*, 186.
21 SKS 27, Papir 254 / EPW 36.
22 SKS 27, Papir 254 / EPW, 37.
23 SKS 27, Papir 254 / EPW, 36.
24 SKS 27, Papir 254 / EPW, 39.
25 SKS 27, Papir 254 / EPW, 39.
26 Oakley, "Consultative Assemblies," 106.
27 SKS 27, Papir 254 / EPW, 40.
28 SKS 27, Papir 254 / EPW, 46.
29 SKS 27, Papir 254 / EPW, 48.
30 SKS 27, Papir 254 / EPW, 48–49.
31 SKS 27, Papir 254 / EPW, 49.
32 SKS 27, Papir 254 / EPW, 50–51.
33 SKS 27, Papir 254 / EPW, 51.
34 SKS 27, Papir 254 / EPW, 48.
35 SKS 27, Papir 254 / EPW, 48.
36 SKS 27, Papir 254 / EPW, 48.
37 SKS 27, Papir 254 / EPW, 47.
38 SKS 27, Papir 254 / EPW, 46–48, my translation.
39 SKS 27, Papir 254 / EPW, 48, my translation.
40 Watkin, *Kierkegaard's Philosophy*, 109, 112.
41 Kirmmse, "Kierkegaard and the End of the Danish Golden Age," 35.

42 Ibid. It is worth noting, however, that Kierkegaard would later distance himself from Heiberg on a number of fronts, particularly regarding the latter's devotion to Hegelianism. Still, Kierkegaard paid favorable attention to the work of Heiberg's mother and wife in *A Literary Review* (1846) and *The Crisis and a Crisis in the Life of an Actress* (1848), respectively.

43 Joseph Westfall, "A, B, and A.F . . . : Kierkegaard's Use of Anonyms," *Kierkegaard's Pseudonyms*, ed. Katalin Nun and Jon Stewart (New York: Routledge, 2016), 32.

44 SKS 14, 13 / EPW, 6.

45 SKS 14, 14 / EPW, 10.

46 SKS 14, 14 / EPW, 10. B's reference to the Irish-Catholic statesman and political activist Daniel O'Connell (1775–1847) is notable here, demonstrating that he believes genuine political reform is possible in modernity. What he is condemning, then, is the error of conflating true reform with journalistic criticism.

47 SKS 14, 14 / EPW, 11.

48 SKS 14, 14 / EPW, 8.

49 SKS 14, 14 / EPW, 9.

50 Watkin, *Kierkegaard's Philosophy*, 145. For more details, see Teddy Petersen, *Kierkegaards polemiske debut: Artikler 1834–36 i historisk sammenhæng* (Odense: Odense Universitetsforlag, 1977), 103–12.

51 Orla Lehmann, "Press Freedom Affair V," *Early Polemical Writings* by Søren Kierkegaard, ed. and trans. Julia Watkin (Princeton, NJ: Princeton University Press, 1990), 139–40.

52 Ibid., 140.

53 Ibid.

54 Ibid., 141.

55 Ibid., 139.

56 SKS 14, 13 / EPW, 7.

57 SKS 14, 14 / EPW, 9.

58 Westfall, "Kierkegaard's Use of Anonyms," 32.

59 SKS 27, Papir 254 / EPW, 52.

60 Johannes Hage, "On the Polemic of the *Flyvende Post*," *Early Polemical Writings* by Søren Kierkegaard, ed. and trans. Julia Watkin (Princeton, NJ: Princeton University Press, 1990), 142.

61 Ibid., 144.

62 Ibid., 145.

63 Ibid.

64 Ibid., 143.

65 SKS 14, 19–21 / EPW, 12–16. "On the Polemic of *Fædrelandet*" is the common title for two short missives, the first published on March 12, 1836, the second on March 15, 1836.

66 SKS 14, 26 / EPW, 23.

67 SKS 14, 23 / EPW, 19.

68 SKS 14, 23 / EPW, 19.

69 SKS 14, 23 / EPW, 19.

70 SKS 14, 23 / EPW, 18.

71 SKS 14, 25 / EPW, 21–22.

72 SKS 14, 29 / EPW, 24.

73 Watkin, "Historical Introduction," xxiii.

74   Ibid.
75   Ibid.
76   SKS 14, 32 / EPW, 29.
77   SKS 14, 32 / EPW, 28.
78   Orla Lehmann, "Reply to Mr. B. of the *Flyvende Post*," *Early Polemical Writings* by Søren Kierkegaard, ed. and trans. Julia Watkin (Princeton, NJ: Princeton University Press, 1990), 158.
79   SKS 14, 33 / EPW, 30–31.
80   Quoted in Kirmmse (ed.), *Encounters with Kierkegaard*, 22–23.
81   Quoted in ibid., 23.
82   See, for example, Garff, *Søren Kierkegaard*, 65–67. Garff believes that the author of these critiques was Peder Ludvig Møller, who would later change Kierkegaard's life (and his own) when he repeatedly ridiculed Kierkegaard in the periodical known as *The Corsair* (*Corsaren*)—a topic that will be discussed in greater detail below.
83   Robert L. Perkins, "Power, Politics, and Media Critique: Kierkegaard's First Brush with the Press," *International Kierkegaard Commentary: Early Polemical Writings*, ed. Robert L. Perkins (Macon, GA: Mercer University Press, 1999), 34.
84   Ibid.
85   Ibid.
86   SKS 27, 198 / EPW, 45–46.
87   Perkins, "Kierkegaard's First Brush with the Press," 29.
88   SKS 21, NB9:42 / JP 6, 6310.
89   SKS 21, NB9:42 / JP 6, 6310.
90   SKS 21, NB9:43 / JP 6, 6311.
91   SKS 24, NB23:50 / JP 6, 6730.
92   Perkins, "Kierkegaard's First Brush with the Press," 44. Kierkegaard calls himself a "*Reflecteur*" in his 1835 talk before the Student Association. See SKS 27, 191, 204 / EPW, 38, 52.
93   Perkins, "Kierkegaard's First Brush with the Press," 44.
94   Petersen, *Kierkegaards polemiske debut*, 112.
95   SKS 17, AA:19 / EPW, 214.
96   Garff, *Kierkegaard*, 74.
97   Ibid., 77–80.
98   See, for example, Josiah Thompson, *The Lonely Labyrinth: Kierkegaard's Pseudonymous Works* (Carbondale: Southern Illinois University Press, 1967).
99   A friend of Hans Christian Andersen put it this way: "You have no idea what a sensation [*Either/Or*] has caused. I think that no book has caused such a stir with the reading public since Rousseau placed his *Confessions* on the altar" (Quoted in Garff, *Kierkegaard*, 217).
100 SKS 14, 49–51, 55–57, 61 / CA, 13–23.
101 Garff, *Kierkegaard*, 214.
102 SKS 7, 569–73 / CUP1, 625–30.
103 SKS 16, 23–27 / PV, 41–44.
104 SKS 16, 25 / PV, 43.
105 SKS 16, 28 / PV, 46.
106 Garff, *Kierkegaard*, 82.
107 SKS 17, DD:208 / EPW, 105.
108 SKS 17, DD:208 / EPW, 113.

109   SKS 17, DD:208 / EPW, 114–15. There are a number of references to "polytechnic students" [*Polyteknikere*] in *Soap-Cellars*, indicating Kierkegaard's awareness of the changing academic culture in Copenhagen. As noted in Chapter 2, Denmark's first technical college, Den Polytekniske Læreanstalt, was founded in 1829. See, for example, Christensen, *Hans Christian Ørsted*, 453–64.

110   SKS 17, DD:208 / EPW, 115.

111   SKS 17, DD:208 / EPW, 116.

112   SKS 17, DD:208 / EPW, 119.

113   SKS 17, DD:208 / EPW, 119–20.

114   SKS 17, DD:208 / EPW, 120–23.

115   SKS 17, DD:208 / EPW, 123. Kierkegaard lists the "horn" as one of the play's characters, describing it as an "organ of public opinion, sometimes used for drinking patriotically, sometimes for blowing patriotically, on which everyone blows a piece when he gets the chance" (SKS 17, DD:208 / EPW, 106). Clearly, then, the "horn" is meant to represent the popular press.

116   SKS 17, DD:208 / EPW, 123.

117   SKS 17, DD:208 / EPW, 124.

118   Garff, *Kierkegaard*, 85.

119   SKS 17, DD:208 / EPW, 124.

120   SKS 13, 15 / PV, 9, emphasis in original.

121   SKS 13, 16 / PV, 10.

122   SKS 13, 16 / PV, 10, my translation.

123   SKS 13, 16 / PV, 10.

124   Howard and Edna Hong describe Kierkegaard's "second authorship" as a "phase" that is "not essentially unconnected with the earlier pseudonymous works, but more concentrated, different in form, with a decisive accent, and also with new pseudonyms" (Howard V. Hong and Edna H. Hong, "Historical Introduction," *The Corsair Affair and Articles Related to the Writings*, ed. and trans. Howard V. Hong and Edna H. Hong [Princeton, NJ: Princeton University Press, 1982], xxxii–xxxiii).

125   See, for example, Garff, *Kierkegaard*, 375–422.

126   Ibid., 378.

127   Ibid.

128   Ibid., 379.

129   Ibid., 385.

130   See P. L. Møller, "Et Besøg i Sorø, Corpusfeuilleton," *Gæa: æsthetisk Aarbog*, ed. P. L. Møller (Copenhagen: Berlingske Bogtrykkeri, 1846), 144–87. Also see CA, 96–104.

131   COR, 101.

132   SKS 14, 83 / COR, 45.

133   SKS 14, 83 / COR, 44–45.

134   SKS 14, 83 / COR, 44–45.

135   SKS 14, 84 / COR, 46.

136   SKS 14, 84 / COR, 46.

137   See, for example, COR, 110.

138   SKS 14, 87 / COR, 47.

139   SKS 14, 87 / COR, 47.

140   SKS 14, 87 / COR, 47.

141   SKS 14, 87 / COR, 47.

142   SKS 14, 87 / COR, 47.

143 SKS 14, 87 / COR, 48.
144 SKS 14, 88 / COR, 49.
145 SKS 14, 88 / COR, 49.
146 SKS 14, 89 / COR, 49.
147 SKS 14, 89 / COR, 50.
148 Garff, *Kierkegaard*, 405.
149 Ibid., 404.
150 Ibid., 405. Some of Kierkegaard's contemporaries apparently agreed with Garff: see *Pap.* VII¹ B 55 / COR, 188–89.
151 Best and Keller, "Reflections on the *Corsair* Affair," 27.
152 *Pap.* VII¹ B 37 / COR, 166.
153 *Pap.* VII¹ B 37 / COR, 166.
154 *Pap.* VII¹ B 37 / COR, 166.
155 *Pap.* VII¹ B 37 / COR, 167.
156 *Pap.* VII¹ B 37 / COR, 167.
157 *Pap.* VII¹ B 37 / COR, 167.
158 *Pap.* VII¹ B 37 / COR, 168.
159 *Pap.* VII¹ B 37 / COR, 170.
160 *Pap.* VII¹ B 37 / COR, 168–69.
161 *Pap.* VII¹ B 37 / COR, 170.
162 *Pap.* VII¹ B 37 / COR, 171–72.
163 *Pap.* VII¹ B 43 / COR, 176.
164 *Pap.* VII¹ B 47 / COR, 177.
165 *Pap.* VII¹ B 54 / COR, 178.
166 *Pap.* VII¹ B 54 / COR, 178.
167 *Pap.* VII¹ B 55 / COR, 181.
168 *Pap.* VII¹ B 54 / COR, 181–82.
169 *Pap.* VII¹ B 54 / COR, 182.
170 *Pap.* VII¹ B 55 / COR, 184.
171 *Pap.* VII¹ B 55 / COR, 185.
172 *Pap.* VII¹ B 55 / COR, 186.
173 *Pap.* VII¹ B 55 / COR, 185–86.
174 *Pap.* VII¹ B 55 / COR, 186.
175 *Pap.* VII¹ B 55 / COR, 190.
176 *Pap.* VII¹ B 55 / COR, 191.
177 *Pap.* VII¹ B 55 / COR, 191.
178 *Pap.* VII¹ B 55 / COR, 190–91.
179 SKS 20, NB2:25 / JP 5, 6007.
180 SKS 20, NB2:25 / JP 5, 6007.
181 SKS 20, NB2:25 / JP 5, 6007.
182 SKS 20, NB2:27 / JP 5, 6008.
183 SKS 20, NB2:27 / JP 5, 6008.
184 SKS 20, NB2:27 / JP 5, 6008.
185 For additional background material, see Best and Keller, "Reflections on the Corsair Affair," 142–44. For more on Gyllembourg's novel itself, see Pattison, *Kierkegaard, Religion and the Nineteenth-Century Crisis of Culture*, esp. 50–71.
186 SKS 8, 59 / TA, 61.
187 SKS 8, 59 / TA, 61.

188   SKS 8, 60 / TA, 62.

189   SKS 8, 60 / TA, 63.

190   SKS 8, 60 / TA, 62–63.

191   SKS 8, 60 / TA, 63, my translation.

192   SKS 8, 64 / TA, 65. It is worth adding that, for Kierkegaard, the only way around this problem is to seek "the highest idea," which underscores the contingent nature of other revolutionary ideals: "From the standpoint of the idea, a person finds definitive rest only in the highest idea, which is the religious" (SKS 8, 63 / TA, 65). Also see Barnett, *Kierkegaard, Pietism and Holiness*, 146–47.

193   SKS 8, 60 / TA, 62.

194   SKS 8, 66 / TA, 68, emphasis in original.

195   SKS 8, 89 / TA, 93, my translation.

196   SKS 8, 86 / TA, 90.

197   SKS 8, 86 / TA, 90.

198   SKS 8, 87 / TA, 91. The Hongs suggest that "as a whole" is a suitable translation of "*en masse in corpore*." However, this rendering elides the Latin phrase *in corpore*, which means "in the body" and thus underscores Kierkegaard's profoundly incarnational understanding of ideal sociopolitical relations. For Kirkegaard, modern politics fails precisely to the extent that it moves away from such an incarnational model.

199   SKS 8, 88 / TA, 92–93.

200   SKS 8, 88 / TA, 93.

201   SKS 8, 89 / TA, 93.

202   SKS 8, 74 / TA, 77, emphasis in original.

203   SKS 8, 74–75 / TA, 77.

204   SKS 8, 75 / TA, 78.

205   SKS 8, 75–76 / TA, 78–79.

206   SKS 8, 76 / TA, 80.

207   SKS 8, 78 / TA, 81.

208   Merold Westphal, "Kierkegaard's Sociology," *International Kierkegaard Commentary: Two Ages*, ed. Robert L. Perkins (Macon, GA: Mercer University Press, 1984), 151.

209   SKS 8, 83 / TA, 87.

210   SKS 8, 80 / TA, 83.

211   SKS 8, 80 / TA, 84.

212   SKS 8, 80 / TA, 84.

213   SKS 8, 81 / TA, 84.

214   SKS 8, 81–82 / TA, 85.

215   SKS 8, 82 / TA, 85.

216   SKS 8, 90 / TA, 94.

217   See also SKS 3, 180–81 / EO2, 185–87, where Kierkegaard's pseudonym Assessor Wilhelm denotes Nero as the epitome of an aesthetic relation to life. According to Wilhelm, Nero is fundamentally a "sensualist," but, precisely for that reason, he lacks the constancy of an ethical worldview and thus remains anxious, "inwardly unfree." The upshot is a predisposition to violent whims—a problem that Kierkegaard will later to attribute to the present age's version of Nero, the *Publikum*.

218   SKS 8, 90 / TA, 95.

219   SKS 8, 90 / TA, 95.

220   Plekon, "Towards Apocalypse," 47.

221 SKS 8, 70–71 / TA, 72–73.

222 SKS 8, 68 / TA, 70.

223 SKS 8, 68 / TA, 71.

224 SKS 8, 72 / TA, 74.

225 SKS 8, 72 / TA, 74.

226 SKS 8, 72 / TA, 74.

227 SKS 8, 72 / TA, 75.

228 SKS 8, 72 / TA, 75.

229 SKS 8, 72–73 / TA, 75.

230 See also SKS 18, JJ:485 / JP 3, 2767, where Kierkegaard levels a similar charge at the publishing industry writ large: "That there are publishers, that there are men whose virtually entire existence expresses that books are a commodity and an author a merchant, is an altogether immoral situation."

231 SKS 8, 81 / TA, 85.

232 SKS 8, 83–84 / TA, 87.

233 SKS 8, 83 / TA, 87.

234 SKS 8, 84 / TA, 88.

235 SKS 8, 85 / TA, 88.

236 SKS 8, 85 / TA, 89.

237 SKS 8, 81 / TA, 84.

238 SKS 8, 84 / TA, 87.

239 The fifth chapter of my book *Kierkegaard, Pietism and Holiness* contends that *A Literary Review* registers a shift in Kierkegaard's understanding of Christian discipleship. Official state religion ("Christendom") seemed to have rendered the pursuit of holiness a private matter, since all citizens were nominally Christian and thus could not be distinguished by their external religious commitments. Yet, in the wake of the *Corsair* affair, Kierkegaard realized that, insofar as one follows the example of Jesus Christ, she will be marginalized and/or persecuted by those who are nominally "Christians." As it turns out, then, the pursuit of holiness *is* a public matter—an insight that led Kierkegaard to retrieve the mystical-cum-Pietist notion of *imitatio Christi*, already adumbrated in the discussion of "the unrecognizables" in *A Literary Review*.

240 SKS 8, 84 / TA, 87–88.

241 SKS 8, 85 / TA, 89.

242 SKS 8, 101 / TA, 91.

243 SKS 8, 102 / TA, 107.

244 SKS 8, 91 / TA, 95–96.

245 SKS 8, 91 / TA, 96.

246 SKS 8, 102 / TA, 107.

247 SKS 8, 85 / TA, 88. Subsequently, in *Works of Love*, Kierkegaard identifies "eternity's equality" with "love [of] the neighbor" (SKS 9, 87 / WL, 81).

248 SKS 8, 101 / TA, 107.

249 SKS 8, 102–03 / TA, 108.

250 SKS 8, 102 / TA, 107.

251 SKS 8, 103–04 / TA, 109.

252 SKS 8, 103 / TA, 109, my translation.

253 SKS 18, JJ:415 / JP 5, 5873.

254 See, for example, Garff, *Kierkegaard*, 727–805.

255   SKS 1, 300 / CI, 262.

256   SKS 1, 301 / CI, 264.

257   SKS 25, NB30:55 / JP 3, 2971. Also see SKS 26, NB32:106 / JP 4, 4235, another 1854 passage that shifts the metaphor: "The public is power, power like bedbugs or a foul smell . . . . What a nauseating kind of blood-lust—the thirst for a man's blood . . . like that of a louse or a legion of lice! The most loathsome of all kinds of tyranny— the tyranny of lice, and the most loathsome of all the bootlickers of tyrants, you timeservers of the tyrants, of the lice: 'the journalists.'"

258   SKS 25, NB30:61 / JP 6, 6886.

259   SKS 25, NB30:61 / JP 6, 6886.

260   SKS 25, NB30:61 / JP 6, 6886.

261   SKS 26, NB32:137a / JP 4, 3886.

262   SKS 26, NB32:137 / JP 4, 3885. Schopenhauer's remark is found the second volume (1844) of *The World as Will and Idea*: "The professional purveyors of opinion, such as journalists and the like, give as a rule only false wares, as those who hire out masquerading dresses give only false jewels." See Arthur Schopenhauer, *The World as Will and Idea*, vol. 2, trans. R. B. Haldane and J. Kemp (Boston: Ticknor and Company, 1888), 269.

263   SKS 26, NB32:137 / JP 4, 3885.

264   SKS 26, NB32:137 / JP 4, 3885.

265   SKS 27, Papir 590 / JP 6, 6968.

266   SKS 27, Papir 590 / JP 6, 6968.

267   SKS 27, Papir 590 / JP 6, 6968.

268   SKS 27, Papir 590 / JP 6, 6968.

269   *Pap.* XI^3 B 120 / JP 6, 6957.

270   *Pap.* XI^3 B 120 / JP 6, 6957.

271   *Pap.* XI^3 B 120 / JP 6, 6957.

272   *Pap.* XI^3 B 120 / JP 6, 6957.

273   *Pap.* XI^3 B 120 / JP 6, 6957.

274   *Pap.* XI^3 B 120 / JP 6, 6957.

275   *Pap.* XI^3 B 246:2 / M, 548. Also see *Pap.* XI^3 B 246:1 / M, 548.

276   SKS 13, 141 / M, 101.

277   SKS 13, 142 / M, 101.

278   *Øieblikket* is a multivalent concept in Kierkegaard's authorship. It is paradigmatically embodied in the person of Christ, whose incarnation reveals the meeting of the eternal and the historical. In turn, this union of infinite and finite, of freedom and necessity, is made the greatest possibility for individual existence (see, especially, *The Sickness unto Death*), whereby a person "consciously relates to the eternal in life, ideally on a moment-by-moment basis" (Watkin, *Kierkegaard's Philosophy*, 168).

279   SKS 13, 141 / M, 101.

280   SKS 13, 141 / M, 101.

281   SKS 13, 141 / M, 101.

282   SKS 13, 141 / M, 101.

283   SKS 13, 405 / M, 341.

284   SKS 13, 405 / M, 341.

285   SKS 13, 405 / M, 342.

286   SKS 13, 406 / M, 342.

287   SKS 13, 408 / M, 344.

288   SKS 1, 281 / CI, 241.

289   SKS 1, 299 / CI, 261.

290   SKS 1, 299 / CI, 261. Tamerlane (or Timur) was a fourteenth-century Turko-Mongol warlord who led military campaigns from Turkestan to the Indian subcontinent and on to the Levant.

291   SKS 1, 299 / CI, 262.

292   SKS 1, 300 / CI, 262.

293   SKS 1, 300 / CI, 262.

294   SKS 1, 302 / CI, 264.

295   SKS 1, 302 / CI, 264.

296   SKS 1, 307–08 / CI, 270–71.

297   SKS 1, 308 / CI, 271.

298   SKS 1, 311 / CI, 275, my emphasis.

299   SKS 1, 311 / CI, 275.

300   SKS 8, 102–03 / TA, 108.

301   George Pattison, *The Philosophy of Kierkegaard* (Chesham: Acumen, 2005), 180.

302   Ibid., 181.

303   Ibid.

304   Ibid., 181–82. In this connection, Pattison mentions Johann Georg Hamann and Gotthold Ephraim Lessing, and Nikolaus Ludwig Graf von Zinzendorf could be added to this list. All three of these "Socratic" predecessors had ties to Pietism. In fact, it is fascinating (but not surprising) that Lessing penned a theological defense of Moravian Pietism entitled *Gedanken über die Herrnhuter* (1784). See Arno Schilson, "Lessing and Theology," *A Companion to the Works of Gotthold Ephraim Lessing*, ed. Barbara Fischer and Thomas C. Fox (Rochester, NY: Camden House, 2005), 161–62. Also see Christopher B. Barnett, "Socrates the Pietist?: Tracing the Socratic in Zinzendorf, Hamann, and Kierkegaard," *Kierkegaard Studies: Yearbook 2010*, ed. Niels Jorgen Cappelørn, Hermann Deuser, and K. Brian Söderquist (Berlin: Walter de Gruyter, 2010), 307–24.

305   Pattison, *The Philosophy of Kierkegaard*, 182.

306   SKS 25, NB30:61 / JP 6, 6886.

307   Pattison, *The Philosophy of Kierkegaard*, 183. Indeed, there is a kind of Socratic irony in the Christian doctrine of Incarnation: "For he hath made him *to be* sin for us, who knew no sin; that we might be made the righteousness of God in him" (2 Cor. 5:21). Of course, such examples could be multiplied.

Chapter 5

1   See "About Google," https://www.google.com/intl/en/about/.

2   Lee Siegel, *Against the Machine: Being Human in the Age of the Electronic Mob* (New York: Spiegel & Grau, 2008), 86.

3   Ibid., 88.

4   Carr, *The Shallows*, 154.

5   Ibid.

6   Siva Vaidhyanathan, *The Googlization of Everything (and Why We Should Worry)* (Berkeley: University of California Press, 2011), 13.

7   Ibid.

8   Carr, *The Shallows*, 150.

9   Quoted in Vaidhyanathan, *Googlization*, 200.

10   Carr, *The Shallows*, 152.

11   See, for example, Jon Stewart, *Kierkegaard's Relations to Hegel Reconsidered* (Cambridge: Cambridge University Press, 2003). Stewart's basic premise is that Kierkegaard's polemics against Hegel are better understood as polemics against Hegelianism, particularly as expressed in the works of some of Kierkegaard's Danish contemporaries, such as Johan Ludvig Heiberg and Hans Lassen Martensen.

12   T. Z. Lavine, *From Socrates to Sartre: The Philosophic Quest* (New York: Bantam, 1984), 208.

13   Quoted in Ibid., 202.

14   Jacques Ellul, *The Technological Society*, trans. John Wilkinson (New York: Vintage, 1964), 52. Ellul and *The Technological Society* will be discussed in greater detail in Chapter 6.

15   Ibid.

16   Ibid.

17   Ibid., 54.

18   Stephen Houlgate, *An Introduction to Hegel: Freedom, Truth and History* (Oxford: Blackwell, 2005), 10.

19   Ibid.

20   Georg Wilhelm Friedrich Hegel, *The Philosophy of History*, trans. John Sibree (New York: Dover, 1956), 137.

21   Ibid., 341.

22   Ibid., 397.

23   Ibid.

24   Ibid., 438–39.

25   Houlgate, *Hegel*, 78.

26   Hegel, *Philosophy of History*, 439.

27   Ibid.

28   Ibid.

29   Ibid., 439–40.

30   Ibid., 440.

31   Ibid.

32   Ibid., 441.

33   Houlgate, *Hegel*, 22.

34   G. W. F. Hegel, *Phenomenology of Spirit*, trans. A. V. Miller (Oxford: Oxford University Press, 1977), 3.

35   John W. Burbridge, *Historical Dictionary of Hegelian Philosophy*, 2nd edition (Lanham, MD: The Scarecrow Press, Inc., 2008), 179.

36   Lavine, *The Philosophic Quest*, 219.

37   Quoted in Merold Westphal, *Transcendence and Self-transcendence: On God and the Soul* (Bloomington: Indiana University Press, 2004), 33.

38   Ibid., 32.

39   The gist of this course has been preserved in lecture form. See Martin Heidegger, "The Onto-Theo-Logical Constitution of Metaphysics," *Identity and Difference*, ed. Joan Stambaugh (Chicago, IL: The University of Chicago Press, 1969), 42–76.

40 Ibid., 18–19. According to Heidegger, "onto-theology" is characteristic of a metaphysics that describes beings in general and also makes them subordinate to a supreme being. For a helpful definition by Heidegger himself, see Martin Heidegger, *Pathmarks*, ed. William McNeill (Cambridge: Cambridge University Press, 1998), 340.

41 Ibid., 23.

42 Heidegger, "The Question Concerning Technology," 311–41.

43 SKS 7, 114 / CUP, 118–19.

44 SKS 7, 116 / CUP, 120.

45 SKS 7, 115 / CUP, 119.

46 Merold Westphal, *Becoming a Self: A Reading of Kierkegaard's Concluding Unscientific Postscript* (West Lafayette, IN: Purdue University Press, 1996), 83.

47 Ibid.

48 SKS 7, 115 / CUP, 119.

49 SKS 7, 118–19 / CUP, 123.

50 SKS 7, 119 / CUP, 124.

51 See, for example, SKS 7, 91–92 / CUP 93, where Climacus links objective thought with a fantastical relation to reality, arguing that the one "who in all his thinking can forget to think conjointly that he is existing . . . makes an attempt . . . to become a book or an objective something that only a Münchausen can become."

52 SKS 7, 120 / CUP, 124.

53 SKS 7, 122–23 / CUP, 130–31.

54 SKS 7, 105 / CUP, 108.

55 SKS 7, 105 / CUP, 108.

56 Jacques Ellul, *Propaganda: The Formation of Men's Attitudes* (New York: Vintage Books, 1973), 84.

57 Admittedly, the word "propaganda" carries negative connotations that exceed the scope of the present discussion; however, Ellul's treatment of the issue sums up Climacus's point nicely. After all, the word "propaganda" is derived from the Latin *propagare* ("to set forth," "to extend"), and its present meaning—"information propagated to further an ideology"—reflects Climacus's criticism of Hegel, not to mention related criticisms broached elsewhere in Kierkegaard's corpus.

58 Stewart, *Kierkegaard's Relations to Hegel Reconsidered*, 2.

59 See, for example, Ibid., 13ff.

60 Craig Detweiler, *iGods: How Technology Shapes Our Spiritual and Social Lives* (Grand Rapids, MI: Brazos Press, 2013), 107.

61 Randall Stross, *Planet Google: One Company's Audacious Plan to Organize Everything We Know* (New York: Free Press, 2008), 9.

62 Detweiler, *iGods*, 109.

63 Quoted in Vaidhyanathan, *Googlization*, 110.

64 Ibid., 174–75.

65 SKS 7, 80–81 / CUP, 80–81.

66 SKS 7, 81 / CUP, 81.

67 SKS 7, 81 / CUP, 81.

68 SKS 7, 81 / CUP, 81.

69 SKS 7, 81 / CUP, 81.

70 See, for example, McLuhan, *Understanding Media*, 7.

71 Vaidhyanathan, *Googlization*, 70. Personalized searching would seem to reflect Google's respect for individuality. Local news and sports scores, for example, are

increasingly proffered in accordance with the user's location. But this trend entails some disconcerting consequences. As Eli Pariser explains, "Our media is [becoming] a perfect reflection of our interests and desires. By definition, it's an appealing prospect—a return to a Ptolemaic universe in which the sun and everything else revolves around us" (Eli Pariser, *The Filter Bubble: How the New Personalized Web Is Changing What We Read and How We Think* [New York: Penguin, 2012], 12). Furthermore, such personalization only doubles down on one's subservience to Google: inasmuch as the latter is the medium through which the user receives pertinent information, this information is objective and *eo ipso* abstracted from the sorts of metaphysical and ethical questions that Climacus deems essential to human flourishing. Google, therefore, does not so much "personalize" one's experience on the internet as assume that all persons want the same kind of experience—namely, that of consuming data.

72   SKS 7, 81 / CUP, 81.

73   SKS 7, 81–82 / CUP, 82. As is well known, Kierkegaard would go on to develop this understanding of the self in *The Sickness unto Death* (1849).

74   SKS 7, 84 / CUP, 85.

75   Vaidhyanathan, *Googlization*, 2.

76   For Hegel, it is "reason" (*Vernunft*), rather than "understanding" (*Verstand*), that enables one to transcend abstract conceptual definitions and, in turn, to view ideas in more nuanced fashion, first with regard to "those contrary terms that are needed to define [their boundaries]" and second "in a unified perspective [that] articulates both the positive and the negative features of their relationship" (Burbridge, *Hegelian Philosophy*, 152). The former is known as dialectical reason, the latter as speculative reason. The point here, however, is just that Hegel envisions a depth—or, perhaps even better, a comprehensiveness—to *Vernunft* that has an analog in Google's own approach to information.

77   Ibid.

78   SKS 7, 116 / CUP1, 121.

79   SKS 7, 111 / CUP1, 115.

80   SKS 7, 111 / CUP1, 115.

81   SKS 7, 111–12 / CUP1, 115.

82   Detweiler, *iGods*, 120.

83   Ibid., 120–21.

84   David Shenk, *Data Smog: Surviving the Information Glut* (San Francisco, CA: Harper Edge, 1997), 11.

85   For a contemporary application of this problem, see, for example, Mark Bauerlein, *The Dumbest Generation: How the Digital Age Stupefies Young Americans and Jeopardizes Our Future (Or Don't Trust Anyone Under 30)* (New York: Tarcher, 2009).

86   SKS 7, 112 / CUP1, 115–16.

87   SKS 7, 113 / CUP1, 117.

88   SKS 7, 105 / CUP1, 109.

89   SKS 7, 114–15 / CUP1, 118–19.

90   SKS 7, 115 / CUP1, 119.

91   Carr, *The Shallows*, 150, 152.

92   Vaidhyanathan, *Googlization*, 14.

93   Detweiler, *iGods*, 115.

94   See "What We Believe: Ten Things We Know to Be True," http://www.google.com/
      about/company/philosophy/.
95   Quoted in Detweiler, *iGods*, 115.
96   Ibid., 117.
97   For example, Google's fiscal results for the third quarter of 2014 indicated
      consolidated revenues of nearly 17 billion dollars, up 20 percent from the same
      quarter in 2013. Patrick Pichette, then Google's CFO, said that further growth was
      expected, particularly in advertising and in "emerging businesses." See "Google
      Inc. Announces Third Quarter 2014 Results," Google Investor Relations, http://
      investor.google.com/earnings/2014/Q3_google_earnings.html (accessed July 18,
      2016). Indeed, by 2018, Google's quarterly revenue had exceeded 30 billion dollars,
      indicating that company continues to grow at an remarkable rate. See Matthew
      Lynley, "Google Beats Expectations Again with $31.15B in Revenue," *TechCrunch*,
      April 23, 2018, accessed December 5, 2018, https://techcrunch.com/2018/04/23/
      google-beats-expectations-again-with-31-15b-in-revenue/.
98   Detweiler, *iGods*, 115.
99   If this claim seems hyperbolic, it is worth underlining that there is, in fact, a Reddit
      community known as "The Church of Google," whose members adhere to the
      following creed: "We at the Church of Google believe the search engine Google is
      the closest humankind has ever come to directly experiencing an actual God (as
      typically defined). We believe there is much more evidence in favour of Google's
      divinity than there is for the divinity of other more traditional gods." The Church
      of Google even boasts a collection of prayers, including one that mimics the Lord's
      Prayer: "Our Google, who art in cyberspace, / Hallowed be thy domain. / Thy
      search to come, / Thy results be done, / On 127.0.0.1 as it is in the Googleplex."
      There is clearly an element of parody here, but the community does insist that to
      use Google is akin to prayer: "Google answers prayers. One can pray to Google by
      doing a search for whatever question or problem is plaguing them." See http://www.
      thechurchofgoogle.org.
100   Carr, *The Shallows*, 121.
101   Ibid., 125.
102   Ibid., 125–26. Intriguingly, Kierkegaard anticipated this turn of affairs in *A Literary
      Review*.
103   Ibid., 138.
104   Ibid., 157, emphasis added.
105   Of course, there are contrary readings—and not just among technophiles. For
      example, Hubert Dreyfus has argued that Wikipedia counterbalances Google's
      "syntactic" approach to Web-based information and, in turn, ensures that "the
      judgment calls of human encyclopedists and librarians" remain relevant in the
      digital era (Dreyfus, *On the Internet*, 128). For that reason, he concludes that
      "pessimism is no longer the order of the day" (ibid.) vis-à-vis fears about Google's
      ostensible elimination of qualitative interaction with data. Yet Carr's findings, at the
      very least, challenge Dreyfus's sanguinity, since they suggest that Google's delivery of
      information literally alters the way that our brains make judgments, even if Google
      does not eliminate judgment altogether. Moreover, from Climacus's perspective,
      Wikipedia can hardly be said to solve the problems raised by Google, because it,
      too, makes the crucial mistake of objectifying information, fostering reflection, and
      ultimately diminishing existential earnestness.

106 See, for example, TA, 68–76.
107 Merold Westphal, "Society, Politics, and Modernity," *The Oxford Handbook of Kierkegaard*, ed. John Lippitt and George Pattison (Oxford: Oxford University Press, 2013), 322.
108 SKS 21, NB8:12 / JP, 235.
109 SKS 5, 17 / EUD, 7, emphasis added.
110 I have treated this issued in greater detail elsewhere: see Barnett, *From Despair to Faith.*
111 SKS 8, 261 / UDVS, 161–62, my emphasis.
112 SKS 8, 262 / UDVS, 162, my translation.
113 SKS 8, 261 / UDVS, 162.
114 George Pattison, *Kierkegaard's Upbuilding Discourses: Philosophy, Literature and Theology* (London, Routledge, 2002), 143.
115 Ibid., 164.
116 For Kierkegaard, "the moment" is not just a measure of time. Rather, when an existing person consciously and in faith relates himself or herself to the eternal, it is a synthesis of temporal and eternal, finite and infinite. This latter understanding of *Øieblikket* is reserved for concrete individual experience and therefore takes Christ—who, in "the fullness of time" (Galatians 4:4), incarnates the eternal—as its exemplar par excellence. Yet, if this is true, then time has a qualitative, subjective depth that cannot be addressed by Google or by other information systems. On the contrary, time is to be fulfilled in ethico-religious practice, which, as Christ himself displays, always already includes *Betragtning.*
117 Carr, *The Shallows*, 207.
118 Ibid.
119 Neil Postman, *Amusing Ourselves to Death: Public Discourse in the Age of Show Business*, 20th Anniversary Edition (New York: Penguin, 2005), 155, 162.
120 Ibid., 156.
121 Pattison, *Thinking about God in an Age of Technology*, 2.
122 Postman, *Amusing Ourselves to Death*, 156–57.
123 Ibid., 157.
124 Martin Heidegger, *Being and Time*, trans. John Macquarrie and Edward Robinson (San Francisco, CA: Harper & Row, 1962), 494.

Chapter 6

1 Hans-Georg Gadamer, *Truth and Method*, trans. Joel Weinsheimer and Donald G. Marshall (London: Bloomsbury, 2013), 289.
2 Roger Poole, "The Unknown Kierkegaard: Twentieth-century Receptions," *The Cambridge Companion to Kierkegaard*, ed. Alastair Hannay and Gordon D. Marino (Cambridge: Cambridge University Press, 1998), 49.
3 See, above all, Harald Høffding, *Søren Kierkegaard som Filosof* (Copenhagen: Philipsen, 1892). Also see Carl Henrik Koch, "Harald Høffding: The Respectful Critic," *Kierkegaard's Influence on Philosophy: Tome I: German and Scandinavian Philosophy*, ed. Jon Stewart (Farnham: Ashgate, 2012), 267–88.
4 Poole, "The Unknown Kierkegaard," 50.

5   See, for example, Heiko Schulz, "A Modest Head Start: The German Reception of Kierkegaard," *Kierkegaard's International Reception: Tome I: Northern and Western Europe*, ed. Jon Stewart (Farnham: Ashgate, 2009), 326–27.
6   Poole, "The Unknown Kierkegaard," 51.
7   Ibid., 50–51, 54.
8   Ibid., 51.
9   See, for example, Thomas F. O'Meara, O. P., *Thomas Aquinas, Theologian* (South Bend, IN: University of Notre Dame Press, 1997) and Judith Wolfe, *Heidegger and Theology* (London: Bloomsbury T&T Clark, 2014).
10 Thomas Merton, *Contemplative Prayer* (London: Herder & Herder, 1969), 24.
11 SKS 7, 85 / CUP1, 85.
12 Robert C. Scharff and Val Dusek (eds.), *Philosophy of Technology: The Technological Condition: An Anthology*, 2nd edition (Malden, MA: Wiley-Blackwell, 2014). The section on "The Historical Background" runs from pages 3 to 87.
13 Michael W. Jennings, Brigid Doherty, and Thomas Y. Levin, "Editors' Introduction," *The Work of Art in the Age of Its Technological Reproducibility, and Other Writings on Media*, ed. Michael W. Jennings, Brigid Doherty, and Thomas Y. Levin (Cambridge, MA: Belknap Press, 2008), 1.
14 Ibid., 2.
15 Ibid., 3.
16 Ibid., 5.
17 Rainer Nägele, "Body Politics: Benjamin's Dialectical Materialism between Brecht and the Frankfurt School," *The Cambridge Companion to Walter Benjamin*, ed. David S. Ferris (Cambridge: Cambridge University Press, 2004), 174n8.
18 Joseph Westfall, "Walter Benjamin: Appropriating the Kierkegaardian Aesthetic," *Kierkegaard's Influence on Philosophy: Tome I: German and Scandinavian Philosophy*, ed. Jon Stewart (Farnham: Ashgate, 2012), 51.
19 Walter Benjamin, "Kierkegaard: Das Ende des philosophischen Idealismus," *Vossische Zeitung*, April 2, 1933. Also see Theodor W. Adorno, *Kierkegaard. Konstruktion des Ästhetischen* (Tübingen: Mohr, 1933).
20 Westfall, "Walter Benjamin," 53.
21 Ibid., 55–56.
22 Walter Benjamin, "The End of Philosophical Idealism," *Walter Benjamin: Selected Writings*, vol. 2, ed. Michael W. Jennings, Howard Eiland, and Gary Smith, trans. Rodney Livingstone, and Others (Cambridge, MA: Belknap Press, 1999), 704.
23 Walter Benjamin, *The Arcades Project*, ed. Rolf Tiedemann, trans. Howard Eiland and Kevin McLaughlin (Cambridge, MA: Belknap Press, 2002), 341.
24 Walter Benjamin, "Central Park," *Walter Benjamin: Selected Writings*, vol. 4, ed. Howard Eiland and Michael W. Jennings, trans. Edmund Jephcott (Cambridge, MA: Belknap Press, 2003), 175.
25 Westfall, "Walter Benjamin," 61.
26 Ibid., 60.
27 Marcia Morgan, *Kierkegaard and Critical Theory* (Lanham, MD: Lexington Books, 2012), 57.
28 Ibid., 56.
29 Ibid.

30   Max Pensky, *Melancholy Dialectics: Walter Benjamin and the Play of Mourning* (Amherst: University of Massachusetts Press, 1993), 11.

31   Ibid., 18.

32   Theodor W. Adorno, *Kierkegaard: Construction of the Aesthetic*, trans. Robert Hullot-Kentor (Minneapolis: University of Minnesota Press, 1989), 8. However, Morgan argues that, ultimately, "Adorno's arguments against Kierkegaard . . . fail" (Morgan, *Kierkegaard and Critical Theory*, 58).

33   Bartholomew Ryan, *Kierkegaard's Indirect Politics: Interludes with Lukács, Schmitt, Benjamin and Adorno* (Amsterdam: Rodopi, 2014), 135–36.

34   Ibid., 135.

35   Ibid., 137. By "indirect politics" Ryan means "the interstitial space between several disciplines," whereby "the exception, the exile and loafer, and the negative foil to all totality" are accommodated (ibid., 1). As a polemicist, who sought to defend the "single individual" from secularist hegemony, Kierkegaard writes "as a citizen (*politikos*) of the city (*polis*), writing within the world and attempting to engage with human beings in the world" (ibid., 2–3). Indeed, it is precisely because Kierkegaard is "anti-, de- and un-political in one sense" that he has come "to be a major influence in certain radical political thinking of the twentieth century" (ibid., 2).

36   Walter Benjamin, "Journalism," *The Work of Art in the Age of Its Technological Reproducibility, and Other Writings on Media*, ed. Michael W. Jennings, Brigid Doherty, and Thomas Y. Levin, trans. Edmund Jephcott, Rodney Livingstone, Howard Eiland, and Others (Cambridge, MA: Belknap Press, 2008), 353.

37   Ibid.

38   Ibid.

39   Ibid.

40   Walter Benjamin, "A Critique of the Publishing Industry," *The Work of Art in the Age of Its Technological Reproducibility, and Other Writings on Media*, ed. Michael W. Jennings, Brigid Doherty, and Thomas Y. Levin, trans. Edmund Jephcott, Rodney Livingstone, Howard Eiland, and Others (Cambridge, MA: Belknap Press, 2008), 356.

41   Ibid., 356–57.

42   Ibid., 355.

43   Ibid., 356.

44   Walter Benjamin, "The Newspaper," *The Work of Art in the Age of Its Technological Reproducibility, and Other Writings on Media*, ed. Michael W. Jennings, Brigid Doherty, and Thomas Y. Levin, trans. Edmund Jephcott, Rodney Livingstone, Howard Eiland, and Others (Cambridge, MA: Belknap Press, 2008), 359.

45   Ibid.

46   Ibid., 360.

47   Of course, Benjamin was by no means blithely optimistic. He offers a "disavowal of the naive optimism which characterized the thinking of the Left between the World Wars, and which would lead the Right to failure" (Philippe Simay, "Tradition as Injunction: Benjamin and the Critique of Historicisms," *Walter Benjamin and History*, ed. Andrew Benjamin [London: Continuum, 2005], 137). In point of fact, Benjamin famously compares historical progress to a *storm*. See, for example, Michael Löwy, *Fire Alarm: Reading Walter Benjamin's "On the Concept of History,"* trans. Chris Turner (London: Verso, 2005).

48   Benjamin, "The Newspaper," 360.

49   Walter Benjamin, "The Work of Art in the Age of Its Technological Reproducibility,"
     *The Work of Art in the Age of Its Technological Reproducibility, and Other Writings
     on Media*, ed. Michael W. Jennings, Brigid Doherty, and Thomas Y. Levin, trans.
     Edmund Jephcott, Rodney Livingstone, Howard Eiland, and Others (Cambridge,
     MA: Belknap Press, 2008), 20–21.

50   Ibid., 22, emphasis in original.

51   Ibid.

52   Ibid.

53   Pattison, *Thinking about God in an Age of Technology*, 231.

54   Benjamin, "The Work of Art," 33, 39.

55   Ibid., 37, emphasis in original.

56   Ibid., 22, 38, 41, emphasis in original.

57   Ibid., 41.

58   Ibid., 36, emphasis in original. With this in mind, Jan Mieszkowski writes, "It is
     on the basis of such claims that Benjamin has continued to be influential for
     left-wing media scholars who strive to reject the unambiguous valorization of high
     art and validate the political and social worth of mass culture" (Jan Mieszkowski,
     "Art Forms," *The Cambridge Companion to Walter Benjamin*, ed. David S. Ferris
     (Cambridge: Cambridge University Press, 2004), 41. Ironically, however, Adorno
     worried that Benjamin placed naive faith in the proletariat, noting that "laughter of a
     cinema audience at the funny tramp with his hat and cane may simply be bourgeois
     sadism" (ibid., 42).

59   Ibid., 28.

60   Eric Ziolkowski, "Introduction," *Kierkegaard, Literature, and the Arts*, ed. Eric
     Ziolkowski (Evanston, IL: Northwestern University Press, 2018), 26.

61   Ibid.

62   Ryan, *Kierkegaard's Indirect Politics*, 175.

63   John D. Caputo, *Radical Hermeneutics* (Bloomington: Indiana University Press,
     1987), 82–83.

64   Quoted in Theodore J. Kisiel and Thomas Sheehan (eds.), *Becoming Heidegger: On
     the Trail of His Early Occasional Writings, 1910–1927* (Evanston, IL: Northwestern
     University Press, 2007), 97–98.

65   Quoted in John van Buren, *The Young Heidegger: Rumor of the Hidden King*
     (Bloomington: Indiana University Press, 1994), 222.

66   Martin Heidegger, "The Word of Nietzsche: 'God Is Dead,'" *The Question Concerning
     Technology and Other Essays*, trans. William Lovitt (New York: Harper and Row,
     1977), 94.

67   Caputo, *Radical Hermeneutics*, 16.

68   Vincent McCarthy, "Martin Heidegger: Kierkegaard's Influence Hidden and in Full
     View," *Kierkegaard and Existentialism*, Kierkegaard Research: Sources, Reception and
     Resources, vol. 9, ed. Jon Stewart (New York: Routledge, 2016), 95.

69   "Dasein" is Heidegger's preferred name for the way of being characteristic of human
     beings, who are unique in their ability to explore the meaning of being. In keeping
     with John Macquarrie and Edward Robinson, whose 1962 English translation
     of Heidegger's *Being and Time* (*Sein und Zeit*, 1927) remains standard, I will not
     italicize Dasein in this discussion.

70   Richard Polt, *Heidegger: An Introduction* (Ithaca, NY: Cornell University Press,
     1999), 118. Whether or not, and to what degree, such a "turn" (*Kehre*) actually took

place in Heidegger's thinking "has become a classic topic in the secondary literature" (ibid., 121).

71 Heidegger, *Being and Time*, 171.
72 Polt, *Heidegger*, 57.
73 See, for example, Heidegger, *Being and Time*, 96, 131.
74 Polt, *Heidegger*, 142.
75 Martin Heidegger, *Contributions to Philosophy (of the Event)*, trans. Richard Rojcewicz and Daniela Vallega-Neu (Bloomington: Indiana University Press, 2012), 98.
76 Ibid.
77 Polt, *Heidegger*, 142.
78 Heidegger, *Contributions to Philosophy*, 100.
79 Ibid., 100–01.
80 Ibid., 94.
81 Polt, *Heidegger*, 143.
82 David Lewin, *Technology and the Philosophy of Religion* (Newcastle upon Tyne: Cambridge Scholars Publishing, 2012), 125, 127.
83 Iain D. Thomson, *Heidegger on Ontotheology: Technology and the Politics of Education* (Cambridge: Cambridge University Press, 2005), 44.
84 Heidegger, "The Question Concerning Technology," 311.
85 Ibid.
86 Ibid., 312.
87 Ibid., 313.
88 Ibid., 317.
89 Ibid.
90 Ibid.
91 Ibid., 318.
92 Frank Schalow and Alfred Denker, *Historical Dictionary of Heidegger's Philosophy*, 2nd edition (Lanham, MD: The Scarecrow Press, Inc., 2010), 49.
93 Thomson, *Heidegger on Ontotheology*, 53.
94 Heidegger, "Question Concerning Technology," 320.
95 Ibid., 321.
96 Ibid., 322.
97 Ibid.
98 Ibid.
99 Ibid., 320–23.
100 Ibid., 323.
101 Ibid., 324.
102 Ibid.
103 Ibid., 330.
104 Ibid.
105 Thomson, *Heidegger on Ontotheology*, 53.
106 Heidegger, "Question Concerning Technology," 331.
107 Ibid., 330.
108 Ibid., 332.
109 Ibid., 333.
110 Quoted in ibid.
111 Ibid.
112 Thomson, *Heidegger on Ontotheology*, 53.

113 See Martin Heidegger, *Discourse on Thinking: A Translation of Gelassenheit*, trans. John M. Anderson and E. Hans Freund (New York: Harper Perennial, 1966), 45–53.

114 Heidegger, "Question Concerning Technology," 341.

115 Lewin, *Technology and the Philosophy of Religion*, 162.

116 Ibid., 145.

117 Martin Heidegger, *The Principle of Reason*, trans. Reginald Lilly (Bloomington: Indiana University Press, 1991), 55.

118 Lewin, *Technology and the Philosophy of Religion*, 147.

119 Schalow and Denker, *Heidegger's Philosophy*, 79.

120 Lewin, *Technology and the Philosophy of Religion*, 147.

121 John Macquarrie, *Existentialism: An Introduction, Guide and Assessment* (London: Penguin, 1972), 169.

122 Ibid., 165.

123 René Descartes, *Meditations on First Philosophy: With Selections from the Objections and Replies*, 2nd Edition, trans. and ed. John Cottingham (Cambridge: Cambridge University Press, 2017), 15.

124 SKS 7, 107 / CUP1, 110.

125 SKS 7, 118 / CUP1, 123.

126 SKS 7, 115 / CUP 1, 119.

127 SKS 18, JJ:14 / JP 5, 5574, my translation.

128 *Pap.* IV B 16 / PF, 235.

129 *Pap.* IV B 16 / PF, 235.

130 SKS 7, 69 / CUP1, 67–68.

131 SKS 13, 165 / M, 123.

132 Schalow and Denker, *Historical Dictionary of Heidegger's Philosophy*, 100.

133 See Alastair Hannay, "Kierkegaard's Levellings and the *Review*," *Kierkegaard Studies Yearbook 1999*, ed. Heiko Schulz, Jon Stewart, and Karl Verstrynge (Berlin: de Gruyter, 1999), 71–95.

134 SKS 27, Papir 586 / JP 2, 1940.

135 Martin Heidegger, *History of the Concept of Time: Prolegomena*, trans. Theodore Kisiel (Bloomington: Indiana University Press, 1985), 282.

136 David Dwan, "Idle Talk: Ontology and Mass Communications in Heidegger," *New Formations* 51 (2003), 113–14.

137 Ibid., 125. Here Dwan is citing Heidegger, *Being and Time*, 166. Also, Dwan's allusion to *The Present Age* is referring to an abridged version of *A Literary Review*: Søren Kierkegaard, *The Present Age*, trans. Alexander Dru (New York: Harper & Row, 1962).

138 Dwan, "Idle Talk," 125.

139 Heidegger, *Being and Time*, 164.

140 Clare Carlisle, "Kierkegaard and Heidegger," *The Oxford Handbook of Kierkegaard*, ed. John Lippitt and George Pattison (Oxford: Oxford University Press, 2013), 435.

141 Schalow and Denker, *Historical Dictionary of Heidegger's Philosophy*, 136. Also see Carlisle, "Kierkegaard and Heidegger," 435–36.

142 Carlisle, "Kierkegaard and Heidegger," 436.

143 Andrew Komasinski, "'Anti-Climacus' Pre-emptive Critique of Heidegger's 'Question Concerning Technology,'" *International Philosophical Quarterly* 54.3 (2014), 269.

144 Ibid., 273.

145 Ibid., 276–77.

146   Ibid., 277.
147   Liselotte Richter, "Kierkegaard und das Zeitalter der Technokratie," *Zeichen der Zeit*, no. 11 (1955), 406.
148   SKS 22, NB13:66 / JP 1, 388.
149   Craig Hanks, "Introduction to Chapter 13," *Technology and Values: Essential Readings*, ed. Craig Hanks (Oxford: Wiley-Blackwell, 2010), 159.
150   Ibid.
151   Herbert Marcuse, *Reason and Revolution: Hegel and the Rise of Social Theory*, 2nd edition (London: Routledge, 2000), 264.
152   Ibid., 264–65.
153   Ibid., 264.
154   Ibid., 266.
155   J. Michael Tilley, "Herbert Marcuse: Social Critique, Haecker, and Kierkegaardian Individualism," *Kierkegaard's Influence on Social-Political Thought*, ed. Jon Stewart, Kierkegaard Research: Sources, Reception and Resources, vol. 14 (London: Routledge, 2011), 139, 142. Tilley notes that critical theorists tended to worry that existentialist critiques of modernity would terminate in fascism, as evinced by the Nazi sympathies of figures such as Emanuel Hirsch and Heidegger. This is surely true, though it is striking that, as Tilley goes on, the figure most responsible for disseminating Kierkegaard's social theory (especially *A Literary Review*) in Germany was Theodor Haecker—a Catholic activist and author who is famous for his *resistance* to Nazism and his membership in the opposition group *die Weiße Rose*. Needless to say, then, this is an exceedingly complex matter, not just in terms of the reception of Kierkegaard's thought but also in terms of the inner meaning of critiques of modern society. Here, again, Heidegger remains a lightning rod for controversy—and rightfully so. Though ambiguities surround Heidegger's relation to Nazism (see, for example, Wolfe, *Heidegger and Theology*, 99–150), there is no denying that Heidegger subscribed to National Socialism for a time. And yet, *pace* critical theorists such as Marcuse, there are strong differences between Kierkegaard and Heidegger, perhaps especially as regards ethical questions. See, for example, Patricia J. Huntington, "Heidegger's Reading of Kierkegaard Revisited: From Ontological Abstraction to Ethical Concretion," *Kierkegaard in Post/Modernity*, ed. Martin J. Matuštík and Merold Westphal (Bloomington: Indiana University Press, 1995), 43–65.
156   Herbert Marcuse, *One-Dimensional Man: Studies in the Ideology of Advanced Industrial Society* (Boston, MA: Beacon Press, 1964), 1.
157   Ibid.
158   Ibid., 3.
159   Ibid., 7.
160   Ibid., 9.
161   Ibid., 11.
162   Ibid., 12.
163   Ibid., 13.
164   Lewin, *Technology and the Philosophy of Religion*, 73.
165   Ibid.
166   Marcuse, *One-Dimensional Man*, 14.
167   Ibid., 12–13.
168   Ibid., 15.

169   See Lewin, *Technology and the Philosophy of Religion*, 76–77.

170   Marcuse, *One-Dimensional Man*, 226.

171   Ibid., 225.

172   Lewin, *Technology and the Philosophy of Religion*, 78.

173   Kierkegaard notoriously stirred up this question during his "attack upon Christendom." On the other hand, while "it is not clear whether Marcuse has a convincing account of the capacity for art to be at once historical and transcendent" (ibid., 93), he has recently been portrayed as a kind of guru for left-wing critiques of the commercialization of art—namely, in the Coen Brothers' 2016 comedy film *Hail, Caesar!*, in which Marcuse (played by John Bluthal) encourages a motley crew of Hollywood actors and writers to ponder "the essence of the dialectic."

174   Donald MacKinnon, "Foreword," *Man against Mass Society*, trans. G. S. Fraser (South Bend, IN: St. Augustine's Press, 2008), i.

175   Jean-Paul Sartre, *Existentialism and Human Emotions* (New York: Citadel Press, 1985), 13.

176   Ibid.

177   Ibid., 15.

178   Thomas C. Anderson, "Atheistic and Christian Existentialism: A Comparison of Sartre and Marcel," *New Perspectives on Sartre*, ed. Adrian Mirvish and Adrian van den Hoven (Newcastle upon Tyne: Cambridge Scholars Publishing, 2010), 45.

179   Ibid.

180   See, for example, Barnett, *Kierkegaard, Pietism and Holiness*, 95–106.

181   Jeanette Bresson Ladegaard Knox, "Gabriel Marcel: The Silence of Truth," *Kierkegaard and Existentialism*, ed. Jon Stewart, Kierkegaard Research: Sources, Reception and Resources, vol. 9 (Farnham: Ashgate, 2011), 199.

182   Indeed, there is a strong Socratic strain Pascal's thought. See, for example, Graeme Hunter, *Pascal the Philosopher: An Introduction* (Toronto: University of Toronto Press, 2013), 221–22.

183   Ibid., 200. The quote from Marcel comes from a 1964 paper that he gave in Paris. Heidegger, Sartre, and Jaspers were also in attendance. See Gabriel Marcel, "Kierkegaard en ma pensée," *Kierkegaard vivant. Colloque organisé par l'UNESCO à Paris due 21 au 23 avril 1964* (Paris: Gallimard, 1966), 64–80.

184   Marcel, "Kierkegaard en ma pensée," 65. The connection to de Lubac is plausible, given that de Lubac himself had a keen interest in the Dane. See, for example, Christopher B. Barnett, "Henri de Lubac: Locating Kierkegaard Amid the 'Drama' of Nietzschean Humanism," *Kierkegaard's Influence on Theology: Tome III: Catholic and Jewish Theology*, ed. Jon Stewart, Kierkegaard Research: Sources, Reception and Resources, vol. 10 (Farnham: Ashgate, 2012), 97–110.

185   Knox, "Gabriel Marcel: The Silence of Truth," 204.

186   Jean Wahl, *Philosophies of Existence: An Introduction to the Basic Thought of Kierkegaard, Heidegger, Jaspers, Marcel, Sartre*, trans. F. M. Lory (New York: Shocken Books, 1969), 24.

187   Ibid.

188   Ibid., my emphasis.

189   Gabriel Marcel, *Man against Mass Society*, trans. G. S. Fraser (South Bend, IN: St. Augustine's Press, 2008), 6.

190   Ibid.

191   Ibid., 6–8.

192   Ibid., 8.

193 Ibid.
194 Ibid.
195 This is the title of the book's third chapter. See ibid., 27–56.
196 Ibid., 33.
197 Ibid., 39.
198 Ibid., 38.
199 Ibid., 39.
200 Ibid.
201 Ibid.
202 Ibid.
203 Ibid., 40.
204 Ibid.
205 Ibid.
206 Ibid.
207 Gabriel Marcel, *The Mystery of Being I: Reflection and Mystery*, trans. G. S. Fraser (Chicago, IL: Henry Regnery Company, 1960), 5.
208 Ibid., 8.
209 Ibid., 7.
210 Marcel, *Man against Mass Society*, 40.
211 Marcel, *The Mystery of Being I: Reflection and Mystery*, 6.
212 Marcel, *Man against Mass Society*, 41–42.
213 Ibid., 41.
214 Marcel, *The Mystery of Being I: Reflection and Mystery*, 6–7.
215 Ibid., 7.
216 Marcel, *Man against Mass Society*, 48.
217 Ibid., 54.
218 Ibid., 54–55.
219 Ibid., 54.
220 See, for example, Steve Fuller, *Post-Truth: Knowledge as a Power Game* (London: Anthem Press, 2018).
221 Jon Stewart (ed.), *Kierkegaard and Existentialism*, Kierkegaard Research: Sources, Reception and Resources, vol. 9 (Farnham: Ashgate, 2011).
222 Jill Graper Hernandez, *Gabriel Marcel's Ethics of Hope: Evil, God and Virtue* (London: Bloomsbury, 2013), 86.
223 Gabriel Marcel, *The Philosophy of Existentialism* (New York: Citadel Press, 1984), 31.
224 Patrick Troude-Chastenet, *Jacques Ellul on Religion, Technology, and Politics: Conversations with Patrick Troude-Chastenet*, trans. Joan Mendès France (Atlanta, GA: Scholars Press, 1998), 4.
225 Sarah Pike Cabral, "Jacques Ellul: Kierkegaard's Profound and Seldom Acknowledged Influence on Ellul's Writing," *Kierkegaard's Influence on Philosophy: Tome II: Francophone Philosophy*, ed. Jon Stewart, Kierkegaard Research: Sources, Reception and Resources, vol. 11 (Farnham: Ashgate, 2012), 139.
226 Quoted in ibid., 140.
227 In fact, Vernard Eller views Kierkegaard and Ellul as "closer than brothers." See Vernard Eller, "Ellul and Kierkegaard: Closer than Brothers," *Jacques Ellul: Interpretive Essays*, ed. Clifford G. Christians and Jay M. VanHook (Urbana: University of Illinois Press, 1981), 52.
228 Cabral, "Jacques Ellul," 142.

229 Quoted in ibid.
230 Jacques Ellul, *Living Faith: Belief and Doubt in a Perilous World*, trans. Peter Heinegg (San Francisco, CA: Harper and Row, 1983), 123.
231 Jeffrey P. Greenman, Read Mercer Schuchardt, and Noah J. Toly, *Understanding Jacques Ellul* (Cambridge: James Clarke & Co, 2013), 11.
232 Ibid., 11, 19.
233 Ibid., 20.
234 Ellul, *The Technological Society*, xxv.
235 Ibid., xxvi.
236 Ibid., 4.
237 Ibid., 5.
238 Ibid.
239 Ibid., 14.
240 Ibid., xxix.
241 Ibid., 17.
242 See Voltaire, *Candide, ou l'Optimisme* (Paris: Sirène, 1759).
243 Ellul, *The Technological Society*, 17.
244 Ibid., 18.
245 Ibid., 19.
246 Ibid., 18–19.
247 Ibid., 19.
248 Ibid., 20.
249 Ibid., 21.
250 Ibid., 420.
251 Ibid., 419.
252 Ibid., 423.
253 Ibid., 424.
254 Ibid.
255 Ibid.
256 Ibid., 55.
257 Jacques Ellul, *Propaganda: The Formation of Men's Attitudes*, trans. Konrad Kellen and Jean Lerner (New York: Vintage Books, 1965), 9.
258 Cabral, "Jacques Ellul," 149.
259 Frédéric Rognon, "Jacques Ellul and Søren Kierkegaard," trans. Lisa Richmond, International Jacques Ellul Society, accessed September 29, 2018, https://ellul.org/ellul-and-kierkegaard/.
260 Ibid.
261 Julia Watkin, *Historical Dictionary of Kierkegaard's Philosophy* (Lanham, MD: The Scarecrow Press, Inc., 2001), 46.
262 David Lovekin, *Technique, Discourse, and Consciousness: An Introduction to the Philosophy of Jacques Ellul* (Bethlehem, PA: Lehigh University Press, 1991), 67.
263 Ibid., 23.
264 SKS 11, 156 / SUD, 41.
265 SKS 11, 155 / SUD, 40. The reference is to King Midas of Phrygia, whose legend was known to and made popular by Aristotle. See Aristotle, *Politics*, trans. Carnes Lord, 2nd edition (Chicago, IL: University of Chicago Press, 2013), 16.
266 Lawrence J. Terlizzese, *Hope in the Thought of Jacques Ellul* (Eugene, OR: Cascade Books, 2005), 56.

267 Ibid.

268 To be sure, neither Kierkegaard nor Ellul would have been dumbfounded by the advent of "transhumanism," a philosophical moment that "seeks the continued evolution of human life beyond its current human form as a result of science and technology" (Max More and Natasha Vita-More, "Roots and Core Themes," *The Transhumanist Reader: Classical and Contemporary Essays on the Science, Technology, and Philosophy of the Human Future*, ed. Max More and Natasha Vita-More [Oxford: Wiley-Blackwell, 2013], 1).

269 Terlizzese, *Hope in the Thought of Jacques Ellul*, 57.

270 SKS 11, 146 / SUD, 29–30.

271 Terlizzese, *Hope in the Thought of Jacques Ellul*, 56.

272 David Skrbina, "Introduction: A Revolutionary for Our Times," *Technological Slavery: The Collected Writings of Theodore J. Kaczynski, a.k.a. "The Unabomber"* (Port Townsend, WA: Feral House, 2010), 30.

273 Pattison, *Thinking about God in an Age of Technology*, 253–54.

274 Jacques Ellul, *The Meaning of the City*, trans. Dennis Pardee (Eugene, OR: Wipf and Stock Publishers, 2011), 7.

275 See, for example, Pattison, *"Poor Paris!,"* 125–30.

276 Pattison, *Thinking about God in an Age of Technology*, 254.

277 Pattison, *"Poor Paris!,"* 141–42.

278 Ibid., 142.

279 Wha-Chul Son, "Are We Still Pursuing Efficiency? Interpreting Jacques Ellul's Efficiency Principle," *Jacques Ellul and the Technological Society in the 21st Century*, ed. Helena M. Jerónimo, José Luís Garcia, and Carl Mitcham (Dordrecht: Springer, 2013), 61.

280 Jacques Ellul, *The Technological Bluff*, trans. Geoffrey Bromiley (Grand Rapids, MI: Eerdmans, 1990), 411.

281 Son, "Interpreting Jacques Ellul's Efficiency Principle," 61.

282 See, for example, *American Philosophy of Technology: The Empirical Turn*, trans. Robert P. Crease, ed. Hans Achterhuis (Bloomington: Indiana University Press, 2001), a collection of essays by leading figures in the "Dutch school" of the philosophy of technology on a number of their American counterparts, including Hubert Dreyfus and Don Ihde.

283 Philip Brey, "Well-Being in Philosophy, Psychology, and Economics," *The Good Life in a Technological Age*, ed. Philip Brey, Adam Briggle, and Edward Spence (New York: Routledge, 2012), 32. In fact, this entire volume is a sustained exercise in relating the latest trends in the philosophy of technology to a number of classical philosophical problems. At the same time, however, it is disappointing that the word "theology" only turns up once in the book, suggesting a postmodern rupture between eudaimonism and theology that a figure such as Kierkegaard might repair.

284 "If Kierkegaard did not exist, he would have to be invented." This line is, of course, adapted from Voltaire. See Voltaire, "Epître à l'auteur du livre des *Trois imposteurs*," *OEuvres complètes de Voltaire*, ed. Louis Moland, vol. 10 (Paris: Garnier, 1877–1885), 402–405.

285 Jon Stewart, "Editor's Introduction: Kierkegaard and the Rich Field of Kierkegaard Studies," *A Companion to Kierkegaard*, ed. Jon Stewart (Oxford: Wiley-Blackwell, 2015), 4.

286 Aidan Nichols, O. P., *Lost in Wonder: Essays on Liturgy and the Arts* (London: Routledge, 2011), 22.

287   Ibid.
288   Ibid., 23. Phenomenology, as a philosophical school, is typically traced back to Franz
      Brentano—a nineteenth-century German thinker (and onetime Catholic priest)
      who sought to recover the concept of "intentionality" in philosophy. Brentano
      taught Edmund Husserl and, indeed, would have a major impact on Heidegger.
289   Ibid., 24.
290   Ibid., 24–25.
291   Peter Šajda, "Romano Guardini: Between Actualistic Personalism, Qualitative
      Dialectic and Kinetic Logic," *Kierkegaard's Influence on Theology. Tome III: Catholic
      and Jewish Theology*, ed. John Stewart (Farnham: Ashgate, 2012), 46–47.
292   Ibid., 45.
293   Ibid., 52.
294   Ibid., 51.
295   With this in mind, it is particularly curious that even an article *directly* concerning
      the reception of *A Literary Review* in Germany fails to mention Guardini. See
      Allan Janik, "Haecker, Kierkegaard and the Early *Brenner*: A Contribution to the
      History of the Reception of *Two Ages* in the German-speaking World," *International
      Kierkegaard Commentary: Two Ages*, ed. Robert L. Perkins (Macon, GA: Mercer
      University Press, 1984), 189–222.
296   Olaf P. Monrad, *Søren Kierkegaard. Sein Leben und seine Werke* (Jena: Diederichs,
      1909), 72.
297   Ibid.
298   Ibid.
299   Oliver O'Donovan, review of *Letters from Lake Como*, by Romano Guardini,
      Studies in Christian Ethics, 8.2 (1995), 104–05. Though it now appears as a "general
      critique," the nine letters comprising *Letters from Lake Como* initially were published
      separately from 1923–25. The current English edition also includes "The Machine
      and Humanity," a paper that Guardini gave at the Munich College of Technology
      in 1959.
300   Romano Guardini, *Letters from Lake Como: Explorations in Technology and the
      Human Race*, trans. Geoffrey W. Bromiley (Grand Rapids, MI: Eerdmans Publishing
      Company, 1994), 7.
301   Ibid.
302   Ibid., 19.
303   Ibid.
304   Ibid., 29.
305   Ibid., 31.
306   Ibid., 32.
307   Ibid., 43.
308   Ibid., 47.
309   Ibid., 47–48.
310   Ibid., 59.
311   Ibid., 62–63.
312   Louis Dupré, "Introduction," Romano Guardini, *Letters from Lake Como:
      Explorations in Technology and the Human Race* (Grand Rapids, MI: Eerdmans
      Publishing Company, 1994), xi, xiii.
313   O'Donovan, review of *Letters from Lake Como*, 104.
314   Andrew Feenberg, *Questioning Technology* (London: Routledge, 1999), 3.

315   Ibid.
316   Ibid., 2–3.
317   SKS 8, 84–85 / TA, 87–89.
318   SKS 8, 103 / TA, 108.
319   SKS 8, 103–04 / TA, 109.
320   SKS 8, 102 / TA, 107.
321   SKS 8, 103 / TA, 108.
322   Guardini, *Letters from Lake Como*, 80.
323   Ibid., 81.
324   Ibid., 81–82.
325   Ibid., 83.
326   Ibid., 85.
327   Ibid., 93.
328   Pattison, *Thinking about God in an Age of Technology*, 40.
329   Pierre Teilhard de Chardin, *The Phenomenon of Man*, trans. Bernard Wall (New York: Harper Perennial, 1976), 219.
330   See, for example, Ernst Mayr, "The Idea of Teleology," *Journal of the History of Ideas* 53.1 (1992), 117–35. Mayr rebuffs the idea that biological teleology can be traced back to any supernatural origin.
331   Michael S. Burdett, *Eschatology and the Technological Future* (New York: Routledge, 2015), 114.
332   Ibid.
333   See Pattison, *Thinking About God in an Age of Technology*, 41.
334   Romano Guardini, *The Faith and Modern Man*, trans. Charlotte E. Forsyth (New York: Pantheon Books, 1952), 65.
335   Wilhelm and Marion Pauck, *Paul Tillich: His Life and Thought* (Eugene, OR: Wipf and Stock, 1989), 4.
336   Ibid., 6.
337   Quoted in Bernard Martin, *The Existentialist Theology of Paul Tillich* (New Haven, CT: College and University Press, 1963), 16.
338   Lee C. Barrett, "Paul Tillich: An Ambivalent Appreciation," *Kierkegaard's Influence on Theology. Tome I: German Protestant Theology*, ed. Jon Stewart (Farnham: Ashgate, 2012), 337.
339   Ibid., 338.
340   Ibid.
341   George Pattison, *Anxious Angels: A Retrospective View of Religious Existentialism* (New York: St. Martin's Press, Inc., 1999), 151.
342   J. Mark Thomas, "Introduction," *Paul Tillich: The Spiritual Situation in Our Technical Society*, ed. J. Mark Thomas (Macon, GA: Mercer University Press, 1988), xiii.
343   Ibid., xiv.
344   John P. Clayton, *The Concept of Correlation: Paul Tillich and the Possibility of a Mediating Theology* (Berlin: de Gruyter, 1980), 191. Clayton especially singles out Tillich's slapdash use of the term *Gehalt*, which bears a "notorious lack of precision" (ibid., 197).
345   Paul Tillich, *Systematic Theology: Volume One* (Chicago, IL: The University of Chicago Press, 1951), 64.
346   Barrett, "Paul Tillich: An Ambivalent Appreciation," 353. Elsewhere Tillich recalls "the shaking impact of [Kierkegaard's] dialectical psychology" during his student

years (Paul Tillich, "Autobiographical Reflections," *The Theology of Paul Tillich*, ed. Charles Kegley and Robert Bretall [New York: Macmillan, 1952], 10–11).

347   Ibid., 355.
348   Ibid., 354.
349   Paul Tillich, *The Interpretation of History* (New York: Charles Scribner's Sons, 1936), 62.
350   Barrett, "Paul Tillich: An Ambivalent Appreciation," 355, 359.
351   Paul Tillich, *Paul Tillich: The Spiritual Situation in Our Technical Society*, ed. J. Mark Thomas (Macon, GA: Mercer University Press, 1988), 25.
352   Ibid., 26.
353   Ibid., 26.
354   Ibid., 27.
355   Ibid.
356   Ibid., 29.
357   Ibid., 30.
358   Ibid.
359   Ibid., 33.
360   Ibid.
361   Ibid., 37.
362   Ibid., 123.
363   Ibid.
364   Ibid., 124.
365   Ibid. See the previous chapter in this study for a fuller exposition of how Kierkegaard's response to Hegel might dovetail with a critique of modern technology.
366   Ibid.
367   Ibid.
368   Ibid., 43.
369   Ibid. Tillich acknowledges this paradox. And, notably, President Dwight Eisenhower would create the National Space and Aeronautics Administration (NASA) a few weeks after "The Lost Dimension in Religion" appeared.
370   Ibid.
371   Ibid.
372   Ibid., 43–44.
373   Ibid.
374   Ibid., 125.
375   Ibid., 136.
376   Ibid., 136–37.
377   Ibid., 135.
378   Ibid.
379   Ibid., 136.
380   Ibid., 137.
381   Robert Inchausti, "Introduction," *Seeds: Thomas Merton*, ed. Robert Inchausti (Boston, MA: Shambala, 2002), xi.
382   Ibid.
383   Ibid., 42.
384   Ibid., xiii.
385   Ibid.

386   Ibid., xv.

387   Ibid.

388   Ibid.

389   Thomas Merton, *The Inner Experience: Notes on Contemplation* (New York: HarperCollins, 2003), 105.

390   Erik Hanson, "Thomas Merton: Kierkegaard, Merton and Authenticity," *Kierkegaard's Influence on Theology. Tome III: Catholic and Jewish Theology*, ed. Jon Stewart (Farnham: Ashgate, 2012), 115.

391   See, for example, Thomas Merton, *The Secular Journal* (New York: Dell Publishing, 1959), 117–21. Also see Thomas Merton, *The Ascent to Truth* (New York: Harcourt, Brace and Company, 1951), 39. Here, in a brief reference, Merton likens Kierkegaard's thought on anxiety and despair to the "two nights" of the Carmelite mystic John of the Cross.

392   Thomas Merton, *The Other Side of the Mountain*, ed. Patrick Hart, O. C. S. O., The Journals of Thomas Merton, vol. 7 (New York: HarperCollins, 1998), 136, 138.

393   Thomas Merton, *Contemplation in a World of Action* (London: George Allen and Unwin, 1971), 31–32, 35.

394   Hanson, "Thomas Merton: Kierkegaard, Merton and Authenticity," 115.

395   See Thomas Merton, *Mystics and Zen Masters* (New York: Farrar, Strauss and Giroux, 1967), 255–80. The reference is from ibid., 263.

396   Ibid.

397   Ibid., 264.

398   Ibid.

399   Ibid., 264–65.

400   Ibid., 265.

401   Thomas Merton, *Conjectures of a Guilty Bystander* (Garden City, NY: Doubleday, 1971), 216–17.

402   Merton, *Mystics and Zen Masters*, 167.

403   See, for example, Hanson, "Thomas Merton: Kierkegaard, Merton and Authenticity," 129.

404   Phillip M. Thompson, *Between Science and Religion: The Engagement of Catholic Intellectuals with Science and Technology in the Twentieth Century* (Lanham, MD: Lexington Books, 2009), 118–20.

405   Quoted in Paul R. Dekar, *Thomas Merton: Twentieth-Century Wisdom for Twenty-First-Century Living* (Eugene, OR: Cascade Books, 2011), 94.

406   Ibid., 98–99.

407   It is intriguing that, in a 1965 letter, Merton lists Kierkegaard and Guardini as "authors who have helped me a lot" (Thomas Merton, *Witness to Freedom: The Letters of Thomas Merton in a Time of Crisis*, ed. William H. Shannon [New York: Farrar, Strauss and Giroux, 1994], 169). However, Merton does not mention Teilhard in this connection.

408   Thomas Merton, *The Seeds of Destruction* (New York: Farrar, Strauss and Giroux, 1964), 323.

409   Ibid., 324.

410   Quoted in Dekar, *Thomas Merton*, 86.

411   This phrase is often translated as "Only a God can save us." See Martin Heidegger, "Nur noch ein Gott kann uns retten," *Der Spiegel* 30 (May 1976), 193–219.

412   Thompson, *Between Science and Religion*, 125.

413 Albert Borgmann, "Contemplation in a Technological Era: Learning from Thomas Merton," *Perspectives on Science and Christian Faith*, 64.1 (2012), 3.

414 SKS 8, 104 / TA, 110.

415 This is not to suggest that Kierkegaard would insist upon (or even approve of) a prominent monastic withdrawal from modern society. On the other hand, some kind of "retreat" is essential to his understanding of Christian praxis. I have begun to disentangle this ostensible paradox (see, for example, Barnett, *Kierkegaard, Pietism and Holiness*, especially Part II, "Holiness in 'The Present Age'"), though what it might mean "on the ground" for a contemporary person remains a stimulating question.

416 Benedicta Ward, "Introduction," *The Desert Fathers: Sayings of the Early Christian Monks*, trans. Benedicta Ward (London: Penguin Books, 2003), ix–x.

417 Ibid., ix.

418 Quoted in *The Desert Fathers: Sayings of the Early Christian Monks*, trans. Benedicta Ward (London: Penguin Books, 2003), 174.

Concluding (Untechnological?) Postscript

1 Merold Westphal, *Becoming a Self* (West Lafayette, IN: Purdue University Press, 1996), 111.

2 Natasha Singer, "How Google Took over the Classroom," *The New York Times*, May 13, 2017, accessed November 11, 2018, https://www.nytimes.com/2017/05/13/technology/google-education-chromebooks-schools.html.

3 Alexa Lardieri, "Electronics in the Classroom Lead to Lower Test Scores," *US News & World Report*, July 27, 2018, accessed November 11, 2018. https://www.usnews.com/news/education-news/articles/2018-07-27/study-cellphones-laptops-in-the-classroom-lead-to-lower-test-scores.

4 Also see Issie Lapowsky, "Google Wants to Save Our Schools—and Hook a New Generation of Users," *Wired*, August 13, 2014, accessed November 11, 2018. https://www.wired.com/2014/08/google-classrooms/.

Works Cited

Works by Søren Kierkegaard

In Danish

Søren Kierkegaards Papirer, vols I-XI-3. Edited by P.A. Heiberg, V. Kuhr, and E. Torsting (Copenhagen: Gyldendalske Boghandel, Nordisk Forlag, 1909–48).
Søren Kierkegaards Skrifter, vols 1–28. Edited by Niels Jørgen Cappelørn, Joakim Garff, Johnny Kondrup, Karsten Kynde, Tonny Aagaard Olesen, and Steen Tullberg (Copenhagen: Gads Forlag, 1997–2013).

In English

Kierkegaard's Journals and Notebooks, vols 1–11. Edited by Niels Jørgen Cappelørn, Alastair Hannay, David Kangas, Bruce H. Kirmmse, George Pattison, Vanessa Rumble, and K. Brian Söderquist (Princeton, NJ: Princeton University Press, 2007–).
Kierkegaard's Writings, vols 1–26. Edited and translated by Howard Hong and Edna Hong (Princeton, NJ: Princeton University Press, 1978–2002).
The Present Age. Translated by Alexander Dru. New York: Harper & Row, 1962.
Søren Kierkegaard's Journals and Papers, vols 1–7. Edited and translated by Howard Hong and Edna Hong (Bloomington: Indiana University Press, 1967–78).

Other sources

Achterhuis, Hans, ed. *American Philosophy of Technology: The Empirical Turn*. Translated by Robert P. Crease. Bloomington: Indiana University Press, 2001.
Adorno, Theodor W. *Kierkegaard: Construction of the Aesthetic*. Translated by Robert Hullot-Kentor. Minneapolis: University of Minnesota Press, 1989.
Adorno, Theodor W. *Kierkegaard. Konstruktion des Ästhetischen*. Tübingen: Mohr, 1933.
Aiken, Mary. *The Cyber Effect: A Pioneering Cyberpsychologist Explains How Human Behavior Changes Online*. New York: Spiegel & Grau, 2016.
Alphabet Investor Relations. "Google Inc. Announces Third Quarter 2014 Results," Google Investor Relations. Accessed July 12, 2018. http://investor.google.com/earnings/2014/Q3_google_earnings.html.
Andersen, Otto. "Denmark." In *European Population: I. Country Analysis*. Edited by Jean-Louis Rallu and Alain Blum, 113–28. Paris: John Libbey Eurotext, 1991.
Andersen, Thorkild. "Kierkegaard-Slægten og Sædding." *Hardsyssels Aarbog* 27 (1933): 26–40.

Anderson, Thomas C. "Atheistic and Christian Existentialism: A Comparison of Sartre and Marcel." In *New Perspectives on Sartre*. Edited by Adrian Mirvish and Adrian van den Hoven, 44–63. Newcastle upon Tyne: Cambridge Scholars Publishing, 2010.

Aristotle. *Political Philosophy*. Oxford: Oxford University Press, 2002.

Aristotle. *Politics*, 2nd edition. Translated by Carnes Lord. Chicago, IL: University of Chicago Press, 2013.

Aristotle. *Politics*. Translated by Benjamin Jowett. New York: Cosimo, Inc., 2008.

Ast, Friedrich. *Grundlinien der Grammatik, Hermeneutik und Kritik*. Landshut: Thomann, 1808.

Backhouse, Stephen. *Kierkegaard's Critique of Christian Nationalism*. Oxford: Oxford University Press, 2011.

Baigrie, Brian Scott. *Electricity and Magnetism: A Historical Perspective*. Westport, CT: Greenwood Press, 2007.

Ball, Michael and David Sunderland. *An Economic History of London, 1800-1914*. London: Routledge, 2001.

Bandle Oscar, ed. *The Nordic Languages: An International Handbook of the History of the North Germanic Languages*, vol. 2. Berlin: de Gruyter, 2005.

Barger, M. Susan and William B. White. *The Daguerreotype: Nineteenth-Century Technology and Modern Science*. Baltimore, MD: Johns Hopkins University Press, 1991.

Barlow, John Perry. "A Declaration of the Independence of Cyberspace." *eff.org*. Accessed June 11, 2017. https://www.eff.org/cyberspace-independence.

Barnett, Christopher. *From Despair to Faith: The Spirituality of Søren Kierkegaard*. Minneapolis, MN: Fortress, 2014.

Barnett, Christopher B. "Henri de Lubac: Locating Kierkegaard Amid the 'Drama' of Nietzschean Humanism." In *Kierkegaard's Influence on Theology: Tome III: Catholic and Jewish Theology*. Edited by Jon Stewart, Kierkegaard Research: Sources, Reception and Resources, 97–110. Farnham: Ashgate, 2012.

Barnett, Christopher. *Kierkegaard, Pietism and Holiness*. Farnham: Ashgate, 2011.

Barnett. Christopher B. "Socrates the Pietist?: Tracing the Socratic in Zinzendorf, Hamann, and Kierkegaard." In *Kierkegaard Studies: Yearbook 2010*. Edited by Niels Jorgen Cappelørn, Hermann Deuser, and K. Brian Söderquist, 307–24. Berlin: Walter de Gruyter, 2010.

Barrett, Lee C. "Paul Tillich: An Ambivalent Appreciation." In *Kierkegaard's Influence on Theology. Tome I: German Protestant Theology*. Edited by Jon Stewart, 335–76. Farnham: Ashgate, 2012.

Bauerlein, Mark. *The Dumbest Generation: How the Digital Age Stupefies Young Americans and Jeopardizes Our Future (Or Don't Trust Anyone under 30)*. New York: Tarcher, 2009.

Benedict of Nursia. *The Rule of Saint Benedict*. Translated by Abbot Parry, OSB. Leominster: Gracewing, 1990.

Benjamin, Walter. *The Arcades Project*. Edited by Rolf Tiedemann. Translated by Howard Eiland and Kevin McLaughlin. Cambridge, MA: Belknap Press, 2002.

Benjamin, Walter. "Central Park." In *Walter Benjamin: Selected Writings*, vol. 4. Edited by Howard Eiland and Michael W. Jennings. Translated by Edmund Jephcott, 161–99. Cambridge, MA: Belknap Press, 2003.

Benjamin, Walter. "A Critique of the Publishing Industry." In *The Work of Art in the Age of Its Technological Reproducibility, and Other Writings on Media*. Edited by Michael W. Jennings, Brigid Doherty, and Thomas Y. Levin. Translated by Edmund Jephcott,

Rodney Livingstone, Howard Eiland, and Others. Cambridge, MA: Belknap Press, 2008.

Benjamin, Walter. "The End of Philosophical Idealism." In *Walter Benjamin: Selected Writings*, vol. 2. Edited by Michael W. Jennings, Howard Eiland, and Gary Smith. Translated by Rodney Livingstone and Others. Cambridge, MA: Belknap Press, 1999.

Benjamin, Walter. "Journalism." In *The Work of Art in the Age of Its Technological Reproducibility, and Other Writings on Media*. Edited by Michael W. Jennings, Brigid Doherty, and Thomas Y. Levin. Translated by Edmund Jephcott, Rodney Livingstone, Howard Eiland, and Others. Cambridge, MA: Belknap Press, 2008.

Benjamin, Walter. "Kierkegaard: Das Ende des philosophischen Idealismus." In *Vossische Zeitung*, April 2, 1933.

Benjamin, Walter. "The Newspaper." In *The Work of Art in the Age of Its Technological Reproducibility, and Other Writings on Media*. Edited by Michael W. Jennings, Brigid Doherty, and Thomas Y. Levin. Translated by Edmund Jephcott, Rodney Livingstone, Howard Eiland, and Others. Cambridge, MA: Belknap Press, 2008.

Benjamin, Walter. "The Work of Art in the Age of Its Technological Reproducibility." In *The Work of Art in the Age of Its Technological Reproducibility, and Other Writings on Media*. Edited by Michael W. Jennings, Brigid Doherty, and Thomas Y. Levin. Translated by Edmund Jephcott, Rodney Livingstone, Howard Eiland, and Others. Cambridge, MA: Belknap Press, 2008.

Berdichevsky, Norman. *An Introduction to Danish Culture*. Jefferson, NC: McFarland & Co., 2011.

Berner, Marie Louis. *Bertel Thorvaldsen: A Daguerreotype Portrait from 1840*. Copenhagen: Museum Tusculanum Press, 2005.

Best, Steven and Douglas Keller. "Modernity, Mass Society, and the Media: Reflections on the *Corsair* Affair." In *International Kierkegaard Commentary: The Corsair Affair*. Edited by Robert L. Perkins, 23–61. Macon, GA: Mercer University Press, 1990.

Bolin, Göran. "Introduction: Cultural Technologies in Cultures of Technology." In *Cultural Technologies: The Shaping of Culture in Media and Society*. Edited by Göran Bolin, 1–15. New York: Routledge, 2012.

Borgmann, Albert. "Contemplation in a Technological Era: Learning from Thomas Merton." *Perspectives on Science and Christian Faith* 64, no. 1 (2012): 3–9.

Botton, Alain de. *The News: A User's Manual*. New York: Pantheon Books, 2014.

Bray, Francesca. "Chinese Technology." In *A Companion to the Philosophy of Technology*. Edited by Jan Kyrre Berg Olsen, Stig Andur Pedersen, and Vincent F. Hendricks, 28–31. Oxford: Wiley-Blackwell, 2009.

Bregnsbo, Michael. "Struensee and the Political Culture of Absolutism." In *Scandinavia in the Age of Revolution: Nordic Political Cultures, 1740-1820*. Edited by Pasi Ihalainen, Karin Sennefelt, Michael Bregnsbo and Patrik Winton, 55–66. Farnham: Ashgate, 2011.

Brey, Philip. "Well-Being in Philosophy, Psychology, and Economics." In *The Good Life in a Technological Age*. Edited by Philip Brey, Adam Briggle, and Edward Spence, 15–34. New York: Routledge, 2012.

Bukdahl, Jørgen. *Søren Kierkegaard and the Common Man*. Translated by Bruce H. Kirmmse. Grand Rapids, MI: Eerdmans, 2001.

Burbridge, John W. *Historical Dictionary of Hegelian Philosophy*, 2nd edition. Lanham, MD: The Scarecrow Press, Inc., 2008.

Burdett, Michael S. *Eschatology and the Technological Future*. New York: Routledge, 2015.

Buren, John van. *The Young Heidegger: Rumor of the Hidden King*. Bloomington: Indiana University Press, 1994.

Burnyeat, Myles, ed. *The Theaetetus of Plato*. Translated by M.J. Levett. Indianapolis, IN: Hackett Publishing Company, 1990.

Cabral, Sarah Pike. "Jacques Ellul: Kierkegaard's Profound and Seldom Acknowledged Influence on Ellul's Writing." In *Kierkegaard's Influence on Philosophy: Tome II: Francophone Philosophy*. Edited by Jon Stewart, Kierkegaard Research: Sources, Reception and Resources, vol. 11, 139–56. Farnham: Ashgate, 2012.

Caputo, John D. *Radical Hermeneutics*. Bloomington: Indiana University Press, 1987.

Carlisle, Clare. "Kierkegaard and Heidegger." In *The Oxford Handbook of Kierkegaard*. Edited by John Lippitt and George Pattison, 421–39. Oxford: Oxford University Press, 2013.

Carlsberg Group. "1811-1870: Founding Carlsberg." *carlsberggroup.com*. Accessed July 8, 2016. http://www.carlsberggroup.com/Company/heritage/Pages/FoundingCarlsberg .aspx.

Carr, Nicholas. *The Shallows: What the Internet Is Doing to Our Brains*. New York: W.W. Norton & Company, Inc., 2011.

Christensen, Dan Charly. *Hans Christian Ørsted: Reading Nature's Mind*. Oxford: Oxford University Press, 2013.

The Church of Google. "Core Beliefs." Accessed June 12, 2018. http://www. thechurchofgoogle.org.

Clark, B.E.G. *Steamboat Evolution: A Short History*. Raleigh, NC: Lulu Press, Inc., 2010.

Clayton, John P. *The Concept of Correlation: Paul Tillich and the Possibility of a Mediating Theology*. Berlin: de Gruyter, 1980.

Crouch, Tom D. *Wings: A History of Aviation from Kites to the Space Age*. New York: W.W. Norton & Company, 2003.

Datablog. "Percentage of Global Population Living in Cities, By Continent." *The Guardian*. Accessed January 1, 2017. https://www.theguardian.com/news/datablog/2009/aug/18/p ercentage-population-living-cities.

Dekar, Paul R. *Thomas Merton: Twentieth-Century Wisdom for Twenty-First-Century Living*. Eugene, OR: Cascade Books, 2011.

Delany, Ella. "Humanities Studies under Strain around the Globe." *New York Times*, December 1, 2013.

Descartes, René. *Meditations on First Philosophy*. Translated by Donald A. Cress. Indianapolis, IN: Hackett Publishing Company, 1993.

Descartes, René. *Meditations on First Philosophy: With Selections from the Objections and Replies*, 2nd edition. Translated and edited by John Cottingham. Cambridge: Cambridge University Press, 2017.

Detweiler, Craig. *iGods: How Technology Shapes Our Spiritual and Social Lives*. Grand Rapids, MI: Brazos Press, 2013.

Dornan, Christopher. "Sounding the Alarm." In *Media and Democracy*. Edited by Everette Eugene Dennis and Robert W. Snyder. New Brunswick, NJ: Transaction Publishers, 1998.

Dostoevsky, Fyodor. *The Idiot*. Translated by Richard Pevear and Larissa Volokhonsky. New York: Vintage Classics, 2003.

Dreyfus, Hubert L. *On the Internet*. London: Routledge, 2009.

Drucker, Peter F. *The Age of Discontinuity: Guidelines to Our Changing Society*. London: Heinemann, 1969.

Dupré, Louis. "Introduction." In *Letters from Lake Como: Explorations in Technology and the Human Race* by Romano Guardini. Grand Rapids, MI: Eerdmans Publishing Company, 1994.

Dwan, David. "Idle Talk: Ontology and Mass Communications in Heidegger." *New Formations* 51 (2003): 113–27.

Dyer, John. *From the Garden to the City: The Redeeming and Corrupting Power of Technology*. Grand Rapids, MI: Kregel Publications, 2011.

Eisenstein, Elizabeth L. *The Printing Press as an Agent of Change*. Cambridge: Cambridge University Press, 1979.

Eller, Vernard. "Ellul and Kierkegaard: Closer than Brothers." In *Jacques Ellul: Interpretive Essays*. Edited by Clifford G. Christians and Jay M. VanHook. Urbana: University of Illinois Press, 1981.

Ellul, Jacques. *Living Faith: Belief and Doubt in a Perilous World*. Translated by Peter Heinegg. San Francisco, CA: Harper and Row, 1983.

Ellul, Jacques. *The Meaning of the City*. Translated by Dennis Pardee. Eugene, OR: Wipf and Stock Publishers, 2011.

Ellul, Jacques. *The Technological Bluff*. Translated by Geoffrey Bromiley. Grand Rapids, MI: Eerdmans, 1990.

Ellul, Jacques. *The Technological Society*. Translated by John Wilkinson. New York: Vintage, 1964.

Ellul, Jacques. *Propaganda: The Formation of Men's Attitudes*. New York: Vintage Books, 1973.

Ellul, Jacques. *Propaganda: The Formation of Men's Attitudes*. Translated by Konrad Kellen and Jean Lerner. New York: Vintage Books, 1965.

Evans, C. Stephen. *Kierkegaard: An Introduction*. Cambridge: Cambridge University Press, 2009.

Evans, C. Stephen and Robert C. Roberts. "Ethics." In *The Oxford Handbook of Kierkegaard*. Edited by John Lippitt and George Pattison. Oxford: Oxford University Press, 2013.

Feenberg, Andrew. *Questioning Technology*. London: Routledge, 1999.

Fukuyama, Francis. *The End of History and the Last Man*. New York: Free Press, 1992.

Fuller, Steve. *Post-Truth: Knowledge as a Power Game*. London: Anthem Press, 2018.

Gadamer, Hans-Georg. *Truth and Method*. Translated by Joel Weinsheimer and Donald G. Marshall. London: Bloomsbury, 2013.

Garff, Joakim. *Søren Kierkegaard: A Biography*. Translated by Bruce H. Kirmmse. Princeton, NJ: Princeton University Press, 2005.

Gilbert, Thomas. "Why a Danish Golden Age?: Structural Holes in 19th Century Copenhagen." In *Kierkegaard Studies: Yearbook 2013*. Edited by Heiko Schulz, Jon Stewart and Karl Verstrynge, 403–34. Berlin: de Gruyter, 2013.

Glazebrook, Trish. *Heidegger's Philosophy of Science*. New York: Fordham University Press, 2000.

Glick, Thomas F. "Islamic Technology." In *A Companion to the Philosophy of Technology*. Edited by Jan Kyrre Berg Olsen, Stig Andur Pedersen, and Vincent F. Hendricks, 32–36. Oxford: Wiley-Blackwell, 2009.

Goldmann, Lucien. *The Philosophy of the Enlightenment: The Christian Burgess and the Enlightenment*. Routledge Revivals, New York: Routledge, 2010.

Google. "About Google." Accessed July 12, 2018. https://www.google.com/intl/en/about/.

Google. "What We Believe: Ten Things We Know to Be True." Accessed July 12, 2018. http://www.google.com/about/company/philosophy/.

Greenman, Jeffrey P., Read Mercer Schuchardt, and Noah J. Toly. *Understanding Jacques Ellul*. Cambridge: James Clarke & Co, 2013.

Grigg, D.B. *Population Growth and Agrarian Change: An Historical Perspective*. Cambridge: Cambridge University Press, 1980.

Grimm, Jacob and Wilhelm Grimm. *Grimm's Complete Fairy Tales*. New York: Barnes and Noble Books, 1993.

Guardini, Romano. *The Faith and Modern Man*. Translated by Charlotte E. Forsyth. New York: Pantheon Books, 1952.

Guardini, Romano. *Letters from Lake Como: Explorations in Technology and the Human Race*. Translated by Geoffrey W. Bromiley. Grand Rapids, MI: Eerdmans Publishing Company, 1994.

Hage, Johannes. "On the Polemic of the *Flyvende Post*." In *Early Polemical Writings* by Søren Kierkegaard. Edited and Translated by Julia Watkin, 142–48. Princeton, NJ: Princeton University Press, 1990.

Hall, Thomas. *Planning Europe's Capital Cities: Aspects of Nineteenth Century Urban Development*. London: E & FN Spon, 1997.

Hamelink, Cees J. *Media and Conflict: Escalating Violence*. New York: Routledge, 2011.

Hanks, Craig. "Introduction to Chapter 13." In *Technology and Values: Essential Readings*. Edited by Craig Hanks, 159–60. Oxford: Wiley-Blackwell, 2010.

Hannay, Alastair. "Kierkegaard's Levellings and the *Review*." In *Kierkegaard Studies Yearbook 1999*. Edited by Heiko Schulz, Jon Stewart, and Karl Verstrynge, 71–95. Berlin: de Gruyter, 1999.

Hanson, Erik. "Thomas Merton: Kierkegaard, Merton and Authenticity." In *Kierkegaard's Influence on Theology. Tome III: Catholic and Jewish Theology*. Edited by Jon Stewart, 111–30. Farnham: Ashgate, 2012.

Hegel, Georg Wilhelm Friedrich. *Phenomenology of Spirit*. Translated by A.V. Miller. Oxford: Oxford University Press, 1977.

Hegel, Georg Wilhelm Friedrich. *The Philosophy of History*. Translated by John Sibree. New York: Dover, 1956.

Heidegger, Martin. *Being and Time*. Translated by John Macquarrie and Edward Robinson. San Francisco, CA: Harper & Row, 1962.

Heidegger, Martin. *Contributions to Philosophy (of the Event)*. Translated by Richard Rojcewicz and Daniela Vallega-Neu. Bloomington: Indiana University Press, 2012.

Heidegger, Martin. *Discourse on Thinking: A Translation of Gelassenheit*. Translated by John M. Anderson and E. Hans Freund. New York: Harper Perennial, 1966.

Heidegger, Martin. *Gelassenheit*. Pfullingen: Günther Neske Verlag, 1959.

Heidegger, Martin. *History of the Concept of Time: Prolegomena*. Translated by Theodore Kisiel. Bloomington: Indiana University Press, 1985.

Heidegger, Martin. "Nur noch ein Gott kann uns retten." *Der Spiegel* 30 (May 1976): 193–219.

Heidegger, Martin. "The Onto-Theo-Logical Constitution of Metaphysics." In *Identity and Difference*. Edited by Joan Stambaugh, 42–76. Chicago, IL: The University of Chicago Press, 1969.

Heidegger, Martin. *Pathmarks*. Edited by William McNeill. Cambridge: Cambridge University Press, 1998.

Heidegger, Martin. *The Principle of Reason*. Translated by Reginald Lilly. Bloomington: Indiana University Press, 1991.

Heidegger, Martin. "The Question Concerning Technology." In *Basic Writings*. Edited by David Farrell Krell, 307–41. London: Routledge, 1978.

Heidegger, Martin. "The Word of Nietzsche: 'God Is Dead.'" In *The Question Concerning Technology and Other Essays*. Translated by William Lovitt, 53–112. New York: Harper and Row, 1977.

Henderson, Harry. *Communications and Broadcasting: From Wired Words to Wireless Web*. New York: Chelsea House, 2007.

Hernandez, Jill Graper. *Gabriel Marcel's Ethics of Hope: Evil, God and Virtue*. London: Bloomsbury, 2013.

Høffding, Harald. *Søren Kierkegaard som Filosof*. Copenhagen: Philipsen, 1892.

Hong, Howard V. and Edna H. Hong. "Historical Introduction." In *The Corsair Affair and Articles Related to the Writings*. Edited and Translated by Howard V. Hong and Edna H. Hong, vii–xxxviii. Princeton, NJ: Princeton University Press, 1982.

Hong, Nathaniel J. and Charles M. Barker, eds. *Søren Kierkegaard's Journals and Papers: Volume 7, Index and Composite Collation*. Bloomington: Indiana University Press, 1978.

Hong, Nathaniel J., Kathryn Hong, and Regine Prenzel-Guthrie, eds. *Cumulative Index to Kierkegaard's Writings*. Princeton, NJ: Princeton University Press, 2000.

Horstbøll, Henrik. "The Politics of Publishing: Freedom of the Press in Denmark, 1770-1773." In *Scandinavia in the Age of Revolution: Nordic Political Cultures, 1740-1820*. Edited by Pasi Ihalainen, Karin Sennefelt, Michael Bregnsbo and Patrik Winton, 145–56. Farnham: Ashgate, 2011.

Houlgate, Stephen. *An Introduction to Hegel: Freedom, Truth and History*. Oxford: Blackwell, 2005.

Hugh of St. Victor. *The Didascalicon of Hugh of St. Victor: A Medieval Guide to the Arts*. Translated by Jerome Taylor. New York: Columbia University Press, 1991.

Hunter, Graeme. *Pascal the Philosopher: An Introduction*. Toronto: University of Toronto Press, 2013.

Huntington, Patricia J. "Heidegger's Reading of Kierkegaard Revisited: From Ontological Abstraction to Ethical Concretion." In *Kierkegaard in Post/Modernity*. Edited by Martin J. Matuštík and Merold Westphal, 43–65. Bloomington: Indiana University Press, 1995.

Inchausti, Robert. "Introduction." In *Seeds: Thomas Merton*. Edited by Robert Inchausti, xi–xvii. Boston, MA: Shambala, 2002.

Idorn, Gunnar M. *Concrete Progress: From Antiquity to the Third Millennium*. London: Thomas Telford Publishing, 1997.

Ihde, Don. *Heidegger's Technologies: Postphenomenological Perspectives*. New York: Fordham University Press, 2010.

Iversen, James D. "The History of Wind Technology in Denmark." In *Danish Culture, Past and Present: The Last Two Hundred Years*. Edited by Linda M. Chementi and Birgit Flemming Larsen, 152–59. Ames, IA: The Danish American Heritage Society, 2006.

Jacobsen, Kurt. "The Great Northern Telegraph Company and the British Empire 1869-1945." In *Britain and Denmark: Political, Economic and Cultural Relations in the 19th and 20th Centuries*. Edited by Jørgen Sevaldsen, 199–229. Copenhagen: Museum Tusculanum Press, 2003.

Janik, Allan. "Haecker, Kierkegaard and the Early *Brenner*: A Contribution to the History of the Reception of *Two Ages* in the German-speaking World." In *International*

Kierkegaard Commentary: Two Ages. Edited by Robert L. Perkins, 189–222. Macon, GA: Mercer University Press, 1984.

Jennings, Michael W., Brigid Doherty, and Thomas Y. Levin. "Editors' Introduction." In *The Work of Art in the Age of Its Technological Reproducibility, and Other Writings on Media*. Edited by Michael W. Jennings, Brigid Doherty, and Thomas Y. Levin. Cambridge, MA: Belknap Press, 2008.

Jespersen, Knud J.V. *A History of Denmark*. Translated by Ivan Hill. Basingstoke: Palgrave Macmillan, 2004.

Juvenal. *Satires I, III, X*. Bristol: Bristol Classical Press, 1982.

Jørgensen, Peter Nicolai. *Bonden i Tivoli: En Historie*. Copenhagen: A.F. Høst, 1844.

Kirmmse, Bruce H. "Biographical Introduction to the English Language Edition." In *Søren Kierkegaard & the Common Man*. Edited and translated by Bruce H. Kirmmse, xi–xviii. Grand Rapids, MI: Eerdmans Publishing Company, 2001.

Kirmmse, Bruce H. *Encounters with Kierkegaard: A Life as Seen by His Contemporaries*. Translated by Bruce H. Kirmmse and Virginia R. Laursen. Princeton, NJ: Princeton University Press, 1996.

Kirmmse, Bruce H. "Kierkegaard and the End of the Danish Golden Age." In *The Oxford Handbook of Kierkegaard*. Edited by John Lippitt and George Pattison, 28–43. Oxford: Oxford University Press, 2013.

Kirmmse, Bruce H. Kierkegaard *in Golden Age Denmark*. Bloomington: Indiana University Press, 1990.

Kisiel Theodore J. and Thomas Sheehan, eds. *Becoming Heidegger: On the Trail of His Early Occasional Writings, 1910-1927*. Evanston, IL: Northwestern University Press, 2007.

Kissmeyer, Anders Brinch. "Carlsberg Group." In *The Oxford Companion to Beer*. Edited by Garrett Oliver, 223–25. Oxford: Oxford University Press, 2012.

Knight, David. "Romanticism and the Sciences." In *Romanticism and the Sciences*. Edited by Andrew Cunningham and Nicholas Jardine, 13–24. Cambridge: Cambridge University Press, 1990.

Knox, Jeanette Bresson Ladegaard. "Gabriel Marcel: The Silence of Truth." In *Kierkegaard and Existentialism*. Edited by Jon Stewart, Kierkegaard Research: Sources, Reception and Resources, vol. 9. Farnham: Ashgate, 2011.

Koch, Carl Henrik. "Harald Høffding: The Respectful Critic." In *Kierkegaard's Influence on Philosophy: Tome I: German and Scandinavian Philosophy*. Edited by Jon Stewart, 267–88. Farnham: Ashgate, 2012.

Komasinski, Andrew. "Anti-Climacus' Pre-emptive Critique of Heidegger's 'Question Concerning Technology.'" In *International Philosophical Quarterly* 54, no. 3 (2014): 265–77.

Lapowsky, Issie. "Google Wants to Save Our Schools—and Hook a New Generation of Users." *Wired*, August 13, 2014. Accessed November 11, 2018. https://www.wired.com/2014/08/google-classrooms/.

Lardieri, Alexa. "Electronics in the Classroom Lead to Lower Test Scores." *US News & World Report*, July 27, 2018. Accessed November 11, 2018. https://www.usnews.com/news/education-news/articles/2018-07-27/study-cellphones-laptops-in-the-classroom-lead-to-lower-test-scores.

Lavine, T.Z. *From Socrates to Sartre: The Philosophic Quest*. New York: Bantam, 1984.

Lees, Andrew and Lynn Hollen Lees. *Cities and the Making of Modern Europe, 1750-1914*. Cambridge: Cambridge University Press, 2007.

Lehmann, Orla. "Press Freedom Affair V." In *Early Polemical Writings* by Søren Kierkegaard. Edited and translated Julia Watkin, 134–41. Princeton, NJ: Princeton University Press, 1990.

Lehmann, Orla. "Reply to Mr. B. of the *Flyvende Post*." In *Early Polemical Writings* by Søren Kierkegaard. Edited and translated by Julia Watkin, 152–59. Princeton, NJ: Princeton University Press, 1990.

Levin, Miriam R. "Dynamic Triad: City, Exposition, and Museum in Industrial Society." In *Urban Modernity: Cultural Innovation in the Second Industrial Revolution*. Edited by Miriam R. Levin, Sophie Forgan, Martina Hessler, Robert H. Kargon and Morris Low, 1–12. Cambridge, MA: The MIT Press, 2010.

Levinson, Jerrold, ed. *The Oxford Handbook of Aesthetics*. Oxford: Oxford University Press, 2003.

Lewin, David. *Technology and the Philosophy of Religion*. Newcastle upon Tyne: Cambridge Scholars Publishing, 2012.

Lovekin, David. *Technique, Discourse, and Consciousness: An Introduction to the Philosophy of Jacques Ellul*. Bethlehem, PA: Lehigh University Press, 1991.

Lowenthal, Leo. *Literature, Popular Culture and Society*. Englewood Cliffs, NJ: Prentice-Hall, 1961.

Löwy, Michael. *Fire Alarm: Reading Walter Benjamin's 'On the Concept of History'*. Translated by Chris Turner. London: Verso, 2005.

Lubrano, Annteresa. *The Telegraph: How Technology Innovation Caused Social Change*. New York: Garland Publishing, Inc., 1997.

Lynley, Matthew. "Google Beats Expectations Again with $31.15B in Revenue." *TechCrunch*. April 23, 2018. Accessed May 12, 2018. https://techcrunch.com/2018/04/23/google-beats-expectations-again-with-31-15b-in-revenue/.

MacKinnon, Donald. "Foreword." In *Man against Mass Society*. Translated by G.S. Fraser. South Bend, IN: St. Augustine's Press, 2008.

Macquarrie, John. *Existentialism: An Introduction, Guide and Assessment*. London: Penguin, 1972.

Malantschuk, Gregor and N.H. Søe. *Kierkegaards Kamp mod Kirken*. Copenhagen: Munksgaard, 1956.

Marcel, Gabriel. "Kierkegaard en ma pensée." In *Kierkegaard vivant. Colloque organisé par l'UNESCO à Paris due 21 au 23 avril 1964*. Paris: Gallimard, 1966.

Marcel, Gabriel. *Man against Mass Society*. Translated by G.S. Fraser. South Bend, IN: St. Augustine's Press, 2008.

Marcel, Gabriel. *The Mystery of Being I: Reflection and Mystery*. Translated by G.S. Fraser. Chicago, IL: Henry Regnery Company, 1960.

Marcel, Gabriel. *The Philosophy of Existentialism*. New York: Citadel Press, 1984.

Marcuse, Herbert. *One-Dimensional Man: Studies in the Ideology of Advanced Industrial Society*. Boston, MA: Beacon Press, 1964.

Marcuse, Herbert. *Philosophy, Psychoanalysis and Emancipation: Herbert Marcuse Collected Papers*, vol. 5. Edited by Douglas Kellner and Clayton Pierce. London: Routledge, 2011.

Marcuse, Herbert. *Reason and Revolution: Hegel and the Rise of Social Theory*, 2nd edition. London: Routledge, 2000.

Martin, Bernard. *The Existentialist Theology of Paul Tillich*. New Haven, CT: College and University Press, 1963.

Marx, Karl. *The Poverty of Philosophy: Answer to the Philosophy of Poverty by M. Proudhon*. Moscow: Progress Publishers, 1955.

Marx, Karl and Friedrich Engels. *Manifesto of the Communist Party*. Translated by Samuel Moore. Chicago, IL: Charles H. Kerr & Co., 1906.

Mayr, Ernst. "The Idea of Teleology." *Journal of the History of Ideas* 53, no. 1 (1992): 117–35.

McCarthy, Vincent. "Martin Heidegger: Kierkegaard's Influence Hidden and in Full View." In *Kierkegaard and Existentialism*. Kierkegaard Research: Sources, Reception and Resources, vol. 9. Edited by Jon Stewart. New York: Routledge, 2016.

McCloskey, Deirdre N. *The Bourgeois Virtues: Ethics for an Age of Commerce*. Chicago, IL: The University of Chicago Press, 2006.

McLuhan, Marshall. *Understanding Media: The Extensions of Man*. Cambridge, MA: The MIT Press, 1994.

Mellor, Anne K. "*Frankenstein*: A Feminist Critique of Science." In *One Culture: Essays in Science and Literature*. Edited by George Levine. Madison: University of Wisconsin Press, 1987.

Merton, Thomas. *The Ascent to Truth*. New York: Harcourt, Brace and Company, 1951.

Merton, Thomas. *Conjectures of a Guilty Bystander*. Garden City, NY: Doubleday, 1971.

Merton, Thomas. *Contemplation in a World of Action*. London: George Allen and Unwin, 1971.

Merton, Thomas. *Contemplative Prayer*. London: Herder & Herder, 1969.

Merton, Thomas. *The Inner Experience: Notes on Contemplation*. New York: HarperCollins, 2003.

Merton, Thomas. *Mystics and Zen Masters*. New York: Farrar, Strauss and Giroux, 1967.

Merton, Thomas. *The Other Side of the Mountain*. Edited by Patrick Hart, O.C.S.O. The Journals of Thomas Merton, vol. 7. New York: HarperCollins, 1998.

Merton, Thomas. *The Secular Journal*. New York: Dell Publishing, 1959.

Merton, Thomas. *The Seeds of Destruction*. New York: Farrar, Strauss and Giroux, 1964.

Merton, Thomas. *Witness to Freedom: The Letters of Thomas Merton in a Time of Crisis*. Edited by William H. Shannon. New York: Farrar, Strauss and Giroux, 1994.

Mieszkowski, Jan. "Art Forms." In *The Cambridge Companion to Walter Benjamin*. Edited by David S. Ferris, 35–53. Cambridge: Cambridge University Press, 2004.

Millward, Robert. *Private and Public Enterprise in Europe: Energy, Telecommunications and Transport, 1830-1990*. Cambridge: Cambridge University Press, 2005.

Mitcham, Carl. *Thinking through Technology: The Path between Engineering and Philosophy*. Chicago, IL: The University of Chicago Press, 1994.

Monaco, James. *How to Read a Film: Movies, Media, and Beyond*. Oxford: Oxford University Press, 2009.

Monrad, Olaf P. *Søren Kierkegaard. Sein Leben und seine Werke*. Jena: Diederichs, 1909.

Mooney, Edward F. "Pseudonyms and 'Style.'" In *The Oxford Handbook of Kierkegaard*. Edited by John Lippitt and George Pattison, 191–210. Oxford: Oxford University Press, 2013.

More, Max and Natasha Vita-More. "Roots and Core Themes." In *The Transhumanist Reader: Classical and Contemporary Essays on the Science, Technology, and Philosophy of the Human Future*. Edited by Max More and Natasha Vita-More, 1–2. Oxford: Wiley-Blackwell, 2013.

Morgan, Marcia. *Kierkegaard and Critical Theory*. Lanham, MD: Lexington Books, 2012.

Myhre, Jan Elvind. "The Nordic Countries." In *European Urban History: Prospect and Retrospect*. Edited by Richard Rodger. Leicester: Leicester University Press, 1993.

Møller, P.L. "Et Besøg i Sorø, Corpusfeuilleton." In *Gæa: æsthetisk Aarbog*. Edited by P.L. Møller, 144–87. Copenhagen: Berlingske Bogtrykkeri, 1846.

Nägele, Rainer. "Body Politics: Benjamin's Dialectical Materialism between Brecht and the Frankfurt School." In *The Cambridge Companion to Walter Benjamin*. Edited by David S. Ferris, 152–76. Cambridge: Cambridge University Press, 2004.

Nichols, Aidan, O.P. *Lost in Wonder: Essays on Liturgy and the Arts*. London: Routledge, 2011.

Nielson, Keld. "Western Technology." In *A Companion to the Philosophy of Technology*. Edited by Jan Kyrre Berg Olsen, Stig Andur Pedersen, and Vincent F. Hendricks, 23–27. Oxford: Wiley-Blackwell, 2009.

Nielsen, L.C. *Fra Johann Snell til vore Dage: Skildringer af Bogtrykkerkunstens Histoire i Odense*. Odense: Milo'ske Boghandels Forlag, 1908.

Nun, Katalin, Gerhard Schreiber and Jon Stewart, eds. *The Auction Catalog of Kierkegaard's Library*. New York: Routledge, 2015.

Oakley, Stewart P. "Absolute Monarchy or Absolutism." In *Historical Dictionary of Denmark*, 25–26. Lanham, MD: The Scarecrow Press, Inc., 1998.

Oakley, Stewart P. "Consultative Assemblies." In *Historical Dictionary of Denmark*, 106–07. Lanham, MD: The Scarecrow Press, Inc., 1998.

Oakley, Stewart P. "Industrialization." In *Historical Dictionary of Denmark*. Edited by Alastair H. Thomas and Stewart P. Oakley, 230–31. Lanham, MD: The Scarecrow Press, Inc., 1998.

O'Donovan, Oliver. "Review of *Letters from Lake Como*, by Romano Guardini." *Studies in Christian Ethics* 8, no. 2 (1995): 104–05.

Oersted, Hans Christian. *The Soul in Nature, with Supplementary Contributions*. Translated by Leonora Horner and Joanna B. Horner. London: Bohn, 1852.

Olsen, Jan M. "For Brewery Giant Carlsberg, It's Back to Basics." *latimes.com*. Accessed July 20, 2016. http://articles.latimes.com/2001/mar/15/business/fi-38042.

O'Meara, Thomas F., O.P. *Thomas Aquinas, Theologian*. South Bend, IN: University of Notre Dame Press, 1997.

Ong, Walter J. *Orality and Literacy*. London: Routledge, 2002.

Ostermann, Johannes. "Our Latest Journalistic Literature." In *Early Polemical Writings: Kierkegaard's Writings I*. Edited and translated by Julia Watkin. Princeton, NJ: Princeton University Press, 1990.

Owens, Joseph. *Cognition: An Epistemological Inquiry*. South Bend, IN: University of Notre Dame Press, 1992.

Pariser, Eli. *The Filter Bubble: How the New Personalized Web Is Changing What We Read and How We Think*. New York: Penguin, 2012.

Pattison, George. *Anxious Angels: A Retrospective View of Religious Existentialism*. New York: St. Martin's Press, Inc., 1999.

Pattison, George. "Kierkegaard and Copenhagen." In *The Oxford Handbook of Kierkegaard*. Edited by John Lippitt and George Pattison. Oxford: Oxford University Press, 2013.

Pattison, George. *Kierkegaard, Religion and the Nineteenth-Century Crisis of Culture*. Cambridge: Cambridge University Press, 2002.

Pattison, George. *Kierkegaard and the Theology of the Nineteenth Century: The Paradox and the "Point of Contact."* Cambridge: Cambridge University Press, 2012.

Pattison, George. *Kierkegaard's Upbuilding Discourses: Philosophy, Literature and Theology*. London: Routledge, 2002.

Pattison, George. *"Poor Paris!": Kierkegaard's Critique of the Spectacular City*. Berlin: Walter de Gruyter, 1999.

Pattison, George. *The Philosophy of Kierkegaard*. Chesham: Acumen, 2005.

Pattison, George. *Thinking about God in an Age of Technology*. Oxford: Oxford University Press, 2005.

Pauck, Wilhelm and Marion Pauck. *Paul Tillich: His Life and Thought*. Eugene, OR: Wipf and Stock, 1989.

Pensky, Max. *Melancholy Dialectics: Walter Benjamin and the Play of Mourning*. Amherst: University of Massachusetts Press, 1993.

Perkins, Robert L., ed. *The Moment and Late Writings*, International Kierkegaard Commentary, vol. 23. Macon, GA: Mercer University Press, 2009.

Perkins, Robert L. "Power, Politics, and Media Critique: Kierkegaard's First Brush with the Press." In *International Kierkegaard Commentary: Early Polemical Writings*. Edited by Robert L. Perkins, 27–44. Macon, GA: Mercer University Press, 1999.

Petersen, Teddy. *Kierkegaards polemiske debut: Artikler 1834-36 i historisk sammenhæng*. Odense: Odense Universitetsforlag, 1977.

Pirenne, Henri. *Medieval Cities: Their Origins and the Revival of Trade*. Translated by Frank D. Halsey. Princeton, NJ: Princeton University Press, 1980.

Plato. *The Republic*. Translated by Desmond Lee. London: Penguin Books, 1987.

Plekon, Michael. "Towards Apocalypse: Kierkegaard's *Two Ages* in Golden Age Denmark." In *International Kierkegaard Commentary: Two Ages*. Edited by Robert L. Perkins, 19–52. Macon, GA: Mercer University Press, 1984.

Polt, Richard. *Heidegger: An Introduction*. Ithaca, NY: Cornell University Press, 1999.

Poole, Roger. "The Unknown Kierkegaard: Twentieth-century Receptions." In *The Cambridge Companion to Kierkegaard*. Edited by Alastair Hannay and Gordon D. Marino. Cambridge: Cambridge University Press, 1998.

Postman, Neil. *Amusing Ourselves to Death: Public Discourse in the Age of Show Business*, 20th Anniversary edition. New York: Penguin, 2005.

RB-Børsen. "Tivoli dropper Carlsberg og Tuborg." *business.dk*. Accessed July 20, 2016, http://www.business.dk/foedevarer/tivoli-dropper-carlsberg-og-tuborg.

Richter, Liselotte. "Kierkegaard und das Zeitalter der Technokratie." *Zeichen der Zeit*, no. 11 (1955): 402–06.

Ritchie, J. Ewing. "Copenhagen as It Was." *The Metropolitan Magazine* 49 (1847): 223–30.

Rodger, Richard. "Theory, Practice and European Urban History." In *European Urban History: Prospect and Retrospect*. Edited by Richard Rodger, 1–18. Leicester: Leicester University Press, 1993.

Rognon, Frédéric. "Jacques Ellul and Søren Kierkegaard." Translated by Lisa Richmond. International Jacques Ellul Society. Accessed September 29, 2018, https://ellul.org/el lul-and-kierkegaard/.

Rojcewicz, Richard. *The Gods and Technology: A Reading of Heidegger*. Albany: State University of New York Press, 2006.

Rose, Michael E. "Society: The Emergence of Urban Britain." In *The Cambridge Historical Encyclopedia of Great Britain and Ireland*. Edited by Christopher Haigh, 276–81. Cambridge: Cambridge University Press, 1985.

Rudgley, Richard. *The Lost Civilizations of the Stone Age*. New York: Touchstone, 1999.

Ryan, Bartholomew. *Kierkegaard's Indirect Politics: Interludes with Lukács, Schmitt, Benjamin and Adorno*. Amsterdam: Rodopi, 2014.

Šajda, Peter. "Romano Guardini: Between Actualistic Personalism, Qualitative Dialectic and Kinetic Logic." In *Kierkegaard's Influence on Theology. Tome III: Catholic and Jewish Theology*. Edited by John Stewart, 45–74. Farnham: Ashgate, 2012.

Sartre, Jean-Paul. *Existentialism and Human Emotions*. New York: Citadel Press, 1985.

Schalow, Frank and Alfred Denker. *Historical Dictionary of Heidegger's Philosophy*, 2nd edition. Lanham, MD: The Scarecrow Press, Inc., 2010.

Scharff, Robert C. and Val Dusek, eds. *Philosophy of Technology: The Technological Condition: An Anthology*, 2nd edition. Malden, MA: Wiley Blackwell, 2014.

Schilson, Arno. "Lessing and Theology." In *A Companion to the Works of Gotthold Ephraim Lessing*. Edited by Barbara Fischer and Thomas C. Fox, 157–84. Rochester, NY: Camden House, 2005.

Schopenhauer, Arthur. *The World as Will and Idea*, vol. 2. Translated by R.B. Haldane and J. Kemp. Boston, MA: Ticknor and Company, 1888.

Schulz, Heiko. "A Modest Head Start: The German Reception of Kierkegaard." In *Kierkegaard's International Reception: Tome I: Northern and Western Europe*. Edited by Jon Stewart, 307–420. Farnham: Ashgate, 2009.

Seybt, Julius, trans. *Percy Bysshe Shelley's poetische Werke in Einem Bande*. Leipzig: Wilhelm Engelmann, 1844.

Sheldrake, Philip. *Spirituality: A Brief History*. Oxford: Wiley-Blackwell, 2013.

Shenk, David. *Data Smog: Surviving the Information Glut*. San Francisco, CA: Harper Edge, 1997.

Siegel, Lee. *Against the Machine: Being Human in the Age of the Electronic Mob*. New York: Spiegel & Grau, 2008.

Simay, Philippe. "Tradition as Injunction: Benjamin and the Critique of Historicisms." In *Walter Benjamin and History*. Edited by Andrew Benjamin, 137–55. London: Continuum, 2005.

Singer, Natasha. "How Google Took Over the Classroom." *The New York Times*, May 13, 2017. Accessed November 11, 2018. https://www.nytimes.com/2017/05/13/technology/google-education-chromebooks-schools.html.

Skrbina, David. "Introduction: A Revolutionary for Our Times." In *Technological Slavery: The Collected Writings of Theodore J. Kaczynski, a.k.a. "The Unabomber,"*16–35. Port Townsend, WA: Feral House, 2010.

Smith, Andrew. "Scientific Contexts." In *The Cambridge Companion to Frankenstein*. Edited by Andrew Smith, 69–83. Cambridge: Cambridge University Press, 2016.

Smith, Edgar C. *A Short History of Naval and Marine Engineering*. Cambridge: Cambridge University Press, 1938.

Smith, Jonathan. *Fact and Feeling: Baconian Science and the Nineteenth-Century Literary Imagination*. Madison: The University of Wisconsin Press, 1994.

Son, Wha-Chul. "Are We Still Pursuing Efficiency? Interpreting Jacques Ellul's Efficiency Principle." In *Jacques Ellul and the Technological Society in the 21st Century*. Edited by Helena M. Jerónimo, José Luís Garcia, and Carl Mitcham, 49–62. Dordrecht: Springer, 2013.

Soulen, Richard N. and R. Kendall Soulen. *Handbook of Biblical Criticism*, 3rd edition. Louisville, KY: Westminster John Knox Press, 2001.

Steiner, Henriette. *The Emergence of a Modern City: Golden Age Copenhagen 1800-1850*. Farnham: Ashgate, 2014.

Stewart, Jon. "Editor's Introduction: Kierkegaard and the Rich Field of Kierkegaard Studies." In *A Companion to Kierkegaard*. Edited by Jon Stewart, 50–65. Oxford: Wiley Blackwell, 2015.

Stewart, Jon, ed. *Kierkegaard and Existentialism*, Kierkegaard Research: Sources, Reception and Resources, vol. 9. Farnham: Ashgate, 2011.

Stewart, Jon. *Kierkegaard's Relations to Hegel Reconsidered*. Cambridge: Cambridge University Press, 2003.

Stewart, Jon. "Kierkegaard's View of Hegel, His Followers and Critics." *A Companion to Kierkegaard*. Edited by Jon Stewart. Oxford: Wiley Blackwell, 2015.

Stewart, Jon. *Søren Kierkegaard: Subjectivity, Irony, and the Crisis of Modernity*. Oxford: Oxford University Press, 2015.

Stross, Randall. *Planet Google: One Company's Audacious Plan to Organize Everything We Know*. New York: Free Press, 2008.

Taylor, Charles. *A Secular Age*. Cambridge, MA: The Belknap Press, 2007.

Teilhard de Chardin, Pierre. *The Phenomenon of Man*. Translated by Bernard Wall. New York: Harper Perennial, 1976.

Terlizzese, Lawrence J. *Hope in the Thought of Jacques Ellul*. Eugene, OR: Cascade Books, 2005.

Thomas, Alastair H. "Press." In *Historical Dictionary of Denmark*. Edited by Alastair H. Thomas and Stewart P. Oakley. Lanham, MD: The Scarecrow Press, Inc., 1998.

Thomas, J. Mark. "Introduction." In *Paul Tillich: The Spiritual Situation in Our Technical Society*. Edited by J. Mark Thomas. Macon, GA: Mercer University Press, 1988.

Thompson, Curtis L. "Speculation/Science/Scholarship." *Kierkegaard's Concepts: Tome VI: Salvation to Writing*. Edited by Steven M. Emmanuel, William McDonald, and Jon Stewart, 65–74. Farnham: Ashgate, 2015.

Thompson, Curtis L. and Joyce M. Cuff. *God and Nature: A Theologian and a Scientist Conversing on the Divine Promise of Possibility*. New York: Continuum, 2012.

Thomson, Iain D. *Heidegger on Ontotheology: Technology and the Politics of Education*. Cambridge: Cambridge University Press, 2005.

Thompson, Josiah. *The Lonely Labyrinth: Kierkegaard's Pseudonymous Works*. Carbondale: Southern Illinois University Press, 1967.

Thompson, Phillip M. *Between Science and Religion: The Engagement of Catholic Intellectuals with Science and Technology in the Twentieth Century*. Lanham, MD: Lexington Books, 2009.

Thorns, David C. *The Transformation of Cities: Urban Theory and Urban Life*. Basingstoke: Palgrave Macmillan, 2002.

Tilley, J. Michael. "Herbert Marcuse: Social Critique, Haecker, and Kierkegaardian Individualism." In *Kierkegaard's Influence on Social-Political Thought*. Edited by Jon Stewart, Kierkegaard Research: Sources, Reception and Resources, vol. 14, 137–46. London: Routledge, 2011.

Tillich, Paul. "Autobiographical Reflections." In *The Theology of Paul Tillich*. Edited by Charles Kegley and Robert Bretall, 3–22. New York: Macmillan, 1952.

Tillich, Paul. *Paul Tillich: The Spiritual Situation in Our Technical Society*. Edited by J. Mark Thomas. Macon, GA: Mercer University Press, 1988.

Tillich, Paul. *The Interpretation of History*. New York: Charles Scribner's Sons, 1936.

Tillich, Paul. *Systematic Theology: Volume One*. Chicago, IL: The University of Chicago Press, 1951.

Troude-Chastenet, Patrick. *Jacques Ellul on Religion, Technology, and Politics: Conversations with Patrick Troude-Chastenet*. Translated by Joan Mendès France. Atlanta, GA: Scholars Press, 1998.

Tudvad, Peter. *Kierkegaards København*. Copenhagen: Politikens Forlag, 2003.

Turkle, Sherry. *Alone Together: Why We Expect More from Technology and Less from Each Other*. New York: Basic Books, 2011.

Tuttle, Howard N. *The Crowd Is Untruth: The Existential Critique of Mass Society in the Thought of Kierkegaard, Nietzsche, Heidegger, and Ortega y Gasset*. New York: Peter Lang, 1996.

Undorf, Wolfgang. *From Gutenberg to Luther: Transnational Print Cultures in Scandinavia 1450-1525*. Leiden: Brill, 2014.

The United States Environmental Protection Agency. "Heat Island Effect." Accessed January 3, 2017, https://www.epa.gov/heat-islands.

Vaidhyanathan, Siva. *The Googlization of Everything (and Why We Should Worry)*. Berkeley: University of California Press, 2011.

Vammen, Hans. "No One Other Than Ourselves? A Character Sketch of Frederik VI and His Régime." In *The Golden Age Revisited: Art and Culture in Denmark 1800-1850*. Edited by Bente Scavenius, 48–55. Copenhagen: Gyldendal, 1996.

Vaughan, Robert. *The Age of Great Cities: Or, Modern Society Viewed in Its Relation to Intelligence, Morals, and Religion*. London: Jackson and Walford, 1843.

Voltaire. *Candide, ou l'Optimisme*. Paris: Sirène, 1759.

Voltaire. "Epître à l'auteur du livre des *Trois imposteurs*." In *OEuvres complètes de Voltaire*. Edited by Louis Moland, vol. 10, 226–30. Paris: Garnier, 1877–85.

Vuchic, Vukan R. *Urban Transit: Systems and Technology*. Hoboken, NJ: John Wiley and Sons, 2007.

Wahl, Jean. *Philosophies of Existence: An Introduction to the Basic Thought of Kierkegaard, Heidegger, Jaspers, Marcel, Sartre*. Translated by F.M. Lory. New York: Shocken Books, 1969.

Ward, Benedicta, trans. *The Desert Fathers: Sayings of the Early Christian Monks*. London: Penguin Books, 2003.

Ward, Benedicta. "Introduction." In *The Desert Fathers: Sayings of the Early Christian Monks*. Translated by Benedicta Ward, vii–xxv. London: Penguin Books, 2003.

Warner, Sam Bass Jr. "When Urban History Is at the Center of the Curriculum." *Journal of Urban History* 18 (1991): 3–9.

Watkin, Julia. *Historical Dictionary of Kierkegaard's Philosophy*. Lanham, MD: The Scarecrow Press, Inc., 2001.

Watkin, Julia. "Historical Introduction." In *Early Polemical Writings: Kierkegaard's Writings I*. Edited and translated by Julia Watkin, vii–xxxvi. Princeton, NJ: Princeton University Press, 1990.

Webb, Simon. *Commuters: The History of a British Way of Life*. Barnsley: Pen and Sword Books, 2016.

Weber, Max. *Die protestantische Ethik und der Geist des Kapitalismus*. Tübingen: Mohr, 1904.

Westfall, Joseph. "A, B, and A.F…: Kierkegaard's Use of Anonyms." In *Kierkegaard's Pseudonyms*. Edited by Katalin Nun and Jon Stewart, 27–38. New York: Routledge, 2016.

Westfall, Joseph. "Walter Benjamin: Appropriating the Kierkegaardian Aesthetic." In *Kierkegaard's Influence on Philosophy: Tome I: German and Scandinavian Philosophy*. Edited by Jon Stewart, 49–66. Farnham: Ashgate, 2012.

Westphal, Merold. *Becoming a Self: A Reading of Kierkegaard's Concluding Unscientific Postscript*. West Lafayette, IN: Purdue University Press, 1996.

Westphal, Merold. "Kierkegaard's Sociology." In *International Kierkegaard Commentary: Two Ages*. Edited by Robert L. Perkins, 133–54. Macon, GA: Mercer University Press, 1984.

Westphal, Merold. "Society, Politics, and Modernity." In *The Oxford Handbook of Kierkegaard*. Edited by John Lippitt and George Pattison, 309–27. Oxford: Oxford University Press, 2013.

Westphal, Merold. *Transcendence and Self-transcendence: On God and the Soul.* Bloomington: Indiana University Press, 2004.

White, Lynn Jr. "Cultural Climates and Technological Advance in the Middle Ages." In *Philosophy of Technology: The Technological Condition: An Anthology.* Edited by Robert C. Scharff and Val Dusek, 511–22. Oxford: Wiley-Blackwell, 2014.

Wolfe, Judith. *Heidegger and Theology.* London: Bloomsbury T&T Clark, 2014.

Woodward, Gordon. "Hjorth, Søren." In *Biographical Dictionary of the History of Technology.* Edited by Lance Day and Ian McNeil, 597–98. London: Routledge, 1996.

Worsøe-Schmidt, Lisbeth. "Spectators in Denmark." In *Enlightened Networking: Import and Export of Enlightenment in 18th Century Denmark.* Edited by Thomas Bredsdorff and Anne-Marie Mai, 23–34. Odense: University Press of Southern Denmark, 2004.

Wyschogrod, Michael. *Kierkegaard and Heidegger: The Ontology of Existence.* New York: The Humanities Press, Inc., 1954.

Ziolkowski, Eric. "Introduction." In *Kierkegaard, Literature, and the Arts.* Edited by Eric Ziolkowski, 3–38. Evanston, IL: Northwestern University Press, 2018.

Index

CPSIA information can be obtained
at www.ICGtesting.com
Printed in the USA
LVHW010218260221
679957LV00012B/250

9 781501 378348